# Of Limits and Growth

## The Rise of Global Sustainable Development in the Twentieth Century

*Of Limits and Growth* connects three of the most important aspects of the twentieth century: decolonization, the rise of environmentalism, and the United States' support for economic development and modernization in the Third World. It links these trends by revealing how environmental NGOs challenged and reformed the development approaches of the U.S. government, World Bank, and United Nations from the 1960s through the 1990s. The book shows how NGOs promoted the use of "appropriate" technologies, environmental reviews in the lending process, development plans based on ecological principles, and international cooperation on global issues such as climate change. It also reveals that the "sustainable development" concept emerged from transnational negotiations in which environmentalists accommodated the developmental aspirations of Third World intellectuals and leaders. In sum, *Of Limits and Growth* offers a new history of sustainability by elucidating the global origins of environmental activism, the ways in which environmental activists challenged development approaches worldwide, and how environmental non-state actors reshaped the United States' and World Bank's development policies.

Stephen J. Macekura is Assistant Professor of International Studies at Indiana University.

# Global and International History

*Series Editors*
Erez Manela, Harvard University
John McNeill, Georgetown University
Aviel Roshwald, Georgetown University

The Global and International History series seeks to highlight and explore the convergences between the new International History and the new World History. Its editors are interested in approaches that mix traditional units of analysis such as civilizations, nations, and states with other concepts such as transnationalism, diasporas, and international institutions.

**Titles in the Series**

Stephen J. Macekura, *Of Limits and Growth: The Rise of Global Sustainable Development in the Twentieth Century*

Michael Goebel, *Anti-Imperial Metropolis: Interwar Paris and the Seeds of Third-World Nationalism*

# Of Limits and Growth

*The Rise of Global Sustainable Development
in the Twentieth Century*

STEPHEN J. MACEKURA

*Department of International Studies, Indiana University*

CAMBRIDGE
UNIVERSITY PRESS

# CAMBRIDGE
### UNIVERSITY PRESS

32 Avenue of the Americas, New York, NY 10013-2473, USA

Cambridge University Press is part of the University of Cambridge.

It furthers the University's mission by disseminating knowledge in the pursuit of education, learning, and research at the highest international levels of excellence.

www.cambridge.org
Information on this title: www.cambridge.org/9781107072619

First published 2015

Printed in the United States of America

*A catalog record for this publication is available from the British Library.*

*Library of Congress Cataloging in Publication Data*
Macekura, Stephen J.
Of limits and growth : the rise of global sustainable
development in the twentieth century / Stephen J. Macekura, Dartmouth College.
pages    cm. – (Global and international history)
Includes bibliographical references and index.
ISBN 978-1-107-07261-9 (hardback)
1. Sustainable development – History – 20th century.    2. Environmental
protection.    3. Sustainable development – Citizen participation.
4. Environmental policy.    I. Title.
HC79.E5M293    2015
338.9'270904–dc23          2015014019

ISBN 978-1-107-07261-9 Hardback

# Contents

# Contents

# Illustrations

# Acknowledgments

No individual deserves more of my gratitude than Melvyn Leffler, who guided this project from its inception as a dissertation to its conclusion as a book. Mel was an ideal mentor during my graduate studies, and his friendship in the years since has helped to sustain my scholarship. Mel always inspired me to endure through challenging times, and he still does.

I also owe tremendous thanks to a number of other terrific scholars who have nurtured this project. Ed Russell introduced me to environmental history and provided incisive criticism at key moments in the growth of the dissertation. Brian Balogh showed me how and why to study governance, and he did so with characteristic good humor. Jennifer Burns encouraged me early in my graduate career, and she continues to be a great colleague for stimulating conversations about the history of economic thought. Will Hitchcock joined the project late, but he provided insightful commentary on many occasions. Josh Yates broadened my disciplinary horizons and stimulated my thinking about culture and political economy, and he became a great friend in the process. Ed Miller, whom I first met as an undergraduate and now know as a terrific colleague and friend, has consistently offered sound professional advice and frequently helped me think through the history of international development.

Brent Cebul and Jamie Allison, two outstanding historians, have been with me from the start of this process. Brent's insightful criticisms and wide-ranging knowledge of American history helped shape this project and continue to aid my work in innumerable ways. Jamie's extensive careful editorial suggestions improved this project greatly and still inform my research and writing. They both aided me in critical ways during the early stages of this book, and I am grateful for their continuing support and, above all, friendship. Here's to many more dinners, drinks, and conversations in the future.

I received tremendous financial support from a number of organizations that made possible the research and writing of this project. I wish to thank the George C. Marshall Foundation, the Society for Historians of American Foreign Relations, the Bankard Fund for Political Economy at the University of Virginia, the Albert Gallatin Graduate Research Fellowship at the University of Virginia, the University of Virginia Society of Fellows, the Gerald R. Ford Presidential Library, the Scowcroft Institute of International Affairs, and the Corcoran Department of History at the University of Virginia. During various stages of the project I had the honor of being a Fellow at the Dickey Center for International Understanding at Dartmouth College, the Institute for Advanced Studies in Culture at the University of Virginia, and the Miller Center for Public Affairs at the University of Virginia. All three institutions are outstanding places for young scholars of U.S. foreign policy, political history, and capitalism and culture to work.

Countless archivists helped me throughout this project. While all deserve commendation, I owe a special thanks to Everlyne Were Makana and Richard Ambani for their help in orienting me to research possibilities in Nairobi. I also benefited from friends who let me sleep on couches or spare beds during extended research excursions. Kate Anderson and Paulina Michnowska opened their home to me during an extended stay in London, as Brad Wolcott, Jillian Rork, Brent Cebul, and Katherine Treppendahl did during trips to Boston.

This book has also benefited from a wide variety of colleagues in the field who have read chapters, commented on conference papers, or provided valuable feedback and advice in other ways. I thank Brent Cebul, Jamie Allison, Richard Tucker, David Ekbladh, David Engerman, Erez Manela, John McNeill, Nick Cullather, Brad Simpson, Amy Sayward, Sarah Snyder, Tom Zeiler, Tore Olsson, Roger Eardley-Pryor, Iris Borowy, Jan-Henrik Meyer, Wolfram Kaiser, Michael Manulak, Stephen Wertheim, Ryan Irwin, Ed Miller, Amanda McVety, and Chris Jones. Daniel Immerwahr, Tom Robertson, Frank Zelko, and Paul Adler deserve special thanks for reading through the entire manuscript and offering constructive feedback along the way. I am greatly appreciative of David Satterthwaite, Lee Talbot, and Jim MacNeill, each of whom took the time to field my many questions and enriched my understanding of environmentalism and international development.

I have had the tremendous good fortune of working with Debbie Gershenowitz at Cambridge University Press. Debbie supported this book from the first day we met, and I am thankful for her thorough editorial work. Along with Debbie, Dana Bricken answered all of my questions and treated this new author with admirable patience. I am also indebted to the insightful anonymous reviewers who read this manuscript.

In Charlottesville, I received support and valuable commentary on this project at various stages from Christian McMillen, Jack Brown, Bernie Carlson, Marc Selverstone, Sid Milkis, Ben Cohen, Victor Nemchenok, Ethan Schrum, Mason Williams, Nir Avissar, Allison Elias, James Wilson, Barin Kayaoglu, Lauren Turek, Kate Geoghegan, Harold Mock, Evan McCormick, Ben Brady, Shannon Nix, Mary Barton, Kelly Winck, Andrew McGee, Laura Kolar, Bart Elmore, Tom Finger, and Leif Frederickson. In Hanover, I benefited greatly from the support and friendship of Jennie Miller, Udi Greenberg, and Gerald Auten during the final phase of this project.

Finally, I thank friends and family who helped me through this process. Trevor Holland, Anna Mikulak, Mike Salter, Rebecca James, Jenna Krumminga, Amy Essigmann, Jason Hartwig, Jonathan Hancock, Jillian Rork, Brad Wolcott, John Bair, Marina McClure, Andrew Martin, Laura Kolbe, Lindsay Turner, and Walt Hunter have all helped to make this project possible. The same is true for my family – Joseph, Mark, Dede, Virginia, Mickey, John, and Marty – who have been unwavering in their support. Allison Quantz came into my life at a late stage of this project, but she improved it in many ways. I am grateful for her guidance, support, and love, and I am especially appreciative for the many hours she spent listening to me talk about this project and the many more she spent reading through drafts. Allison, thank you.

# INTRODUCTION

# NGOs and the Origins of "Sustainable Development"

In the summer of 1956, Russell Train, a U.S. Tax Court judge, visited East Africa in the hopes of seeing and hunting some of the region's many big-game animals (Figure 1). Two years later, Train returned to the region for a similar safari. Train enjoyed the first trip, which he had spent enthusiastically tracking leopards and pursuing a trophy elephant tusk. However, he came away startled and deeply worried from the second one. Extensive poaching by native hunters, widespread clearing of land for settlement, and the realization that new postcolonial leaders might dissolve game reserves and parks established in the colonial era alarmed Train. "With the native races assuming more and more control over the destiny of the African continent, the fate of the wildlife becomes increasingly uncertain," Train wrote to family and friends upon his return home. "The need is desperate to act now," he continued, "before this magnificent heritage which belongs to all the world is lost forever."[1] Decolonization, and in particular the loss of Western control over Africa's wildlife, seemed to imperil the continent's natural flora and fauna.

In the fall of 1960, Julian Huxley, a British scientist and former official with the United Nations (UN), took a trip similar to Train's. Huxley ventured to East Africa, where he hoped to document the state of the region's wildlife protection programs. Much like Train, Huxley came away stunned. He shared Train's fears of decolonization. Everywhere he went, he saw the transfer of power from colonial authorities to new nationalist leaders as a threat to the imperial protection arrangements.

[1] Russell and Aileen Train, "Back to Africa: 1958," 1959, box 1, Russell E. Train Papers, Manuscript Division, Library of Congress [hereinafter cited as Train Papers].

FIGURE 1: Aileen B. Train and Russell E. Train on safari in Kenya, 1956, with a leopard shot by Russell E. Train. Courtesy of Russell Train Papers, Manuscript Division, Library of Congress.

Hoping to engender widespread concern back home for these issues, Huxley penned a series of articles for a London newspaper, the *Observer*. In these pieces, he juxtaposed images of exotic animals and bucolic landscapes with hyperbolic headlines and descriptions portraying Africa's wildlife in a dire situation. "The issue is this," Huxley asserted, "whether Africa's wild life and wild nature can survive, or whether they will be destroyed or whittled down to a poor remnant by the rising tides of over-population and industrial and other 'development.'"[2] Huxley feared that leaders of postcolonial nations would soon clamor for economic development, which would make the African situation seem far more troubling.

Train's and Huxley's concerns reveal many important themes from the mid-twentieth century. Many Western conservationists looked to what observers termed the "developing world" and saw disturbing trends. Decolonization and economic development seemed to pose such a serious threat to wild flora and fauna all over the world that individuals such as Train perceived a "need" to act on behalf of the nonhuman world to help

[2] Julian Huxley, "The Treasure House of Wildlife," *Observer*, November 13, 1960, 23–4.

it survive. Underlying these notions was a belief that such exotic flora and fauna did not necessarily belong to any one nation, but as Train suggested, "to all the world." External interventions could thus be justified to protect wildlife if an individual nation failed to do so. These arguments proved to be quite powerful. Over the second half of the twentieth century such global environmental imperatives would frequently conflict with national sovereignty in a world where power was increasingly being allocated to nation-states.[3]

Additionally, beneath Train's and Huxley's statements lurked a powerful tension between economic development and environmental protection. Development, they assumed, was a linear process that necessitated a view of nature as a static entity, designed only for human exploitation. As they understood it, development meant the removal of barriers to human action and economic growth. By contrast, the kind of environmental protection they sought demanded limits on human freedom, to preserve and protect the natural world from unheeded human use.[4]

---

[3] Although most histories of environmentalism tend to focus on movements within national borders, this book highlights the global origins of leading Western environmental activist organizations. It expands on recent works in this vein such as Thomas Robertson, *The Malthusian Moment: Global Population Growth and the Birth of American Environmentalism* (New Brunswick, NJ: Rutgers University Press, 2012); Frank Zelko, *Make It a Green Peace! The Rise of Countercultural Environmentalism* (New York: Oxford University Press, 2013); Ramachandra Guha, *Environmentalism: A Global History* (New York, Longman, 2000); Ramachandra Guha and Juan Martinez-Alier, *Varieties of Environmentalism: Essays North and South* (London: Earthscan Publications, Ltd., 1997); John McCormick, *The Global Environmental Movement*, 2nd ed. (Chichester: John Wiley & Sons, 1995). The literature on American environmentalism is too long to cite in full here, but excellent starting points are Adam Rome, "'Give Earth a Chance': The Environment Movement and the Sixties," *The Journal of American History*, Vol. 90, No. 2 (2003), 525–4; Samuel P. Hays, *Beauty, Health, and Permanence: Environmental Politics in the United States* (Cambridge: Cambridge University Press, 1987); Michael Egan and Jeff Crane, eds., *Natural Protest: Essays on the History of American Environmentalism* (New York: Routledge, 2009).

[4] The history of development has a rich historiography that has grown tremendously in recent years. For general studies on the origins and evolution of international development, see Michael Cowen and Robert Shenton, *Doctrines of Development* (New York: Routledge Press, 1996); Gilbert Rist, *The History of Development: From Western Origins to Global Faith* (London: Zed Books, 2008); James C. Scott, *Seeing Like a State: How Certain Schemes to Improve the Human Condition Have Failed* (New Haven: Yale University Press, 1998); H. W. Arndt, *Economic Development: The History of an Idea* (Chicago: The University of Chicago Press, 1987); Joseph Morgan Hodge, *Triumph of the Expert: Agrarian Doctrines of Development and the Legacies of British Colonialism* (Athens: Ohio University Press, 2007); Amy L. S. Staples, *The Birth of Development: How the World Bank, Food and Agriculture Organization, and the World Health Organization Changed the World, 1945–1965* (Kent: The Kent State University Press, 2006). On development in U.S. foreign relations, see David C. Engerman, Nils Gilman,

How Train and Huxley responded to these concerns was also indicative of a significant trend in the postwar era, the growth of international non-governmental organizations (NGOs). Both men helped to found NGOs: the African Wildlife Leadership Foundation (AWLF) in Train's case, and the more influential International Union for the Conservation of Nature (IUCN) and the World Wildlife Fund (WWF) in Huxley's. Environmental activists such as Train and Huxley believed that national governments had not effectively pursued environmental protection or were simply unwilling to do so, and thus they needed new institutions to pressure governments to adopt environmental policies. Moreover, decolonization and development were global problems; nations across the world strove for self-determination and rapid economic growth. Train and Huxley figured that it was necessary to form NGOs that were global in scope and purpose. Their subsequent activism transcended national borders and covered much of the world.[5]

Mark H. Haefele, and Michael E. Latham, eds., *Staging Growth: Modernization, Development, and the Global Cold War* (Amherst: The University of Massachusetts Press, 2003); Nils Gilman, *Mandarins of the Future: Modernization Theory in Cold War America* (Baltimore: Johns Hopkins University Press, 2003); Vernon Ruttan, *United States Development Assistance Policy: The Domestic Politics of Foreign Aid* (Baltimore: The Johns Hopkins University Press, 1996); Michael Latham, *Modernization as Ideology: American Social Science and "Nation Building" in the Kennedy Era* (Chapel Hill, NC: University of North Carolina Press, 2000); Amanda Kay McVety, *Enlightened Aid: U.S. Development as Foreign Policy in Ethiopia* (New York: Oxford University Press, 2012); Michael E. Latham, *The Right Kind of Revolution: Modernization, Development, and U.S. Foreign Policy from the Cold War to the Present* (Ithaca: Cornell University Press, 2011); David Ekbladh, *The Great American Mission: Modernization and the Construction of an American World Order* (Princeton: Princeton University Press, 2010); Nick Cullather, *The Hungry World: America's Cold War Battle Against Poverty in Asia* (Cambridge: Harvard University Press, 2011). This book pushes the history of development in new directions by elucidating the environmental critique of development and showing how lending institutions transformed as a result of environmental NGO lobbying efforts from the 1970s and beyond. In so doing, it integrates insights from diplomatic and environmental history. On this point, see *Diplomatic History*, Special Edition on Environmental History, Vol. 32, No. 4 (September 2008), 407–673.

5 The environmental NGOs discussed in this book took the entire globe as an object of governance, moved freely across borders, filled their staff rosters with cosmopolitan elites from many nations, sought to use supranational or transnational institutions to establish global standards for development practice, and attempted to reform foreign aid and development policies of all regions and nations. By focusing on such actors, their ideas, their actions, and the extent to which their activism reshaped national and international institutions, this book presents one way of writing a history of transnational activism that keeps an analytic eye toward both non-state actors and state policy. For other recent works on non-state actors and international politics, see Sarah B. Snyder, *Human Rights Activism and the End of the Cold War: A Transnational History of the Helsinki Network* (Cambridge University Press, 2011); Matthew Evangelista, *Unarmed Forces: The Transnational*

As NGOs attempted to promote environmental protection worldwide over the ensuing decades, the tension between environmental and development objectives emerged as a major theme of international politics. From the late 1960s onward, controversies raged over how development policies should integrate environmental protection measures. When the developed countries proposed international agreements over environmental problems, developing countries fired back with claims of neo-imperialism and calls for financial compensation and increased development aid. When developing countries demanded their right to unfettered economic growth, developed countries claimed that the "Global South" was selfishly scuttling international cooperation. All the while, NGOs advocated for the United States, the World Bank, and the United Nations to promote development projects that emphasized ecological limitations. These debates all revolved around a single question: What kind of development policies would reconcile the desire for economic development with the necessity of environmental protection?

*Of Limits and Growth* explores how some of the largest and most influential international and U.S. based NGOs endeavored to answer this question over the second half of the twentieth century. This book begins by uncovering how concerns about decolonization and a global push for economic growth in the developing world motivated Western reformers to form international environmental NGOs. Many of these groups sought to continue colonial era protection arrangements, and many of them emerged to replace imperial authorities in postcolonial game reserves and national parks. However, as the allure of development captivated many leaders in these countries, and as Western countries increasingly offered foreign aid for economic development in the hopes of winning allies in the global Cold War, environmental issues received little attention. NGO officials struggled to convince nationalist leaders to adopt environmental protection policies during the 1950s and 1960s.

*Movement to End the Cold War* (Ithaca: Cornell University Press, 1999); Akira Iriye, *The Global Community: The Role of International Organizations and the Making of the Modern World* (Berkeley: The University of California Press, 2002); Matthew Connelly, *Fatal Misconception: The Struggle to Control World Population* (Cambridge: Harvard University Press, 2008); Erez Manela, "Reconceiving International History," *Reviews in American History*, Vol. 37, No. 1 (March 2009), 69–77; Erez Manela, "A Pox on Your Narrative: Writing Disease Control into Cold War History," *Diplomatic History* Vol. 34, No. 2 (April 2010); Matthew Hilton, *Prosperity for All: Consumer Activism in an Era of Globalization* (Ithaca: Cornell University Press, 2009).

Following their early difficulties to promote environmental protection in the so-called Third World countries, NGOs refocused their activism on the lenders of development aid, particularly the United States, the World Bank, and the United Nations. Environmentalists believed that existing development approaches used by major donor governments, such as the United States, and international development agencies, such as the World Bank, would wreak havoc on the nonhuman world. After all, it was becoming clear that Western industrial development over the previous century had wrought tremendous environmental consequences. By the mid-twentieth century, air and water pollution, excessive resource exploitation, rapid population growth, and many more issues threatened ecosystems around the globe. To minimize such destruction in the developing countries, prominent NGOs – such as the IUCN, the WWF, the International Institute for Environment and Development (IIED), Friends of the Earth International (FOEI), Volunteers in Technical Assistance (VITA), the Environmental Defense Fund (EDF), and the Natural Resources Defense Council (NRDC) – attempted to reform existing international development policies in a number of ways. They advocated for the use of small-scale, "appropriate" technologies; the incorporation of environmental reviews in the lending process; the adoption of development planning models on the basis of ecological principles; and international cooperation around environmental issues at the United Nations Conference on the Human Environment in 1972 and the Rio Earth Summit in 1992.

This book shows that through these reform efforts NGOs gave rise to the concept and discourse of "sustainable development" in the 1980s as a way to link developmental aspirations with environmental concerns. *Of Limits and Growth* argues that the origins of the sustainability idea can only be understood by examining how environmental NGOs transformed the practices of major development lending institutions – particularly the U.S. government, the World Bank, and the United Nations – during the 1970s and 1980s. Organizations such as VITA and the WWF seized on opportunities created by shifts toward privatization in foreign aid, as they earned government support to carry out development projects. FOEI, the EDF, and the NRDC became potent lobbying groups that swayed congressional opinion and mounted effective legal campaigns against governing institutions. The IUCN and the IIED leveraged personal connections and professional expertise to shape the agendas and outcomes of major conferences. From the time of Train's and Huxley's trips to East Africa through the rise of sustainable development discourse in the 1980s, these civil society groups dynamically coevolved with leading development institutions, altering both the content of foreign aid policies and the nature of NGO advocacy strategies.[6]

These reforms exposed both the possibilities and the limitations of focusing on institutional changes within development lenders. In so doing they raised critical questions about the role of NGOs in international politics. In reforming development policies, leading environmental groups created a variety of legal and political mechanisms to make lending agencies accountable for the ecological consequences of their projects. The new relationships forged between environmental advocacy groups and governing institutions ensured this accountability. Yet the slow implementation of new environmental protection measures, coupled with the close relationship between major NGOs and centers of power, led some development experts and activists to wonder whether the accountability

---

[6] This book focuses closely on the dynamic interactions between governing institutions and private actors. It looks *within* the U.S. Agency for International Development, the World Bank, and the United Nations as much as "beyond the state" to investigate the personal and structural relationships formed between large institutions and NGOs in the sphere of development policy. By highlighting institutions as venues where private activism and public power meet, this book demonstrates how NGOs reformed public policy, how the institutionalization of the environmental movement into large NGOs altered its tenor and character, and how the close ties with governing ultimately shaped the meaning of "sustainable development." My approach draws on insights from American Political Development (APD) and International Relations (IR) scholarship on institutional change, advocacy networks, and environmental NGOs. See, for instance, Edmund P. Russell, "The Strange Career of DDT: Experts, Federal Capacity, and Environmentalism in World War II," *Environmental History*, Vol. 40, No. 4 (Oct. 1999), 770–96; Brian Balogh, *Chain Reaction: Expert Debate and Public Participation in American Commercial Nuclear Power, 1945–1975* (Cambridge: Cambridge University Press, 1991); Paul Pierson and Theda Skocpol, eds., *The Transformation of American Politics: Activist Government and the Rise of Conservatism* (Princeton: Princeton University Press, 2007); McGee Young, *Developing Interests: Organizational Change and the Politics of Advocacy* (Lawrence: University of Kansas Press, 2010); Andrew Hurrell and Benedict Kingsbury, eds., *The International Politics of the Environment: Actors, Interests and Intuitions* (Oxford: The Clarendon Press, 1992); Margaret E. Keck and Kathryn Sikkink, *Activists Beyond Borders: Advocacy Networks in International Politics* (Ithaca: Cornell University Press, 1998); Paul Wapner, *Environmental Activism and World Civic Politics* (Albany: State University of New York Press, 1996). On the need to look "beyond" the state in diplomatic and international history, see Matthew Connelly, "Seeing Beyond the State: The Population Control Movement and the Problem of Sovereignty," *Past & Present*, Vol. 193, No. 1 (December 2006), 197–233. This book is not a comprehensive history of all environmental NGOs worldwide, nor does it focus on local environmental NGOs in the Global South that organize around developmental issues. On environmentalism activism around the world, see, for instance, Guha, *Environmentalism: A Global History* and Guha and Martinez-Alier, *Varieties of Environmentalism*.

achieved came at the expense of more open access and democratic representation in major development institutions.

Likewise, the rise of the sustainability discourse came through a process of negotiation and compromise that left some wondering whether or not the concept offered a truly new approach to development. As many environmentalists have celebrated, sustainable development planning provided for the incorporation of ecological science into public policy.[7] Yet sustainable development also derived from a process of political accommodation in which officials in leading environmental NGOs consciously sought to include the concerns of intellectuals and other elites from the developing world. By the late 1970s, leaders in the environmental community came to support poverty eradication, the pursuit of socioeconomic equality between countries, and economic development as a political right for developing nations to a far greater extent than when Train and Huxley first made their trips to East Africa and largely focused on maintaining imperial protection programs. Environmental thought incorporated developmental aspirations as much as development thinking and practice addressed ideas of environmental protection. NGOs used the phrase "sustainable development" to encapsulate this intellectual compromise.

Although the phrase only became widely used in the 1980s, there is a long history behind sustainable development ideas and practices. Historians have pointed to the early twentieth-century conservation movement that stressed the "wise use" of natural resources to serve the greatest number of people for the greatest amount of time and to the mid-twentieth-century idea of "maximum sustained yield" that allowed for resource use within a given ecosystem's regenerative capacities. Still others have gazed further back, finding "sustainable" thinking and practices in traditions as diverse as eighteenth-century German soil science and medieval Christian theology.[8]

---

[7] The United Nations' World Commission on Environment and Development made this point clear in its popular 1987 report, *Our Common Future*: "The ability to anticipate and prevent environmental damage requires that the ecological dimensions of policy be considered at the same time as the economic, trade, energy, agricultural, and other dimensions. They should be considered on the same agendas and in the same national and international institutions." [Online] Available: http://www.un-documents.net/ocf-ov.htm. Accessed August 18, 2014.

[8] For scholarship that addresses the meaning and origins of sustainable development, see Sharachchandra M. Lele, "Sustainable Development: A Critical Review." *World Development*, Vol. 19, No. 6 (1991), 607–21; Charles V. Kidd, "The Evolution of Sustainability," *Journal of Agricultural and Environmental Ethics*, Vol. 5, No. 1 (1992),

Such accounts, however, do not explain why or how the concept "sustainable development" emerged in the 1970s, or why the phrase became so popular in the 1980s and beyond. *Of Limits and Growth* argues instead that it gained traction because it offered a way to reconcile the deep international tensions over development and environmental protection that had proliferated after World War II. The sustainability discourse took hold because it allowed leaders to acknowledge general environmental imperatives while also sanctioning aspirations for continued economic development. By the 1980s the phrase had acquired multiple definitions, and many national policy makers used it to suggest the compatibility of environmental protection with a growth-oriented, market economy. Infused with this optimistic meaning that elided calls for greater resource transfers from the wealthy countries to the Global South – which many NGO officials believed was a necessary component for realizing sustainable development plans – the sustainability discourse did little to persuade leaders in powerful countries to alter the balance of power in international politics. Although talk of sustainable development pervaded the 1992 Rio Earth Summit, decades-old debates between developed countries and the Global South over foreign aid levels, the virtues of increased regulation, and who should bear the costs of environmental protection still bedeviled negotiations over global agreements such as the emerging United Nations Framework Convention on Climate Change.

By the 1990s, environmental NGOs could celebrate their role in compelling many changes in the practice of international development, but they also had to confront the ongoing and serious challenges to environmental protection worldwide. NGOs' activism reshaped the lending policies and strategies of the United States, the World Bank, and the UN system. Environmentalists also introduced the language of sustainability into international politics. The environmental movement, however, remained trapped between developing countries' emphasis on national sovereignty and economic growth and the continued refusal of the developed world – and the United States in particular – to invest the substantial financial resources necessary to protect the global environment.

The story told here recounts many discussions and debates over ideas about both economic growth and ecological limits, but it also emphasizes

1–26; John Robinson, "Squaring the Circle? Some Thoughts on the Idea of Sustainable Development," *Ecological Economics*, Vol. 48, No. 4 (2004), 369–84; Paul Warde, "The Invention of Sustainability," *Modern Intellectual History*, Vol. 8, No. 1 (2011), 153–70; Thomas Ebben, "The History of Sustainability: Tracing Back a Legal Concept," unpublished paper in author's possession.

the growth of environmental NGOs and, ultimately, the limits of their influence. Recapturing this history of environmentalists' engagement with international development is significant, because it helps to illuminate a perplexing dilemma. Over the past forty years the environmental movement has strengthened, diversified, and seen tremendous institutional gains. Yet the state of the global environment remains as precarious as it did decades earlier.[9] *Of Limits and Growth* helps to explain why, after the rise of sustainable development discourse, this is still the case.

* * *

This book is comprised of three parts. The first part consists of three chapters that explore the origins of the postwar global environmental activism and its relationship to decolonization and international development policy through the early 1970s. Chapter 1 uncovers the origins of the IUCN and the WWF in the late 1940s and shows how their efforts to promote environmental protection conflicted with the rise of foreign aid policies for economic development and early theories of economic growth. Chapter 2 moves from offices in Fontainebleau and London, the founding sites for the IUCN and the WWF, to East Africa, where NGOs officials made their most concerted effort to sell the conservation cause in the developing world. Although their efforts to promote environmental protection in postcolonial states foundered, many reformers learned from their mishaps. By the end of the 1960s they began to target the sources of development aid – lending agencies in the United States, Western Europe, and international institutions. Chapter 3 explores the growing connections between environmental protection, foreign aid, and international politics by analyzing the 1972 UN Conference on the Human Environment in Stockholm. Many activists hoped the event would spark a worldwide commitment to environmental protection, yet debates between the Global South and the United States and Western European nations over responsibility for bearing the costs of environmental protection thwarted many environmentalists' aspirations for generating deep and lasting international cooperation between all countries. As a result, NGOs redoubled their own efforts to reconcile aspirations for economic growth with environmental limits.

In Part II, *Of Limits and Growth* explores a single question: How have NGOs attempted to reform international development policy and practice

---

[9] James Gustav Speth has also stressed the importance of recognizing this dilemma. See James Gustav Speth, *Red Sky at Morning: America and the Crisis of the Global Environment* (New Haven: Yale University Press, 2004), 8–9.

to be ecologically sustainable? Chapters 4, 5, and 6 explore three ways in which NGOs challenged existing development approaches during the 1970s and 1980s. Each chapter focuses on an environmental critique of development and elucidates how environmentalists attempted to alter the way in which development agencies lent foreign aid. While these efforts generally unfolded contemporaneously and involved many of the same activists and NGOs, Part II separates out each critique to analyze in depth the origins, evolution, and outcomes of these three ways in which activists altered development thought and practice.

Chapter 4 examines one approach to reforming development policy – substituting environmentally and socially "appropriate" technologies for the capital-intensive, large-scale projects of the past. It reveals how a handful of NGOs lobbied the U.S. government to promote small-scale technologies in its foreign aid lending, but also how the government officials' preoccupation with using technologies to spur local entrepre-neurialism came to overshadow the holistic, environmental message that reformers had championed. Chapter 5 highlights how NGOs successfully pressured the U.S. government and the World Bank to incorporate formal environmental reviews in the project approval process during the 1970s and 1980s. Making these governing institutions accountable only to powerful NGOs, however, led many observers to wonder whether the campaigns resulted in non-state actors carrying too much influence over the lending process and unjustly circumvented recipient countries' sover-eignty. Chapter 6 presents a third case of how environmentalists reformed development approaches by tracing NGOs' efforts to promote "sustain-able development" planning within developing nations and foreign aid agencies. In this reform process many environmentalists came to accom-modate the developmental aspirations of leaders and experts from Third World countries, which generated fierce battles over the purpose of envir-onmental protection within leading NGOs. This chapter demonstrates how these tensions came into sharp relief amid the IUCN's drafting of the *World Conservation Strategy*, a guidebook for ecologically based devel-opment and the first to use the phrase "sustainable development" as a compromise between developmental and environmental imperatives. It also reveals the challenges that arose while implementing national con-servation strategies based on the document.

After exploring these case studies of reform, Part III of this book charts the proliferation of the new sustainability discourse amid the persistence of older problems about foreign aid, the costs of environmental protec-tion, and North-South politics. Chapter 7 exposes the acrimonious debates over environmental and development politics at the 1992 UN Earth Summit in Rio de Janeiro. Despite all the reforms of the intervening decades, the chapter shows that many of the same problems, particularly the North-South conflict, pervaded the Rio gathering. Although a new set of environmental concerns – particularly global climate change – gave the meeting an added urgency, to the chagrin of many environmentalists, consensus over international agreements for issues such as climate change proved elusive for many of the same reasons that had hampered negotiations in Stockholm. The Conclusion reflects on how NGOs reformed the conduct and content of international development policies, but it also stresses the enduring challenges of reconciling a continued desire for economic growth with environmental protection. It illuminates the evolution of NGOs' legitimacy, power, and purpose in shaping global environmental protection and development efforts.

* * *

The conflicts between environmental NGOs, leaders from the developing world, and development lending agencies began in the mid-twentieth century, but still persist. In the twenty-first century, as people across the world wrestle with the myriad and profound challenges that stem from global climate change, many talk of "sustainable development" as a way to tie together environmental concerns with a desire for continued material abundance and high standards of living. Yet the vagueness and ubiquity of the phrase make it easy to overlook the history that gave rise to the concept and discourse in the first place. A historical perspective on the relationship between environmental protection and economic development illuminates why the sustainable development synthesis emerged when it did, what its advocates intended for the concept to mean, and why the tensions that continue to plague the sustainability idea were present at its inception. *Of Limits and Growth* thus chronicles how two generations of reformers identified, defined, and sought to redress the environmental challenges of the twentieth century.

To illuminate the myriad ways in which environmentalists worked to reshape global development thought and practice, this book connects individuals and their ideas to the institutions they used to challenge existing development approaches and implement new ones. It reveals the origins of the "sustainable development" discourse *and* exposes important policy changes that environmental NGOs pursued in reforming international development. Focusing on NGOs, their reform efforts, and changes in development policy elucidates how and why the peculiar institutional web that defines contemporary environmental policy making evolved in the way that it did. After all, national governments, international institutions, and NGOs now dominate the politics of global environmental protection and international development. To understand how those institutions govern, the policy options they have before them, and the challenges they face in reconciling environmental concerns with economic aspirations, we must first turn to the turbulence of the late 1940s amid both the optimism for economic growth worldwide and the nascent concern over global environmental degradation.

# PART ONE

# ORIGINS

I

# The Rise of International Conservation
# and Postwar Development

In the early months of 1948, Julian Huxley felt optimistic. As the most devastating war in human history faded from view, the reconstruction of his native Britain slowly took shape. At the same time, the new international organization he had been selected to lead, the United Nations Education, Social, and Cultural Organization (UNESCO), was getting off the ground. A highly regarded scientist, writer, and internationalist, Huxley held high hopes for UNESCO. He believed his new organization would usher in an era of more harmonious relations between different nations, cultures, and individuals. World War II had shown humankind at its most destructive; now was a time for the world to create new institutions that would revive common bonds between disparate societies, bring advances in science to bear upon pressing social and economic problems, and link together the world's brightest minds in the hopes of crafting a lasting peace. UNESCO, Huxley wrote, would "help the peoples of the world to mutual understanding and to a realization of the common humanity and common tasks which they share, as opposed to the nationalisms which too often tend to isolate and separate them." Huxley dedicated the better part of his postwar career to bringing about just such an understanding.[1]

Amid all the social problems that Huxley hoped to address with UNESCO was an issue close to his heart but one that found only a handful of supporters worldwide in 1948: the devastation of natural flora and fauna. The world wars not only shattered many illusions about the

[1] Quoted in Julian Huxley, UNESCO: Its Purpose and Its Philosophy (London: The Frederick Printing Co., Ltd., 1946), 13.

relationship between human societies. They also called into question the relationship between humankind and nature. War alters the nonhuman environment in substantial ways, a fact made all the more apparent by the particular destructiveness of the technologies used during World War II.[2] To Huxley, the war's impact on the environment represented the culmination of longer trends of destruction, despoliation, and exploitation. Since the late nineteenth century, rapid economic and social development in the United States, Europe, and Japan had spurred wide-scale environmental change. Industrialization, urbanization, increasing use of natural resources, and rapid worldwide population growth all threatened the natural world.

In the postwar world, Huxley believed he could use international institutions to generate greater public concern over such issues, bring together like-minded scientists and experts from all over the world to study landscape depreciation and species loss, and pressure reticent governments to take aggressive action in the name of environmental protection. Postwar international conservation flowered from the roots Huxley laid down in UNESCO. Within a decade and a half after the War, Huxley and a team of like-minded experts – such as the British ornithologists E. Max Nicholson and Peter Scott, German zoologist Bernhard Grzimek, Swedish zoologist Kai Curry-Lindahl, Belgian administrator Jean-Paul Harroy, and American scientist Harold "Hal" Coolidge – had created organizations to institutionalize international conservation. They established the International Union for the Conservation of Nature (IUCN) and the World Wildlife Fund (WWF), two of the largest and most significant non-governmental organizations (NGOs) of the postwar period. Although they were not professional activists – only a few, including Hal Coolidge, would serve as full-time, salaried NGO officials – Huxley and his associates' work in the 1940s and 1950s provided the foundation for a significant postwar development: the rise of a global network of NGOs focused on environmental issues.

Huxley and his colleagues believed that there were two main purposes for NGOs. First, NGOs would influence national governments and international institutions to make policy changes. Second, NGOs would bring together transnational networks of reformers and experts to share

[2] On war and the environment in general, see Richard Tucker and Edmund Russell, eds., *Natural Enemy, Natural Ally: Toward an Environmental History of War* (Corvallis: Oregon State University Press, 2004) and Richard Tucker, "War and the Environment," in J. R. McNeil and Erin Stewart, eds., *A Companion to Global Environmental History* (London: Blackwell Publishing, 2012).

information, discuss major issues of the day, and facilitate work on the ground worldwide. Huxley and his colleagues envisioned their work as fundamentally global in scope. They believed the protection of nature, especially distinctive landscapes and wildlife, required international coordination and cooperation. It was not enough for one community or nation to take measures on behalf of saving endangered flora and fauna; they argued that such nonhuman entities belonged to the whole of humankind. In making such statements, NGO officials also implied that if a local community, region, or nation-state threatened some part of the nonhuman world, external interventions were necessary to protect the environment and could trump national sovereignty. "Protection of nature is a matter of vital concern to all nations, and the furthering of it is primary concern of no single effective international agency," the IUCN's constitution explained. Given this absence of a single institution to promote such protective measures, the founders of the IUCN and the WWF believed that they had to educate the public, lobby governments, and establish international guidelines for worldwide nature protection "in order that the future peace, progress, and prosperity of mankind may be assured."[3]

However, as international conservation began to develop some political momentum in the postwar years, so too did another important idea. As part of the emerging postwar international order during the late 1940s and 1950s, the concept of "development" entered the lexicon of academics, policy makers, and new nationalist leaders alike. No longer would countries be defined by colonizers and colonized, trapped in a fixed hierarchy of exploiter and exploited. In its place emerged a logic of development, which placed all nations on a linear track. Fully "developed" nations, such as the United States, stood at the end of the line, while "developing" or "underdeveloped" nations moved upward through time trying to reach the top. In this process, countries strove to overcome the conditions of "underdevelopment" through industrialization, urbanization, and mass consumption.

These shared assumptions spread across the world at mid-century as the global Cold War took shape. In developmental thinking, communism and capitalism were not just ideal social ends but also conditional means, two alternative political economies and worldviews that nations could use to pursue material abundance. With European empires crumbling, both

[3] "Text of the Constitution of the International Union for the Protection of Nature," in *International Union for the Protection of Nature: Established at Fontainebleau, 5 October 1948* (Brussels: IUCN, 1948), 16. Pamphlet viewed at the International Union for the Conservation of Nature Library [hereinafter cited as IUCN Library], Gland, Switzerland.

the United States and the Soviet Union invested heavily in the developing world in the 1950s and 1960s in the hopes that their system would win hearts and minds to earn strategic partners in a global Cold War. Leaders of countries in the Global South often accepted such aid, as they, too, aspired for rapid development. Although conflicts arose over means to achieve development, the leadership of all nations held rapid economic growth rates, high living standards, and increasing national wealth as common goals to pursue.

While there were many differences between different political economies of development, there was a critical common set of assumptions about the relationship between humans, technology, and nature. In the developer's mindset, wild nature – natural resources, wildlife, and the land itself – was to be made "legible" and productive through the use of organizational power (be it states or firms) and technology to harness the powers of nature.[4] People, by and large, understood nature in economic terms. Policy makers saw natural resources less as partial components of complex ecosystems than as commodities waiting to be extracted from the land for human use. Development, conceived in this way, often led to the wasteful use of plant and animal species, habitat loss, and a general deterioration of the natural world.[5]

These facts alarmed Huxley and his network of conservationists. World War II had shown how a potent mixture of nationalism, the quest for natural resources for economic expansion, and modern industrial technologies could ravage the natural world. Huxley and his colleagues feared that postwar desires for rapid economic growth would lead to greater environmental devastation. In particular, the founders of the IUCN and the WWF worried that newly independent nations in the developing world would dismantle the national parks and game reserves that colonial authorities had set up in earlier periods and embrace wasteful, exploitative patterns of development. They feared that these new nations might follow the destructive path taken by the industrial powers of the West. Like many postwar civil servants, conservationists spoke in a

---

[4] I borrow the concept of "legibility" of nature from Scott, *Seeing Like a State*.

[5] For the longer history of the "imperial" view, as well as other epistemologies for understanding the natural world, see Donald Worster, *Nature's Economy: A History of Ecological Ideas* (Cambridge: Cambridge University Press, 1994). On the relationship between environmentalism and American liberalism, see the introduction in Keith Woodhouse, *A Subversive Nature: Radical Environmentalism in the Late-Twentieth-Century United States* (Ph.D. Dissertation, University of Wisconsin–Madison, 2010). On the relationship between liberalism and American development policy, see Latham, *Modernization as Ideology*.

progressive, value neutral, internationalist language about the universal appeal of wildlife and importance of wise use resource management.[6] In practice their actions in the developing world often served to reinforce and preserve colonial arrangements in the turbulent decolonization process. Fear of short-term political change motivated them as strongly as optimism over the possibilities of long-term cultural transformation.

The focus and strategy of postwar NGOs reflected these concerns. Although conservationists in the IUCN and the WWF often spoke of "the earth" or "the world" as the object of their activism, in practice they focused much of their early activities trying to shore up existing colonial relationships in the developing world, particularly Africa. At the heart of these efforts lie two competing ideas about environmental protection: preservation (thought of as separating nature from the market through strict regulatory legislation, such as national parks) and conservation (the rational management of natural resources).[7] One of the distinctive characteristics of the IUCN and the WWF was that they called for, from their inception, reconciliation between developmental goals of economic progress with the necessity of environmental protection. Yet although IUCN officials, and Huxley in particular, often spoke of the need to reconcile both desires to preserve and conserve natural resources in the postcolonial world, in actuality by the early 1960s no reconciliation had occurred. Leaders in the developing world and officials in major lending countries, particularly the United States, thus placed a low priority on preservation and conservation compared to other developmental objectives. The tensions between donor agencies, nationalist leaders, and international conservationists such as Huxley exposed a sharp divide

---

[6] On internationalism in the postwar world see Mark Mazower, *No Enchanted Palace: The End of Empire and the Ideological Origins of the United Nations* (Princeton: Princeton University Press, 2009). On postwar "progressive" internationalism, see Staples, *The Birth of Development*.

[7] This book refers to NGOs in the early postwar years as "conservation" organizations and their members as "conservationists" because NGOs often described themselves in that way and because they held strong beliefs about the importance of conserving natural resources as well as preserving natural spaces. In instances when NGOs promoted policies that placed greater emphasis on preserving natural spaces over the judicious management of natural resources, particularly in the case of creating national parks, terms such as "preservationist" or "protectionist" are used. The term "environmental" or "environmentalist" became widespread in the 1960s and 1970s, and many NGOs began using those words as umbrella terms to encapsulate all concerns for the state of the natural world. For a longer elaboration of the historical (and historiographical) use of "conservation" and "preservation," see Richard White, "American Environmental History: The Development of a New Historical Field," *Pacific Historical Review*, Vol. 54, No. 3 (August 1985), 297–335.

between the national imperatives of economic growth and the universal arguments for environmental protection put forth by IUCN and WWF officials. After a decade and a half of advocacy, the future for international conservation remained uncertain.

## THE POSTWAR CONTEXT, I: AN ERA OF INTERNATIONAL INSTITUTION BUILDING

As World War II drew to a close, Julian Huxley fixed his attention on the problems of postwar recovery and future reconstruction. He was troubled by the fact that Western Europe, a society that he had come to admire for its scientific advances and aesthetic tastes, had nearly destroyed itself in a half-decade of brutal warfare. Huxley believed that parochial, often virulent nationalism had been an important motivating force behind the conflict. Growing up in a wealthy and famous family (his great-uncle, Matthew Arnold, was a well-known writer, as was his brother, Aldous), Huxley had the opportunity to travel extensively, which encouraged him to think globally about political issues. Huxley wanted to embed countries in webs of international institutions that could mitigate their destructive tendencies and facilitate constructive interactions to combat the narrow self-interest that often led nations to war. Like many architects of the postwar international order, Huxley hoped to provide expert guidance on topics such as economic development, agricultural production, and political mediation by bringing new scientific research to bear on social ills.[8]

In particular, he championed the United Nations as a model for future international cooperation and governance. Attempts at international governance were not new, but the United Nations held particular importance in the early postwar period for national leaders attempting to redress the parochialism and narrow-minded nationalism that had ravaged the interwar years.[9] Officially created by an international charter in April 1945 and ratified by the five permanent members of the Security Council (France, the Soviet Union, China, Great Britain, and the United States), the UN embodied the hopes of Huxley and many others who saw the new organization as an evolutionary expansion of the ill-fated League of Nations and a harbinger of future international cooperation.[10]

[8] On his thought, see Richard Samuel Deese, *Ecology and the Gospel of Progress: Julian and Aldous Huxley in the American Century* (Ph.D. Dissertation, Boston University, 2007).

[9] Ibid., chapter 3.

[10] On the founding of the UN, see Paul Kennedy, *The Parliament of Man: The Past, Present, and Future of the United Nations* (New York: Random House, 2006), part I, and Jussi

*architects of the postwar international order*

The United Nations' founding was a mixture of high-minded idealism and calculated realism. Article 1 stated that, *inter alia*, the new organization would seek "to take effective collective measures for the prevention and removal of threats to the peace" and "to achieve international co-operation in solving international problems of an economic, social, cultural, or humanitarian character, and in promoting and encouraging respect for human rights and for fundamental freedoms for all without distinction as to race, sex, language, or religion." However, Article 2 noted that "nothing contained in the present Charter shall authorize the United Nations to intervene in matters which are essentially within the domestic jurisdiction of any state or shall require the Members to submit such matters to settlement under the present Charter."[11] Put another way, at the founding of the United Nations, a discernable tension existed between the aspirations of elite-driven international governance and the entrenched power of national sovereignty. This tension pervaded the rest of the century, and it underscored much of the difficulties international NGOs would face when attempting to bring their ideas to bear upon international institutions and national governments.

In spite of the power afforded to nation-states, the UN charter and the early years of the organization did seem to achieve many of the internationalists' goals. In elaborating on the powers of the UN's Economic and Social Council, the charter stated in Article 71, "The Economic and Social Council may make suitable arrangements for consultation with non-governmental organizations which are concerned with matters within its competence. Such arrangements may be made with international organizations and, where appropriate, with national organizations after consultation with the Member of the United Nations concerned."[12] The Article distinguished "non-governmental organizations" as a category of political and social organization different from the intergovernmental organizations established under the new charter. In time, the category became an umbrella term to describe all private, nonprofit entities. In the immediate context, Article 71 created the institutional framework for

M. Hanhimaki, *The United Nations: A Very Short Introduction* (Oxford: Oxford University Press, 2008), chapter 1.

[11] Quoted from *Charter of the United Nations:* chapter 1: *Purposes and Principles.* [Online] Available: http://www.un.org/en/documents/charter/index.shtml. Accessed October 25, 2010.

[12] Quoted from *Charter of the United Nations:* chapter 10: *The Economic and Social Council.* [Online] Available: http://www.un.org/en/documents/charter/index.shtml. Accessed October 25, 2010. See also Kennedy, *The Parliament of Man,* 217–18.

NGOs to become part of the UN system, and, eventually, shape UN legislation and activities.

The UN's Economic and Social Council also emphasized cultural internationalism, and promoted an agency within the UN system to work on disseminating information and advocating causes that spoke to a kind of universal uplift. Although the most important functions of the UN began in the realm of peacekeeping and humanitarian relief, early efforts to incorporate education, economic development, and scientific knowledge would have long-lasting effects for the organization. The UN's founders believed education, intellectual cooperation, and new methods to promote shared values were necessary to establish peace. "Since wars begin in the minds of men," British Prime Minister and UNESCO supporter Clement Atlee explained, "it is in the minds of men that the defences [sic] of peace must be constructed."[13]

This softer side of international organization came to flourish through a number of UN specialized agencies such as the Food and Agricultural Organization (FAO) and the World Health Organization (WHO), as well as through the International Bank for Reconstruction and Development (World Bank) and the International Monetary Fund (IMF), and the General Agreement on Tariffs and Trade (GATT). Taken together, these organizations reflected a belief that top-down elite guidance, international cooperation, and engagement with international institutions would modulate the parochialism of the 1930s. By focusing on economic and social issues as well as political issues, the creation of these organizations also implied that many policy makers hoped to use such expertise and coordination to relieve the conditions of deprivation and desperation that gave rise to radical ideologies and political upheaval. The goal was not to erode national sovereignty but to provide international frameworks in which national self-interest could be geared toward shared goals through incremental change.[14]

Julian Huxley's early postwar activities reflected many of these aspirations. Throughout much of 1946, Huxley eschewed his scientific research and prolific writing to serve as an administrative head of a loose body of

---

[13] Quoted in H. H. Krill De Capello, "The Creation of the United Nations Educational, Scientific, and Cultural Organization," *International Organization*, Vol. 24, No. 1 (Winter 1970), 19.

[14] On international institutions and development, see Staples, *The Birth of Development*. On the WHO, see Chorev, *The World Health Organization between North and South*. On GATT, see Thomas W. Zeiler, *Free Trade, Free World: The Advent of GATT* (Chapel Hill: University of North Carolina Press, 1999). On the World Bank, see Chapter 5 of this book.

scientists, educators, policy makers, and other men and women of letters. He worked with a preparatory committee tasked with constructing a "cultural" side of the UN, which established the Educational, Scientific, and Cultural Organization (UNESCO) in 1945. Huxley became the organization's executive director in early 1947, a position he embraced with great enthusiasm.[15] In his leadership role, Huxley pushed for the organization to develop a strong scientific component, lobbying for including the "S" ("Scientific") in the organization's name.[16] He thought that such knowledge could transcend ideological divisions and be deployed to solve most problems, from low agricultural productivity to conflict resolution. "The application of science provides most of the material basis for human culture," Huxley claimed, "and also that the practice and the understanding of science need to be integrated with that of other human activities."[17] He wanted UNESCO to champion the application of the most modern scientific advances in the name of human progress. Accordingly, in its early years UNESCO used its small budget to fund scientifically backed literacy campaigns in areas controlled by the UN's mandate system.[18]

UNESCO was emblematic of the larger constellation of international organizations created in the postwar years born from a progressive faith that held that applying expertise could transform the world for the better. The individuals who staffed the World Bank, the FAO, and the WHO often shared Huxley's assumptions and values. They thought that human progress was a linear and measurable phenomenon; many sought to circumscribe competitive nationalism; they believed in the benefits of nondiscriminatory trade and modest governmental management of market forces; and many thought they could employ advances science and technology to bear on perplexing social problems.[19]

The rise of such organizations reveals two salient aspects of the thinking held by internationalists of Huxley's generation. For one, they signified a faith held by many reformers that international organizations were fundamentally necessary to guide, manage, and resolve future conflicts. Scientific and technological advances seemed to homogenize life

[15] Huxley, *UNESCO: Its Purpose and Its Philosophy.*
[16] Mazower, *No Enchanted Palace*, 95.
[17] Huxley, *UNESCO: Its Purpose and Its Philosophy*, 7.
[18] Krill De Capello, "The Creation of the United Nations Educational, Scientific, and Cultural Organization," 23.
[19] Staples, *The Birth of Development*, 6.

experiences and economic systems and dissolve old differences, so that everything from agricultural production to disease prevention to wildlife protection could be negotiated and defined at the international level and then applied to local situations with a modicum of adjustments. Second, this set of assumptions about scientific knowledge and historical under-standing nurtured a belief that the Western experience of industrializa-tion, economic management, and political modernization could be used to encourage the development of the entire world.

### THE POSTWAR CONTEXT, II: RELIEF, RECONSTRUCTION, AND THE RISE OF DEVELOPMENT

The rise of postwar development thinking derived from both humanitar-ian and strategic motivations. Many of the civil servants who served in international institutions hoped to overcome persistent deprivation, scar-city, and instability in the "underdeveloped" world through the applica-tion of Western knowledge and techniques. However, these organizations also sought to promote open and interconnected economies, cultural exchange, and liberalism against the threats posed by totalitarian foes – National Socialist or Soviet Communist. A more prosperous, intercon-nected, and cooperative world would improve humankind's lot, but it would also contain and isolate the autarkic and imperialistic tendencies of totalitarian states. Economic development stood at the intersection of these dual objectives. It would improve material welfare worldwide while creating vibrant national economies and stable nations that would enlarge the international community along liberal, capitalist lines. In this line of thinking, ideals and interests were mutually supportive.[20]

In addition to these international institutions designed for develop-ment, in the early postwar years many nations designed programs to promote coordination of the global economy, promote liberal capitalist polities worldwide, and guard against the autarkic practices that had contributed to World War II. In the United States, the postwar years witnessed the creation of the national security state, an enlargement of federal power in foreign policy making. Among the many changes in foreign relations during this time were the founding of the Central Intelligence Agency, the consolidation of national security policy in the

---

[20] On the strategic purpose of development assistance and foreign aid, see Ruttan, *United States Development Assistance Policy.*

Department of Defense, and a global system of military bases able to respond to any threat around the globe.[21]

Among these transformations in American foreign policy was a new emphasis on foreign aid. To curtail communist expansion in Europe, promote open liberal trading systems, and rebuild struggling nations, programs such as the Truman Doctrine and Marshall Plan offered relief and reconstruction aid to Europe. These programs built on earlier relief and economic aid efforts, such as the Institute for Inter-American Affairs (IIAA) of the early 1940s and the United Nations Relief and Recovery Administration (UNRRA) of the 1940s, but greatly expanded the role of federal spending abroad and explicitly married economic assistance to grand strategy. In the fourth point of his 1949 inaugural address, President Truman announced for the first time that the United States would take as a formal objective the economic and social development of what he termed the "underdeveloped" world – the countries of Asia, Africa, and Latin America.[22] The greatest fears in foreign policy circles surrounding natural resources in the 1940s and 1950s were not potential exhaustion, mismanagement, or exploitation, but rather that the countries might fall into the Soviet orbit and fuel an expansive, imperial totalitarian state.[23]

The Point Four program, which emerged from Truman's 1949 inaugural, marked the first time a president had made so strong a commitment to the economic development of other countries.[24] Point Four created a

[21] On post–World War II foreign policy, see Melvyn Leffler, *A Preponderance of Power: National Security, the Truman Administration, and the Cold War* (Stanford: Stanford University Press, 1992); Michael J. Hogan, *A Cross of Iron: Harry S. Truman and the Origins of the National Security State, 1945–1954* (Cambridge: Cambridge University Press, 1998); John Lewis Gaddis, *Strategies of Containment: A Critical Appraisal of American National Security Policy during the Cold War, Revised and Expanded Edition* (Oxford: Oxford University Press, 2005).

[22] On the Marshall Plan, see Michael Hogan, *The Marshall Plan: America, Britain, and the Reconstruction of Western Europe, 1947–1952* (Cambridge: Cambridge University Press, 1987); Robert Wood, "From the Marshall Plan to the Third World," in Melvyn P. Leffler and David S. Painter, eds., *The Origins of the Cold War: An International History*, 2nd ed. (New York: Routledge, 1994), 239–50.

[23] On postwar thinking about natural resources and national security, see Leffler, *A Preponderance of Power*, introduction; Alfred E. Eckes, Jr., *The United States and the Global Struggle for Minerals* (Austin: University of Texas Press, 1979).

[24] Truman Inaugural Address, January 20, 1949. [Online] Available: http://www.trumanli brary.org/whistlestop/50yr_archive/inagural20jan1949.htm. Accessed October 12, 2010. On the precedents to Point Four, see David Ekbladh, *The Great American Mission*, chapter 1; Merle Curti and Kendall Birr, *Prelude to Point Four: American Technical Missions Overseas, 1838–1938* (Madison: The University of Wisconsin Press, 1954).

small bureaucracy with the expressed purpose of transferring American expertise to spur the economic development of the so-called underdeveloped world.[25] By providing American expertise or guaranteeing loans for development projects, Point Four officials believed that they could catalyze economic transformations, enrich developing nations, and create sustainable markets for goods manufactured by recovering European nations. In so doing, they would enlarge the liberal, capitalist trading area and establish societies that would turn away from communist influence. Point Four was a small weapon in the early phase of the Cold War, but it was a weapon nonetheless.[26]

Following the creation of Point Four, the idea of development soon captivated leaders across the globe. "Few subjects," explained Willard Thorp, the U.S. delegate to the UN's Economic and Social Council, "excite the imagination more than economic development. To many, these words signify economic progress, more of the better things of life for more people. . . . These words capture the imagination of people everywhere, in the most developed countries as well as those less developed or only partially development."[27] High-minded rhetoric proliferated in the West as expectations rose across the developing world. Foreign aid for economic development seemed to hold the power to alleviate the persistent material scarcity that had plagued humankind for millennia.

---

[25] In this book, I use "developing countries," "Global South," and "Third World" interchangeably, as many key actors from around the world did so during the latter half of the twentieth century. There are problems with using any single term to capture the complexity and shifting alliances between the countries outside of the United States, Canada, Europe, Japan, and the Soviet Union. But all three terms appeared during the 1960s and 1970s. When one term is more appropriate than another, such as when describing the self-conscious activism of Third World countries in the 1970s, I use that term. After all, for many years under consideration here, the Third World was "a project," in Vijay Prasad's terminology, which bound much of the world together in a tenuous but potent informal alliance. Vijay Prashad, *The Poorer Nations: A Possible History of the Global South* (London: Verso, 2012), 1. On the problems of geographic categories in general, see Martin W. Lewis and Kären E. Wigen, *The Myth of Continents: A Critique of Metageography* (Berkeley: University of California Press, 1997).

[26] On the history of the Point Four program, see Stephen Macekura, "The Point Four Program and International Development Policy," *Political Science Quarterly*, Vol. 128, No. 1 (Spring 2013), 127–60; Stephen Macekura, "Point Four and the Crisis of Foreign Aid in the 1970s" in Robert Devine, ed., *Harry S. Truman and Foreign Aid* (Kirksville, MO: Truman State University Press, 2015), 73–100.

[27] Press release #558, February 25, 1949, United States Mission to the United Nations, File G.X. 26/1 "Economic Development Technical Assistance – Jacket 1," The United Nations Office at Geneva Registry Collection [hereinafter cited as UNOG Registry Collection], Geneva, Switzerland.

Despite the shared enthusiasm for the process of development, individual projects reflected a lack of consensus among what types of policies best promoted economic development and protected American interests. Development models go in and out of style, depending on theoretical fashion and specific historical circumstances. In very general terms, though, the late 1940s and 1950s experienced a mixture of land reform efforts, community development, and infrastructure building (particularly dam building), which often were designed to increase agricultural production. Assuring export-based economies would, for the United States and Western Europe, tend to liberalize developing nations and thereby reinforce the liberal capitalist configuration of the international system. Reforming the cultural patterns and worldview of peasantry in these largely agrarian societies would also lay the groundwork for industrial take-off, with wealthy, industrial society symbolizing the apogee of progress and modernity to which most nations aspired.[28]

This latter point is critical. Dams and other large capital-intensive projects symbolized modernity, power, and prestige.[29] In the United States, many development officials looked to instances of America's own successful development projects, such as the Tennessee Valley Authority's (TVA) mixture of public and private control, grassroots labor and organization, and broad scope, as evidence for the ways large technologies could harness, exploit, and repurpose nature toward given social and political ends. Projects such as the TVA demonstrated to these officials that high science, engineering acumen, and capital investment could generate new wealth, dissolve social problems via prosperity, and offer evidence of growth for national elites seeking to tell narratives of growing prestige and influence.[30] Julian Huxley himself marveled at the TVA, a

[28] On the variety of early developmental models, see Cullather, *The Hungry World*; Arndt, *Economic Development: The History of an Idea*, chapter 3; Robert A. Packenham, *Liberal America and the Third World: Political Development Ideas in Foreign Aid and Social Science* (Princeton: Princeton University Press, 1973), chapter 1; Latham, *Modernization as Ideology*, chapter 2. On the cultural implications of development, see Cullather, *Hungry World*; Escobar, *Encountering Development*; Rist, *The History of Development*, chapters 4–6. On community development, see Daniel Immerwahr, *Thinking Small: The United States and the Lure of Community Development* (Cambridge: Harvard University Press, 2014).

[29] Nick Cullather, "Damming Afghanistan: Modernization in a Buffer State," *The Journal of American History*, Vol. 89, No. 2 (September 2002), 512–37; Daniel Klingensmith, *"One Valley and a Thousand": Dams, Nationalism, and Development* (New Delhi: Oxford University Press, 2007).

[30] On the TVA's place in development history, see Ekbladh, *The Great American Mission*, chapters 2–6.

"most remarkable piece of planning and execution," often encouraging leaders of developing nations to whom he spoke to adopt such systems.[31] He even wrote a book about it.[32]

Moreover, the success of such projects was measured by another set of abstractions. Economic statistics, particular gross national product (GNP), became the primary way for measuring – and defining – national economic health and national viability in the 1950s. GNP was "the key yardstick of the Cold War – and of the twentieth century. Around the world, national income became the measure of national success, the ranking system for wealth, and a proxy for well-being. It ranked developed as well as developing countries, set the dividing line between them, and defined the goals for national economic policies the world over."[33]

Concurrent with this came a new emphasis on "economic growth" as the proper measure for the dynamism of a society. In the United States, growth became a policy goal to achieve full employment and minimize social conflict through the promise of ever-growing prosperity. Growth soon became the object of policy makers' aspiration in Europe, too. The Organization for European Economic Cooperation (OEEC) used the phrase "economic growth" for the first time in 1956, and its successor organization, the Organization for Economic Cooperation and Development (OECD), placed the phrase among its official objectives four years later.[34] In the early 1950s, generating, maintaining, and guiding growth had become the overwhelming focus among development

[31] Julian Huxley, "Population and Conservation: Lecture II," from lectures at the University of Ghana, 1961, box 175, Huxley Papers, 1899–1980, MS 50, Woodson Research Center, Fondren Library, Rice University [hereinafter cited as Huxley Papers].

[32] Julian Huxley, *TVA: Adventure in Planning* (Surrey, UK: The Architectural Press, 1943).

[33] Quoted in David Engerman, "Bernath Lecture: American Knowledge and Global Power," *Diplomatic History*, Vol. 31, No. 4 (September 2007), 615–21. On statistical thinking, economics, and the rise of a measurable "national economy," see Timothy Mitchell, "Economists and the Economy in the Twentieth Century," in George Steinmetz, ed., *The Politics of Method in the Human Sciences: Positivism and Its Epistemological Others* (Durham: Duke University Press, 2005); Timothy Mitchell, *Rule of Experts: Egypt, Techno-Politics, Modernity* (Berkeley: University of California Press, 2002); Daniel Speich, "The Use of Global Abstractions: National Income Accounting in the Period of Imperial Decline," *Journal of Global History*, Vol. 6, No. 1 (2011), 7–28; Daniel Speich, "Travelling with the GDP through Early Development Economics' History," in *Working Papers on The Nature of Evidence: How Well Do Facts Travel?* No. 33/2008, London School of Economics, Department of Economic History, September 2008. On the growth mantra in America, see Robert M. Collins, *More: The Politics of Economic Growth in Postwar America* (Oxford: Oxford University Press, 2000).

[34] Mark Mazower, *Dark Continent: Europe's Twentieth Century* (London: Penguin Press, 1998), 301.

economists, too.[35] By the time Walt Rostow's famous development tract *The Stages of Economic Growth* came out in 1960, economic growth had transformed from a new statistical construct to a policy goal and political gospel.[36]

National leaders in the developing world – such as India's Jawaharlal Nehru, Kwame Nkrumah in Ghana, and Gamal Abdel Nasser in Egypt – embraced this growth mindset and held rapid economic growth as a primary aim for their countries. Likewise, they believed that increasing GNP was the primary measure of their nation's vitality.[37] The global spread of economic growth as a political objective thus had multiple sources. Cold War competition often impelled the United States and the Soviet Union to intervene in the developing world and promote their respective models of modernization.[38] National leaders had their own purposes for pursuing developmental ends as well, and they turned to large, capital-intensive development projects in the name of revolutionary nationalism. Such nationalism was especially pronounced for leaders attempting to throw off the shackles of colonialism and make their nations powerful, and by extension, modern.

Seeking to fulfill nationalist aspirations as their foremost goal, young nationalists often leveraged their position between the two superpowers to gain as much assistance as possible, regardless of its ideological source. In Ghana, Nkrumah willfully played the Soviet bloc off the United States and Britain to garner Western support for a hydrological dam project on the Volta River, explaining that "either we shall modernize with your interests and support—or we shall be compelled to turn elsewhere." Nationalist leaders, too, recognized the symbolic value of big development projects in constructing nationalist narratives, as they internalized some of modernization's most basic precepts, from the use of expertise, the power of technology to spark social change, and the submission of nature toward human ends. Nyerere hailed Western support for a massive hydroelectric plant by claiming that "schemes such as this one are in fact the bricks and mortar evidence of the revolution which our country is

---

[35] H. W. Arndt, *The Rise and Fall of Economic Growth: A Study in Contemporary Thought* (Melbourne: Longman Cheshire Pty Limited, 1978), chapters 3 and 4.

[36] W. W. Rostow, *The Stages of Economic Growth: A Non-Communist Manifesto* (Cambridge: Cambridge University Press, 1960).

[37] Engerman, "Bernath Lecture: American Knowledge and Global Power," 619.

[38] Westad, *The Global Cold War*. See also Charles S. Maier, "The World Economy and the Cold War in the Middle of the Twentieth Century," in Melvyn P. Leffler and Odd Arne Westad, eds., *The Cambridge History of The Cold War: Volume I, Origins* (Cambridge: Cambridge University Press, 2010), 44–66.

deliberately and purposefully undergoing. It represents the application of science to the needs of the people." The ends of development, economic growth, and progress, coupled with the means of using capital-intensive, high-technology, large-scale projects that required domination of the natural world, were shared by developers in the United States and Europe *and* by leaders of developing nations alike.[39]

It is not surprising that early development projects left ecological considerations far down the list of priorities, since the primary objectives of development were to create economic growth measured in terms of national production and income and symbols of national prestige. Where would the protection of nature fit into development plans, if at all? Why should national leaders protect the natural environment at all, if doing so would hinder their larger developmental goals? Julian Huxley and his colleagues pondered these questions, and in the postwar years they struggled to find satisfying answers to them.

### THE BIRTH OF GLOBAL WILDLIFE PROTECTION: JULIAN HUXLEY AND THE IUCN

Huxley and his colleagues had an ambivalent relationship with development. On the one hand, they believed that societies everywhere could be improved by planned development programs guided by enlightened elites. As early as 1942, Huxley envisioned a world in which development, "planned on a world scale," would uplift struggling peoples out of desperation and poverty. Huxley dreamed of an "international economic union" that would transfer aid to developing nations, helping them to increase economic productivity and educate their citizens. He wanted such an organization to organize primary product exporters and oversee the distribution of raw materials to avoid the autarkic trading activities that had dominated the 1930s. In addition, Huxley foresaw "cultural self-determination," and international exchange of ideas and people through a "League of Free Peoples," a forerunner to UNESCO.[40]

Likewise, Huxley and his colleagues had a strong faith in the power of science to solve social ills. Huxley believed technical solutions could be

---

[39] Quotes from Heather J. Hoag and May-Britt Öhman, "Turning Water into Power: Debates over the Development of Tanzania's Rufiji River Basin, 1945–1985," *Technology and Culture*, Vol. 49, No. 3 (July 2008), 631–2.

[40] Julian Huxley, "Forging of the Peace Aims," unpublished manuscript, box 65, Huxley Papers; letter from Joseph Needham to Julian Huxley, October 16, 1947, box 17, Huxley Papers.

devised to solve almost any problem in society. He claimed that one of UNESCO's foremost goals was to "promote the international application of science to human welfare." He used the organization to promote projects, from literacy drives to rainforest exploration, which brought Western experts to distant locations in the name of economic and social development.[41] In striving to bring scientific knowledge to bear on existing social problems, Huxley assumed a leading role in mid-century eugenics (he served as president of the Eugenics Society from 1959 to 1962, and was a Life Fellow in the organization from 1925 until his death), as a means to explore potential ways to curb rapid population growth.[42] Huxley held complicated views about race, as well. He often explained his support for eugenics in race-neutral language, and he spoke out against racial prejudice. At UNESCO he supported major projects that emphasized that there was no scientific basis for racial inferiority or discrimination. However, his paternalism and faith in expert-driven management would greatly shape the conservation approaches he later supported in Africa, policies that often led to racially discriminatory practices.[43]

Huxley recognized that unimpeded economic development imperiled wildlife and often led to wasteful use of finite natural resources. In the early postwar years, many like-minded environmental experts, such as American ecologist William Vogt and conservationist Fairfield Osborn, Jr., warned in popular books about the dangers of unheeded development and global population growth.[44] He agitated in every one of UNESCO's formative gatherings for the new organization to collect and organize scientific knowledge so that it could be applied to rationalize resource use without "causing soil exhaustion or erosion ... or by ruining natural beauty or causing the extinction of striking or interesting species of

[41] Julian Huxley, "UNESCO: THE First Year," 1947, box 66, Huxley Papers. The project, proposed by Huxley in preparatory meetings in 1946, was approved at a UNESCO Conference in Beirut in 1948 and formally begun at a Conference in Florence in 1950, at the same time UNESCO commissioned a new scholarly periodical, the *Journal of World History*, to emphasize comparative histories of world civilizations. Unpublished manuscript by Julian Huxley, 1963, box 81, Huxley Papers. On the *History of Humanity*, see S. J. De Laet, ed., *History of Humanity* (London: Routledge, 1994).

[42] Malthusian fears animated mid-century conservation, a topic recently illuminated in Robertson, *The Malthusian Moment*. On the global movement for population control, see Connelly, *Fatal Misconception*.

[43] On Huxley, UNESCO, and race, see Stefan Kühl, *For the Betterment of Race: The Rise and Fall of the International Movement for Eugenics and Racial Hygiene* (New York: Palgrave Macmillan, 2013), 138–41.

[44] Robertson, *The Malthusian Moment*, chapter 2.

animals and plants."[45] Huxley was not opposed to the basic tenets of development; he believed in notions such as linear progress, the need for economic growth, and the virtues of scientific expertise. He just wanted to carve out a space for environmental protection within the development mindset.[46]

In his first few years with UNESCO, Huxley discovered that it was difficult to rally UN experts and government officials to spend large amounts of money to fund conservation activities. So he wanted to create a broader and more powerful international organization to promote conservation and establish a consistent source of funding to educate governments on the value of such practices.[47] To pursue this end, he organized and chaired a subcommittee within UNESCO called the Wild Life Conservation Special Committee.

The subcommittee established three features that became central to international conservation NGOs. For one, it organized cooperation among a number of leading ecologists (including scientific luminaries such as Arthur Tansley, Charles Elton, Owain Richards, and Edward Salisbury). Second, the committee declared that conservation had to link ecological science to public policy, although it also had to make the limitations of the science clear to a world that believed that technology could fix everything. And third, the group proclaimed that science should be used to protect endangered flora and fauna and conserve necessary resources. The subcommittee implied that its goal was not only protection but also the enhancement of wildlife populations. Its members supported the rational use of resources through careful research and planning on an international scale. Huxley's efforts to promote scientific management of land and natural resources were, according to a fellow conservationist, "perceived to be the exciting dimensions of post-war reconstruction."[48] After all, if many believed that control and exploitation of natural resources had been a precipitating cause of the previous war, appropriate use of resources would be a cornerstone of peaceful relations in the postwar world. Huxley used the language of progressive era conservation – the wise

---

[45] Huxley, *UNESCO: Its Purpose and Its Philosophy*, 28.

[46] On Huxley's years at UNESCO, see Glenda Sluga, "UNESCO and the (One) World of Julian Huxley," *Journal of World History*, Vol. 21, No. 3 (2010), 393–418.

[47] This was the case in Huxley's difficulty in raising funds for a biological research station on the Galapagos, which reinforced the need for a fund-raising conservation organization. "Memorandum for the Members of the Galapagos Committee Established in London on 15th July, 1958," box 81, Huxley Papers.

[48] Martin Holdgate, *The Green Web: A Union for World Conservation* (London: Earthscan Publications, Ltd., 1999), 17.

use of resources for the greater good – to describe his vision for rational management. The committee, in Huxley's mind, would help reticent governments realize this goal.

The subcommittee also spurred Huxley's efforts to launch an international conservation organization. Frustrated that UNESCO could not offer enough institutional support to preservationists and conservationists, in his last few months as director, Huxley devoted a great deal of effort to creating alternative venues for those concerned with international conservation. In the summer of 1947, Huxley organized a gathering with fellow European conservationists called the International Conference for the Protection of Nature, to lay the groundwork for a UNESCO conference the next year. The meeting brought together scientists who dealt with the "natural world" – biologists, zoologists, physiologists – and connected them in a network to share information and research, promote learning and new experiments, and create an international hub of intellectual activity designed to promote the conservation of natural resources.[49]

The UNESCO meeting took place in Fontainebleau, France, in October 1948, attended by representatives from 18 governments, 7 international organizations, and 107 national nature protection groups. The American delegation, led by Harold "Hal" Coolidge of the National Research Council and William Vogt of the Conservation Foundation, drafted an early constitution for a new group called the International Union for the Protection of Nature (IUPN), which it changed a few years later to the International Union for the Conservation of Nature and Natural Resources (IUCN). The founding document contained similar concepts and much of the same thinking vocabulary that Huxley had used at UNESCO. The organization sought to help preserve "the entire world biotic community" and all its natural resources. It also hoped to arrest the most disturbing aspects of development. "Civilization," the founding document continued, had achieved "its present high development by finding ever more effective means for exploiting these resources."[50] There needed to be some kind of countervailing force to this push for development, the IUCN founders argued, some way for concerned individuals to have their voices heard and to promote their interests in major institutions, such as the UN.

49 Ibid.
50 Tony Mence, "IUCN: How It Began, How It Is Growing Up" (Gland: International Union for the Protection of Nature and Natural Resources, 1981), 8–9, IUCN Library; Holdgate, *The Green Web*, 17–9. The IUPN changed its name to the IUCN in 1956.

Since all nations at the time seemed to strive for this style of exploitative development, the founders agreed that a new and fundamentally global organization was necessary to ensure that wise management of resources and cautious preservation of select natural landscapes replaced injudicious accumulation and wasteful use. "Conservation and rational utilization of natural resources can develop only within the broad limits of international cooperation," one of the organization's early members explained.[51] Its founders accordingly designed the IUCN to "promote and recommend national and international action in respect to the preservation in all parts of the world of wildlife and the natural environment ... by appropriate legislation such as the establishment of national parks, nature reserves and monuments and wild life refuges, with special regard to species threatened with extinction."[52] They would provide the scientific knowledge for new legislation in all national governments and promote international treaties and conventions, as the conservationists in the IUCN believed the entire planet required enlightened stewardship.

The IUCN built upon a smattering of earlier efforts to protect the wildlife of the colonial world. In the early twentieth century, conservation organizations had been largely national in scope and often restricted to protecting specific wildlife, such as sea birds. The few international organizations focused exclusively on imperial possessions. The first international environment agreement was signed in 1900 as the Convention for the Preservation of Wild Animals, Birds, and Fish in Africa by Great Britain, France, Germany, Italy, Portugal, and the Belgian Congo. To enforce this accord, the experienced hunters and naturalists who managed colonial parks formed the Society for the Preservation of the Wild Fauna of the Empire (SPWFE) in 1903.[53] Founder of Switzerland's first national park, Paul Sarasin, and a Dutch scientist, P. G. Van Tienhoven, had led much more narrow efforts to institutionalize nature protection after

---

[51] This sentence comes from a speech by renowned Soviet conservationist G. P. Dementiev, a member of the IUCN, during a speech at a workshop of conservation. G. P. Dementiev, "Conservation of Fauna," address before the IUCN Permanent Commission on Conservation Education, Nairobi Kenya, September 12–13, 1963, box 81, Huxley Papers.

[52] Tony Mence, "IUCN: How It Began, How It Is Growing Up" (Gland: International Union for the Protection of Nature and Natural Resources, 1981), 8–9, IUCN Library.

[53] British groups such as the East Riding Association for the Protection of Sea Birds (1867) and the Society for the Protection of Birds (1889) and in the United States, the Sierra Club (1892) led the way.

World War I. The IUCN expanded on these older organizations to spread the preservation and conservation message to the rest of the world.[54]

These early conservationists held idealized and romantic views of nature that inspired protection schemes predicated on colonial power. Many early conservationists saw Africa as a virtual Garden of Eden. In the minds of park managers and big-game hunters, exotic wildlife, large swaths of land yet to be developed, and hunter-gatherer populations contrasted vividly with the polluting, artificial landscapes of industrialized Europe. Much of the conservation activity in colonial possessions was directed toward preserving the paradisiacal vision of a wondrous landscape.[55]

The founders of the IUCN shared many of these assumptions of earlier conservationists, but the organization they created varied from its predecessors in a number of ways. Rather than focusing on single species, the IUCN cast a wider intellectual net. From its birth, the IUCN stressed the need to maintain a "balance of nature" and, in Huxley's words, an "equilibrium" between conservation and development. Two parallel conferences held at the temporary UN headquarters at Lake Success, New York, brought over 4,000 experts from around the world to "discuss how to apply the techniques of resource conservation and utilization to the development that was so essential to the post-war world." A resolution sent to the UN's Economic and Social Council in 1949 included language that would appear in the UN's definition of "sustainable development" forty years later, proclaiming the "urgent significance of ecology" to help planners "maintain for future generation the natural resources indispensable to their subsistence."[56] Thus, the IUCN from its start was committed

---

[54] Mence, *How It All Began*, 3–4, IUCN Library. See also Richard Tucker, "Preserving Nature's Remnant: Americans and Tropical Wildlife Conservation to 1941," unpublished book chapter in author's possession.

[55] David Anderson and Richard Grove, eds., *Conservation in Africa: People, Policies, and Practice* (Cambridge: Cambridge University Press, 1987), 4–5; Richard Grove, *Green Imperialism: Colonial Expansion, Tropical Island Edens, and the Origins of Environmentalism, 1600–1860* (Cambridge: Cambridge University Press, 1996).

[56] Holdgate, *The Green Web*, 41–2. On the history of UNESCO's early support for these gatherings, see Anna-Katharina Wöbse, "'The World After All Was One': The International Environmental Network of UNESCO and IUPN, 1945–1950," *Contemporary European History*, Vol. 20, No. 3 (August 2011), 331–48; John McCormick, "The Origins of the World Conservation Strategy," *Environmental Review*, Vol. 10, No. 3 (Autumn 1986), 177–8. On the two conferences, see Thomas Jundt, "Dueling Visions for the Postwar World: The UN and UNESCO 1949 Conferences on Resources and Nature and the Origins of American Environmentalism," *Journal of American History*, Vol. 101, No. 1 (June 2014), 44–70.

to preservation, outlined by the American delegation's wording of the initial constitution, and wise use conservation, as indicated in their early correspondence with the UN.

The IUCN was also broader in purpose and personnel than earlier conservation organizations. Composed of a large network of scientists, specialists, academics, and journalists, the organization had a more varied membership base than the earlier organizations stocked with hunters and naturalists. Moreover, the founders designed it to become a "union" in a very broad sense. It was a home for scientists concerned with all international conservation and protection issues, but also an organization that individuals, other NGOs, or even national governments (such as the United Kingdom) could join as members. Its purposes varied, too, and its scope extended more than just advocacy and oversight. The scientists who joined up worked in the three major areas, organized into "Commissions": the Species Survival Commission, which charted the status of endangered fauna around the globe; the World Commission on Protected Areas, which identified and kept track of the status of protected regions (national parks) and pressured national governments to include more such spaces; and the Commission of Environmental Law, which kept tabs on legal changes and became a standard bearer for crafting policy measures to protected natural spaces.[57] IUCN officials saw themselves as global experts capable of establishing principles and rules for all nations to follow.

The ambitious agenda and broad institutional structure that made the IUCN distinct created a variety of problems. Although it claimed itself to be an international organization with global reach, its representation from outside Europe and the United States was extremely low in its initial years. IUCN's membership ranged from the United States to Western Europe to the Soviet Union, but was primarily composed of Northern Europeans and Americans. The organization's secretary-general was Jean-Paul Harroy, a Belgian administrator who had worked extensively in colonial Belgian Congo; its first president was Charles Bernhard from the Swiss League for the Protection of Nature; its first vice presidents were Hal Coolidge (USA), Roger Heim of the Museum National D'Histoire Naturelle (France), and Henry Maurice of London's Zoological Society (UK). Aside from one Peruvian and one Argentine, all of the members of the Executive Board were from northern Europe or the United States.[58]

[57] Holdgate, *The Green Web*, vi.
[58] "Text of the Constitution of the International Union for the Protection of Nature," 28–9, IUCN Library.

Hence, the IUCN had what one former secretary-general called an "identity crisis" from the outset: How could an organization founded by a handful of largely Northern European scientists claim to be "global" in its character?[59]

The organization also struggled financially in its first decade and a half of existence. Initial funding from UNESCO kept the organization afloat. The IUCN sought to cover its basic operating expenses through membership dues. However, delinquency in payments and a constantly changing membership base, not to mention the organization's expanding ambitions, rendered this plan untenable. As the organization expanded to include more international gatherings, it remained solvent only through critical eleventh-hour donations (largely from American philanthropists), often secured by the assiduous lobbying of Hal Coolidge. It took decades for the IUCN to figure out an effective way to ensure consistent and reliable funding.[60]

From its inception, the IUCN struggled, as well, to reconcile its dual objectives of landscape preservation and resource conservation. In the early 1950s, environmental protection largely meant the same thing it did fifty years earlier: setting aside wild spaces (areas with minimal human presence) through governmental action. Promoted by early advocates such as John Muir, protectionism took the form of national parks, wildlife refuges, and game reserves. Many of the scientists in the IUCN, including Huxley, derived their understanding of the natural world through early and mid-twentieth-century writings from those such as Frederic Clements and Arthur Tansley. What the IUCN activists took away from the early scholarly literature on modern ecology was a sense that mankind was inherently destructive and threatening, and that nature was pure and tended toward stable, climax vegetation systems. Consequently, the best way to militate against mankind's destructiveness was to carve out artificial spaces – national parks and game reserves – and limit the human activity therein. The visceral memories of the global devastation during World War II only reinforced such notions.[61]

[59] Holdgate, *The Green Web*, 39.
[60] "Text of the Constitution of the International Union for the Protection of Nature," 29–30, IUCN Library.
[61] On preservation, see Roderick Nash, *Wilderness and the American Mind*, 3rd ed. (New Haven: Yale University Press, 1982); McCormick, *The Global Environmental Movement*, 2nd ed., chapter 1. On the rise of popular images of mankind as a destructive force toward nature, see Thomas Robertson, "'This Is the American Earth': American Empire, the Cold War, and American Environmentalism,"

Resource conservation, by contrast, focused on using nature for human ends, not its separation into national parks. Often called "wise use," resource conservation required planning, management, and organizational techniques – often led by educated experts – to ensure no aspect of the natural world – whether coal for factory use, water for irrigation, or animals for meat – would be exhausted. Forestry organizations, such as the United States' under Gifford Pinchot, often pioneered conservation programs.[62] Both preservation and conservation called for an active role for government, both believed in expert guidance, both required scientific knowledge to manage the natural world, and both, by the 1950s, were present in colonial administration policies.[63] Yet there was an important difference: Preservation implied cutting off nature from human settlement and utilization, while conservation encouraged use of the land, albeit wise use guided by scientific management that harmonized human needs with ecological restraint. While IUCN officials spoke about both methods, in practice, especially in the developing world, they placed greater emphasis on preservation.

Nevertheless, at the Fontainebleau conference in 1948 contentious debates arose over whether to use the word "protection" or "conservation" in the organization's name. "Protection" won initially. In debates among its members, it was evident that the International Union for the *Protection* of Nature melded a concern for protecting seemingly "wild" nature – flora and fauna – with a progressive notion of maximum resource utilization. In 1956, the organization changed its name officially to the International Union for the *Conservation* of Nature and Natural Resources (IUCN) to emphasize this point and to mitigate criticism from within that it only sought narrow "protectionism." IUCN officials sought to ensure that endangered species would be protected under national laws, but it also sought broad legal frameworks to ensure wise use of raw

---

*Diplomatic History* Vol. 32, No. 4 (September 2008), 564–7. On early ecology, see Arthur G. Tansley, "The Use and Abuse of Vegetational Concepts and Terms," *Ecology*, Vol. 16 (1935), 284–307; and Frederic Clements, "Nature and Structure of Climax," *Journal of Ecology*, Vol. 24 (1936), 252–84. On the influence of these thinkers on members of the IUCN and the WWF, see Sally Jeanrenaud, *People-Oriented Approaches in Global Conservation: Is the Leopard Changing its Spots?* (London: International Institute for Environment and Development (IIED) and Brighton: Institute for Development Studies (IDS), 2002), 11–12.

[62] On conservation, see Samuel Hays, *Conservation and the Gospel of Efficiency*; McCormick, *The Global Environmental Movement*, 2nd ed., chapter 1.

[63] On colonial policies, see William Beinart and Lotte Hughes, *Environment and Empire* (Oxford: Oxford University Press, 2007).

materials to prevent exhaustion and potentially violent competition over scarce resources.[64]

A final dilemma for the new organization was its imperial roots. IUCN's founder saw it as a progressive, forward-looking institution based on principles of cooperation, not coercion. However, many of its early leaders had been colonial administrators who still privileged their efforts in former colonies over other places. In the 1930s and 1940s, Julian Huxley had worked for the British Colonial Office in Africa on both educational and scientific projects.[65] The IUCN's inaugural director-general, Jean-Paul Harroy, a Belgian preservationist and diplomat, had extensive experience as a game warden in the Belgian Congo. Working closely with Harroy was another Belgian, Victor Van Straelen, who chaired the IUPN's Program Committee and helped to shape its agenda. Van Straelen, in addition, had served in a colonial capacity in Central Africa, where he had been instrumental in setting up the first gorilla sanctuary in the Congo.[66] Harroy's early goals were to increase prestige for the young organization, achieve a global reach, and disseminate information and educate the public, especially in the developing world about the benefits of preservation, conservation techniques, and applying coordinated ecological research.[67] The latter objective was particularly pressing, as many members feared decolonization would destabilize the existing relationships under the mandate system. If World War II was the formative experience in spurring Huxley's desire for a new international organization for nature protection, the imperial experience was the key historical force that shaped the young organization's collective character.

At its start, then, the IUCN held many conflicting characteristics. These conflicts, though, were not lost on its founders. Members realized that Harroy's vision for the group was not of "an activist pressure group." Rather, he envisioned a network of elite experts who could leverage their collective knowledge and experience to ensure game reserves and protected areas from the colonial era would receive the same status in a postcolonial world. Since the organization was made up primarily of European and a few American scientists, some in the organization feared that it would seem imperial, endeavoring "from the outside to propose (or impose) themselves and their techniques" on "autonomous peoples of

---

[64] Holdgate, *The Green Web*, 17–19.
[65] Hodge, *Triumph of the Expert*, 257.
[66] Mence, *How It All Began*, 8, IUCN Library; Jean-Paul Harroy, "Victor Van Straelen: An International Conservationist," *Oryx*, Vol. 7, Issue 5 (1964), 212.
[67] Holdgate, *The Green Web*, 40.

the tropics."[68] This realization alone could only go so far. In many ways, the early projects of the IUCN ended up being just that kind of neo-imperial imposition on developing countries.

## "THE MOST URGENT INTERNATIONAL CONSERVATION PROBLEM OF THE PRESENT TIME": THE IUCN AND THE AFRICA SPECIAL PROJECT

Much of IUCN's work, in fact, focused on colonial mandates in Africa. During the organization's early years, Julian Huxley traveled frequently in the British protectorates, bird-watching and meeting with imperial science authorities to discuss the fate of the landscapes he and his wife came to love so well. During much of the 1950s, the IUCN sponsored field surveys in nations throughout East Africa. The region became the focus of one of IUCN's earliest projects, Huxley's most famous works on conservation, and a seminal site in the history of development and environmental protection.

After all, African leaders desired rapid material progress during the postwar years, which added urgency to decolonization. Colonial rule left many nations deeply impoverished, and many new postcolonial leaders' credibility hinged on their ability to alleviate suffering, generate wealth, and establish prestige.[69] This desire to develop rapidly brought the problems facing African nations closer to the focus of leading American policy makers. The Manichean divisions of the Cold War meant that the potential political instability wrought by independence could point in one of two directions – free, open, capitalist governments friendly to the West, or closed, centralized, communist governments looking toward the Soviet Union. Vice President Richard Nixon visited the continent in 1957 – the first trip by a senior American official to Africa since the end of World War II – and concluded in a report to President Dwight Eisenhower that "the course of [Africa's] development ... could well prove to be the decisive factor in the conflict between the forces of freedom and international communism." President John Kennedy echoed this sentiment. Between 1958 and 1962, the United States increased total contributions

---

[68] Ibid.

[69] On the colonial origins of development, see Frederique Apffel-Marglin and Stephen Marglin, eds., *Decolonizing Knowledge: From Development to Dialogue* (New York: Oxford University Press, 1996);

Michael Cowen and Robert Shenton, *Doctrines of Development* (New York: Routledge Press, 1996).

to Africa from $110 million to $519 million, from around 2 percent of its overall aid expenditures to 8 percent.[70] Although still a small component of the United States' aid strategy, Africa increasingly became both a symbol of the challenges facing the so-called underdeveloped world and a physical site where competing visions of modernity played out.

However, modernization was not strictly an imposition of one view of nature and growth by powerful donor nations on docile recipient nations. More powerful than any particular policy was a set of assumptions about growth, progress, nationhood, and nature that shaped the developmental objectives of U.S. officials and nationalist leaders alike. As new nations emerged from the shackles of colonialism clamoring for economic growth and modernization, it was unclear whether conservation would be included in their nationalist projects. In this context the IUCN officials tried to inject ecological considerations into developmental goals.[71] In particular, they turned their attention to East Africa, formerly under German and British control, and to the young governments working toward full independence.

East African wildlife had long attracted nature-watchers and big-game hunters. One such enthusiast was a middle-aged American tax court judge named Russell E. Train, who began taking safaris in Kenya during the late 1950s. Active in American conservation society circles and an advocate for national parks, Train and his wife, Aileen, visited colonial East Africa in the hopes of seeing some of the most pristine wild landscapes in the world – and shooting an elephant (Figure 2).[72] Enthralled by his first safari in 1956, Train returned a couple years later. The second time around, Train worried about the future of the region's flora and fauna after encountering fewer animals on his hunting trips. He blamed the East Africans for the situation. "The ever-increasing native population, always hungry for more land and seemingly indifferent to the fate of the wildlife," he explained to friends upon his return home, was "the main problem" preventing the kind of preservation and conservation programs that he thought necessary to protect wildlife for viewing, rational use, and managed hunting.[73] Spurred into action by these concerns, from his offices in Washington, DC, in 1961 he created the African Wildlife Leadership Foundation (AWLF), which would later become the

---

[70] Michael Clough, *Free at Last?: U.S. Policy Toward Africa and the End of the Cold War* (New York: Council on Foreign Relations Press, 1992), 5–8.

[71] Holdgate, *The Green Web*, 57–71.

[72] Train 1956 Africa Safari, typed transcription of travel notes, box 1, Train Papers.

[73] Russell and Aileen Train, "Back to Africa: 1958," 1959, box 1, Train Papers.

FIGURE 2: Russell E. Train, Kenya, 1958, elephant tusks weighing 101 and 102 pounds. Courtesy of Russell Train Papers, Manuscript Division, Library of Congress.

influential African Wildlife Foundation, to promote environmental protection throughout the continent.[74]

Other elite American and European conservationists also worried about the African situation. Peter Scott, a British artist and conservationist who hosted a BBC show called *Look*, visited Uganda in 1956. What he saw startled him. Insufficient staffing and funding plagued national parks; local people shot at wildfowl without a proper appreciation for managing population size; tribal hunting and poaching seemed to decimate animal populations. "I cannot overstress the urgency of these conservation problems," Scott wrote in his final report. "The fate of Africa's wildlife hangs in the balance," and a ten-year plan for national park expansion, crafted by Scott and like-minded conservationists, "must be vigorously followed up if this unique heritage of the African people is to be preserved for their enjoyment and for the enjoyment of all mankind in generations to come."[75]

[74] Raymond Bonner, *At The Hand of Man: Peril and Hope for Africa's Wildlife* (New York: Alfred A. Knopf, 1993), 57–60.

[75] "Notes arising from a short visit to Uganda in January 1956," by Peter Scott, National Archives of the United Kingdom [hereinafter cited as NA-UK], records created and

Between Train's early trips in the late 1950s and the creation of the AWLF in 1961, Julian Huxley made another excursion to East Africa. In 1960, the IUCN commissioned Huxley to travel to East Africa and make recommendations for how to shape their policy recommendations for the region. Along the way, he wrote three long pieces for the *Observer*. Huxley's articles struck an ominous tone, with each offering lengthy descriptions of the African environment and the dire situation it faced. Huxley described a bleak state of affairs, but one not without hope. "The Africans (or some of them)," he explained, "are beginning to realize the value of wild life for themselves, as a source of much-needed meat, of revenue from visitors, game licenses, or ivory, or finally of national pride and international prestige." He then celebrated the work of the FAO, the UNESCO, and the IUCN, implying that their work would be instrumental for making the future of African wildlife an issue of concern on the international stage.[76]

In his final report on the trip to the IUCN, later published as a book, Huxley presented a succinct call for classical conservation, in spite of the demands the young nation was making on local inhabitants to develop the land for agricultural production. He explained:

The term "utility" should not be confined to customary types of development and land use. ... It should be regarded as "useful," and is certainly valuable, to preserve land from deterioration, to maintain forest cover, to keep habitats for scientific study, and to conserve wildlife to attract those who want to enjoy it in natural surroundings. In any modern planning, the concept *of utility* in the customary sense must give way to the over-all concept of *value* – not only utilitarian value, but also physiological value, social value, scientific value and enjoyment value. *Enjoyment value* applies notably to wild life and natural scenery.[77]

Put another way, Huxley believed land should not solely be legible in the market or for the state's productive capacities. Rather, certain lands had a particular aesthetic and emotional "value" – a "mixture of wonder, sheer pleasure, fascinated interest, refreshment and uplifting of sprit, and sense of fulfillment or enhancement of life," in his effusive description – that required governing authorities to ward off and protect. In addition, he turned to his own NGO, the IUCN, to convince nations that protecting

inherited by the Nature Conservancy, the Nature Conservancy Council and English Nature [hereinafter cited as FT], 3/593.

[76] Julian Huxley, "The Treasure House of Wildlife," *Observer*, November 13, 1960, 23–4.

[77] Julian Huxley, *The Conservation of Wild Life and Natural Habitats in Central and East Africa* (Paris: UNESCO, 1961), 21–2.

land was necessary. He believed environmental protection could also be used to generate wealth. Much of his argument rested on a burgeoning global phenomenon: international tourism.

Advances in air travel had expanded opportunities for global tourism by mid-century.[78] With a few landing strips and qualified personnel to direct traffic, airplanes from Europe and the United States shrunk time and space, carrying wealthy tourists interested in seeing African wildlife. For the IUCN, tourism was a silver bullet – it ensured some degree of economic benefit from setting aside productive land. Huxley believed that "if the wild life of Africa is properly conserved in National Parks and similar reserves, and adequate accommodation, access, and viewing facilities are provided, an increasing number of visitors from all parts of the world will undertake the modern equivalent of pilgrimage to enjoy the spectacle, and revenue from tourism could become one of the mainstays of the economy of all East African countries."[79] He claimed that national parks could be a source of national prestige, and thus could help developing nations earn an important symbol of modern nationhood.[80]

Promoting preservation and encouraging tourism became central goals of the IUCN. Huxley believed that the promise of foreign exchange earned through tourism might entice developing nations to create more national parks.[81] Bernhard Grzimek, IUCN member and former director of the Frankfurt Zoo, agreed with Huxley's concerns. Noting that in 1959 tourist revenues in East Africa amounted to $22 million (U.S. dollars) (among the largest sources of foreign exchange for the region) and that "more and more tourists will be searching for places where they can see animals in the wild," he encouraged the construction of more park infrastructure and tourist amenities. In addition, he called for a more vigorous

---

[78] Iriye, *Global Community*, 22–3. For studies of how air travel shaped and was shaped by American geopolitical interests, see Jenifer Van Vleck, *Empire of the Air: Aviation and American Ascendancy* (Cambridge: Harvard University Press, 2013).

[79] Julian Huxley, "Wild Fauna and Flora of Africa as a Cultural and Economic Asset, and the World Interest Therein," in *Conservation of Nature and Natural Resources in Modern African States: A Report of a Symposium Organized by CCTA and IUCN and Held Under the Auspices of FAO and UNESCO at Arusha, Tangayika, September 1961*, IUCN Publications new series No. 1 (Morges, Switzerland: International Union for the Conservation of Nature and Natural Resources, 1963), 204.

[80] See Huxley, "Wild Fauna and Flora of Africa as a Cultural and Economic Asset, and the World Interest Therein," in *Conservation of Nature and Natural Resources in Modern African States*.

[81] Ibid., 206.

international campaign to stir interest in African wildlife by playing down the dangers and difficulties of visiting the continent.[82]

The hopes that tourism would provide a source of profit for young nations were not unfounded. Colonial administrators had established a variety of expansive national parks throughout Africa. The Nairobi National Park in Kenya, located just outside the capital, drew many visitors who stayed in the city. More stunning landscapes of the lush and verdant Queen Elizabeth Park and the towering Murchison Falls in Uganda drew visitors further inland. And air traffic was increasing to Nairobi – thirteen international airlines reached the city in 1959. However, it was unrealistic to think that even improvements in hotels and roadways would lead to the staggering tourist growth necessary to meet the foreign exchange needs of developing countries. East Africa was but a small share of the global tourist market. In 1959, just over 64,000 tourists came to East Africa, compared to over 4 million who visited Austria, for instance, or the 1.3 million who visited the Netherlands, or the 126,000 who visited Turkey.[83]

In 1960, the IUCN launched its first major program, the African Special Project (ASP), to promote conservation by making the case that tourism revenues for wildlife were a valuable part of any modernization program. IUCN officials started the ASP under the assumption that "the accelerated rate of destruction of wild fauna, flora and habitat in Africa" was "the most urgent international conservation problem of the present time." The IUCN hoped to protect national parks and faunal reserves and to manage wildlife stocks on lands outside existing parks and reserves. The ASP would attempt to pursue both goals by undertaking surveys of wildlife and flora in Africa, hosting a major conservation conference, and drafting a charter on wildlife preservation and conservation.[84] At root, the ASP was designed "to convince African leaders and African public opinion of the importance to their new countries of conservation practices based on ecological knowledge."[85] Africa's wildlife was in peril, and as

[82] Bernhard Grzimek, "Value of the Tourist Industry," in *Conservation of Nature and Natural Resources in Modern African States*, 190. On Grzimek's work, see Thomas Lekan, "*Serengeti Shall Not Die*: Bernhard Grzimek, Wildlife Film, and the Making of a Tourist Landscape in East Africa," *German History*, Vol. 29, No. 2 (June 2011), 224–64.

[83] Grzimek, "Value of the Tourist Industry," 191.

[84] IUCN, "General Statement: IUCN's Africa Special Project (ASP) 1960–1963," May 1, 1961, box 107, Huxley Papers.

[85] "African Special Project (ASP), 1960–1963, Report of the IUCN Working Group," by E. B. Worthington, June 1960, folder "African Special Project," box 365, Flora and

the IUCN founders saw it, they had to persuade Africans to take the threat more seriously.

The ASP derived from a realization that most Africans did not share the same values related to preservation and conservation as did Western nature lovers. "The African thinks of game in terms of a potential source of much needed food for himself and his family and, not unnaturally, he regards it his by right of inheritance," wrote Uganda's game warden in 1960. "The future of survival of wildlife will depend entirely on the co-operation of the African, and we shall only get this co-operation provided that we must accept the concept of game as a food crop."[86] African governments, although they claimed to support conservation and preservation, often made little effort to instruct their populations about such issues. In Kenya, for instance, the Game Advisory Committee, tasked with overseeing all policies related to wild game, was "ineffective" according to the IUCN, because of "lack of preparation for meetings, which are, themselves, poorly attended and infrequent." Likewise, financial problems made wildlife education almost nonexistent throughout Kenya.[87]

The ASP sought to redress these problems in three stages. In Stage I, FAO's Forestry Officer for Africa, Gerald G. Watterson, toured sixteen countries in Africa with a variety of other scientists to study the state of conservation efforts in newly independent or soon-to-be independent countries. Stage II planned a major conservation conference, to be held in Tanganyika. Stage III created a specialized staff unit within the IUCN to "help interested African governments help themselves to develop wildlife management and wildlife tourism policy and practice." It was an ambitious program. Stage III alone would cost, at a minimum, $30,000 per year – an amount that far surpassed the funds the organization had in 1960.[88]

Thus, the IUCN's constant budgetary and personnel problems required resolution, and in many ways the fate of the organization depended on it. Promoting tourism and encouraging preservation and conservation efforts in the developing world infused the organization with a clear

Fauna International Archives [hereinafter cited as FFI archives], Flora and Fauna International, Cambridge, United Kingdom.

[86] "Wildlife Conservation and Management in Areas of Uganda Outside the National Parks," 1960 report by J. H. Blower, NA-UK, FT 3/592.

[87] "Confidential Report IUCN/ASP-9/Kenya," February 19, 1961, 9, folder, "African Special Project," box 365, FFI Archives.

[88] "Report on the African Special Project (ASP)," *IUCN Bulletin*, No. 1, Vol. I (August 1961), 1–3.

mission, but it lacked consistent funding and had inadequate personnel to mobilize public support and pressure governments. The organization also required better public outreach to ensure that its scientific discussions could shape public discourse and government policy. If IUCN wanted to win hearts and minds in Africa, it needed a more effective public strategy. Communication with skeptical and assertive African leaders was a major challenge. To address these many issues, Huxley soon formed a new organization.

## FUNDING THE CAUSE: THE BIRTH OF THE WWF AND CONSOLIDATION OF GLOBAL CONSERVATION

Huxley's writings for the British newspaper the *Observer* gained him international attention. With his typical lucid prose and admiration for wildlife, Huxley's articles described stunning topography and glorious flora and fauna. In dramatic flights of fancy, he described how overzealous developers using new farming technologies coupled with inadequate government resources imperiled Africa's wildlife. Poorly funded but inspired conservationists tried in vain to thwart the tides of change. To a British public long saturated with gruesome and hyperbolic tales of the Mau-Mau uprising, the articles offered an alternative depiction of East Africa.[89] They were a tremendous success.

Huxley used the articles as platforms to support a new charitable trust he was getting off the ground. In late 1960, Victor Stolan, a concerned London businessman, implored Huxley to create a new conservation body capable of raising vast sums of money. Huxley and Stolan turned to Huxley's friend Max Nicholson of Britain's Nature Conservancy to get the program off the ground. On September 11, 1961, the men, in typical Huxley style, convened a regal meeting on the bucolic north shore of Lake Geneva in Morges, Switzerland. There they announced the creation of a charitable trust that would serve as a fund-raising arm for IUCN and potentially, other like-minded NGOs. Well-known conservationists such as Peter Scott, American philanthropist Godfrey Rockefeller, IUCN official and experienced African conservation specialist E. B. Worthington, and British advertising executive Guy Mountfort helped get the organization going. Capitalized with donations of £13,000 (British pounds), a new public face for international conservation was born with the World

---

[89] Bonner, *At the Hand of Man*, 60–2.

*WWF started out as a fundraising agency* [handwritten note in left margin]

Wildlife Fund (WWF).[90] The WWF, unlike the IUCN, focused on raising money. It was "principally an agency for helping fund other international conservation efforts," recalled Russell Train, a founding trustee of the WWF's U.S. National Appeal.[91] Prince Philip, Duke of Edinburgh, the first president of WWF's United Kingdom office, explained that the WWF "was like the Cancer Research Fund – it raised money, and gave it to the experts to get on with."[92]

The founding charter focused heavily on protecting wildlife and wild places: "A fundamental responsibility of civilized man is to ensure that the wild creatures of this earth have adequate suitable wild lands set aside for them and safeguarded against damage, disturbance, or exploitation by Man." What was new in the WWF's stated purpose would be the scope of management for these wild spaces. "It is the duty of each country to ensure this," the document continued, but this was not enough. It was also the responsibility of the United Nations to "keep watch over its fulfillment."[93] The new organization sought to pressure national governments to adopt protection measures. It had a small international secretariat based in Switzerland that oversaw all activities and coordinated fund-raising, but it also established national branches to raise money and cull ties with policy makers.[94]

More than anything else, the foremost goal of the organization was to raise money. Conservation and preservation organizations had had political success in Europe, the United States, and some colonies in promoting national parks and game reserves, but they needed more resources. The "remaining missing element" in international conservation explained a confidential memo circulated by the WWF's founders was "money – real

---

[90] "Saving the World's Wildlife, Note of a Meeting held at 19, Belgrave Square, SW I, at 2:30 pm on Thursday, 27th July, 1961," box 120, Huxley Papers; Max Nicholson, "The First World Conservation Lecture," *The Environmentalist*, Vol. I (1981), 110–11; McCormick, *The Global Environmental Movement*, 46–8; Holdgate, *The Green Web*, 81–3.

[91] The WWF U.S. National Appeal reflected the group's ties to elite networks, as well. In addition to Train, who knew Nicholson and Huxley through the IUCN, the WWF-US Appeal included noted conservationists such as Hal Coolidge, Fairfield Osborn, and Dillon Ripley as well as famous businessmen such as John Olin and Max McGraw (head of the McGraw-Edison Company). Russell Train, "WWF/CF 90/07," History of the Conservation Foundation, unpublished report, Wildlife Information Center, World Wildlife Fund–United States (WWF-US) Office, Washington, DC.

[92] Holdgate, *The Green Web*, 85.

[93] "Saving the World's Wildlife: Draft World Wild Life Charter, Revised Version, 3/7/61," box 120, Huxley Papers.

[94] Notes of a meeting held on April 25, 1961, Preparatory Committee for "Saving the World's Wildlife," box 120, Huxley Papers.

money in worthwhile amounts – not the petty cash to which such bodies have become accustomed to limit their ambitions, with disastrous results for wildlife."[95] At early preparatory meetings, delegates spent a great deal of time talking about fund-raising strategies. Its founders conceived of the WWF as a "fuel tank" with a "petrol pump to fill and refill" other like-minded organizations and conservation projects. Other organizations, such as the IUCN, had "failed utterly in facing and tackling the problem of finding adequate resources for conservation," and thus "a new approach by new minds" was essential.[96] Nicholson and Huxley wanted the WWF to be a charitable trust, and they set it up in Switzerland with this in mind. To raise the money they desired, the WWF sought to cultivate wealthy individuals with a known appreciation for wildlife, such as Prince Albert, Duke of Edinburgh, and the Kennedy family. The IUCN and early conservation efforts were professional in the sense that they were formal institutions staffed by professional scientists, but the WWF was professional in the sense that it would have employees whose sole profession was that of international conservationists. It adumbrated the rise of professional interest group NGOs who would come to wield significant power by the end of the century.

In its early months, the WWF's leaders secured funds from a variety of wealthy European and American donors. Among their early publicity efforts, they published French and English glossy, colorful translations of an illustrated German conservation magazine, *Das Tier*. They also held film festivals to promote movies such as Bernhard Grzimek's popular documentary on the African wildlife situation, *Serengeti Shall Not Die*.[97] And they started to plan bigger events. To draw global attention to their cause, they announced a conference on the urgent necessity of protecting wildlife in the developing world, to be held in Arusha, Tanganyika – the original phase II of IUCN's African Special Project. The WWF provided the financial muscle and public attention necessary to spur the IUCN's activities in Africa. Through its success in fund-raising and publicity, the WWF ensured that the IUCN and the cause of global conservation would continue into the near future.

[95] "How to Save the World's Wildlife," Confidential WWF memo, 1961, box 120, Huxley Papers.

[96] "World Wildlife Fund: Save the World's Wildlife," draft constitution, 1961, box 120, Huxley Papers.

[97] "How to Save the World's Wildlife," Confidential WWF memo, 1961, box 120, Huxley Papers. On the role of films in shaping Western perceptions of wildlife, see Gregg Mittman, *Reel Nature: America's Romance with Wildlife on Film* (Seattle: University of Washington Press, 2009).

## CONCLUSION: INTERNATIONAL ENVIRONMENTAL
## PROTECTION AND DEVELOPMENT IN CONFLICT

In the postwar years, global events shaped environmental thought in a number of important ways. International conservationists such as Julian Huxley made a significant cognitive leap about how they considered the relationship between themselves, the rest of the world, and political boundaries. NGO members such as Huxley often spoke of "the planet" or "the earth" as an object of governance. Alongside this construction of the earth as a coherent social unit, conservationists implied that wildlife belonged to the whole of humanity, not any one particular nation. Environmentalists interpreted these developments as evidence that nation-states could no longer stand alone – or be trusted – to ensure the protection of the environment. Effective management of the natural world required new ideas, new relationships, new institutions, all of which would help create coherent way of militating against the most fearsome aspects of decolonization and development.

To accomplish these goals, the IUCN and the WWF turned to established networks of like-minded activists and colonial officials with experience in game and park management to defend existing protection arrangements in the developing world. In many ways, members of the early postwar international NGOs hoped to continue many imperial protection programs into the postcolonial world. Many wildlife enthusiasts concerned with Africa's flora and fauna worried that leaders of developing countries could not be trusted to maintain the old arrangements or that nationalist elites would ignore the protection of the natural environment in their eagerness to pursue rapid economic development. The uncertainty and urgency of decolonization motivated Western activists, and in turn NGOs built upon and reinforced imperial power dynamics, informed by paternalistic and racial assumptions about the superiority of Western management practices, in the hopes of bringing stability and certainty to the future of African environmental protection.

At the time of the WWF's founding in the early 1961, though, international conservation efforts were still in their infancy. Huxley and his colleagues had succeeded in creating an institutional architecture to promote environmental protection worldwide. Uncertainty reigned, however, as the developmental goals of nations around the world seemed to leave little room for conservationist and preservationist thinking.

Although the IUCN, the WWF, and a variety of other conservation organizations worked assiduously over the next decade to make national parks, game reserves, and conservation policies a hallmark of new nations, particularly in East Africa, their efforts quickly encountered formidable challenges.

2

# Parks and Poverty in Africa

## *Conservation, Decolonization, and Development*

Although officials in environmental non-governmental organizations
(NGOs) such as the International Union for the Conservation of Nature
(IUCN) and World Wildlife Fund (WWF) often spoke about reconciling
conservation and development, in practice their policies were unsuccessful
at doing so. As the two leading international conservation organizations,
the IUCN and WWF were formally global in their scope. Yet much of
their activity involved continuing and expanding upon colonial-era
arrangements, particularly national parks, in East Africa. NGO officials
and their allies ran into extensive difficulties in promoting environmental
protection in the postcolonial nations of the region. As East African
leaders increasingly asserted their desire to carve out their own path
toward economic development, the IUCN's and WWF's hopes for preservation clashed with the objectives and aspirations of the new countries'
leaders and their counterparts in foreign aid agencies. Consequently,
during the 1960s the policies put forth by NGOs became even more
marginal to the larger developmental objectives of national governments
and development lenders alike.

The IUCN and WWF, along with a variety of other Western activists,
primarily attempted to persuade emerging nationalist leaders to adopt a
preservationist set of policies. They promoted the creation of national
parks, or areas of state-protected "wild" nature, that were legally cut off
from human use. In emerging postcolonial states, this approach often
meant maintaining and expanding existing parks and game reserves that
had been set up by colonial authorities. IUCN and WWF leaders
feared that independence movements would destabilize the relationships
between government and citizens. It was unclear whether new nations

54

would maintain and expand on the national parks, game reserves, and scattered conservation schemes that had been created in the colonial era. Many of the IUCN's early officials had cut their teeth working in imperial game reserves or nature protection schemes. As the process of decolonization accelerated, these officials, now working in NGOs, wanted to ensure the policies they had put in place during the colonial era would continue into the future. American conservationists found themselves allied with former imperial officials in the hope of preserving the colonial game reserves and national parks in East Africa. Conservationists claimed that national parks managed through scientific principles and elite guidance could produce real wealth, primarily through tourist dollars. NGO officials argued that parks, both for aesthetic and economic reasons, should be a vital component of the development process.[1]

American and European activists, however, were unable to win support from nationalist leaders. NGOs could not convincingly link arguments for preservation with leaders' state-building objectives. Development, after all, is both an economic and a symbolic project. The high-intensity, large-scale development projects that national leaders championed, such as extensive railroad networks or hydroelectric dams, held greater cultural power and economic benefit for developing nations aspiring for wealth and prestige than did national parks or elaborate programs of environmental protection. Employing grandiose and universalistic rhetoric, NGO officials often claimed Africa's unique wildlife and landscapes belonged to the whole of humanity. African leaders did not share this view and often opted instead for policies aimed at maximizing

[1] On incidents of early national parks and colonial reserves that forcibly displaced local inhabitants in order to create an image of "wild" nature that did not include human beings, see Mark Dowie, *Conservation Refugees: The Hundred-Year Conflict between Global Conservation and Native Peoples* (Cambridge: MIT Press, 2009); Jane Carruthers, *The Kruger National Park: A Social and Political History* (Pietermaritzburg, South Africa: University of Natal Press, 1995); Karl Jacoby, *Crimes Against Nature: Squatters, Poachers, Thieves, and the Hidden History of American Conservation* (Berkeley: University of California Press, 2001); Roderick Neumann, "Ways of Seeing Africa: Colonial Recasting of African Society and Landscape in Serengeti National Park," *Ecumene*, Vol. 2, No. 1 (1995), 149–69; Roderick Neumann, *Imposing Wilderness: Struggles Over Livelihood and Nature Preservation in Africa* (Berkeley: University of California Press, 2002); John F. Reiger, *American Sportsmen and the Origins of Conservation*, 3rd ed. (Corvallis: Oregon State University Press, 2001); Mark Spence, *Dispossessing the Wilderness: Indian Removal and the Making of the National Parks* (New York: Oxford University Press, 1999); Lekan, *"Serengeti Shall Not Die"*; David Anderson and Richard Grove, "The Scramble for Eden: Past, Present, and Future in African Conservation," in David Anderson and Richard Grove, eds., *Conservation in Africa: People, Policies, and Practice* (Cambridge: Cambridge University Press, 1987), 1–12.

national power and prestige. In particular, controversies surrounding national parks in postcolonial Tanzania and Uganda, respectively, reveal the stark differences between a preservationist approach couched in universalistic rhetoric and a development mindset based on advancing national interests. By the late 1960s, the IUCN's and WWF's few successes in East Africa were more tenuous than when the decade began.

Frustrated though they were, leading NGO officials learned from their experiences. The frequent clashes with nationalist leaders demonstrated to environmental NGOs that for conservation and preservation policies to endure, they needed to engage leaders in developing nations more actively and target their lobbying efforts on donor countries offering development assistance. Following their disappointments in East Africa, NGOs reoriented their advocacy strategy toward lobbying international institutions and development lending agencies. This shift presented new opportunities over the following years for non-state actors to exercise influence over governing institutions and the course of development assistance policy.

## PUSHING PARKS: THE ARUSHA DECLARATION AND POSTCOLONIAL PRESERVATION

Africa had long held a special place in the conservationists' imagination, with its awesome landscapes and distinctive big-game wildlife.[2] The postcolonial era was no different. Fund-raising success and decolonization led the IUCN and WWF to focus their attention on the continent in unprecedented ways. Between 1961 and 1964, the WWF raised $1.9 million (U.S. dollars). About half of the grants went to Africa for protected areas, species protection, education, and research.[3] As former IUCN President Martin Holdgate said of the 1960s, "This period was, in many ways, the Era of Africa."[4] IUCN's staff, in particular Huxley, focused much of their efforts on ensuring that newly independent African states would continue the national parks and game preserves that colonial authorities had established. "The 'wind of change' was now blowing through Africa," recalled WWF founder Max Nicholson as he invoked British Prime Minister Harold McMillan's famous metaphor. "With imminent decolonization," Nicholson feared, "it was widely predicted

---

[2] On the place of Africa in the environmental imagination, see Anderson and Grove, eds., *Conservation in Africa.*
[3] Holdgate, *The Green Web*, 85.
[4] Ibid., 71.

that conservation of wildlife would be amongst the first casualties."[5] Such expressions were a common refrain, and men such as Julian Huxley, Russell Train, and Nicholson groped for solutions to these ominous changes.

To stave off their worst fears over decolonization, conservationists attempted to persuade new national leaders to adopt preservation and conservation policies in their new national agendas. In 1961, the IUCN sponsored a conference in Arusha, Tanganyika, on the importance of protecting animal species.[6] The gathering, hatched by Huxley and Nicholson, brought together leading IUCN and WWF officials, erstwhile colonial park managers and game wardens, and representatives from a number of African political parties. Born out of a sense that "the accelerated rate of destruction of wild fauna, flora, and habitat in Africa ... was the most urgent conservation of the present time," conference organizers hoped to persuade future leaders of the necessity of conservation and draw worldwide attention to these claims of imminent danger. It also provided a road map for future action. The pressing problems required two solutions, as the IUCN saw it: "first, conservation of the national parks and faunal reserves; and second, the management of wildlife stocks on lands outside the existing parks and reserves, especially on those lands not suited to agriculture" (Figure 3).[7]

Huxley and his colleagues found a willing partner to pursue such policies in the dynamic Julius Nyerere. Nyerere was a successful political organizer and powerful orator who would become a leader in Tanganyika's, and later, Tanzania's, government. While studying in Scotland during the early 1950s, Nyerere became interested in the history of Western socialist thought, which would shape his thinking and activism for decades to come. After his studies Nyerere returned to his homeland to start a teaching career, in addition to involving himself in many civic and political organizations. In 1953 he became president of the civic-minded Tanganyika Africa Association, which he later expanded and transformed into a political group called the Tanganyika African National Union (TANU), which mobilized support for Tanganyikan national sovereignty. Eventually turning to politics full time in the late 1950s, Nyerere won a seat in Tanganyika's legislature in the first colonial

---

[5] Max Nicholson, "The First World Conservation Lecture," *The Environmentalist*, Vol. I (1981), 110.

[6] The conference was co-organized by the Commission for Technical Cooperation in Africa (CCTA), South of the Sahara.

[7] "Chapter 1: Origins and Aims," in IUCN, *Conservation of Nature and Natural Resources in Modern African States*, 9.

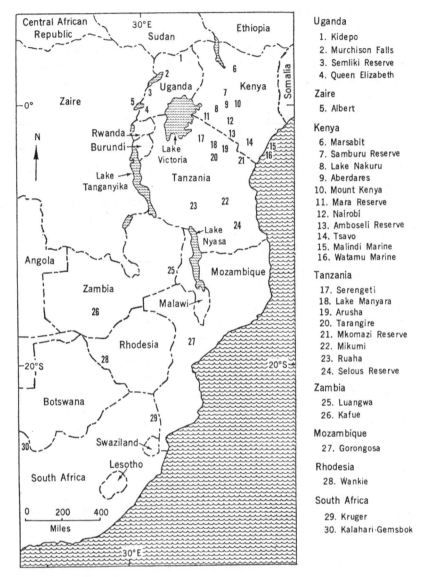

FIGURE 3: National parks and game reserves in East Africa, ca. 1970. Redrawn map, original by Norman Myers. Courtesy of *Science*.

elections and became chief minister after more elections in 1960. Following independence in 1961, the well-liked and respected Nyerere became prime minister. When Tanganyika became a republic the following year, Nyerere became the country's first president.

Nyerere's personal correspondence with NGO officials suggested that he would include many conservation policies in his country. In a note to IUCN officials, Nyerere stated that his government's first budget increased the Game Department's provisions by 40 percent to improve national park facilities and staff, changed the name of the relevant ministry from "Lands and Surveys" to "Lands, Surveys, and Wildlife," and promised to open a new national market later in the year at the famous Ngurdoto Crater.[8] Bernhard Grzimek, the NGO-affiliated filmmaker behind *Serengeti Shall Not Die*, interviewed Nyerere multiple times before the conference and came away impressed with the young leader. He reported back that Nyerere himself did not care much for watching or hunting game animals, but the young leader knew that "Europeans and Americans enjoy this" and suggested that "wild animals" would be "Tanganyika's third most important source of revenue after sisal and diamonds."[9]

Although IUCN officials corresponded in private with Nyerere, in public they prepared an extravagant international launch event for the WWF. Nicholson and Huxley hoped to spur an initial fund-raising drive for the new organization at the Arusha Conference. In what was largely a publicity stunt, they crafted a "Declaration of a State of Emergency," in which African leaders, notably Nyerere, proclaimed the importance of protecting wildlife for developing nations worldwide. Scientists and conservationists from the United States and Western Europe would sign the declaration in a show of support. However, when Nyerere received the draft declaration, he balked at the thought that conservation should be spoken of in such grave terms. After a few exchanges, Nyerere agreed to open the Arusha Conference with a "Manifesto," later identified as a founding document of African conservation. Although many at the time held the Manifesto to be Nyerere's own words, it was in fact written by Nicholson and an advertising executive hired by the WWF.[10]

With a mixture of preservationist and conservationist sentiment and a tinge of alarm, the document bore many similarities to Huxley's own writings and contained many common tropes of conservationist thinking vis-à-vis Africa. Read aloud at the conference by a local chieftain speaking on Nyerere's behalf, the Manifesto connected East Africa's wildlife to a broader global imperative. "The survival of our wildlife is a matter of

---

[8] Julius Nyerere to IUCN board, Arusha Manifesto, box 109, Huxley Papers.
[9] Quoted in Holdgate, *The Green Web*, 73.
[10] Raymond Bonner, *At the Hand of Man: Peril and Hope for Africa's Wildlife* (New York: Alfred A. Knopf, 1993), 64–5; Julius Nyerere to IUCN board, Arusha Manifesto, box 109, Huxley Papers.

grave concern to all of us in Africa," the declaration began. "Wild creatures amid the wild places they inhabit are not only important as a source
of wonder and inspiration but are an integral part of our natural resources
and of our future livelihood and well-being ... conservation of wild life
and wild places not only affects the Continent of Africa but the rest of
the world as well."[11] The document placed Africa at the center of a global
crisis by claiming that the continent's wildlife was in peril and demanded
that all nations needed to take steps to ensure the protection of the
endangered flora and fauna.

To redress such problems, the document encouraged cooperation
between young African nations and experts in the developed world.
"The conservation of wildlife and wild places calls for specialist knowledge, trained manpower and money and we look to other nations
to cooperate in this important task," the declaration proclaimed, and
with this Nyerere largely agreed.[12] Nyerere welcomed the presence of
the IUCN and WWF because of their commitment to building up
Tanganyika's tourism industry, which had become a growing source of
earning foreign exchange for neighboring Kenya. Education programs
sponsored by the IUCN and WWF also helped to convince the peasants
and pastoralists who supported Nyerere's nationalist TANU party that
parks and nature tourism were to their "own ultimate advantage."[13]
Money from NGOs was also spent on a bizarre array of marketing
gimmicks, from a short film about a young Maasai boy who traveled to
Yellowstone National Park to learn the emotional and economic value of
national parks to a series of posters designed by a French artist that
emphasized the "national pride" of having such parks.[14] Such efforts
provided rhetorical fodder for Nyerere's nationalist narratives, with the
IUCN and WWF footing the bill.

Nyerere also accepted the IUCN's and WWF's entreaties because of the
larger political strategy he had adopted during Tanganyika's transitional
phase toward full independence. From the late 1950s until around 1962,
Nyerere largely favored a gradualist policy toward independence. He
hoped that maintaining close relations with Britain would ensure consistent foreign aid, prevent a major exodus of skilled civil servants, and build
up British resolve, especially among more liberal elements in Parliament,
to support majority rule elsewhere in the continent. In this "strategy

[11] "Arusha Manifesto," Julius Nyerere to IUCN board, box 109, Huxley Papers.
[12] Ibid.
[13] Neumann, *Imposing Wilderness*, 140–2.
[14] Ibid., 141.

of dependence," Nyerere calculated that close cooperation with the British and with other Western officials and experts was more prudent than adopting a confrontational push for immediate independence.[15] Although the WWF's founders believed they had a found a willing ally who would stand in the vanguard of conservation efforts, Nyerere's political calculations and nationalist aspiration would evolve, increasingly leaving the WWF leaders far more isolated than they anticipated.

### EARLY PROBLEMS IN PARKS: THE PERSISTENCE OF COLONIAL POLICIES

In the short term, the Arusha Conference emboldened the WWF. Looking to generate greater financial support from donors back in Europe and the United States, shortly after the event the WWF launched a media campaign emphasizing how inaction would lead to extreme environmental degradation. They purchased front page space in the *Daily Mirror* in October 1961, running the headline "Doomed – to disappear from the face of the earth due to Man's FOLLY, GREED, NEGLECT" with a picture of large rhinoceros below, a symbol to big-game hunters worldwide. The campaign worked well, raising £30,000 (British pounds).[16] At the same time, the WWF funded and organized a new scheme in Uganda called "Making African Wildlife Pay," wherein for £500 pounds (airfare included) visitors from Europe could take shooting and sightseeing safaris. Prince Bernhard of the Netherlands, who had been named the nominal president of the WWF, went on the inaugural excursion.[17] In 1961 and 1962, the WWF put its new funds to use in East Africa, purchasing swaths of land in Tanganyika to add to the Ngurdoto Crater National Park.[18]

The WWF's early projects and objectives, however, often imperiled peoples living near or around protected territories, especially indigenous groups. In East Africa, national parks particularly threatened the Maasai. A traditionally nomadic people, the Maasai hunted across large stretches of land between Kenya and Tanganyika. Many national parks and game reserves had closed off this traditional hunting territory, creating severe

---

[15] The nature of the "strategy of dependence" is explained in much greater detail in Cranford Pratt, *The Critical Phase in Tanzania: 1945–1968: Nyerere and the Emergence of a Socialist Strategy* (Cambridge: Cambridge University Press, 1976), chapters 3–5.

[16] Bonner, *At the Hand of Man*, 66–7.

[17] The World Wildlife Fund, "World Wildlife News No. 1," 1962, box 120, Huxley Papers.

[18] The World Wildlife Fund, "World Wildlife News No. 6," ibid.

tensions between colonial authorities, local government officials, and the Maasai during the colonial era. These tensions continued into the early 1960s, as Maasai hunters continued to use their traditional lands much to the chagrin of conservationists. Kenya's burgeoning guerrilla war further destabilized these areas, resulting in many nomadic peoples seeking sanctuary within park territory.[19]

IUCN and WWF officials frequently called for such parks to restrict access to the Maasai. They celebrated efforts to clear the "wild" spaces of human inhabitants, often using racially charged language to do so. Bernhard Grzimek, for instance, had lauded efforts by parks in the former Belgian Congo to move indigenous tribes from game reserves. Declaring the Serengeti a "primordial wilderness," Grzimek argued that no people, "not even natives," should be permitted to live within its national park space. That Maasai had used the land for centuries seemed only to add urgency to Grzimek's concerns. "We Europeans must teach our black brothers to value our own possessions," and not "because we are older and cleverer, but because we do not want them to repeat our mistakes and ours sins," such as overexploitation of game, even if that meant pushing off indigenous peoples from using and living on land they had regarded as their own.[20]

Conservationists also castigated the Maasai for "irrational," wasteful use of the land. Lee Talbot of the IUCN criticized the nomads for overgrazing with "herds of economically worthless cattle." "As they move into the Serengeti," he wrote, they "bring the desert with them, and the wilderness and wildlife must bow before their heads."[21] Colonial policy reflected such views. In the late 1940s, British colonial authorities had written up a "bill of rights" for Maasai living within their jurisdiction. While these laws explicitly protected customary rights of Maasai to graze certain parts of the Serengeti, the bill left it to the discretion of park officials to allow Maasai to exercise traditional rights. As a result, frequent clashes occurred between government officials and Maasai tribesmen.[22]

By the 1950s, although various advocates within East Africa called for greater protection of the Maasai under colonial law, many conservationists

[19] See Neumann, *Imposing Wilderness*, 102–54; Beinart and Hughes, *Environment and Empire*, 278–81.
[20] Quoted in Dowie, *Conservation Refugees*, 24–5. On Grzimek's forays into East Africa, see Lekan, "*Serengeti Shall Not Die.*"
[21] Holdgate, *The Green Web*, 74.
[22] Neumann, *Imposing Wilderness*, 134–6.

argued for greater restrictions on the native population. As one petition produced by North American conservation organizations put it, "We argue that the basic inherent right of the African is to have his natural heritages protected and defended even from his own errors." By the mid-1960s, it was clear that "there would be no place for people in Tanzania's parks."[23] And the Maasai recognized this fact, too. By the early 1970s, some Maasai had taken to slaughtering rhinoceros in game reserves, in the words of one writer, as "a protest against land alienation for wildlife preservation."[24] The IUCN's and WWF's early efforts at preservation and conservation in Africa were conceptually hamstrung by an idealized portrait of "wild nature" that removed humans from the natural world and marginalized non-Western methods of land tenure.

Although conservationists' ideas about nature protection conflicted with long-held land use patterns of indigenous peoples, IUCN and WWF officials often appealed to larger imperatives – the fate of endangered wildlife, a notion of a shared global responsibility to protect the natural world – in justifying interventions that undermined claims to self-determination. The Arusha Declaration made clear that conservation and protection of wildlife and wild spaces "affects the Continent of Africa but the rest of the world as well." Yet the rest of the world in the early 1960s did not share such sentiments. While local conflicts over land use simmered, a larger conflict was brewing. National leaders in the developing world and policy makers in the West increasingly promoted national development plans premised on rapid economic growth that left little space for protection and preservation of the natural world. The IUCN's and WWF's ongoing efforts to engineer preservation projects in East Africa soon revealed the challenges of promoting environmental protection in the context of rapid modernization.

## THE MODERNIZATION MINDSET: USAID
## AND FOREIGN AID TO TANGANYIKA

To understand how the United States came to play an active role in African development, it is important to recount how development

[23] Ibid., 138.
[24] David Collett, "Pastoralists and Wildlife: Image and Reality and Kenya Maasailand," in Anderson and Grove, eds., *Conservation in Africa*, 144. On other tensions between the modernizing state and the Maasai, see Leander Schneider, "The Maasai's New Clothes: A Developmentalist Modernity and Its Exclusions," *Africa Today*, Vol. 53, No. 1 (2006), 101–29.

assistance became an increasingly significant role in the Cold War during the late 1950s and early 1960s. Much of the lasting infrastructure of U.S. international development assistance and foreign aid was set up between 1955 and 1965. In the United States, Point Four had merged into the Mutual Security Assistance in 1955, uniting technical assistance and community development programs with military aid. In the early 1960s, foreign aid programs were reorganized even more fundamentally. Under the Foreign Assistance Act of 1961, President John F. Kennedy announced the creation of the Agency for International Development (AID) within the State Department as part of a broader effort to make foreign economic aid a more central component of U.S. foreign policy.

AID refocused development funding from short-term fixes and crisis responses to long-term funding on a country-by-country basis. "Uneven and undependable short-term financing" of existing development programs weakened their effectiveness, Kennedy explained. "Piecemeal projects, hastily designed to match the rhythm of the fiscal year are no substitute for orderly long-term planning," the president continued, and the ability "to make long-range commitments has enabled the Soviet Union to use its aid program to make developing nations economically dependent on Russian support – thus advancing the aims of world communism."[25] AID would provide long-term planning, more consistent funds, and more elaborate oversight to produce "self-sustained growth" in developing nations. A greater focus on development aid took hold in international institutions, too. In 1958, UN officials set up SUNFED – the Special United Nations Fund for Economic Development, which became the institutional base of the UN's Development Programme. The World Bank established the International Finance Corporation (IFC) to promote private investment in the developing world in 1956, and in 1960 it created the International Development Association (IDA) to offer loans at below-market rates. The World Bank subsequently created regional development banks for Africa (1964) and Asia (1966).[26] In less than a decade, an elaborate network of international institutions had been set up to finance worldwide development.

Behind this elaborate network of institutions lay a common set of assumptions and ideas about what constituted proper development. For the United States, the foremost objective in Tanganyika, as was often the

[25] "Special Message to the Congress on Foreign Aid," March 22, 1961, John F. Kennedy, *Public Papers of the President*, 1961–63. [Online] Available: http://www.presidency.ucsb .edu/ws/?pid=8545. Accessed February 14, 2011.

[26] Rist, *The History of Development*, 90.

case elsewhere in the developing world, was the "success of responsible and stable government," and by extension, "the denial of sensitive areas of government and economy to the [Soviet] bloc."[27] The United States sought to achieve these dual goals by raising standards of living. The primary way to achieve higher standards of living was through spurring economic growth, which in practice often meant increased industrial and agricultural production. In general, the success of such policies was measured in terms of increasing per capita income and gross national product (GNP).[28] For policy makers at all levels in the United States, this kind of development was understood as just one tool of many in its diplomatic arsenal. Foreign aid directed toward development was a means to an end: a noncommunist, stable, liberal world order.

Changing circumstances in the Cold War led policy makers to place these ideas into policy. The "winds of change" that had led to early postwar decolonization swept across Africa and Southeast Asia. Many of the nascent nations looked to the Soviet Union as a model of growth, as the Soviet Union had experienced the most rapid rises in standard of living in human history over the previous five decades.[29] Following Stalin's death in 1953, Nikita Khrushchev reconceived Soviet strategy toward the developing world, viewing national elites less as "stooges" (in Stalin's terminology) and more as potential allies in a global socialist coalition. The Soviet Union sent aid to Algerian rebels, India, Egypt, Indonesia, and many other nations, and Soviet leaders toured many post-colonial nations offering promises of centralized infrastructure development of the variety that had transformed the U.S.S.R in the 1920s and 1930s.[30] By the end of the decade, communist China got in on the act as well, claiming solidarity with oppressed rural nations and offering billions of dollars in aid, particularly to emerging African nations.[31] Worries of

---

[27] "Country Assistance Strategy for Tanganyika," February 17, 1963, USAID Documents Experience Clearinghouse. [Online] Available: http://dec.usaid.gov/index.cfm. Accessed March 12, 2011.

[28] On the evolution of thinking about using either industrialization or agriculture to achieve to development, see Cullather, *The Hungry World*, chapters 3–7.

[29] The Soviet Union/Russia doubled the average life expectancy from 32 to 65 between 1900 and 1950, a remarkable leap in comparison with any other country. United Nations: Demographic Yearbook, Historical supplement. [Online] Available: http://unstats.un.org/unsd/demographic/sconcerns/mortality/mort2.htm. Accessed April 1, 2012.

[30] Latham, *The Right Kind of Revolution*, 42.

[31] Warren Weinstein and Thomas H. Henriksen, *Soviet and Chinese Aid to African Nations* (New York: Praeger Publishing, 1980); Sergey Mazov, *A Distant Front in the Cold War: The USSR in West Africa and the Congo, 1956–1964* (Washington, DC: Woodrow Wilson Center Press, 2010); Timothy Naftali and Aleksandr A. Fursenko, *Khrushchev's*

potential Soviet influence in the late 1940s gave way to fears over real Soviet activity by the early 1960s.

Developing countries, though, saw development as both a means and an end. As a process, rapid economic development was the way to throw off colonial shackles and make a modern, powerful nation worthy of international respect. It also offered a way for governments, such as Nyerere's in Tanganyika, to ensure domestic political stability and power. From raising standards of living to remaking Tanganyikan society through placing Africans in posts held by colonial expatriates, the success of Nyerere and the ruling TANU party hinged on effective development. Creating such a society was also the goal of the process. Leaders such as Nyerere wanted a wealthy, productive nation to ensure that the development process would continue. While U.S. policy makers wanted to ensure stability and alliance, nationalist leaders often cared less about waging Cold War than achieving their domestic aspirations.

The conservationists in IUCN and WWF found themselves in between the United States, the lending agencies, and the developing nations. Officials in these NGOs saw development as part of a process of national growth, but one that required interventions to protect natural areas and the environment from deterioration. By increasing protection for the natural world, they wanted to change, albeit slightly at first, the means by which development was pursued. The divergent goals and means were evident from the start in Tanganyika, especially after the country moved toward declaring formal independence.

While independence loomed in political terms, economic ties continued to bind Tanganyika to Europe, particularly Great Britain and West Germany, and the United States. The country required a vast amount of foreign aid in order to achieve its developmental objectives. Following independence in 1961, the young government called for a three-year development plan of $67 million. Although its territorial expanse equaled France and Germany combined, Tanganyika had only 9.5 million people, with a per capita income of $56, among the lowest in Africa at the time of independence. Initially, Great Britain offered one-half of the required funds for the three-year plan, with the United States offering another $10 million in loans and grants through various institutions.[32]

*Cold War: The Inside Story of an American Adversary* (New York: W. W. Norton and Company, 2007).

[32] "Country Assistance Strategy for Tanganyika," February 17, 1963, USAID Documents Experience Clearinghouse. [Online] Available: http://dec.usaid.gov/index.cfm. Accessed March 12, 2011.

Tanganyika was one of the first recipients of AID funding, and the projects AID put forth represented a mélange of contemporary development thinking. Throughout much of the 1950s and 1960s, achieving a high GNP with rising per capita income marked developmental success.[33] In Tanganyika, AID defined export crops (particularly sisal, cotton, and sugar) as being "of the greatest significance to the country's economic growth."[34] Beginning in 1961, AID funded specific projects "concerned with increasing per capita income based upon higher agricultural production." It offered multiple grants valued in hundreds of thousands of dollars to consolidate peasant land holdings into larger-scale agricultural plots. AID also established agricultural training centers to teach modern farming techniques, to introduce a number of hybrid strains of wheat, and to encourage wide-scale wheat production.[35] By 1963, AID was giving $12.8 million a year to Tanganyika, making it one of eight nations in Africa receiving more than $10 million in foreign aid.[36]

At the same time, AID funded community development programs based on training local workers to oversee agricultural production, a common feature of development projects aimed at engineering a social transformation among the peasantry.[37] "The main threat to the present Government," AID's country survey of Tanganyika concluded, "lies in those elements of the indigenous society for whom economic development and African political leadership ... are not proceeding rapidly enough under the present regimes."[38] Raising agricultural production and transforming peasants into large-scale farmers would help stem the instability upon which revolutionary nationalists or communists might thrive.

---

[33] Engerman, "Bernath Lecture: American Knowledge and Global Power," 615–21.

[34] Country Assistance Program: Tanganyika, Department of State, Agency of International Development, October 1963, 11–17, USAID Documents Experience Clearinghouse. [Online] Available: http://dec.usaid.gov/index.cfm. Accessed March 12, 2011.

[35] "Project Agreement between AID and the Government of United Republic of Tanganyika and Zanzibar," June 30, 1964, box 1, Office of International Training, African Branch, Agency for International Development, Tanzania PPROJ/SUBJ FY1960–71, RG 286, Records of the Agency for International Development, National Archives and Records Administration II, College Park, MD [hereinafter cited as NARA II].

[36] "Memorandum from the President's Special Assistant (Dungan) to President Kennedy," March 6, 1963, *Papers Relating to the Foreign Relations of the United States* [hereinafter cited as *FRUS*], *Vol. XXI, Africa, 1961–63* (Washington, DC: GPO, 1995), 329–30.

[37] On community development, see Cullather, *The Hungry World*, chapter 3; Immerwahr, *Thinking Small*.

[38] Country Assistance Program: Tanganyika, Department of State, Agency of International Development, October 1963, 1–6, USAID Documents Experience Clearinghouse. [Online] Available: http://dec.usaid.gov/index.cfm. Accessed March 12, 2011.

Unsurprisingly, then, the IUCN's and WWF's desire to set aside valuable land to create national parks in the hopes of encouraging tourist dollars was low on AID's general priorities for economic development. The project plans offered no major grants or loans to national parks, for such efforts remained far beyond the agency's purview. Without such aid, NGOs themselves would increasingly seek to fill the void. In the minds of Huxley, Nicholson, and other conservationists, this lack of attention from major development lending agencies provided part of the justification for creating the WWF in the first place. IUCN and WWF officials viewed their own projects, such as the purchase of land to expand Ngurdoto Crater National Park, with added urgency. Because neither nationalist leaders nor American developers assigned priority to wildlife and landscape protection, the IUCN and WWF sought other ways to promote their cause.

### DREAMS OF A FUTURE FOR CONSERVATION: THE CASE OF THE CAWM

One way in which the IUCN and WWF hoped to promote environmental protection measures was by training interested young Africans in park management and conservation, seizing an opportunity created by the absence of qualified personnel in transitional, postcolonial governance. One of the most pressing concerns of postcolonial regimes was that existing governments often did not represent the people they purported to govern, as they remained staffed by colonial elites. In Tanzania, Nyerere sought to overcome this challenge through a rapid "Africanization" of civil servants, by which he meant the removal of British officials from various posts and their replacement with black Africans. Foreign aid agencies offered help with this transition, recognizing its importance to young leaders. AID proclaimed one of its project goals to be "assisting in Africanization, maintenance, and improvement of the public service," and offered a grant to create an "Institute of Public Administration" to train administrative and executive personnel.[39] A survey commissioned by AID and led by a team of American scholars and Rockefeller Foundation experts proclaimed that a "critical shortage" of "high-level manpower" – professionals, administrators, clerical staff, teachers, and supervisors.

---

[39] "Country Assistance Strategy for Tanganyika," February 17, 1963, USAID Documents Experience Clearinghouse. [Online] Available: http://dec.usaid.gov/index.cfm. Accessed March 12, 2011.

Given that many postcolonial nations were primarily agricultural producers, emphasis needed to be placed on training agricultural experts capable
of overseeing new development projects.[40]

NGO officials recognized the urgency of this problem, but also saw it
as an opportunity to promote a new generation of wildlife managers and
generate greater public support for conservation issues. Thus, in 1963,
through start-up funds from Russell Train's AWLF and a small grant from
AID, a group of conservationists established the College of African
Wildlife Management (CAWM). CAWM fit right in with AID's desire
for trained experts to help guide the "Africanization" process, and seemed
to ease conservationists' concern about handing control of parks over to
African nations.[41]

Train realized the momentum behind Nyerere's Africanization and
similar trends in the region. Major Bruce Kinloch, a former member
of the British Indian Army and Game Warden for both Uganda and
Tanganyika, told delegates at the Arusha Conference that nationalist
leaders' call for "rapid Africanisation [sic] of the civil services" presented
urgent problems for national parks and conservation efforts. "Not only
are we faced with having to introduce the long overdue properly organised
formal training facilities for intermediate and junior wildlife staff,"
Kinloch complained, "but now we also have the problem of having to
locate, attract, train, and establish suitable African officers in the senior
posts in the immediate future, instead of progressively and steadily as
had hitherto been foreseen."[42] Officials such as Kinloch envisioned that
CAWM would redress this problem. Russell Train hoped the school
would stem "the pressure for Africanization of government services"
and to "meet the threat" that imperial European game managers would
be "replaced by completely untrained Africans."[43] NGO officials realized
the momentum behind the transition toward local control, but used

---

[40] Study Committee on Manpower Needs and Educational Capabilities in Africa,
"Summary Report: Study of the Manpower Needs, Educational Capabilities, and
Overseas Study," August 31, 1965, USAID Documents Experience Clearinghouse.
[Online] Available: http://dec.usaid.gov/index.cfm. Accessed March 12, 2011.

[41] In a celebratory remembrance for a WWF-US tribute to Train in 1994, CAWM's first
director, Hugh Lamprey, recalled that USAID provided its funds at "Russ' prompting."
Hugh Lamprey, "Russell Train: Recollections by Hugh Lamprey," July 7, 1994, box 60,
Train Papers.

[42] Major B. G. Kinloch, "The Urgent Need for Formalised Training Facilities for Wildlife
Management Personnel in the Africa of To-Day," in *Conservation of Nature and Natural
Resources in Modern African States*, 190.

[43] Russell Train, unpublished essay, Fall 1963, box 53, Train Papers.

CAWM as a way to exert influence over the course and direction of the transfer of power. Beneath this rhetoric lurked highly racialized assumptions, as well. Train and his colleagues often implied that Africans were not only unwilling but also unable to manage wildlife on their own and thus required guidance and oversight from Europeans.[44]

Train also hoped the college would resolve another problem – nationalists in East Africa did not seem to care about preserving wildlife in the way that Europeans and Americans did. John Owen, director of the Tanganyika National Parks, believed that East Africa's wildlife belonged to all of humanity, but worried that Africans did not share such universalism. "The scientific value of National Parks is probably too remote a concept to be got across with much effort at present," Owen explained at the Arusha Conference, "as is also the idea that Tanganyika owes it to the rest of mankind to preserve [animals as] a world asset." Preservation was a tough sell. "Those in daily contact with animals, whether they are persons whose crops are raided by elephants or hunters hungry for meat, are stony soil for propaganda," he added.[45] Other conservation elites agreed. Speaking of the largest park in Kenya, Train lamented that "practically no Africans ever visit it."[46] Profits from European tourism were "necessarily indirect in nature" and "not readily observable by average Africans." Conservationists felt they needed to encourage Africans to take an interest in wildlife. "If African peoples are ever going to develop a real commitment to parks and wildlife," Train argued, "their national parks must belong to them in fact as well as in name ... the park must become of direct, personal interest to the Africans, and this means utilization of the parks by Africans."[47] A new effort needed to be made, he figured, to instill preservationist values in the people of East Africa.

To stir up interest in preservation, Train's AWLF launched a major education campaign after establishing CAWM. Created with guidance from Julian Huxley, Train's organization built a public education office outside the Nairobi National Park in Kenya. Likewise, the AWLF, working in tandem with Tanganyika National Parks, funded an "Information Unit" equipped with a mobile projector to show films and other visual

[44] On racial stereotypes and the formation of racial identity around East Africa's parks, see Neumann, *Imposing Wilderness*.

[45] J. S. Owen, "Awakening Public Opinion to the Value of the Tanganyikan National Parks," in *Conservation of Nature and Natural Resources in Modern African States*, 262.

[46] Russell Train, unpublished essay, Fall 1963, box 53, Train Papers.

[47] Ibid.; "Wildlife Conservation and Management," Project Report, June 30, 1965, box 10, Office of International Training, African Branch, Agency for International Development, Tanzania PPROJ/SUBJ FY1960–71, RG 286, NARA II.

aids to African schoolchildren lauding the value of wildlife.[48] Train's organization also made a variety of posters that attempted to tie preserving nature to national prestige, with slogans, written in Swahili, such as "Our National Parks are the envy of the world – be proud of them" and "Our National Parks bring good money into Tanganyika – preserve them."[49] If national parks were going to be components of postcolonial development, NGO officials came to believe that local culture needed to change.

Changing cultural norms was a difficult task, and the CAWM's early years were fraught with struggles that reflected its myriad purposes. Although the school sought to engender a widespread appreciation for the aesthetic and economic value of wildlife conservation among young Africans, it had difficulty attracting potential African game managers. An early report written by Train noted that a typical student attending the school neither "speaks nor reads English," and "has no background whatsoever in game matters." The chief instructor, a British biologist named Hugh Lamprey, who came originally to East Africa to research wildlife migrations, spent most of his nights offering rudimentary language education. The considerable bureaucratic red tape in the new Tanganyikan government made it difficult to use AID's grant money, which had to be filtered through appropriate ministries. The grant money from AWLF and WWF, which went directly to Lamprey, covered basic operating costs in the school's first few years.[50]

Train's fellow conservationists were much more interested in the school than was Nyerere's government. While visiting Nairobi for the ninth annual World Assembly of the IUCN, Train led an extensive tour of CAWM. Train walked around the school grounds with U.S. Secretary of the Interior Stewart Udall, UC Berkeley Professor Starker Leopold (son of Aldo Leopold), IUCN researcher Lee Talbot, and other conservation luminaries, introducing the tour group to students and showing off the school's curriculum. Amid all the activities, though, Train and his crew never met with representatives of the Kenyan, Ugandan, or Tanganyikan government. Aside from a young African student who was studying game management at Michigan State University, the African with whom Train

[48] Train, unpublished essay, Fall 1963, box 53, Train Papers.
[49] J. S. Owen, "Awakening Public Opinion to the Value of the Tanganyikan National Parks," in *Conservation of Nature and Natural Resources in Modern African States*, 263.
[50] Russell Train, "Memorandum to Trustees, African Wildlife Leadership Foundation," 1963, box 53, Train Papers.

spent the most time was his safari driver.[51] Rarely did Nyerere or any important ministers visit the school during such showcase moments or otherwise. CAWM was designed for an "Africanized" future, but its early years reflected more of its colonial heritage.

The school's travails were indicative of a larger economic problem. National parks and game preserves had not become larger priorities for Nyerere's government because there was little evidence that actual revenues from tourism would match the conservationists' promises. Even leading multilateral lending organizations believed the emphasis on protectionism was misplaced. A World Bank mission sent to examine the possibilities of development aid to Tanganyika reported in 1961 that "sentimentality over game cannot be expected to influence Africans in the areas concerned in favor of the protection of animals from hunting and the reservation of large areas of land – even dry, tsetse-infested land. So far, revenue from tourists is not enough to provide a very persuasive argument."[52] The IUCN's and WWF's efforts had not produced a message that compellingly linked the preservation of natural spaces with economic growth, and thus they had failed to engender consistent support from both the national government and local people. In place of "sentimental" protection, the World Bank mission recommended funding for integrated game cropping systems focused on food production.[53]

As the 1960s wore on, Nyerere embraced a more aggressive and rapid development agenda for his country. When Nyerere announced a new Five Year Plan in 1964, he identified three long-term goals to be achieved by 1980. He wanted to raise per capita income to $126, attain self-sufficiency in trained manpower, and raise life expectancy from the present 35 to 40 years to 50 years. To spur these changes, the plan focused on agricultural production, building new villages, and industrial development via in agricultural processing and manufactured consumer goods. It depended on foreign assistance and private foreign investment, as Nyerere's government needed short-term capital. "The need to show economic progress is a political reality," AID officials said of the Five Year Plan. "The crucial question is whether progress can be achieved quickly enough under the Plan to avoid the dangers of despair and

[51] Ibid.

[52] *The Economic Development of Tanganyika: Report of a Mission Organized by the International Bank for Reconstruction and Development at the Request of the Governments of Tanganyika and the United Kingdom* (Baltimore: The Johns Hopkins University Press, 1961), 296–7.

[53] Ibid., 297.

a grasping at alternative extremist approaches."[54] Policy makers in Washington believed U.S. assistance was necessary to prevent Nyerere from turning to the Soviet bloc.

AID's development plans resembled Nyerere's in that they left little room for preservation and conservation. U.S. officials identified two "basic weaknesses" in the Tanganyikan economy: the "need for greater cash crop production and the need to industrialize."[55] American development experts consistently focused funding for agricultural production through a variety of planting schemes, education, and public works projects, believing that "the prospects for stability rest on the rapidity with which demands for economic development can be met."[56] Tourism appeared only as a marginal component in AID's overall planning, with only a few hundred dollars allocated for equipment and maintenance of national parks. By the mid-1960s, what little money arrived for the purposes of spurring tourism came from China.[57] While CAWM would help with the second goal, it was difficult to see how adding more national parks would help otherwise if tourist dollars did not materialize as IUCN and WWF officials had claimed.

Recognizing their growing marginalization, WWF and IUCN stepped up their campaign to encourage protection and conservation policies in the postcolonial world. In 1963, the WWF teamed with the Commission for Technical Co-operation in Africa (CCTA), an organization of erstwhile colonial authorities. The CCTA had endeavored to oversee scientific exchanges and development projects in the early 1950s when international institutions paid little interest to sub-Saharan Africa. With nominal support from African leaders such as Nyerere, the two organizations produced an "African Charter for the Protection and Conservation of Nature," which attempted to provide a guiding policy framework for how young nations should treat their natural landscapes. "Rational

[54] Agency for International Development, "Country Assistance Program: United Republic and Tanganyika and Zanzibar," October 1964, 1–5, USAID Documents Experience Clearinghouse. [Online] Available: http://dec.usaid.gov/index.cfm. Accessed March 12, 2011.

[55] Ibid., 11–13.

[56] Ibid., 1–6.

[57] In 1966, for instance, the largest AID project to Tanzania related to the parks was a $400 loan for equipment in Serengeti. By contrast, according to AID, China offered over $150,000 to the Ministry of Information and Tourism, with AID offering no substantial projects in that field. Agency for International Development, "Country Assistance Program FY 1968: Tanzania, Part II," October 1966, 89, USAID Documents Experience Clearinghouse. [Online] Available: http://dec.usaid.gov/index.cfm. Accessed March 12, 2011.

exploitation based on specific and well-proven scientific rules is the only satisfactory means of complying with both moral obligations and legitimate material interests," the Charter asserted. It also created many stipulations about enforcing existing national parks and game reserves and establishing new spaces and to require any large-scale development projects, such hydroelectric dams or wide-scale agricultural schemes, to be reviewed systematically by "all the specialists concerned, including biologists."[58] Although clear and declarative, the document had minimal legal power and in no way bound states to action.

By the 1960s, the Arusha Conference, projects such as CAWM, and the CCTA charter revealed the limitations of the IUCN's and WWF's strategy. On the one hand, the IUCN continued to promote preservation of existing "wild" areas, places of spectacular beauty and distinctive wildlife that needed state protection from the market. On the other hand, the IUCN and Huxley also promoted "scientific management" of resources, a line of thinking dating from progressive-era conservation. Proponents believed that finite natural resources, such as animals that could be used as protein sources, required careful management and coordination by scientific experts. And although the IUCN framed both strands of thought as part of a larger program of reconciling conservation and development, it often emphasized the former. Promoting national parks, often at the expense of indigenous people, was the defining feature of major environmental NGOs from their early years in Africa.

Huxley's own writings consistently emphasized defending and expanding wildlife, parks, and game reserves, rather than a more integrative model that placed human resource use at the center of its platform.[59] Although IUCN members such as Huxley often claimed that creating a tourist industry around shielded flora and fauna was both the most necessary and most beneficial step a developing nation could take to secure the dual purposes of protecting the environment and earning valuable foreign exchange, such arguments generally fell on deaf ears in both the Nyerere administration and among leading donor agencies, such as AID.[60] But WWF's growing financial support and increasing international

[58] "African Charter for the Protection and Conservation of Nature," CCTA/CSA, Publication No. 91, June 1963, box 109, Huxley Papers. On the CCTA, see Isebill V. Gruhn, "The Commission for Technical Co-operation in Africa, 1950–1965," *The Journal of Modern Africa Studies*, Vol. 9, No. 3 (Oct. 1971), 459–69.

[59] Julian Huxley, "Wild Life and World Enjoyment," 1963 and Julian Huxley, "Wild Life as a Resource," both propose national parks and game reserves as the primary solutions to problems of conservation. Both can be found in box 81, Huxley Papers.

[60] Neumann, *Imposing Wilderness*, 124–5.

profile ensured that it would continue to pressure governments and pursue its own projects. The prospects for the future of environmental protection were unclear. "A good beginning has been made, especially in establishing national parks, where for the moment the wild animals are safe," Huxley wrote in 1965. "But the future is still very insecure."[61]

### NATIONALIST NIGHTMARES: MODERNIZATION, INTERNATIONAL TENSIONS, AND NYERERE'S UJAMAA

As conservationists struggled to promote their cause, Julius Nyerere became increasingly preoccupied with the politics of postcolonial rule. Uncertainty and flux defined the process of moving from partial to full political autonomy, and Nyerere spent much of his time in the mid-1960s attempting to shape the regional politics of East Africa. In 1963, Nyerere tried and failed to create a pan-East African federation led by Kenya and Tanganyika. Later in that year, neighboring island Zanzibar became fully independent under the leadership of an Arab-led minority party, although a bloody uprising of African nationalists followed shortly thereafter. To ensure that Zanzibar adopted a nonaligned stance similar to Tanganyika and because of deep affinities Nyerere held with the Africans on the island, Nyerere and Tanganyikan officials negotiated a union between the two nations. They created a new formal political entity, called Tanzania, in late 1964. In the process, Nyerere focused increasingly on promoting pan-African solidarity and closer ties between majority-rule black African nations.[62]

Elsewhere in the region, tumultuous events soon followed. In late 1964 and early 1965, rumblings from Ian Smith, Rhodesia's white minority leader, suggested that he planned a unilateral declaration of independence and sought to establish an apartheid state in his nation. Smith's posturing infuriated Nyerere, who had long been an advocate of black African unity and racial liberalism. The Tanzanian leader wrote a personal letter to President Lyndon Johnson, asking for the United States to support some kind of punitive UN action against Rhodesia, explaining, "Africa simply cannot afford to wait for the slow attrition of power from Mr. Smith's government. The immediate dangers to us all – but especially to Zambia – are too great."[63] The presence of an apartheid state threatened to

---

[61] Julian Huxley, "Notes on UNESCO," 1965, box 84, Huxley Papers.

[62] Pratt, *The Critical Phase in Tanzania, 1945–1968*, 136–9.

[63] Quoted in Robert Rakove, "A Genuine Departure: Kennedy, Johnson, and the Nonaligned World" (Ph.D. Dissertation, University of Virginia, December 2008), 462.

undermine black independence and destabilize the economic health of landlocked Zambia, a small nation located southwest of Tanzania and north of Rhodesia. Highly dependent upon copper exports, Zambia feared the loss of critical transportation routes through Rhodesia.[64]

Nyerere, seeing an opportunity to extend his influence over the region and redirect trade routes through his nation (and thereby bypassing white settler states), proposed the construction of a vast railroad network from Zambia through Tanzania. In the quest for national economic growth, symbols of political power, and international prestige, governments in Africa often turned to large-scale development projects. Nyerere's railroad exemplified this mindset. In early 1965, Nyerere turned to the United States and Great Britain to ask for extensive financial support to build the railroad. Initially, President Johnson was willing to cooperate with a survey; however, when Tanzanian officials asked for a commitment to build the road, Johnson refused to finance the construction.[65] Following the rejections, in a move common among nonaligned nations, Nyerere turned to China for financing. Nyerere visited the country in early 1965, and Chinese Premier Zhou Enlai made a visit to Tanzania later that same summer in the hopes of laying the groundwork for a major bilateral assistance agreement.[66] He and Zhou Enlai gradually worked out the terms of the contract for the railroad, which ended with 1,163 miles of track laid by hundreds of thousands of workers (more than a quarter of whom were Chinese).[67] The project ultimately consumed 20 percent

[64] On the history of U.S. policy toward white rule in Southern Africa during the Cold War, see Thomas Borstelmann, *Apartheid's Reluctant Uncle: The United States and Southern Africa in the Early Cold War* (New York: Oxford University Press, 1993); Thomas Noer, *Cold War and Black Liberation: The United States and White Rule in Africa, 1948–1968* (Columbia, MO: University of Missouri Press, 1985); Andrew DeRoche, *Black, White, and Chrome: The United States and Zimbabwe, 1953–1998* (Trenton, NJ: Africa World Press, Inc., 2001); Philip Muehlenbeck, *Betting on the Africans: John F. Kennedy's Courting of African Nationalist Leaders* (Oxford University Press, 2012); Sue Onslow, ed., *Cold War in Southern Africa: White Power, Black Liberation* (New York: Routledge, 2009).

[65] "Memorandum from Ulric Haynes of the National Security Council Staff to the President's Special Assistant for National Security Affairs (Bundy)," June 15, 1965, *FRUS*, 24: 304.

[66] Peter J. Schraeder, *United States Foreign Policy Toward Africa: Incrementalism, Crisis, and Change* (Cambridge: Cambridge University Press, 1994), 202. Robert Rakove has shown how nonaligned nations, such as Tanzania, could often play donor nations off one another. Rakove, "A Genuine Departure," 357.

[67] George T. Yu, "The Tanzania-Zambia Railway: A Case Study in Chinese Aid to Africa," in Warren Weinstein and Thomas H. Henriksen, *Soviet and Chinese Aid to African Nations* (New York: Praeger Publishing, 1980), 117–44.

of Chinese aid to Africa during the Maoist era, and 10 percent of its overall aid to noncommunist nations.[68]

The celerity with which Chinese authorities accepted Nyerere's plans alarmed policy makers in the Johnson administration. Two members of the National Security Council (NSC) staff, Robert Komer and Ulric Haynes, wrote an urgent memo to President Johnson following the visits, claiming that "a major Chicom bridgehead in East Africa could be highly painful" for American interest in the region.[69] Already by 1966, U.S. officials were referring to Nyerere as "mercurial and fiercely independent," claiming his Tanzania was "the bastion of radicalism in East Africa."[70]

The railroad case caused friction between the United States and Tanzania governments, but it also came to symbolize a period in which Nyerere became increasingly aggressive in his nationalistic ambitions. In another "Arusha Declaration" produced in 1967, Nyerere proclaimed that his *Ujamaa* platform would henceforth serve as the blueprint for Tanzania's future. *Ujamaa*, a Swahili word for familyhood and community, presented a comprehensive restructuring of development goals. Nyerere presented an indigenous vision for the nation that emphasized forced villagization, on the basis of principles of mutual respect, common property, and a collective obligation for all people to work.[71] The declaration embodied the principles of national self-sufficiency and self-determination, and it bore the hallmark of Nyerere's own increasingly socialistic thinking.[72] Crucially, too, unlike the Arusha Declaration of

---

[68] Michael Adas, *Dominance by Design: Technological Imperatives and America's Civilizing Mission* (Cambridge: The Belknap Press of Harvard University Press, 2006), 259.

[69] "Memorandum from Robert W. Komer and Ulric Haynes of the National Security Council Staff to President Johnson," July 12, 1965, *FRUS*, 24:800–1.

[70] "Paper Prepared in the Department of State, undated" (Summer 1967), *FRUS*, 24: 374. Larry Grubbs argues that American officials increasingly perceived Nyerere as a "typically emotional African" when diplomatic tensions between Tanzania and the United States became more frequent. Larry Grubbs, *Secular Missionaries: Americans and African Development in the 1960s* (Amherst: University of Massachusetts Press, 2009), 156–7.

[71] See Scott, *Seeing Like a State*, chapter 7; Goran Hyden, *Beyond Ujamaa in Tanzania* (London: Heineman, 1980).

[72] On Nyerere and socialism, see Pratt, *The Critical Phase in Tanzania, 1945–1968*, chapters 7 and 8; Norman O'Neill, "Politics and Development Strategies in Tanzania," in Norman O'Neill and Kemal Mustafa, eds., *Capitalism, Socialism, and the Development Crisis in Tanzania* (Aldershot, UK: Gower Publishing Company, Ltd., 1990), 1–21. On Nyerere's perception that postcolonial Tanzania was moving away from his own aspirations for a democratic and egalitarian society, see Rodger Yeager, *Tanzania: An African Experiment* (Boulder: Westview Press, 1982), chapter 4.

1961, this document was penned entirely by Nyerere himself, and made no mention to wildlife preservation or natural resource conservation.[73]

Similarly, Nyerere had decided, over the course of events during the mid-1960s, to abandon the old ties to Europe and the United States and pursue a foreign policy of nonalignment.[74] He worried, as did many in the TANU, about his country's growing dependence on foreign aid; 83 percent of Tanzania's 1964–65 development budget came from foreign loans and grants.[75] Nonalignment and self-sufficiency became reinforcing, Nyerere looked inward to build the society he had envisioned free from foreign constraints and in accordance with his own ideals. Nyerere was a nationalist in 1967, just as he had been in 1961, but changing circumstances, domestic pressures, and foreign policy crises led him to adopt less cooperative means to achieve his goals. The nationalism he expressed by the late 1960s augured poorly for conservationists, whose difficulties in encouraging environmental protection only intensified.

## PARKS IN PERIL: NGO FRUSTRATIONS
## AT THE END OF THE DEVELOPMENT DECADE

In spite of difficulties garnering local support for their projects, the WWF continued to grow in size and scope. Fund-raising, which had been the IUCN's bête noire, was not an issue for the WWF. The organization leveraged both its personal connections to wealthy individuals in Europe and the United States as well as an elaborate marketing campaign of television specials, sponsored film viewings, and countless publications to generate donations (largely from the United States and Great Britain). In 1967 alone, the international secretariat was able to allocate more than $600,000 to international projects, introducing fifty-six new WWF-funded projects, such as CAWM, into the developing world. Africa remained far ahead of other developing continents in receiving money. From 1962 to 1967, Africa received $381,280 in grants, an amount surpassed only by Europe and North America. And it had the highest number of operative WWF projects – sixty-five – of any continent in the world.[76]

[73] Julius, Nyerere, "The Arusha Declaration: Socialism and Self-Reliance," January 29, 1967, reprinted in Nyerere, *Freedom and Socialism*, 231–50.
[74] Andrew Coulson, *Tanzania: A Political Economy* (Oxford: Clarendon Press, 1982), 180.
[75] Yeager, *Tanzania*, 55.
[76] Fritz Vollmar, ed., *The Ark Under Way: Second Report of The World Wildlife Fund, 1965–67* (Lausanne: Heliographia S.A., 1968), 48–9.

As the continent's postcolonial game wardens and park officials scrambled to ensure the long-term viability of their programs, they turned to the WWF for help. By 1967, the WWF was in some instances funding entire national parks. For example, WWF paid $16,910 in 1967 to keep up Meru National Park until the Kenyan National Parks could assume and afford full control of its operations.[77] Similarly, when poaching became rampant in some African parks and reserves, the WWF ended up covering expenses for extensive anti-poaching efforts. In Queen Elizabeth National Park in Uganda, WWF funded the transfer of six sets of radio transceivers from the New York Zoological Society, numerous firearms, and three airplanes to create a "mobile anti-poaching unit" to detect, track, and if necessary, attack potential poachers. After two years of operation, the director of Ugandan National Parks reported that poaching was still widespread, and that "an aircraft based permanently in the Queen Elizabeth Park" was necessary. Backed by the East African Wildlife Society, it secured such funds.[78] With this new influx of capital came more tourists (83,000 arrivals in all of East Africa in 1963 compared to 152,000 in 1967), although Kenya received the most benefits of the growth. Of the 152,000 tourists who came in 1967, approximately 117,000 arrived in Kenya, with the rest split between Tanzania and Uganda.[79] And although tourism was increasing throughout the region, it was unclear whether the upward trend would continue and whether tourism could be relied upon as a foundation for national developmental strategies.

Amid these changes, conservation and preservation remained a small portion of overall development projects. Moreover, the assertive nationalism from Nyerere and other leaders magnified the concerns of Huxley and his fellow conservationists' concerns. The IUCN's and WWF's protection efforts foundered in East Africa. In late 1965, Tanzania broke off relations with Great Britain over London's support of white rule in Rhodesia. A few months later in early 1966, as Nyerere was beginning to intensify his rhetoric of self-determination, Great Britain announced it would cut off all new foreign aid to the country. This presented a major problem for conservationists, as Tanzania's National Parks had come to rely on a small infusion of British development funds to cover the costs of

---

[77] Ibid., 96–7.
[78] Ibid., 114–15.
[79] Joseph P. B. M. Ouma, *Evolution of Tourism in East Africa, 1900–2000* (Nairobi: East African Literature Bureau, 1970), 27.

hiring qualified workers beyond what the WWF itself could afford.[80] Meanwhile, formal control over the parks was never set in stone, as administrative control did not fully rest with the Tanzanian government, since many workers were paid through these outside grants and park managers often had more allegiance to their particular parks than the national government. Fearing that lowering salaries from British to "African" levels would lead to many resignations and worried that he would not be able to attract new recruits, Tanzania's Director of National Parks, John Owen, went on a whirlwind tour of Western Europe and the United States to raise enough money to keep the parks system afloat.[81]

While funding problems left the parks in a perilous state throughout 1966 and 1967, a major crisis erupted in 1968. Britain's decision to halt all new foreign aid in 1966 hit one group of people particularly hard: pensioners. Up to that point, British officials working in the Tanzanian government had their pensions paid for by Tanzania, which in turn relied on British aid to help cover the mounting costs of doing so. By 1968, however, Nyerere's government decided that the cost was too much to bear, and subsequently announced it would no longer pay British civil servant pensions. In response to the gesture, Britain announced it would stop all aid whatsoever from going to Tanzania, save for a few exceptions.[82]

Nyerere's decision, which he framed in the vocabulary of "Africanization" of government, alarmed conservationists. So too did Britain's reaction. Conservationists' greatest fears were coming true: local authorities were seizing control of national parks, just like any other department. By ceding what remained of their prior control over the parks to the "Africanizing" Tanzanian government, conservationists worried that they had increasingly little recourse to ensure the protection of flora and fauna as they saw fit.[83]

---

[80] Funding also came in small grants from donor governments, particularly Germany and Canada, before British aid arrived in 1965. "Tanzania National Parks," November 1966, National Archives of the United Kingdom [hereinafter cited as NA-UK], records created or inherited by the Department of Technical Co-operation, and of successive Overseas Development bodies [hereinafter cited as OD] 16/669.

[81] Ibid.

[82] "An Appeal to the British Government for the Continuance of H.M.G.'s Support of the British Officers of the Tanzania National Parks," by John Owen, June 26, 1968, NA-UK, OD 16/1668.

[83] J. S. Owen to George Rogers, August 23, 1968, NA-UK, OD 16/1669; "An Appeal to the British Government for the Continuance of H.M.G.'s Support of the British Officers of the Tanzania National Parks," by John Owen, June 26, 1968, NA-UK, OD 16/1668.

In response, John Owen, who had long been associated with the IUCN and WWF (he had been a delegate and speaker at the original Arusha Conference), leapt into action. He traveled to London to meet with officials in the Ministry of Overseas Development (MOD). He argued that the pension dilemma would exacerbate the problems exposed in 1966–67. Existing British workers employed by the parks, he claimed, would leave with their financial future uncertain; new recruits would be hard to come by; the young crop of CAWM students were not yet ready to take control. MOD officials explained the withdrawal of aid would take some time and would not have a tremendous immediate effect on anyone. They also told Owen that the parks were a Tanzanian institution, and thus required Tanzanian oversight. Owen was incredulous. MOD officials noted that he intended "to pull out every stop to prevent withdrawal of support, basing his case primarily on the value to the world of preserving East Africa's unique wildlife and that Britain's support of this aim is a moral responsibility which she cannot shed." And more pointedly, Owen "seemed to have no idea that it was a neo-colonialist conception to infer that, whatever the views of the Tanzanian Government, it was simply up to the British government to impose British staff on the Parks, and their consequent departure, would in itself bring the Parks to ruin."[84] They made a persuasive argument. Owen had to turn to other means to support his cause.

After arriving back in Tanzania, Owen pressured the British government to grant an exception to the national parks during their withdrawal of aid. Since the parks were, in the words of British officials, a "wholly Tanzanian institution," no such exception could be made.[85] Undaunted, Owen claimed that to draw public attention to his cause – attention from Tanzanians, Europeans, and Americans – he would launch a "protest march" from Mikumi National Park to Dar es Salaam, wherein Owen would walk more than 180 miles in the hopes of convincing concerned parties abroad to pressure Britain to continue its aid to the parks. The stunt did not go over well with Tanzanians or the British government. Officials in London wryly called Owen's trek the "Long March," and believed it accomplished little. Owen, after all, had only a handful of supporters joining him. Moreover, although Owen had dismissed it as insignificant, British workers in Tanzania had already secured a promise

---

[84] R. H. Hobden to M. G. Smith, "Withdrawal of Support under BESS for National Parks," July 9, 1968, NA-UK, OD 16/668.

[85] J. S. Owen to George Rogers (House of Commons), August 23, 1968, NA-UK, OD 16/1669.

of some financial support for parks from the Ford Foundation. More importantly, Tanzanians themselves showed little interest in Owen's efforts and greeted him with more hostility than gratitude. According to multiple sources in Tanzania, Owen greatly overstated the support in Tanzania for his actions. Influential Tanzanians in Dar es Salaam were "certainly opposed" to Owen's spectacle, which many believed would bring unwanted attention on the nation.[86]

Since his personal efforts were ineffective, Owen turned to his connections with the WWF and IUCN in the hopes of reaching more influential officials. He started at the top. In early November 1968, Prince Bernhard, still president of the WWF, wrote a personal letter to British Prime Minister Harold Wilson. Bernhard expressed concern that British personnel would abandon the parks, which would be a "serious blow" to conservation in East Africa.[87] Wilson's staff crafted a warm and receptive response letter to Bernhard, although they were clear in stating that as a Tanzanian institution, the parks were the ultimate purview of Tanzanians, not British aid officials.[88] In Dar es Salaam, word of Bernhard's letter riled many British and Tanzanians alike. It was "unexpected and unwelcome," for the prince had already irritated Tanzanian officials by sending multiple letters imploring them to keep British staff on board by offering higher salaries. More so than previous letters, the one to Wilson "offended Tanzanian government susceptibilities" because it suggested Tanzania could not look after its own affairs and might complicate the aid relationship even further by reinstating the old relationship.[89]

Following Prince Bernhard's campaign, Max Nicholson wrote directly to Sir Geoffrey Wilson, Britain's secretary of overseas development. In a desperate tone employing hyperbolic language and peculiar logic, Nicholson argued that the Tanzanian parks were not, in fact, the provenance of Tanzania. Rather, the British government had "not appreciated that the National Parks . . . are in no way accountable for the misdeeds of the Government of Tanzania, but are in fact carrying out a trusteeship task on behalf of the whole world in preserving the unique environment" of Tanzania. The parks, which Nicholson called "probably the most

---

[86] W. F. Grieve to B. T. Holmes, October 4, 1968, NA-UK, OD 16/1669.

[87] Prince Bernhard to Harold Wilson, November 8, 1968, NA-UK, Records of the Prime Minister's Office [hereinafter cited as PREM], 13/2415.

[88] Harold Wilson to Prince Bernhard, November 25, 1968, NA-UK, PREM 13/2415.

[89] Telegram 947, November 27, 1968, Dar es Salaam to FCO, "Technical Assistance to Tanzania (National Parks)," NA-UK, PREM 13/2415.

important in the whole world," needed a small fund of money to maintain the British officials working there. He suggested there might be "international repercussions" for Britain if it did not support the parks more robustly, although he did not articulate what the consequences would be.[90] Through his letter, it was evident that concerns over an "Africanized" future for the parks remained just as pressing for conservationists at the end of the 1960s as they had at the beginning of the decade. Nicholson's arguments of a trusteeship for the globe, of the universal value of national parks for an imagined global community, had yet to win over hearts and minds in Africa or Great Britain, but they augured a shift in thinking that would reshape NGO strategy in the coming years.

The parks remained in an uncertain state through the next few years. With Owen unable to secure funding from Great Britain, the Tanzanian National Parks Board of Trustees moved toward what they called "localization." Localization meant hiring more graduates from CAWM to look after the parks, as the Board noted that CAWM was "the backbone of our local service in the Parks." Owen stayed on as director until 1971, when the first Tanzanian director of the parks took command. Although now fully a "Tanzanian institution," the fact that most park employees came through CAWM ensured that the parks still would continue to rely, albeit less directly, on the WWF and IUCN.[91] The small size of CAWM coupled with official ambivalence toward the prior debacle shrouded Tanzania's parks in uncertainty for the near future.

As officials in the IUCN and WWF dealt with the crisis in Tanzanian parks, similarly troublesome developments percolated in neighboring Uganda, as well. Colonial conservationists and their postcolonial supporters had long celebrated the Murchison Falls region as one of the continent's greatest wonders. Located just inland from the shores of Lake Albert in northern Uganda, where the White Nile courses through a narrow gorge, the falls produce one of the most powerful torrents of water in the region. The area around the falls also holds some of the continent's largest wildlife, including giraffes, white rhinos, and lions. For the conservationists in the IUCN and WWF, Murchison Falls represented the aesthetic ideal of a primeval wilderness and the essence of Africa's staggering flora and fauna. For contemporary nation builders, the river and falls had more than aesthetic and ecological value. In their

---

[90] E. M. Nicholson to Sir Geoffrey Wilson, February 13, 1969, NA-UK OD 16/1669.
[91] Neumann, *Imposing Wilderness*, 142.

minds, it was a tremendous store of energy for a country desperate to build infrastructure.

The area surrounding Murchison Falls had been protected as a national park, but in 1965 Uganda's government launched a new five-year plan for industrial development that called for a widespread increase in power use.[92] According to engineering surveys, the Nile, which declined precipitously across Uganda, held within it some 4,500 megawatts (MW) that could be tapped through damming. A number of sites held the possibility for dams to produce 100–150 MW each, but Murchison Falls, by far the most lucrative place, held upwards of 600 MW.[93] Moreover, Uganda President Milton Obote came from the nearby district of Lango, and the possibility of a major infrastructure project to express both his political power and commitment to his region of origin further enticed him.[94]

The proposed dam alarmed many conservationists. Peter Scott, a founding member of the WWF who had done an early survey of conservation in Uganda back in 1956, wrote frantic letters to the British engineering and construction firms charged with building the dam, asking them to halt their progress and search for alternative sites.[95] Russell Train, whose AWLF had provided extensive funds for a colonial-era national park surrounding the falls, had nervous dinners with multiple Ugandan ministers in the hopes of convincing them to stop the Murchison project. Train was set to invest $50,000 in a conservation education program at Murchison Falls, and worried that the dam would scuttle the project.[96] Hugh Elliot, an IUCN official, contacted multiple officials in Uganda and affirmed IUCN's position on the issue, namely that Murchison Falls was off limits to any kind of development.[97] Prince Bernhard, too, expressed dismay over the project and inquired about potential alternatives.[98]

The constant lobbying and pressure from the conservationists slowed developments of the Murchison Falls project, but the delay was short lived. In 1967 and early 1968 an alternative site on the Nile, at Bujagali, went under serious consideration, but in July 1968, the Ugandan government elected to go ahead with the Murchison Falls site. Once again, conservationists used personal connections to people in government

---

[92] Letter, unknown author to Prince Bernhard, August 18, 1965, NA-UK, FT 3/593.

[93] Robert Davis to Hugh Elliot, May 1969, NA-UK, FT 3/593.

[94] Many British officials shared this opinion. "R. M. K. Slater to D. R. Love," February 12, 1971, NA-UK, FCO 31/1061.

[95] A. A. Joy to H. E. O. Hughes, March 19, 1971, NA-UK, FCO 31/1061.

[96] Russell Train to Francis X. Katete, September 18, 1965, NA-UK, FT 3/593.

[97] Hugh Elliot to A. A. Ojere, August 2, 1965, NA-UK, FT 3/593.

[98] Letter, unknown author to Prince Bernhard, August 18, 1965, NA-UK, FT 3/593.

to slow down the project. E. B. Worthington, a well-established IUCN scientist who had worked in East Africa for many years, wrote to President Obote lamenting his project. Worthington was not against all dams, per se, but Murchison Falls was "an area where no building or human construction should ever be."[99]

Russell Train, on behalf of the WWF and the IUCN, also wrote to Obote imploring the president to halt his construction plans. Eschewing the hyperbolic language of arguments focused on the aesthetic and scientific value of the park, Train argued that the dam was a threat to tourism in a manner reminiscent of arguments Julian Huxley had made a decade earlier. He explained that revenues earned from park visitors would bring needed foreign exchange to the nation if given proper time. By 1974, Train claimed, the park "would be worth over $15 million to the economy." Building the dam, he insisted, would actually cause Uganda to "lose $10 million in foreign exchange per year, or $200 million over the entire construction period" because of the potential harm it would do to wildlife tourism. He added that other options, including nuclear, would make the dam obsolete in a few years and proposed new sites – Bujagali, Buyala, Kalagala – that could provide hydroelectric power without altering a cite of natural value as important as Murchison Falls.[100] Such economic figures had merit, too. The World Bank had questioned the immediate economic value from building a dam there, and Bank President Robert McNamara even visited the site where he called for a full "objective" study of the dam's proposed ecological impacts.[101]

However, Obote's steadfast commitment to building at Murchison Falls for both economic and symbolic reasons remained strong. "To hell with animals and to hell with tourists, to hell with Murchison Falls!" declared Erisa Kironde, chairman of Uganda's Electricity Board in 1970. Murchison Falls had been a tourist boon for Uganda, but the power and prestige that could be gleaned from the proposed dam proved too powerful of a draw. "The Uganda Electricity Board," one reporter wrote, "has become the very symbol of the modernity the nation aspires to; there is a spurious progressive quality to the attitude ... expressed by UEB Chairman Kironde."[102] Despite estimates from conservationists that

[99] E. B. Worthington to President Milton Obote, July 31, 1968, NA-UK, FT 3/593.
[100] Russell Train to Milton Obote, August 22, 1968, box 83, David Brower Papers, Bancroft Library, University of California, Berkeley [hereinafter cited as Brower Papers].
[101] "The Murchison Falls Hydroelectric Project," February 20, 1970, NA-UK, FT 3/593.
[102] Jamie Sutton, "Murchison Falls Need Not Die," *Not Man Apart*, Vol. 1, No. 3 (February 1971), 17–20.

construction would cost the country up to $200 million in lost tourist
dollars, such arguments carried little weight. In 1970, the government
moved forward with the project, despite IUCN and WWF officials' personal entreaties.

Conservationists tried to rally public opinion by taming their critiques
and appealing to the universal value of Murchison Falls. Peter Scott
explained to officials in government and members of Parliament, "I am
in no way against selling electrical equipment or engineering know-how,
or helping Uganda; nor I am in favor of holier-than-thou attitudes. I'm just
against major development in National Parks."[103] Scott, Fraser Darling,
and Julian Huxley coauthored a notice for WWF members and wrote an
editorial for the *Times* in which they argued a similar point.[104] In it, the
authors suggested that the tide of world opinion was on their side: "The
project is wholly against accepted international precepts in the management of national parks, precepts which are being greatly reinforced at
the present time by world opinion on quality of the environment."[105] Such
worldwide sentiment, they hoped, would convince Uganda's leadership
of the aesthetic, economic, and political value of preserving Murchison
Falls from human use, arguments Huxley and his allies had been making
about African wildlife for more than a decade.

The project moved forward, however, even surviving a change of
government. In 1970, General Idi Amin overthrew Obote's government.
Amin was "keen" on the project in 1971, especially because it would
help bring into the fold of his new states the restive Acholi tribes of the
northern region around Murchison. He sought financial support from
the UK to go on with the dam.[106] He kept Kironde on board at the
influential Electricity Board, and Kironde remained committed to the
project. And this was in spite of growing opinion that the dam would
serve no immediate economic interests. British officials quoted a World
Bank official who believed Uganda would be "quite wrong to bank on
economic growth through the medium of industrial expansion," based on
increased power from Murchison. "What they should be concentrating
on was agriculture," according to the official, but he did not deny "the

---

[103] Peter Scott to Lord Aldington, March 26, 1970, NA-UK, FT 3/593.
[104] Letter to the editor of the *Times*, "The Murchison Falls," February 20, 1970, NA-UK FT
3/593. The editorial appeared on May 6, 1970.
[105] "Memorandum from Peter Scott to members of IUCN/WWF," May 12, 1970, NA-UK,
FT 3/593.
[106] "Confidential memorandum regarding Booth's letter of March 5 to Purcell," NA-UK,
FCO 31/1061.

greater political attractiveness of industrial, as opposed to agricultural development."[107]

Politics did slow construction of the project at Murchison Falls. E. B. Worthington lobbied a Dr. Banage, minister of Animal Industry, Game, and Fisheries and an ally of Amin, to revive the old Bujagali project for its potential political windfalls. Coincidentally, Amin began increasingly framing his rule as a corrective to the excesses of Obote's tenure. According to British officials, an increasing part of Amin's strategy in 1971 was to criticize Obote for "favouritism" toward Lango and the North. In response, the British officials believed that this impelled the general's decision to delay the Murchison Falls project as his administration looked into Bujagali with greater interest.[108]

The project was in doubt, but it was not a clear-cut victory for conservationists. The fate of their parks was still unknown and uncertain. Although General Amin had agreed to slow developments, his reasoning had little to do with a personal concern for conservation. Far from it. As he held up construction, his troops began to use animals in the Murchison area as target practice, slaughtering game throughout the area. The IUCN, WWF, and AWLF took heart because Amin had delayed construction of the dam. Amin's actions, however, did not reflect a widespread concern for wildlife.[109]

At the end of the decade, IUCN's and WWF's efforts in East Africa remained precarious. Preservationist measures, particularly national parks and game reserves, held a tenuous place in the overall development plans of new nations. Projects such as CAWM or the AWLF's park around Murchison Falls were tenuous and difficult to sustain as long as money was injected from the outside, usually from the IUCN and WWF.[110] NGOs themselves often had to scramble just to preserve what they had helped to build. To promote their cause, they had to rely on what little financial leverage they could muster and personal persuasion. They struggled to convince nationalist leaders that wildlife should hold a special place in their countries' future. Nor had they won over politicians to the idea that potential tourist dollars would outstrip the costs of setting aside

---

[107] A. A. Joy to H. E. O. Hughes, March 19, 1971, NA-UK, FCO 31/1061.

[108] R. M. K. Slater to D. R. Love, February 12, 1971, NA-UK, FCO 31/1061.

[109] Jamie Sutton, "Murchison Falls Need Not Die," *Not Man Apart*, Vol. 1, No. 3 (February 1971), 17–20. See also Bonner, *At the Hand of Man*, 101–2, which describes General Amin's decision to slaughter 2,000 elephants and 4,000 hippos to deal with overpopulation in Murchison Falls.

[110] Neumann, *Imposing Wilderness*, 142.

vast swaths of land from people, the marketplace, and state extraction. The growing tensions between national governments and the large-scale development projects they pursued and the WWF's and the IUCN's calls for preservation powerfully demonstrated that these NGOs had not effectively reconciled through policy environmental concerns and developmental aspirations.

When decolonization loomed at the start the 1960s, the IUCN, the WWF, and other conservation organizations feared what might happen to existing national parks and game reserves, and hoped that their personal connections could bring about a harmonious, universal recognition of the need for the protection of nature. By the end of the decade, the realities of economic nationalism and developmental imperatives had dashed their hopes and provoked some of their worst nightmares.

### CONCLUSION: DIVERGENT INTERESTS AND CONFLICTING GOALS

By the end of the 1960s, a panoply of institutions were working on the ground in East Africa to help facilitate the development process. The U.S. government, largely under the aegis of AID, was carrying out a variety of projects. And as they had before independence, conservationists were working on the ground in East Africa helping to maintain underfunded parks and the fledgling CAWM at Mweka. However, so too were Chinese engineers, laying railways and extending their influence in the developing world. And former British and German imperial officials worked to maintain old relationships in new nations. National governments run by black Africans, in countries such as Tanzania and Uganda, were becoming increasingly assertive, intransigent, and steadfast in aspiring to a robust nationalism. The trenchant, assertive tone of Nyerere's *Ujamaa* had obscured the deferential ventriloquist act of the WWF's Arusha Declaration.

Tanzania had relied heavily on commodity exports and foreign aid (largely from Great Britain) to keep itself solvent and productive. To free itself from dependence on global commodity prices and foreign investment, Nyerere aspired to financial autonomy and political prestige. And achieving both of these meant shunning existing international relationships in favor of an inward-looking fiscal policy. Tanzania still accepted donations from the WWF and the AWLF to expand its national parks, but nationalization of old European estates for village land became more of a priority for Nyerere's government in the late 1960s. Tourism increased in Tanzania, from 400 visitors in 1956 to 52,000 in 1972, but it did not bring the whirlwind, transformative profits its proponents had claimed. Although national parks remained in place in East Africa, especially in Kenya and Tanzania, they did so in part through the funding efforts of international NGOs such as the WWF. Indeed, much tourism came through NGO activity. More than a hundred chartered photo safaris in Tanzania during the 1960s and early 1970s came from Bernhard Grzimek's Frankfurt Zoological Society. Little of this money, however, trickled down to local communities.[111] Notwithstanding Nyerere's welcoming gesture toward WWF in 1961, the *Ujamaa* Declaration of 1967 was a symbol of the divergent interests and conflicting goals in the debates over development and environmental protection in years to come.[112]

Having failed to convince national leaders to incorporate a preservationist or conservationist ethos into their development programs, NGOs increasingly turned to international institutions and lending agencies to reform the sources of development funding. Writing to Robert McNamara in 1971, Max Nicholson explained that "several of us involved in international conservation are feeling that the time has come to initiate somewhat more overt high level co-operation in averting such unfortunate situations as have arisen for example, over ... Murchison Falls."[113] It was unclear to Nicholson how to achieve further high-level cooperation, and whether, for the time being, the IUCN and WWF could marshal enough power to pursue their objectives effectively. A need to focus on the source of development lending was becoming clearer to NGO officials, as was the need to expand the scope of the advocacy beyond the expansion of national parks and other protected areas.

By the late 1960s, IUCN and WWF were no longer alone in promoting international conservation causes. A series of events and intellectual trends in the West highlighted a growing environmental consciousness by the mid-1960s. Threatening ecological problems – pollution, nuclear fallout, and population growth – endangered all nations. Scientific data seemed to suggest that populations in the developing world were growing at numbers that would exhaust the planet and create conflict for land,

---

[111] Lekan, "*Serengeti Shall Not Die*," 259.

[112] On the global impact and legacy of *Ujamaa*, see chapter 8 in Rist, *History of Development*. See also Neumann, *Imposing Wilderness*, 148–50.

[113] E. M. Nicholson to R. S. McNamara, April 16, 1971, box 2, E. Max Nicholson Papers, Royal Geographical Society, London, United Kingdom [hereinafter cited as Nicholson Papers].

water, and resources.[114] Huxley's articles in British newspaper, films such as *Serengeti Shall Not Die*, education campaigns in the industrialized world, and scientific studies on conservation and preservation in Africa did little to reshape the thinking of nationalist leaders, but these efforts did help invigorate new constituencies of concerned, environmentally minded citizens and governments in the industrialized North.

In the immediate postwar years, environmental NGOs had attempted to draw attention to many ecological problems facing the developing world by leveraging personal connections, often tied to colonial relationships. By the late 1960s, members of the IUCN, the WWF, and other activist groups could look optimistically at a rapidly growing generation of environmental activists emerging across the United States and Europe. The environmental movement of the 1960s and 1970s would also look to the Global South and perceive many of the same problems that Julian Huxley and his colleagues had decades earlier. The growing public awareness of environmental issues in the 1960s seemed to offer an opportunity to encourage all nations to come together and create new policies capable of reconciling environmental protection measures with global aspirations for economic development. One event, in particular, soon encapsulated this optimism. Proposed in 1968 and planned for June 1972, the United Nations Conference on the Human Environment (UNCHE) became the symbol of hope for environmentalists across the globe.

[114] Connelly, *Fatal Misconception*.

# 3

# "The World's Most Dangerous Political Issue": The 1972 Stockholm Conference and the Politics of Environmental Protection

"The relationship between man and his environment is undergoing profound changes in the wake of modern scientific developments" began a resolution put before the UN's General Assembly on December 3, 1968. These profound changes were global in scope and presented harrowing problems for people across the world. Rapid population growth and industrialization in developing countries coupled with continued economic growth in the developed world created concerns about potential exhaustion of important raw materials, especially energy sources. Industrial air and water pollution had no regard for boundaries between states, igniting complicated diplomatic disputes and endangering natural systems and human well-being. Excessive use of technologies, such as industrial fertilizers and nuclear power plants, with potentially deleterious unintended consequences imperiled human health and threatened the very material abundance of contemporary society that such technologies had helped to create.[1]

Alarmed by these events, leaders of major states began to take notice of the environmental problems that activists such as Julian Huxley and Russell Train had been worried about for years. Riding the tide of environmental concern sweeping the developed world in the 1960s, the Swedish government put forth a proposal to convene an international conference, under UN auspices, to bring all nations together to address these environmental problems. Backed by the General Assembly on

[1] Resolution 2398 (XXIII), December 3, 1968, UN General Assembly, 23rd session. [Online] Available: http://www.un.org/Depts/dhl/resguide/specenv.htm. Accessed January 7, 2011.

*What was meant by the "human environment"?*

December 3, the UN called for the June 1972 meeting to be dedicated to the "human environment." It was necessary, the UN resolution claimed, to "focus the attention of Governments and public opinion on the importance and urgency of this question and also to identify those aspects of it that can only or best be solved through international cooperation and agreement."[2] The gathering, to be held in Stockholm, Sweden, was designed to do just that.

The Stockholm Conference also signaled the rapid broadening of what quickly became called the "environmental movement." Whereas the World Wildlife Fund (WWF) and the International Union for the Conservation of Nature (IUCN) had focused mostly on engaging developing nations and relied mostly on personal leverage to generate support among individual national leaders, by the late 1960s a broader movement, buoyed by a new generation of activists, turned to grassroots activism to promote policy changes in donor governments and new environmental values in the United States and Europe. This prompted cleavages within the wider environmental movement. The IUCN and the WWF defined much of the Stockholm agenda and developed close ties with government delegations. Newer NGOs, by contrast, found themselves without such institutional footholds and much of their activities in Stockholm focused on grassroots mobilization outside conference walls.[3]

The Stockholm Conference also exposed new ideological, political, and social differences within environmental NGOs. While some members of the IUCN and the WWF relied heavily on older modes of thinking about conservation and preservation, particularly progressive resource

---

[2] The human environment was a broad phrase that referred to a variety of issues in the late 1960s and early 1970s that seemed to be linked together – overpopulation, hunger, famine, resource exhaustion, pollution, and environmental degradation.

[3] Scholars have generally analyzed Stockholm as a binary between state action on the inside and a "global community" of activists outside the conference. The argument for minimal NGO influence appears most explicitly in Stephen Hopgood, *American Foreign Environmental Policy and the Power of the State* (Oxford: Oxford University Press, 1998). See also McCormick, *The Global Environmental Movement*, 121–4; J. Brooks Flippen, "Richard Nixon, Russell Train, and the Birth of Modern Environmental Diplomacy," *Diplomatic History*, Vol. 32, No. 4 (September 2008), 613–38 and Bramble and Porter, "Non-Governmental Organizations and the Making of US International Environmental Policy"; Morphet, "NGOs and the Environment." The phrase "global community" comes from Iriye, *Global Community*. The term "global community" refers to interactions among international or transnational individuals and groups pursuing a kind of world order not entirely defined by military power and national interests. See also Barry Buzan, *From International to World Society? English School Theory and the Social Structure of Globalization* (New York: Cambridge University Press, 2004).

management and the wilderness ideology underlying national parks, from the late 1960s onward many environmentalists shifted to focus on critiquing the underlying assumptions of modernization – the purpose of development, the measurements of progress, and the use of industrial technologies. For these activists, Stockholm was less a culmination of decades of work on conservation than a moment to begin calling into question newer issues such as North-South equity, ending the conflict in Vietnam, and the use of nuclear power in peace and war. There was no such thing as a global environmental movement, but rather a myriad of environmentalists with different priorities and different points of emphasis.

   The gathering at Stockholm reinforced the fact that NGOs faced many challenges as they struggled to inject environmental concerns into development policy. While there was international consensus over support for some issues, such as the need for a global monitoring system for environmental problems, efforts to reform international development policies brought more discord than cooperation. The meeting evoked profound political tensions between developed countries, such as the United States, major nations of the Third World, primarily Brazil and India, and environmental NGOs over the relationship between environmental protection and economic development. Global comity over environmental protection was elusive because the most pressing issues – particularly financing environmental reforms in poorer nations – laid bare deep-seated tensions between the North and the South over questions of justice and equality in the global economy.[4] The United States was at the center of these controversies. The Nixon administration had taken up international environmental issues because the president's advisors assured him it was a "nonpolitical" issue that could earn domestic and international goodwill. However, the debates surrounding the conference ensured, to the administration's dismay, that any global environmental accord would be bound up with the future of foreign aid, international development policy, and questions of power and equality in the international system.

   The most significant legacies of Stockholm lie in the concepts that emerged from these debates and how environmental NGOs responded to them. Although the Nixon administration and the developing nations achieved some basic objectives at the gathering, more tensions were raised

---

[4] Global issues are those that affect all societies, often irrespective of national boundaries, such as narcotics trafficking, population growth, disease, human rights, and environmental degradation. On the rise of "global issues," see Daniel Sargent, *A Superpower Transformed: The Remaking of American Foreign Relations in the 1970s* (New York: Oxford University Press, 2015).

than problems solved. The Stockholm Conference left unresolved questions over how best to balance national economic interests with global environmental imperatives although the concepts of "development" and "environmental protection" became intertwined. As a result, officials in environmental NGOs came to believe that the fate of worldwide environmental protection measures would be tied to the extent to which they could make international development policy take ecological considerations into account. They recognized the importance of seeking strategic alliances with key policy makers and institutions in the industrialized North, as well as embracing, to varying degrees, the arguments made by those from developing nations.

While many environmentalists celebrated the symbolic value of Stockholm and the few agreements it produced, all NGOs viewed the meeting as a starting point for future activism aimed at reforming development policies in the industrialized North to incorporate ecological considerations. Many activists, too, came to promote environmental protection in the language of development – conservation *for* development, as the IUCN described it.[5] Stockholm exposed the challenges of seeking state-centric solutions for problems global in scope, and further convinced environmental NGOs of the necessity of finding policies capable of reconciling the desire for economic growth with a recognition of environmental limits.

## THE GLOBAL ENVIRONMENTAL MOMENT

The Stockholm Conference's origins date back to 1965, when the UN General Assembly formally designated a symbolic "International Cooperation Year." To help substantiate the concept, President Lyndon B. Johnson agreed to rededicate the United States to "the ideal and practice of international cooperation" by hosting a conference in December to explore the various ways in which the United States engaged the rest of the world.[6] For a president and administration that had recently

---

[5] "Conservation for Development" was the title and theme of the IUCN's Twelfth Technical Meeting, held concurrently with its eleventh General Assembly meeting held in Banff, Canada, from September 11–16, 1972. Hugh F. I. Elliott, ed., *IUCN's Twelfth Technical Meeting, Banff, Alberta, Canada, 12 to 15 September 1972: Papers and Proceedings* (Morges, Switzerland: IUCN, 1973), IUCN Library.

[6] Lyndon Johnson, "Message to the White House Conference on International Cooperation," November 29, 1965. [Online] Available: http://www.presidency.ucsb.edu/ws/?pid=27386# axzz1Obpq5wf2 Accessed June 7, 2011.

increased its involvement in an undeclared war in Southeast Asia, the conference was, in a cynical view, a thinly veiled and ineffective way to deflect negative public opinion. However, the meeting also bespoke a group of policy makers gradually coming to terms with a variety of seemingly new problems – population growth, increasingly interdependent national economies, disease epidemics, resource exhaustion, pollution – for which international cooperation and global management seemed necessary.[7] Assistant Secretary of State for International Organization Affairs Richard Gardner explained, "A generation ago much of the international cooperation on the 1965 agenda did not exist. Modern science, with its awesome powers of creation and destruction, had not yet made cooperation so possible or so imperative."[8]

Among a variety of other topics during the Johnson administration's White House Conference on International Cooperation (WHCIC), the conservation of natural resources received extensive attention as environmental concern had recently swept the nation.[9] Many conservation NGOs sent representatives to the meeting in the hopes of shaping deliberations.[10] Russell Train was one such representative. Train was becoming a major player in American conservation circles, having resigned as a U.S. Tax Court judge in the summer of 1965 to work with his African Wildlife Leadership Foundation and the Conservation Foundation full time.[11] At the WHCIC, he sat on the Natural Resources Committee, where he suggested a number of innovative conservation proposals that would,

---

[7] The first volume in the *Foreign Relations of the United States* [hereinafter cited as *FRUS*] series to use the phrase "global issues" appears in the Johnson administration, and covers issues such as population growth, human rights, hijacking, water for peace, and cooperation in space. *FRUS, 1964–68, Volume XXXIV, Energy Diplomacy and Global Issues.* [Online] Available: http://history.state.gov/historicaldocuments/frus1964-68v34. Accessed June 10, 2011.

[8] Richard N. Gardner, "Introduction" in Richard N. Gardner, ed., *Blueprint for Peace: Being the Proposals of Prominent Americans to the White House Conference on International Cooperation* (New York: McGraw-Hill, 1966), 1.

[9] Rachel Carson's *Silent Spring* generated widespread interest in 1963 and the Wilderness Society successfully lobbied Congress to pass the Wilderness Act, which set aside over 9 million acres of federal land as formally protected areas. Gottlieb, *Forcing the Spring,* 79–80; Mark Harvey, *Wilderness Forever: Howard Zahniser and the Path to the Wilderness Act* (Seattle: University of Washington Press, 2005).

[10] Memorandum from the Under Secretary of State (Ball) to President Johnson, September 22, 1965, *FRUS, 1964–68, Volume XXXIV, Energy Diplomacy and Global Issues.* [Online] Available: http://history.state.gov/historicaldocuments/frus1964-68v34/d274. Accessed June 10, 2011.

[11] Russell E. Train to George T. Bowdoin, July 14, 1965, box 8, Train Papers, Manuscript Division Library of Congress.

seven years later, be central to the platform at the Stockholm meeting. Train called for an "International Trust for the World Heritage."[12] The trust, which spoke to many of the challenges he and his colleagues were experiencing in trying to maintain control over East Africa's parks, would "identify, establish, develop, and help manage natural areas and archaeological sites of unique value to the world community" by setting aside land holding valuable natural or cultural sites as national parks. The Committee also demanded training programs for officials in developing nations, institutes for resource use analysis, and an international treaty on endangered species.[13]

Joining Train was an influential expert on international development policy, a British economist named Barbara Ward. Ward had become a respected journalist for the *Economist* during the 1950s, and she wrote widely on issues pertaining to economics, global development, and international politics. By the early 1960s, she emerged as a leading voice on the political and economic aspects of international development. She also held close connections to many policy makers; Ward was a personal friend and informal foreign policy advisor to presidents Kennedy and Johnson. A devout Catholic, Ward worked to mobilize developed nations to increase their foreign aid commitments to the Global South in the hopes of reducing global poverty. At the meeting in Washington, her presence helped to ensure that participants focused on the global dimensions of the contemporary problems and the importance that the developing world would play in any future accords.[14]

While Train and Ward's work at the White House's conference had little effect on policy at the time, the solutions for global natural resource management issues put forth at the conference bore a striking similarity to solutions being discussed by the IUCN and the WWF. The two organizations had begun actively pursuing international cooperation and consensus as a means to deal with global environmental issues. By the late 1960s, the

[12] J. Brooks Flippen, *Conservative Conservationist: Russell E. Train and the Emergence of American Environmentalism* (Baton Rouge: Louisiana State University Press, 2006), 54. Train worked on the idea with the committee's chair, Joseph L. Fisher, president of the research institute Resources for the Future. The proposed Trust would, in essence, be for the entire world what the 1964 Wilderness Act had been for the United States.

[13] Richard N. Gardner, "Introduction," in Gardner, ed., *Blueprint for Peace*, 17; 140–57.

[14] FK to Ward, October 8, 1959, box 2, Barbara Ward Papers, Georgetown University Special Collections Library, Washington, DC [hereinafter cited as Ward Papers]; David Satterthwaite, *Barbara Ward and the Origins of Sustainable Development* (London: IIED, 2006), 43–6; Barbara Ward, *Spaceship Earth* (New York: Columbia University Press, 1966).

IUCN and the WWF had grown considerably, and their leading members were taking advantage of the growing official interest in conservation members. In January 1965, Peter Scott, a British WWF official active in African conservation circles, and U.S. Secretary of the Interior Stewart Udall designed an international scientific conference on environmental matters with a scope far beyond the narrow focus on parks and other protected areas that the IUCN and the WWF had promoted in the past. Their efforts, bolstered soon by the addition of Raymond Dasmann, a young ecologist who led the Conservation Foundation's International Program, resulted in a 1968 gathering dubbed the "Biosphere Conference." The symposium reflected growing interest in the new concept of "biosphere," itself a testament to the growing body of ecological science that suggested interconnectedness among all living things on earth. It was a milestone in promoting international sharing and public presentation of scientific knowledge for issues ranging from toxic pollution to ocean management to questions of achieving a "dynamic balance" between human use of the environment and preserving natural systems.[15]

Additionally, in the late 1960s the IUCN and the WWF underwent major changes in their personnel and purpose to focus more on working with officials in developed nations and international institutions. Julian Huxley, who had turned 80 in 1967, had stepped back from a leadership role as new leaders rose to the fore. At a meeting held in New Delhi in November 1969, the IUCN reached what former director Martin Holdgate called a "turning point." The IUCN's Programme and Budget Committee, now staffed by younger members such as Lee Talbot, adopted revised formal objectives. The organization now sought to formulate major statements and declarations related to international conservation, advise governments more actively, and consult national agencies on preservation and conservation. These objectives reflected what the IUCN had already been doing, especially vis-à-vis developing countries – it only made that mission more explicit. The IUCN had been formed as a network of scientists hoping to share data and exchange information; after 1969, it sought to influence public policy more directly.[16]

---

[15] Holdgate, *The Green Web*, 96–7; Harold J. Coolidge, "World Biosphere Conference: A Challenge to Mankind," *IUCN Bulletin*, Vol. 2, No. 9 (October/December 1968), 66; *Use and Conservation of the Biosphere: Proceedings of the Intergovernmental Conference of Experts on the Scientific Basis for Rational Use and Conservation of the Resources of the Biosphere, Paris, 4–13 September 1968* (Paris: UNESCO, 1970).

[16] Holdgate, *The Green Web*, 108–9.

This lobbying role became apparent as a new generation of leaders came to the IUCN. In 1970, the organization appointed Dr. Gerardo Budowski, a scientist affiliated with UNESCO, as its director general. Beneath him, Frank Nicholls, an administrator working for the United Nations Development Programme (UNDP), was named deputy director-general. Ray Dasmann, the head of the Conservation Foundation's International Foundation, became the IUCN's senior ecologist. Together, these men replaced Huxley's generation, whose work experience often came in colonial park management or scientific research. The new group was, Holdgate remembered, "a far cry from the old-style, informal, 'family.'"[17] Their professional backgrounds in management and governance signaled that the IUCN was positioning itself to lobby more aggressively and build stronger ties with government officials.

This new base of funding and personnel also underwrote a broadening of the organizations' scope. The IUCN and the WWF continued to support projects across the world and offered direct financial support for national parks.[18] The organizations also enthusiastically endorsed Train's idea for the World Trust. To date the IUCN, working with UN officials, had begun keeping track of the status of national parks worldwide, but the Trust opened up new management opportunities for an international body to oversee the maintenance of current and future protected spaces.[19] By the end of the 1960s, important members of the organization critiqued the most basic assumptions of the development process, as part of a "crisis of modernization" when many reformers questioned orthodox development thinking.[20] In the early days of the WWF, its members "hadn't become involved in the causal factors which make conservation measures necessary, like human overpopulation, environmental pollution, poverty, high technology agriculture, and so on," claimed Peter Scott.[21] At the Second International Congress of the World Wildlife Fund in 1970, Max

---

[17] Ibid., 110. The WWF expanded, as well. See Bonner, *At the Hand of Man*, 67–71.

[18] Fritz Vollmar, ed., *The Ark Under Way: Second Report of The World Wildlife Fund, 1965–67* (Lausanne: Heliographia S.A., 1968), 46.

[19] "Appendix XII: International Commission on National Parks Resort [sic] 1966–1969," in *Tenth General Assembly: Vol. II, Proceedings and Summary of Business* (Morges, Switzerland: IUCN, 1970), 116–17. [Online] Available: http://www.iucn.org/knowledge/publications_doc/publications. Accessed November 14, 2011; Holdgate, *The Green Web*, 109.

[20] Ekbladh, *The Great American Mission*, chapter 7.

[21] "Speech by Sir Peter Scott at the 20th Anniversary Celebrations of WWF," n.d., folder C.1225, Sir Peter Markham Scott Papers, Department of Manuscripts and University Archives, Cambridge University, Cambridge, UK [hereinafter cited as Scott Papers].

Nicholson proclaimed, "Worldwide efforts to promote continuous economic growth through the hasty application of large scale modern technology are cumulatively creating greater environmental problems, such
as global pollution, on a scale for which no practical solutions are yet
in view."[22]

However, rather than work primarily with leaders in the developing
world, as they had in East Africa, major NGOs turned their attention
to the developed world. Frustrated by their difficulties in convincing
nationalist leaders to adopt environmental protection policies on a wide
scale, environmental groups believed that they could have more success
by lobbying the countries that provided development assistance. For
instance, to redress the problems he laid out at the WWF's Second
International Congress, Nicholson resolved to place new emphasis on
working directly with lending agencies.[23] These shifts toward professional
lobbying and criticizing the basic assumptions of the development process
were subtle but significant changes for the IUCN and the WWF.

The IUCN's and the WWF's new focus mirrored the emergence of a
broad-based environmental movement in the United States and Western
Europe. Whereas a desire for "wise use" of natural resources and the
protection of endangered wildlife and landscapes had animated the
founders of the IUCN and the WWF, a growing set of concerns sparked
the environmentalist movement of the 1960s. Carson's *Silent Spring* in
1962 revealed the deleterious effects of chemical pollution. Air and
water pollution, soil erosion, and oil spills all became visible signs of
environmental degradation, especially in the suburbs.[24] The unintended
consequences of industrial technologies sparked concerns for making
environmental risk and technical information accessible to the public.[25]
Images of ecological destruction and severe poverty from the developing
world stirred fears of Malthusian limits, aided by the proliferation of
middle-class television watching.[26] Influential congressmen, such as

---

[22] Max Nicholson remarks, Summary of the Seventh Session, The Second International
Congress of the World Wildlife Fund Meeting in London, November 1970, box 107,
Huxley Papers.

[23] Ibid.

[24] Rome, *The Bulldozer in the Countryside.* On environmentalism in the 1960s generally,
see Rome, "Give Earth a Chance."

[25] Egan, *Barry Commoner and the Science of Survival.*

[26] Robertson, "This Is the American Earth." TV spurred interest not only in environmental
issues, but many other global issues, as well. See James Schwoch, *Global TV: New Media
and the Cold War, 1946–69* (Urbana and Chicago: University of Illinois Press, 2009).

Wisconsin Senator Gaylord Nelson and Maine Senator Edmund Muskie took interest in environmental issues.[27]

With the growing national interest in environmental issues, grassroots movements swelled.[28] In 1960, the total membership of major American environmental NGOs was 123,000; by 1969, the leading organizations had approximately 819,000 members.[29] By 1970, polls showed that nearly 70 percent of Americans thought air and water pollution were significant problems requiring government action.[30] Interest in the global environment increased, too; large American NGOs, such as the Sierra Club and Conservation Foundation, established "international" wings.[31] Similarly, new international groups, such as Greenpeace, formed to offer more radical expressions of environmental activism.[32] Compared to the state of international conservation at the time of the IUCN's founding in the late 1940s, the environmental movement – now termed "environmentalism" in common parlance – in the late 1960s was far more diverse in its scope and generated far more popular support in the United States and Western Europe.[33]

The contours of the emerging environmentalism were evident in a new NGO, Friends of the Earth (FOE), founded by the iconoclastic American environmentalist, David Brower. A wildlife enthusiast from a young age, Brower became a significant environmental voice during World War II. Witnessing how the war denuded mountains and polluted valleys in Italy, he placed "wilderness at the top" of his agenda when he returned home

[27] J. Brooks Flippen, *Nixon and the Environment* (Albuquerque: University of New Mexico Press, 2000), 5–9.

[28] Adam Rome, "The Genius of Earth Day," *Environmental History*, Vol. 15, No. 2 (April 2010), 194–204.

[29] Lee Talbot, "The Quest for Environmental Sustainability: The Coevolution of Science, Public Awareness, and Policy," in Larry L. Rockwood, Ronald E. Stewart, and Thomas Dietz, eds., *Foundations of Environmental Sustainability: The Coevolution of Science and Policy* (New York: Oxford University Press, 2008), 13. The numbers reflect the sum of membership numbers for the Sierra Club, the National Audubon Society, the National Wildlife Federation, the Wilderness Society, the National Parks Conservation Association, the Izaak Walton League, the Defenders of Wildlife, the Nature Conservancy, and the WWF – all of which were founded in 1961 or earlier.

[30] John C. Whitaker, *Striking a Balance: Environment and Natural Resources Policy in the Nixon-Ford Years* (Washington, DC: American Enterprise Institute, 1976), 8.

[31] *IUCN Bulletin*, Vol. 2, No. 7 (April/June 1968), 53.

[32] Zelko, *Make It a Green Peace*.

[33] "Environmentalism" serves as an umbrella term for this diverse movement of activists and groups concerned with the state of the nonhuman world, and is thus broader in its scope than either "conservation" or "preservation," the terms that IUCN and WWF officials had used to describe themselves in the 1950s and 1960s.

and took a full-time job at the Sierra Club. He became executive director in 1952. Among other changes, Brower pushed for an international section for the group focused on global issues such as population growth, and protested major development projects in the United States.[34] Over time, however, Brower's leadership style frustrated other Sierra Club officials, and he resigned amid controversy in 1969.[35] He then formed two organizations: the League of Conservation Voters, which sought to influence domestic elections, and Friends of the Earth (FOE), a tax-exempt organization that encouraged grassroots mobilization behind a wide range of causes typical to the new environmentalism, such as curtailing energy use and protesting nuclear power.[36]

The creation of FOE was significant because it marked the growing interest in global activism and increasing debates over the proper tactics for environmental groups. Although Brower founded the group in 1969 as a domestic organization, it quickly expanded to include chapters in Sweden, France, and the United Kingdom. In 1971, Brower established an "international secretariat," called Friends of the Earth International (FOEI) to oversee the chapters.[37] FOEI embodied Brower's famous phrase, "think globally, act locally."[38] The new umbrella organization faced deep questions over how far to coordinate local chapters and which tactics to employ in pursuing its causes. For instance, FOEI members sought UN accreditation to have an active role at Stockholm, but they also wanted to focus on local mobilization and agitation. The tensions between seeking political influence with centers of power and building up grassroots credibility were also apparent in Brower himself, who cultivated an identity as a passionate outsider. Speaking once of Brower, Russell Train quipped, "Thank God for David Brower. He makes it so

---

[34] David Brower, *For Earth's Sake: The Life and Times of David Brower* (Salt Lake City: Peregrine Smith Books, 1990), 87–128; Gottlieb, *Forcing the Spring*, 81–2.

[35] On Brower's departure from the Sierra Club, see Gottlieb, *Forcing the Spring*, 81–2.

[36] "David Brower: Environmental Activist, Publicist, and Prophet," 260–1. Regional Oral History Office, Sierra Club Oral History Series, The Bancroft Library, University of California Berkeley. [Online] Available: http://www.archive.org/details/environmentalactoo browrich. Accessed November 12, 2011; report on first conference: Paris and Foret de Rambouillet – France, FRG, Italy, Swiss, United Kingdom, and the United States showed up, January 23–24, 1971 – Les Amis de la Terre, box 84, Brower Papers.

[37] "David Brower: Environmental Activist, Publicist, and Prophet," 260–1. Regional Oral History Office, Sierra Club Oral History Series, The Bancroft Library, University of California Berkeley. [Online] Available: http://www.archive.org/details/environmentalactoo browrich. Accessed November 12, 2011.

[38] Paul Wapner, *Environmental Activism and World Civic Politics*, 123–4; "David Brower: Environmental Activist, Publicist, and Prophet," 256–7.

easy for the rest of us to be reasonable," to which Brower responded, "Thank God for Russell Train. He makes it so easy for anyone to appear outrageous."[39] The tensions between pursuing grassroots activism and maintaining a professionalized, hierarchical institution persisted for years.

While Brower's new groups had a different platform and advocacy style than the IUCN and the WWF, all environmental organizations of the era shared two common traits – interest in international development and excitement about the Stockholm Conference. A December 1968 conference on the "Ecological Aspects of International Development" held in northern Virginia demonstrated that many environmentalists worried about international development policies and practice. Unlike the UNESCO Biosphere Conference run by IUCN officials, "Little concern had ever been given to anticipating ecological costs and side-effects, to say nothing of having such factors serve as inputs to decision-making in development projects," the editors of the conference report claimed.[40] Barry Commoner derided the disruptive effects advanced technologies had on ecosystems in the developing world. "The rescue rope offered to developing nations by modern science and technology," he argued, was "intrinsically unsound."[41] Lee Talbot of the IUCN called for greater local participation, claiming that "any development must take into account the culture of the people involved."[42] Russell Train, one of the meeting's hosts, conduced the entire event down to one sentence. "Our immediate purpose," Train told delegates, "is to build the clearest possible case for the inclusion of ecology in the development planning and decision-making process."[43]

In this context, Stockholm seemed important because of the growing perception that the global ecological crisis was only worsening. In 1968, a Stanford researcher named Paul Ehrlich released a book entitled *The Population Bomb*, in which population growth in the developing world

---

[39] J. Flippen, *Conservative Conservationist*, 60–1.

[40] Taghi Farvar and John P. Milton, "Foreword," in M. Taghi Farvar and John P. Milton, eds., *The Careless Technology: Ecology and International Development* (Garden City, New York: The Natural History Press, 1972), xiii.

[41] Barry Commoner, "On the Meaning of Ecological Failures in International Development" in Farvar and Milton, eds., *The Careless Technology*, xxii–xxiii. Commoner's ideology is explored fully and carefully in Egan, *Barry Commoner and the Politics of Survival*.

[42] Lee M. Talbot, "Ecological Consequences of Rangeland Development in Masailand, East Africa," in Farvar and Milton, eds., *The Careless Technology*, 695.

[43] Train, "Introduction to the Conference," in Farvar and Milton, eds., *The Careless Technology*, vii.

was depicted as a ticking time bomb.[44] Speaking at an international conference in 1971, David Brower warned of impending cataclysm. "We are headed for a technological epidemic, combined with a larcenous attack by this generation on the earth's biological capital that should serve many generations of mankind and of other living things," he claimed, because of an "almost irrational race for sources of energy to make his life more convenient, whatever else it may cost."[45] Despite their differences on the proximate causes of the global ecological problems, few doubted that a major crisis was nigh. Environmentalists viewed Stockholm as a global Earth Day, a single event to focus worldwide attention to the impending crises.

Many activists believed that international cooperation and some form of global governance were necessary in order to confront environmental problems. The editors of the *New Scientist*, a respected international science journal, claimed, "The fact is that the classical nation state is largely irrelevant in the environmental crisis," and individual national laws were insufficient without "a genuine supranational community and a degree of world government."[46] At its 1970 General Assembly, the IUCN reiterated and reemphasized that one of its most important purposes was "to encourage and assist in the making of coordinated legislation and international conventions to govern the utilization and treatment of soil, water, air, flora and fauna, to minimize pollution, and to protect the landscape in general and ecosystems of special interest in particular."[47] No less an establishment figure than George Kennan agreed. Writing in *Foreign Affairs* in 1970, the former U.S. ambassador to the Soviet Union called for a supranational institution to manage environmental issues.[48]

The idea that international cooperation was a first step toward saving the earth led many to anticipate the Stockholm meeting with great hope.

---

[44] Paul Ehrlich, *The Population Bomb* (New York: Ballantine Books, 1968). Malthusian fears of population outstripping food and other resources had long been a strand of environmental thought, but Ehrlich's book added a sense of cataclysmic urgency. See Robertson, *The Malthusian Moment*.

[45] David Brower, remarks at the "International Conference on Environmental Future," held in Helsinki and Jyvaskyla, Finland, June 27 to July 3, 1971, box 85, Brower Papers.

[46] *New Scientist*, Vol. 54, No. 798, 1 June 1972, 475.

[47] "Appendix XVIII: Declarations," *Tenth General Assembly: Vol. II, Proceedings and Summary of Business* (Morges, Switzerland: IUCN, 1970), 155. [Online] Available: http://www.iucn.org/knowledge/publications_doc/publications. Accessed November 14, 2011.

[48] George Kennan, "To Prevent a World Wasteland: A Proposal," *Foreign Affairs*, Vol. 48, No. 3(April 1970), 410.

Former IUCN President Martin Holdgate recalled the dominant feeling leading up to the conference "was that environmental issues had 'broke through.'" Holdgate explained that this enthusiasm derived from the fact that "for the first time the environment was being discussed by the world's governments as a subject in its own right."[49] Likewise, Barbara Ward, who had become increasingly active in environmental circles, wondered aloud in a speech to conference participants "whether we may not be present at one of those turning points ... when the human race begins to see itself and its concerns from a new angle of vision." Many years later she recollected that "those of who were there experienced ... a feeling that at last we were getting going."[50] Barry Commoner referred to the conference as a moment of "global motherhood," a coming together of diverse peoples in recognition that humanity's relationship with Mother Earth had soured.[51]

Thus, by the end of the 1960s, environmental groups began critiquing the most basic assumptions of development and looked toward the Stockholm Conference as the first step toward a collective response to global crisis. They also had further reason for optimism leading up to the conference. It seemed that major states were starting to take environmental issues seriously. Nowhere was this more evident than in the United States, where the administration of Richard Nixon had initiated a series of international solutions for global environmental issues.

## RICHARD NIXON, RUSSELL TRAIN, AND U.S. INTERNATIONAL ENVIRONMENTAL POLICY

On April 10, 1969, President Richard Nixon spoke before the North Atlantic Council on its twentieth anniversary. "NATO is needed," Nixon began, "and the American commitment to NATO will remain in force and it will remain strong. We in America continue to consider Europe's security to be our own." He then spoke at length about détente, describing ways in which the allies could begin arms control talks with the Soviet Union. Then Nixon took an unexpected turn. He talked about quality of life, social reform, and, most strikingly, environmental issues. "On my recent trip to Europe I met with world leaders and private citizens

---

[49] Quoted in McCormick, *The Global Environmental Movement*, 120.
[50] Ibid.
[51] Barry Commoner, "Motherhood in Stockholm," *Harper's*, Vol. 244, No. 1465 (June 1972), 49–54.

alike," Nixon explained, "and I was struck by the fact that our discussions were not limited to military or political matters. More often than not our talks turned to those matters deeply relevant to our societies – the legitimate unrest of young people, the frustration of the gap between generations, the need for a new sense of idealism and purpose in coping with an automating world." NATO, Nixon asserted, needed to address these concerns. He proposed the creation of the "Committee for the Challenges of Modern Society" (CCMS), which would give institutional expression to NATO's new dimension. "We are not allies because we are bound by treaty," Nixon said. "We bind ourselves by treaty because we are allied in meeting common purposes and common concerns."[52] Nixon suggested that nations faced common environmental problems such as air and water pollution, soil erosion, and loss of wildlife, and accordingly "nonpolitical," nonideological solutions could be pursued jointly.[53]

Nixon's speech to NATO was derived from the president's recent embrace of environmental politics. Shortly after his 1968 election, Nixon created a series of task forces to deal with a variety of issues facing the nation, which opened up opportunities for private actors to help define the administration's approach to public policy issues. Nixon's advisers recommended a group on the environment, for which they suggested a familiar name in conservation to serve as chairman: Russell Train. Train, a silk-stocking Republican with many personal ties to Washington, soon

---

[52] Richard Nixon, "Address at the Commemorative Session of the North Atlantic Council, April 10, 1969." [Online] Available: http://www.presidency.ucsb.edu/ws/?pid=1992. Accessed February 10, 2009. For a more complete exploration of the CCMS, see Jacob Darwin Hamblin, "Environmentalism for the Atlantic Alliance: NATO's Experiment with the Challenges of Modern Society," *Environmental History*, Vol. 15, No. 1 (2010), 54–75.

[53] Richard Nixon, "Address at the Commemorative Session of the North Atlantic Council, April 10, 1969." [Online] Available: http://www.presidency.ucsb.edu/ws/?pid=1992. Accessed February 10, 2009. Nixon and his advisers knew that the Soviet Union faced serious environmental problems, which made a bilateral agreement seem possible. By 1970 the Soviet Union was spending nearly $7 billion annually on water pollution measures, $5 billion annually to stop rampant soil erosion, and trying desperately to modernize its environmental bureaucracy. See J. R. McNeill, "The Biosphere and the Cold War," in Melvyn Leffler and Odd Arne Westad, eds., *The Cambridge History of the Cold War* (Cambridge: Cambridge University Press, 2010); Flippen, "Richard Nixon, Russell Train, and the Birth of Modern Environmental Diplomacy," 626; Douglas R. Weiner, *Models of Nature: Ecology, Conservation, and Cultural Revolution in Soviet Russia* (Pittsburgh: Pittsburgh University Press, 2000). See also Telegram 27061 from the Department of State to the Mission to North Atlantic Treaty Organization, the Mission to the United Nations European Office, and to UNESCO, Washington, February 24, 1970, *FRUS, 1969–1976*, Vol. E-1, [Online] Available: http://www.state.gov/r/pa/ho/frus/nixon/e1/46441.htm. Accessed February 10, 2009.

joined up. Amidst the younger, more aggressive environmentalists, the well-connected and well-respected Train seemed more amenable to elites. He quickly became the most important environmental figure in the administration.[54]

Political considerations drove Nixon's decision to adopt an environmental platform. In early December 1968, after examining public opinion polls, Train submitted to the president a memorandum saying that Nixon could garner more domestic support by taking environmental concerns seriously.[55] The president then appointed Train to the newly created Environmental Quality Council (soon renamed the Council on Environmental Quality, or CEQ) and instructed him to investigate ways to show that his administration was concerned about environmental matters. Nixon himself may have cared little for the environment, but as a politician Nixon was deeply aware of its potential to earn him votes.[56] In a few short months, Nixon oversaw a massive expansion of the environmental bureaucracy.[57]

Nixon and his advisers saw environmental legislation as a way to help restore faith in political institutions in the wake of domestic protests. Many groups that had protested peacefully in the early 1960s were adopting more hostile and bellicose approaches. Finding many allies within environmental movement, youthful protestors criticized capitalism, government, and the ineffectiveness of their leaders.[58] The rising anger over the United States' continued war in Vietnam stoked the flames of protest. Similar dissent occurred in Western Europe, Eastern Europe, and China as demonstrators questioned the ability of their leaders to create the utopian societies they had envisioned. The legitimacy of the nation-state itself seemed to be in question, and political leaders across the globe sought to craft policies that could assuage the protestors, protect their own domestic power, and stabilize their societies. Many NATO countries entered into the CCMS discussions with an eye toward this turbulence at home.[59]

---

[54] Flippen, *Conservative Conservationist*, 49.

[55] "Report of the Task Force on Resources and Environment (Train), December 5, 1968," box 305, Daniel Patrick Moynihan Papers, Manuscript Division, Library of Congress [hereinafter cited as Moynihan Papers].

[56] Flippen, "Richard Nixon, Russell Train, and the Birth of Modern Environmental Diplomacy," 617.

[57] For a detailed description of the federal environmental institutions created by Nixon, see Whitaker, *Striking a Balance*.

[58] On the ties between the student movement and the environmental movement and the place of radical environmentalism within both, see Woodhouse, *A Subversive Nature*.

[59] Suri, *Power and Protest*, chapter 5.

To lead the CCMS, Nixon turned to Harvard professor and urban policy specialist Daniel Patrick Moynihan, who linked together issues of environmental protection, social unrest, and quality of life. For Moynihan, CCMS was a progressive step on the part of the administration to redress a common set of issues – pollution, loss of fertile land to erosion, student dissent – that threatened stability and standards of living in much of the industrialized world. It was also a way to revitalize ties between the United States and many of its European allies in NATO, which had become increasingly strained over the Vietnam War.[60] Russell Train told Kissinger that substantive action on environmental issues could create a "positive image" of the United States abroad that would contrast with the "large number of divisive issues" in which the United States was involved.[61] Environmental politics held symbolic power for the new administration. Nixon even presented CCMS as a tool to help improve relations between the Cold War superpowers.[62]

Although environmental diplomacy became only a minor component of détente with the Soviet Union, between early 1969 and Nixon's visit to Moscow in 1972, much of the environmental bureaucracy worked toward this end.[63] On matters of bilateral environmental diplomacy, Russell Train led the way. In early 1972, Train began a series of lunch meetings with Soviet Ambassador Anatoly Dobrynin to outline a U.S.-U.S.S.R. agreement on environmental protection. When Nixon arrived in Moscow in May 1972, he signed the U.S.-U.S.S.R. Agreement on Cooperation in the Field of Environmental Protection. In an effort to maximize publicity,

---

[60] Ibid., 321. For background on the connection between Lyndon Johnson's Vietnam policies and his diplomacy with Europe, see Thomas Alan Schwartz, *In the Shadow of Vietnam: Lyndon Johnson and Europe* (Cambridge: Harvard University Press, 2003). See also Lawrence Kaplan, *NATO and the United States: The Enduring Alliance* (Boston: Twayne Publishers, 1988), chapter 6.

[61] Quoted in Hopgood, *American Foreign Environmental Policy and the Power of the State*, 76. For more on CCMS, see Jacob Darwin Hamblin, "Environmentalism for the NATO Alliance: NATO's Experiments with the 'Challenges of Modern Society,'" *Environmental History*, Vol. 15 (January 2010), 54–75; Stephen Macekura, "The Limits of Global Community: The Nixon Administration and Global Environmental Politics," *Cold War History*, Vol. 11, No. 4 (2011), 489–518.

[62] Nixon and his advisers were aware that the Soviet Union faced serious environmental problems, which made a bilateral agreement seem both practical and useful. On the Soviet environment, see Weiner, *Models of Nature*.

[63] On détente and environmental issues, see Glenn E. Schweitzer, "Environmental Protection and Soviet-American Relations," in Robert Jervis and Seweryn Bialer, eds., *Soviet-American Relations After the Cold War* (Durham: Duke University Press, 1991), 225–30.

upon his return to Washington, Nixon hosted a number of photo ops with Train, lauding the agreement as a wedge into the other issues of the détente process.[64]

The optimism surrounding the détente agreement carried over to the Nixon administration's preparations for the Stockholm gathering. Nixon viewed the conference as another means to cull together international support over global issues. Speaking before the UN General Assembly in 1969, Nixon proclaimed that through such efforts the international community might launch "new national and international initiatives toward restoring the balance of nature and maintaining our world as a healthy and hospitable place for man."[65] In an address to Congress on foreign policy, Nixon also described the conference as a key component of future international cooperation.[66] Likewise, Secretary of State Rogers acknowledged that the United States recognized "the need for greater involvement of the international community in pollution control and for greater coordination in international efforts to protect the environment."[67] The Stockholm meeting signified one method for giving institutional expression of the interrelatedness of environmental problems.[68]

---

[64] Russell E. Train to Martin J. Hillenbrand, November 16, 1971, box 24, Train Papers. For a thorough overview of Train's efforts in creating the Soviet treaty, see Flippen, "Richard Nixon, Russell Train, and the Birth of Modern Environmental Diplomacy"; Train, *Politics, Pollution, and Pandas*, 126–7. To oversee these activities, the accord established a Joint Committee of Environmental Protection, which convened annually to discuss research progress. Train met with Soviet representatives annually for much of the rest of the decade. "Remarks by Russell Train, US Delegation, First Meeting of the US-USSR Joint Committee for Cooperation in the Field of Environmental Protection, House of Unions, Moscow, September 18, 1972," box 23, Train Papers; memorandum of meeting between Train and Podgorny, November 19, 1976, box 18, Train Papers.

[65] Nixon before the 24th Session of the UN General Assembly at the UN, New York, September 18, "Strengthening the Total Fabric of Peace," Department of State *Bulletin*, October 6, 1969, 301.

[66] "US Foreign Policy for the 1970's: A New Strategy for Peace, by Richard Nixon, February 18, 1970," reprinted in Department of State *Bulletin*, March 9, 1970, 287–8.

[67] Secretary of State Rogers, "US Foreign Policy in a Technological Age," made before the Panel of Science and Technology of the House Committee on Science and Astronautics, January 26," Department of State *Bulletin*, February 15, 1971, 198–202.

[68] This sentiment was expressed frequently by both Christian Herter, Jr., assistant secretary of state for environmental affairs, and Bush leading up to the conference. See "US to Back Global Policy on Pollution," *New York Times*, March 12, 1970, 16; "Bush Asks World Unit Action on Problems of Environment," *Chicago Tribune*, March 17, 1971, A3. Institutionalizing international issues was part of the Nixon and Kissinger's attempts to build multipolarity to reduce tensions and deepen and stabilize international order. On their strategy, see Gaddis, *Strategies of Containment*, 274–81; Sargent, *A Superpower Transformed*, introduction.

Many officials saw the Stockholm Conference in a similar light to the CCMS and other international initiatives. In particular, for many the meeting represented an opportunity to revive youthful enthusiasm for the UN, too. Newly appointed UN Representative George H. W. Bush emphasized that building a dynamic environmental program might revitalize young peoples' interest and faith in the UN.[69] Similarly, Maurice Strong, a Canadian diplomat and secretary-general of the UN conference, embarked on a speaking tour to universities and youth forums. He admitted that the industrialized North caused most of the world's pollution problems and said that the forthcoming meeting might offer a chance to rectify such past failings.[70]

The preparations for Stockholm also reflected some of the ways in which the ideas held by non-state actors came to influence the administration's foreign policy. Conservationists with years of experience outside the state were now beginning to work in official governmental capacities. Because Nixon assigned a low priority to the actual content of environmental policies, Russell Train had significant leeway in deciding which issues would come to the fore at Stockholm. As a result of his efforts, the U.S. delegation's goals closely resembled those of the IUCN and the WWF.[71] Train worked closely with Lee Talbot of the IUCN, whom Train had brought to the CEQ to serve as its senior scientist. The two crafted a long list of objectives. The most significant was a UN-based financial pool to fund international research on environmental matters, based on voluntary contributions from UN members with a five-year target of raising $100 million.[72] They also sought to further efforts for a "World Heritage Trust" of endangered places around the world overseen by UNESCO, the establishment of an international referral center to exchange environmental information, a moratorium on whaling, and a nongovernmental mechanism to provide scientific advice to individuals and the UN system. Each of these became goals for the U.S. delegation in

---

[69] "Bush Suggests UN Program," *New York Times*, March 16, 1971, 33.

[70] "Industrial Nations Blamed for Pollution," *New York Times*, August 29, 1971, 11.

[71] Conflicts immediately arose between officials at the State Department, such as Herter, and those more closely tied to the White House, such as Russell Train. See Hopgood, *American Foreign Environmental Policy and the Power of the State*, 67–77, for a longer narration of the bureaucratic conflict that pervaded the lead-up to Stockholm.

[72] "UN Conference on Human Environment Scope Paper," box 15, Train Papers; McCormick, *The Global Environmental Movement*, 115; and *Stockholm and Beyond: Report of the Secretary of State's Advisory Committee on the 1972 United Nations Conference on the Human Environment*, Department of State (Washington, DC, 1972), 129.

preparatory meetings, and each had been put forth by Train earlier in the
1960s and had been supported previously by the IUCN.[73]

Train quickly set about to incorporate these ideas into policy. Train
convinced Nixon to place the World Heritage Trust in his 1971 environmental message to Congress. "Such an initiative," Nixon said, "can add a
new dimension to international cooperation. Confronted with the pressures of population and development, and with the world's tremendously
increased capacity for environmental modification, we must act together
now to save for future generations the most outstanding natural areas as
well as places of unique historical, archaeological, architectural, and
cultural value to mankind."[74] Talbot, serving as cochair for the U.S.
delegation during the preparatory meetings, put the Trust idea and
Train's other objectives on the conference agenda through preparatory
communications in 1970.[75] Likewise, IUCN Director-General Gerardo
Budowski consulted the U.S. delegation's advisory committee on the Trust
idea, relaying IUCN's past work on similar projects and how the NGO
envisioned the Trust working in action.[76] Thus, the U.S. platform and the
conference agenda reflected the positions and objectives of the IUCN and
its members.

There was one component of the American platform, though, that
came from above Train, and proved more significant than any others – a
firm refusal on the administration's part to accept any increase in foreign
aid funding for development issues. Nixon, at the behest of National
Security Adviser Henry Kissinger, stipulated that the delegation could
only make firm rhetorical commitments to the proposed fund. The delegation could agree to any general statements or agreements that sought to
"conserve or improve" the environment, but only insofar as such statements did not incur any further financial commitments. Moreover, Nixon

---

[73] "Memorandum from the President's Assistant for National Security Affairs (Kissinger) to
President Nixon, Washington, June 8, 1972," *FRUS, 1969–1972*, Vol. IV. [Online]
Available: http://history.state.gov/historicaldocuments/frus1969-76veo1/d323. Accessed
February 10, 2011.

[74] Richard Nixon, "Special Message to Congress Proposing the 1971 Environmental
Program," February 8, 1971, *Public Papers of the President*. [Online] Available: http://
www.presidency.ucsb.edu/ws/?pid=3294. Accessed June 14, 2011.

[75] Russell E. Train, "International Environmental Policy: Some Recollections and
Reflections," in Rockwood, Stewart, and Dietz, eds., *Foundations of Environmental
Sustainability*, 45.

[76] Gerardo Budowski, "Statement for the Advisory Committee on the 1972 United Nations
Conference on the Human Environment (The Baker Committee), U.S. Department of
State, Washington, DC, November 22, 1971," folder C.1001, Scott Papers.

instructed the delegation to reject any plans proposed by developing nations, especially any efforts to increase the previously agreed-upon 1% GNP donation to the UN Development Programme (UNDP).[77] The delegation would thus support concrete action emanating from the meeting, but only for limited purposes that were deemed acceptable to the United States' interests.

These stipulations comported with key components of Nixon and Kissinger's general strategy toward international development. In the wake of the Vietnam quagmire, the administration generally sought to avoid direct confrontation with the "Third World" as a bloc of nations with ostensibly common interests.[78] Nixon feared that development aid would further entangle the United States in the Global South. Writing to Secretary of State Rogers, Nixon said that he was "concerned about the tendency of our aid programs and, indeed, of the activities of our personnel overseas, in general, to draw us into a deep involvement in the domestic politics of developing countries."[79] In response, Nixon advocated private investment and multilateral banks to facilitate capital flows for development instead of direct federal funding.[80] In this context of redirecting development assistance through private channels, Nixon made clear that raising overall governmental expenditures on foreign aid would not be part of the Stockholm Conference.

This policy not only reflected Nixon's strategy toward the Global South, but also the reality of increasing congressional limitations on foreign aid. As the nation's economic downturn in the early 1970s continued and the war in Vietnam dragged on, public support waned for funding costly international initiatives.[81] Congress annually cut foreign aid programs, which led Nixon to further emphasize the role of private enterprise and multilateral lending institutions, such as the World Bank.

---

[77] "UN Conference on Human Environment Scope Paper," box 15, Train Papers.

[78] As Odd Arne Westad has argued, the United States' debacle in Vietnam had colored much of Nixon's thinking that developing nations were a source of disorder in the international system. Odd Arne Westad, *The Global Cold War: Third World Interventions and the Making of Our Times* (Cambridge: Cambridge University Press), 194–202.

[79] "Letter from President Nixon to Secretary of State Rogers, April 12, 1969," *FRUS, 1969–1972*, Vol. IV. [Online] Available: http://www.state.gov/r/pa/ho/frus/nixon/iv/15573.htm. Accessed April 19, 2009.

[80] Hal Brands, "Economic Development and the Contours of U.S. Foreign Policy: The Nixon Administration's Approach to Latin America, 1969–1974," *Peace and Change*, Vol. 33, No. 2 (April 2008), 243–73.

[81] Alfred E. Eckes, Jr. and Thomas W. Zeiler, *Globalization and the American Century* (Cambridge: Cambridge University Press, 2003), 181–95.

Congress also reduced the president's requests for UNDP funding every year in office. In 1971, Office of Management and Budget Director George Shultz recommended reductions in UNDP contributions as a component of Nixon's New Economic Policy, to which Nixon ultimately agreed.[82] In addition, Nixon annually decreased the size of the Agency for International Development (AID) as a symbol to Congress that he was willing to reduce federal expenditures overseas.[83] Although Nixon openly spoke of humanitarian reasons for foreign development aid, the actual implementation of his development policies reflected a narrow concern for American self-interest that sought to limit the role of federal aid to the Global South.[84]

Creating rules that denied support ipso facto for any counterproposal from the developing countries proved portentous for future debates at the conference. Although Train could celebrate the progress of both Nixon initiatives, global consensus over the necessity of environmental protection proved more elusive. CCMS and détente gatherings met with success because they were small in scope and because they spoke directly to problems shared by the advanced industrial economies of the United States, Western Europe, and the Soviet Union – countries at a comparable stage of economic development. The Stockholm Conference, by contrast, sought to include all nations, East and West, North and South. Developing nations, in contrast to the North, adopted a more cautious, defensive attitude toward the need for environmental protection and

---

[82] "Memorandum from President's Assistant for National Security Affairs (Kissinger) to President Nixon, September 20, 1971," *FRUS, 1969–1976*, Vol. V. [Online] Available: http://history.state.gov/historicaldocuments/frus1969-76v05/d261. Accessed April 19, 2009. On Nixon's "New Economic Policy" and the tumultuous period of economic policy making in the late summer and fall of 1971 more broadly, see Allen J. Matusow, *Nixon's Economy: Booms, Busts, Dollars, and Votes* (Lawrence: University Press of Kansas, 1998), chapter 6.

[83] William P. Rogers, "The U.S. Foreign Assistance Program and Current International Realities," Department of State *Bulletin*, August 20, 1973, 292. AID's overall employment dropped 44 percent between 1968 and 1973, cited in "The Budget of the United States Government – Fiscal Year 1974," Department of State *Bulletin*, February 19, 1973, 213–4. See Carol Lancaster, *Foreign Aid: Diplomacy, Development, and Domestic Politics* (Chicago: University of Chicago Press, 2007), 75–8.

[84] In a special message to Congress Nixon spoke about the need to emphasize humanitarian motives in foreign aid; Richard Nixon, "Special Message to the Congress on Foreign Aid," May 28, 1969, *Public Papers of the President*. [Online] Available: http://www .presidency.ucsb.edu/ws/index.php?pid=2073. Accessed April 22, 2009. On the decline of Nixon's commitments to the developing world, see Cullather, *The Hungry World*, 254–5 and Ekbladh, *The Great American Mission*, 220–3.

harbored a deep disdain for the methods that environmentalists in the North used to promote conservation. Attempts to gain short-term political benefits on the environmental issue ran up against long-standing tensions over foreign aid policies, economic inequality, and national sovereignty.

### THE LEAD-UP TO THE CONFERENCE: THE CHALLENGE FROM THE SOUTH

In the lead-up to Stockholm, a series of political disputes created an atmosphere of uncertainty and acrimony. A seating controversy over East Germany nearly derailed the conference, as the Soviet Union, the United States, and Great Britain quarreled over convoluted UN rules governing conference participation. Likewise, questions over whether the People's Republic of China would attend the conference as a full participant took attention away from the environmental issues under review.[85] A more substantive criticism of the conference's intentions and implications, however, emerged from developing nations in the Global South. These countries formed a loose coalition known as the Group of 77 (G-77) at the UN Conference on Trade and Development (UNCTAD). They sought to defend their common economic interests and enhance their leverage in multilateral negotiations. The G-77 wanted to alter the rules of the global economy to favor their interests, such as by more deeply legitimating their sovereign control over activities, such as extraction of natural resources.[86] They approached the gathering in Stockholm with similar intent.

Brazilian officials stood out among developing countries in taking a major role in criticizing environmental protection in the conference's buildup. In the summer of 1970, the Brazilian delegation circulated a working paper saying that Brazil would not support any restrictive environmental policies put forth by the developed nations. Environmental regulations, the paper claimed, must "be planned as a means to promote development

---

[85] For more on the seating controversy and the PRC question, see Macekura, "The Limits of Global Community," 503–5.

[86] Stephen Krasner, *Structural Conflict: The Third World Against Global Liberalism* (Berkeley: University of California Press, 1985). UNCTAD and the UN Law of the Seas (UNCLOS) discussions became two early sites for their politicking in the late 1960s, but by the 1970s the Group of 77 was involved in most UN activities. See also Rist, *The History of Development*, chapters 9 and 10.

and not as an obstacle and a barrier to the rising expectations of the underdeveloped world."[87] At a meeting of the UN's Economic and Social Council in June 1970, Brazilian delegates "dismissed the fashionable concern for the environment in the industrialised [sic] countries as a diversionary manoeuvre by the major aid donors," much to the chagrin of their counterparts from the United States and Europe.[88] Brazilian leaders worried that pollution standards imposed by the UN or through an international treaty would thwart Brazil's economic growth, impair its ambitions toward regional power, and imperil future flows of development assistance. To help allay such concerns, U Thant, the UN secretary-general, subsequently approved four regional meetings of experts to ensure developing nation participation in the preparatory work for Stockholm.[89] Nevertheless, the Brazilian delegation's arguments quickly sparked a larger debate focused on two main issues: additionality and compensation.

Although many leading developing nations chided the Brazil's aggressive tone, they nonetheless rallied behind its main arguments. In late 1970, the Chilean delegation put forth an amendment to a draft resolution that reiterated Brazil's criticism and called for "additional resources" for the Global South to cover the costs of environmental protection. Soon dubbed "additionality," the concept of increasing foreign aid transfers to help developing countries pay for environmental regulations became quite popular among the G-77. By the end of 1970, according to one participant, by stressing the notion that environmental protection would necessarily impair development plans by dramatically increasing costs the

---

[87] Quoted in Lars-Göran Engfeldt, *From Stockholm to Johannesburg and Beyond: The Evolution of the International System for Sustainable Development Governance and Its Implications* (Stockholm: Ministry of Foreign Affairs, Sweden, 2009), 45.

[88] "Memorandum: The Human Environment, the Developing Countries, and U.K. Aid," September 24, 1970, 7, NA-UK, FCO 55/390.

[89] Under the guidance of Maurice Strong, the first seminar was hosted by the Economic Commission for Asia and the Far East (ECAFE) in Bangkok, August 17–23, 1971; the second by the Economic Commission for Africa (ECA) in Addis Ababa, August 23–28, 1971; the third by the Economic Commission for Latin America (ECLA) in Mexico City, September 6–11, 1971; and the fourth by the UN Economic and Social Office in Beirut (UNESOB), September 27 to October 1, 1971. "Note on Preparation for the UN Conference on the Human Environment by the Secretary-General," November 13, 1970, UN General Assembly Document A/8065/Add.1, published in Yvonne I. Nichols, ed., *Source Book: Emergence of Proposals for Recompensing Developing Countries for Maintaining Environmental Quality, IUCN Environmental Policy and Law Paper No. 5* (Morges: IUCN, 1973), 34.

developing countries had "planted the seeds ... [of] the implied conflict between environment and development concerns."[90]

Over the following year, it became clear that inserting the "additionality" qualifications into preparatory discussions did not allay Brazil's concerns. Developing countries also demanded "compensation" in the form of financial contributions to restore trade positions of any developing country adversely affected by the adoption of environmental measures taken by industrialized trading partners.[91] A diplomat in the Brazilian embassy wrote to Christian Herter, Jr., in early 1971 that many high-level officials in the Brazilian government still talked about repudiating any environmental agreement on the grounds that any international standards represented an unfair imposition of Northern problems onto Latin America.[92] Similarly, a U.S. intelligence report noted that "Brazil's official policy, reflected in preliminary discussions, places developmental goals above pollution control ... [and] those who make policy ... are in close agreement and claim international standards will be used to keep the developing nations dependent."[93] After stating such criticisms publicly, Brazil sought to gain support among its neighbors and other developing nations to thwart the perceived incursions of the industrialized North into the industrializing South.

Policy makers in the United States were well aware of the growing challenge coming from Brazil and its allies. Prior to the conference, U.S. officials sought to co-opt the rising tide of dissent by directly addressing the issue. As he reasserted the need for vigorous pollution control laws, Ambassador Bush continued speaking about the Global South. "On the world scale, we must help the developing nations to get their necessary share of the world's rising economic activity, while taking care that the

---

[90] Engfeldt, *From Stockholm to Johannesburg and Beyond*, 46–7; "Notes: General Issues and Considerations Pertaining to the Concept of Additionality," "G.X 34/3 'Environment: UN (World) Conference on the Human Environment – Sweden 1971 – Correspondence' – Jacket 1," UNOG Registry Collection.

[91] "'The Concept of Compensation,' Environmental Regulations and Effects on Trade with the Developing Countries," 1972, G.X 34/3; "Environment: UN (World) Conference on the Human Environment – Sweden 1971 – Correspondence – Jacket 1," UNOG Registry Collection.

[92] "Letter From the Scientific Attache (Hudson) at the Embassy in Brazil to the Director of the Office of Environmental Affairs (Herter), February 12, 1971," *FRUS, 1969–1976*, Vol. E-1. [Online] Available: http://www.state.gov/r/pa/ho/frus/nixon/e1/46490.htm. Accessed February 10, 2009.

[93] "Intelligence Note RARN-7 Prepared by the Bureau of Intelligence and Research, Washington, March 2, 1972," *FRUS, 1969–1976*, Vol. E-1. [Online] Available: http://www.state.gov/r/pa/ho/frus/nixon/e1/46505.htm. Accessed February 10, 2009.

sum total of that activity does not irreversibly damage our common life-support system, this planet earth." He continued, "For this we will need new research, new global monitoring systems, and new international restraints on pollution."[94] The administration took seriously the developing countries' arguments, but Bush did not explain how to help realize their demands.

As Bush made efforts to calm the nerves of the leaders of developing nations, so too did the UN General Assembly. In December 1971, they passed a resolution calling that "no environmental policy should adversely affect the present or future development possibilities of the developing countries." In addition, it stated, rather vaguely, "the burden of the environmental policies of developed countries cannot be transferred ... to the developing countries," which seemed to leave open some room for compensatory financial relief for developing nations for lost revenue that might accrue from added environmental standards.[95] Unsurprisingly, the United States and Britain protested the resolution.[96]

Nongovernmental activists and other interested scholars took a proactive stance to resolve such conflicts, as well. Barbara Ward, now teaching at Columbia University, organized two conferences with David Runnalls, a political science graduate student, on the topic of environment and development. The first, which Ward convened at Columbia in 1970, produced an influential report and featured some of the leading development economists in the West, such as W. Arthur Lewis and Albert Hirschman; influential environmental experts, including Lester Brown of the Overseas Development Council and Max Nicholson of the IUCN; and leading scholars from the Global South such as the Pakistani economist Mahbub ul Haq, Indian economist and banker I. G. Patel, and Egyptian economist Samir Amin. It was the first of its kind to incorporate development economists from the South and environmentalists into substantive discussion.[97]

An even more influential gathering occurred the following year under the leadership of Maurice Strong, a Canadian oil executive and chairman

---

[94] George Bush, U.S. Rep. to UN, "Environment and Development: The Interlocking Problems," July 5, 1971, Department of State *Bulletin*, 21–2.

[95] Quoted in United Nations, Report of the Secretary-General to the Third Session of the Preparatory Committee, UN Doc A/CONF.48/PC.11 (New York: United Nations, 1971).

[96] McCormick, *The Global Environmental Movement*, 112.

[97] Satterthwaite, "Barbara Ward and the Origins of Sustainable Development," 10–12. The report was published as Barbara Ward, J. D. Runnalls, and Lenore D'Anjou, eds., *The Widening Gap: Development in the 1970s* (New York: Columbia University Press, 1971).

of the Stockholm Conference. Like many future international environmental figures, Strong's formative experiences lay in the developing world. A trip to East Africa in 1951 at the age of twenty-two sparked within him a life-long concern about international development and environmental protection. Although Strong spent much of his early professional career working in the oil industry, he was also active in various capacities at the UN and served as head of the Canadian International Development Agency in the late 1960s. Renowned as a thoughtful leader and stellar administrator, Strong was well respected in the development community, including among elites and intellectuals from the Global South. Strong's appointment as chairman of the Stockholm Conference received widespread acclaim at the time, as many observers believed he could use his experience with the UN, connections with development experts, and sterling reputation to reconcile the tensions between North and South, and between environmentalists and development specialists.[98]

As chairman, Strong worked assiduously to generate constructive discussions between the warring factions. In June 1971, he and Barbara Ward gathered an international group of experts – many of whom had attended Ward's 1970 conference at Columbia – in Founex, Switzerland, to examine the development/environment tensions in depth. The concluding document, entitled the Founex Report, asserted that the major problems facing developing countries were of a "different kind" than the ecological issues plaguing the industrialized North. Most of the environmental problems facing the developing world, the report claimed, were issues such as disease, poor sanitation, and substandard housing. In all of those instances, "Development becomes essentially a cure for their major environmental problems."[99] It underscored arguments in behalf of additionality and compensation, and demanded that developed nations reassure the South that "growing environmental concern will not hurt the continued development of the developing world."[100] The report encapsulated the belief that the right to economic self-determination and national sovereignty trumped all other imperatives. Notwithstanding concessions to the developing world regarding their ability to forego environmental protection in the name of economic development, the report won large

---

[98] Maurice Strong, *Where on Earth Are We Going?* (New York: Texere, 2000), 81–6; Holdgate, *The Green Web*, 111.

[99] "Development and Environment: Founex, Switzerland, June 4–12, 1971" (Mouton, France: École Pratique des Hautes Études, 1971), 6–7.

[100] Ibid., 34.

support from NGOs, such as David Brower's Friends of the Earth, for
embracing environmental issues, social justice, and poverty reduction all
at once.[101]

Major industrialized nations grappled with the Founex Report in
late 1971 and early 1972, but made only cosmetic gestures to allay the
developing nations' concerns. In August 1971, the U.S. Agency for
International Development (AID) announced an ecological advisory committee, but it left little in the way of concrete restrictions.[102] In September
1971, Nixon sent Republican Senator Howard Baker on an 18-day tour of
developing nations to "dispel notions that environmental legislation
would retard economic growth."[103] Daniel Patrick Moynihan tried to
defuse the "paranoid-style" of less-developed country (LDC) politics by
pressuring the conference secretariat to state that it was not "sponsoring
an anti-development conference."[104] In February 1972, U.S. officials met
with representatives from leading Western European nations and the
World Bank to discuss how they might respond publicly to the Founex
Report, but ended up agreeing only that any additional costs incurred by
developing nations for adopting environmental standards would be paid
through existing aid programs. There would be no "additionality" or
"compensation" in the form of new or increased development assistance
from donor nations.[105] The U.S. delegation to Stockholm called for a
"new development strategy" with "environmental considerations," but
offered little explanation of what either would entail.[106]

The Founex Report also did little to blunt the Group of 77's criticisms.
In fact, by late 1971, the report had emboldened developing nations. In a
statement to the UN, a Brazilian diplomat lauded the conference secretariat for making "environment and development" a key talking point at
Stockholm, but maintained that developing nations had an unalienable
right to use as much of their own resources as possible and in any way they

---

[101] On FOE's support of Founex's conclusions, see Homer Page, "Where Will the
Stockholm Conference Get Us?" *Not Man Apart*, Vol. 2, No. 5 (May 1972), 8–9.
[102] "Environment and Development Committee Established by AID," Department of State
*Bulletin*, August 9, 1971, 158.
[103] "Senator Baker Studies Environment Attitudes of Developing Countries," Department
of State *Bulletin*, September 6, 1971, 260.
[104] "Daniel Patrick Moynihan statement, US Representative to Stockholm Committee II,
November 29, 1971," box 324, Moynihan Papers.
[105] "DAC Meeting on the Environment, 23 February 1972," NA-UK, FCO 55/836.
[106] Department of State, "Documents for the UN Conference on the Human Environment"
(Springfield, VA: National Technical Information Service, 1972), 297–8.

deemed fit during the early stages of development.[107] Brazil reaffirmed this idea at a conference in Lima, arguing that developed countries were responsible for pollution and seeking to retard the South's development; that environmental problems in the developing world stemmed from underdevelopment; and that along with "additionality," the North should provide "compensation" to developing nations to finance environmental programs in the South.[108] These principles amounted to an unambiguous attack on top-down international environmental protection and made "additionality" and "compensation" the sine qua non of any major agreement at Stockholm.

In the weeks just prior to the opening of the Stockholm Conference, criticism reached a fever pitch. The Organization for African Unity (OAU), an amalgam of African states, listed a series of grievances against Stockholm along the lines of the Brazilian critique. OAU nations claimed global environmental standards would impinge on their sovereignty.[109] Similarly, another group of developing nations tried to extract concessions regarding Stockholm's potential for establishing pollution standards during a five-week gathering in Chile sponsored by the United Nations Conference on Trade and Development, but failed to do so.[110] An informal meeting between Maurice Strong, Christian Herter, and representatives from major nations such as Brazil and the United Kingdom met on May 3rd and 4th to discuss further the draft resolutions for the conference and the plans for the environmental fund. No new ideas or resolutions emerged from the discussion.[111]

As the Stockholm Conference neared, the increasingly virulent criticisms from developing nations left environmentalists in an uncomfortable place. Nationalistic divisions threatened to undermine international cooperation at a time when such partnership seemed most necessary. While some environmentalists hoped for the best, others assumed a more

---

[107] "Statement by the Brazilian Representative, Mr. Bernardo de Azevedo Brito, Item 11 of the Agenda, United Nations Conference on the Human Environment," Economic and Social Council Fifty-First Session, Co-ordination Committee, July 1971, G.X 34/3; "Environment: UN (World) Conference on the Human Environment – Sweden 1971 – Correspondence – Jacket 1," UNOG Registry Collection.

[108] U.S. Department of State telegram Lima 6774, November 15, 1971, box 324, Moynihan Papers; "Environmental Issues in the General Assembly, 1971," ibid.

[109] Claire Sterling, "Rich and Poor Nations Collide: World Politics and Pollution Control," *The Washington Post*, May 26, 1972, A24.

[110] Ibid.

[111] "UN Conference on the Human Environment: Informal Meeting in Geneva, 3/4 May," meeting notes, NA-UK, FCO 55/840.

pessimistic view. Although the meeting originally represented "global motherhood," Barry Commoner wrote in early 1972 that the North-South and East-West conflicts had cast a pall over the event that rendered the entire "global" project seemingly meaningless. Commoner called international environmental protection "the world's most dangerous political issue," since environmental issues brought into focus "the long-standing, unresolved conflicts that trouble the world."[112] The nonpolitical issue could not escape politics, after all.

## PREMATURE HOPES AND FUNDAMENTAL DIFFERENCES: THE STOCKHOLM CONFERENCE

The Stockholm Conference opened on June 6, 1972, to much fanfare. In the first few days of the meeting, though, there was heavy focus on events outside the conference walls on what one writer dubbed an "environmental smorgasbord."[113] Popular NGOs, such as FOE, the IUCN, and the WWF, had booths at the well-attended Environmental Forum, which hosted lively debates and educational seminars.[114] Less well-known NGOs without formal UN recognition organized around a variety of topics, adumbrating the big-tent protests that would follow most international conferences later in the century.[115] Swarms of protestors condemned "ecocide," the United States' use of chemical warfare in Vietnam; the People's Forum, backed by a variety of Swedish leftist groups, hosted rallies; and the Hog Farm, a pseudo-commune founded by American hippies that very much resembled the muddiest days of the Woodstock festival, presented Maurice Strong with a fully grown pig at the end of the festivities. Although these groups often presented

---

[112] Commoner, "Motherhood in Stockholm," 49–54.

[113] Norman J. Faramelli, "Toying with the Environment and the Poor: A Report on the Stockholm Environmental Conferences," *Environmental Affairs*, Vol. 2, No. 3 (Winter 1972), 469–70.

[114] "Letter from Lennart Daleus to FOE," box 85, Brower Papers.

[115] The formal way NGOs can influence the UN is through "accreditation," which affords NGOs consultative status with ECOSOC (a standing committee within ECOSOC determines which NGOs get this access). See Kennedy, *The Parliament of Man*, 216–20. At Stockholm only a few groups had ECOSOC accreditation, but fifty-two NGOs attended as consultants at least one of the four preparatory meetings. And the IUCN and the WWF, in contrast to the many protestors with no formal UN status outside the conference, staffed national delegation with environmental experts and attended as participants some of the Preparatory Committee's intergovernmental working groups. Morphet, "NGOs and the Environment," 125–6.

trenchant critiques of modern society, their tactics did not win them much legitimacy from the larger, well-represented NGOs. Raymond Dasmann, who had organized an IUCN panel at the Environmental Forum, recalled finding himself "in the awkward position of agreeing with much of what the rebels wanted to accomplish while disagreeing with their methods for achieving their goals."[116]

The diversity of these groups illustrated divisions among environmental activists. David Brower, one of the featured speakers at the Environmental Forum who also participated in many proceedings inside the UN gathering, listened assiduously to Train speaking about the proposed World Heritage Trust. Although Brower supported the Trust idea, the close ties between WWF officials and international elites rankled him. As Train spoke, Brower derisively scribbled down that the WWF's "VIP treatment" was "elitist" and tendentiously referred to the organization, which had long hailed itself as savior for the world's wildlife, as the "golden ark."[117] While all conservationists could rally behind Train's Trust idea, differences emerged over how far NGOs would push the more contentious issues about the root causes of environmental degradation.[118] The parallel conferences at Stockholm suggested that the "new" environmentalism that linked grassroots mobilization with questions of social justice, economic rights, and international power relations was now challenging the "old" technical and scientific conservation and preservation (Figure 4).

A variety of serious environmental problems loomed beneath these tactical and intellectual debates. In Stockholm, environmentalists pointed to many trends that threatened the entire globe. Urbanization created staggering amounts of solid waste; population growth stoked fears of

---

[116] Raymond Dasmann, *Called by the Wild: The Autobiography of a Conservationist* (Berkeley: University of California Press, 2002), 145. NGOs interacted with the main conference, as well. Working in tandem with *Ecologist* magazine, FOE staff produced an eight-page daily newspaper for conference delegates to educate them on such controversial issues and keep them abreast of debates happening outside the main conference building. David Brower and Barbara Ward wrote books for the conferences with the same title, *Only One Earth*. Ward's book, which she coauthored with noted scientist René Dubos, was the first of many such introductions she would write for UN conferences. "David Brower to Ansel Adams, November 24, 1972," Brower Papers; Satterthwaite, "Barbara Ward and the Origins of Sustainable Development," 10–11; *The Stockholm Conference: Only One Earth. An Introduction to the Politics of Survival* (London: Earth Island Limited, 1972); Barbara Ward and René Dubos, *Only One Earth: The Care and Maintenance of a Small Planet* (New York: W.W. Norton, 1972).

[117] David Brower, notes on "World Heritage Trust Scheme," box 85, Brower Papers.

[118] Paul R. Ehrlich, "A Crying Need for Quiet Conferences: Personal Notes from Stockholm," *Bulletin of the Atomic Scientists*, Vol. XXVIII, No. 7 (September 1972), 30–2.

FIGURE 4: Christian Herter and Russell Train meet with NGO representatives at the Stockholm Conference. Courtesy of Russell Train Papers, Manuscript Division, Library of Congress.

land and food scarcity; large-scale industrial agriculture required the use of dangerous pesticides on a vast scale. Discussions over increased regulations for a range of issues – such as international whaling, ocean dumping, and the use of nuclear and chemical weapons – pervaded the preparatory meetings leading up to Stockholm. The release of the apocalyptic *Limits to Growth* report in 1972 evoked tremendous anxiety about resource exhaustion worldwide, particularly for key energy sources such as coal and petroleum. The need for cheap, bountiful energy had drawn many policy makers to nuclear power, which in turn sparked many environmentalists' fears about its potential risks to ecosystem viability and human health. The fact that leaders from the G-77 demanded economic growth sparked concerns that these issues, all too apparent in Europe and the United States, would soon subsume the Global South, too.[119]

---

[119] These concerns all appeared in Ward and René Dubos, *Only One Earth: The Care and Maintenance of a Small Planet.*

Although many environmentalists protesting throughout the streets of Stockholm clamored for action on these issues, within the halls of the official conference national delegations replayed the debates that plagued the lead-up to the conference. Chinese delegates spoke frequently about the growing inequalities between the developing nations and the industrialized West.[120] Delegates from developing nations dismissed World Bank President Robert S. McNamara's claim that current development models would eventually redress global inequalities.[121] Numerous speakers from developing nations accused the industrialized North of exploiting the national resources of the South.[122] Brazil, India, and others argued before a special committee on environment and development for the two core principles of additionality and compensation.[123] Their efforts resulted in the two concepts appearing as nonbinding "principles" in the final conference report, but as "principles" they had no enforcement mechanism.[124] Nor were they welcomed by the United States. New York Senator and U.S. delegation member James L. Buckley explained that the United States "does not provide compensation" for cyclical fluctuations in business activity, changes in consumer tastes, and technological developments. He saw "no reason to single out for special treatment declines which may result from measures taken for the protection of the environment."[125]

Representatives from multiple countries assailed the U.S. delegation. Tanzanian officials, led by Julius Nyerere, elicited a flurry of diplomatic activity among the Western allies when its delegation called for declarations against colonialism and apartheid. Furious at the political gesture, British and American delegates tried to eliminate the Tanzanian

---

[120] Claire Sterling, "Chinese Attack on US Endangers Declaration on Environment," *The Washington Post*, June 11, 1972.

[121] "Prophets of Doom Come on Strong but Ecology Talks Sideline Them," *Los Angeles Times*, June 15, 1972, A16.

[122] "United Nations Conference on the Human Environment: Report to the Senate," (Washington, DC: GPO, 1972), 57–8. See also the "Development and the Environment" section of the "Proceedings of the Conference," *Report of the United Nations Conference of the Human Environment*. [Online] Available: http://www.unep.org/Documents.Multi lingual/Default.asp?DocumentID=97&ArticleID=1497&l=en. Accessed April 22, 2009.

[123] "Rich Nations Urged to Bear Cost for Clean Environment," *Chicago Tribune*, June 8, 1972, A2; Patricia Rambach, "Report from Stockholm," *Sierra Club Bulletin*, Vol. 57, No. 7 (July 1972), 22.

[124] "Rich Nations Urged to Bear Cost for Clean Environment," *Chicago Tribune*, June 8, 1972, A2.

[125] Quoted in Sally Jacobson, "II. A Call to Environmental Order," *Bulletin of the Atomic Scientists*, Vol. XXVIII, No. 7 (September 1972), 24.

provisions, but abstained from voting in the committee responsible for finalizing the declaration.[126] Equally frustrating for the United States, many countries decried American use of chemical and biological warfare in Vietnam, a topic that dominated the parallel NGO conferences. The U.S. delegates successfully kept the war in Southeast Asia away from major negotiations, but talk about the conflict filled hallways and pervaded media reports.[127] When Swedish Prime Minister Olaf Palme raised the Vietnam issue, a visibly rankled Russell Train rebuffed him: "The United States has worked long and hard to make this conference a success. The raising of a highly charged issue by the prime minister can only do a disservice to this objective."[128]

NGOs, too, soon challenged the U.S. delegation's platform. In a statement to the plenary session on June 12, a collection of NGO members and activists, led by Barbara Ward and American anthropologist Margaret Mead, strongly criticized existing notions of development. In the development process, there needed to be "a greater emphasis on non-material satisfactions ... and, above all, altruism in the pursuit of the common good." Ward and Mead argued that technical fixes – more production – would not solve developmental problems, because a balance between environment and development "can be achieved only if we face honestly the problem of social justice and redistribution." More concretely, they called for a tiny percent of GNP to be allocated in grants and low interest for long-term loans for concessionary assistance and for additional flows of capital assistance from the developed nations to offset costs in the developing world.[129] Ward and other NGO representatives had taken the Founex Report to heart, and their declaration was more similar to that document than Train's platform for the U.S. delegation.

The conference ended in dramatic fashion. Indian Prime Minister Indira Gandhi gave a concluding speech that garnered several standing ovations. She proclaimed that poverty, not pollution, was the foremost

---

[126] "Confidential Telegram, Stockholm to UKMIS New York, June 12, 1972: Following for Environment Delegation," NA-UK, FCO 55/842.

[127] Faramelli, "Toying with the Environment and the Poor," 471–2. See also "United Nations Conference on the Human Environment: Report to the Senate."

[128] "US Losing Argument to Poor Nations," *The Washington Post*, 8 June 1972, A29.

[129] "NGO Plenary Declaration," Reprinted in Special Issue: The Stockholm Conference, *Not Man Apart*, Vol. 2, No. 7 (July 1972), 8–10. The Pearson Report refers to the findings of a 1967 World Bank commission, staffed by scholars from around the world, to assess past World Bank lending policies and make prescriptions for future programs. Lester B. Pearson, *Partners in Development: Report of the Commission on International Development* (New York: Praeger Publishers, 1969).

FIGURE 5: Are not poverty and need the greatest polluters? Indian Prime Minister Indira Gandhi speaks to the Stockholm Conference, June 14, 1972. Courtesy of UN Photo Library.

global problem of the era. "Pollution is not a technical problem," she proclaimed. "The fault lies not in science and technology as such but in the sense of values of the contemporary world which ignores the rights of others and is oblivious of longer perspective." Simple mechanisms, such as standards created for air and water pollution, would not solve deeper problems. Priorities and values needed to change. The industrialized North, she concluded, had no right to impose international standards that could impair the growth and development of the Global South (Figure 5).[130]

The Stockholm Conference produced a formal declaration, written by representatives from official delegations. The "Declaration on the Human Environment," listed twenty-six principles. Many reflected the concerns of the developing countries. Principle 1 incorporated Tanzania's request and included a condemnation of "apartheid, racial segregation, discrimination, colonial and other forms of oppression and foreign domination." Principles 11 and 12 embodied the "additionality" and "compensation" concerns. They reaffirmed the right of nations to seek development as they

[130] Indira Gandhi's speech reprinted in *India News*, clipping from box 15, Train Papers.

so desired without being hampered by environmental policies and called for additional resources to cover the costs of new environmental safeguards.[131] These principles were important symbolic additions, but they had no teeth. Rhetorical and symbolic gains for the Global South, important though they were, left few practical achievements and opened up space for future discord.[132]

The conference also produced an "Action Plan" with a list of specific recommendations. The plan included an environmental fund to establish a new specialized agency within the UN. Some participants feared that a new environmental agency would overstep the bounds of existing organizations. In fact, in July 1971, outgoing UN Secretary-General U Thant had issued a report claiming that "no unnecessary new machinery should be created."[133] Existing UN agencies wanted to fold environmental concerns into their own activities. The United States and the United Kingdom, by contrast, wanted the fund to serve as a centralized, coordinating body with the ability to fund its own projects.[134] The conference secretariat ultimately sided with the U.S. and UK delegations. Endorsed by Maurice Strong, the Action Plan called for the environmental fund to set up a global information-sharing network, Earthwatch, and a new specialized agency that later became the United Nations Environment Program (UNEP).[135] Strong, Barbara Ward, and many other environmentalists celebrated the creation of the UNEP as a major victory.[136]

The plan also promised to fund family-planning activities, expand data collection facilities, and convene for future conferences. Other issues, such

---

[131] "Declaration on the Human Environment," in *In Defence of the Earth: The Basic Texts on Environment: Founex, Stockholm, and Cocoyoc*, UNEP Executive Series, No. 1 (Nairobi: UNEP, 1981), 45.

[132] IUCN officials culled together a briefing book on the history of the environment-development debate, to serve as a basis for future discussions that might "mitigate the apprehensions of developing countries that measures to control environmental degradation and to enhance environmental quality will be detrimental to their development and trade." Yvonne I. Nichols, ed., *Source Book: Emergence of Proposals for Recompensing Developing Countries for Maintaining Environmental Quality, IUCN Environmental Policy and Law Paper No. 5* (Morges: IUCN, 1973).

[133] Quoted in United Nations, Report of the Secretary-General to the Third Session of the Preparatory Committee, UN Doc A/CONF.48/PC.11 (New York: United Nations, 1971).

[134] "Proposed United Nations Environment, The Case for a UK Contribution," NA-UK, T341/419; "Draft Brief for ECOSOC 53 Resumed and For Item 47 of Provisional Agenda for 27th General Assembly," 1972, NA-UK, T341/419.

[135] "A Summary of UNEP Activities, Report No. 8" (New York: UNIPUB, 1980), 4–5.

[136] McCormick, *The Global Environmental Movement*, 125.

as the World Heritage Trust, the trade of endangered species, a moratorium on whaling, and standards on marine waste dumping received widespread support, but required separate agreements to be formally established.[137] Russell Train had suggested the Trust idea back in 1965 and the IUCN had been promoting all of these issues over the previous decade. Through allies on national delegations, these ideas had been realized as policies at Stockholm. The Action Plan won almost universal support; China was the only nation not to sign it.[138]

The U.S. delegation accomplished Nixon and Kissinger's main goals, but delegates left the conference frustrated about the controversies it had stoked and the future conflicts it augured. Train dutifully reported to Nixon that the U.S. delegation had achieved all of the administration's major objectives – the creation of the UN environmental fund, the World Heritage Trust, the global environmental monitoring program, and a moratorium on whaling. Yet he also lamented the likelihood of future conflicts. Environmental issues could not be discussed without impinging on the development aspirations of the LDCs, said Train.[139] He was right. The Action Plan left unanswered many conceptual questions, and it did little to reconcile the desire for economic growth with the need for environmental protection.

The U.S. delegation, moreover, was unable to thwart criticism from the Global South. Nixon and Kissinger had instructed the U.S. delegation to vote against any measures that would increase financial aid to the developing nations.[140] This stipulation left the U.S. delegation hamstrung for much of the conference. Developing nations frequently offered resolutions during debates, but U.S. representatives often rebuked their proposals without offering any explanation. In a final report to Congress, delegation members Senators Claiborne Pell and Clifford Case stated that the

---

[137] UNESCO created the World Heritage Trust in November 1972. In the same month, an international agreement was reached on marine dumping. On that process, see Jacob Darwin Hamblin, "Gods and Devils in the Details: Marine Pollution, Radioactive Waste, and an Environmental Regime circa 1972," *Diplomatic History*, Vol. 32, No. 4 (September 2008), 539–60. The Convention on International Trade in Endangered Species of Wild Fauna and Flora (CITES), which began as an IUCN project in 1963, was signed in March 1973.

[138] "Memorandum to the President, UN Conference on Human Environment, June 19, 1972," box 17, Train Papers.

[139] Memo, Russell Train to Richard Nixon, June 19, 1972, *FRUS, 1969–1976*, Vol. E-1. [Online] Available: http://history.state.gov/historicaldocuments/frus1969-76veo1/d324. Accessed June 14, 2011.

[140] "UN Conference on Human Environment Scope Paper," box 15, Train Papers.

restrictions imposed by Nixon and Kissinger had made it "impossible" for the U.S. delegation to express its views on development. They claimed it was imperative for the United States to "work within a multilateral framework to help developing nations choose a growth pattern that will yield a combination of low environmental risk and high economic gain for the general economy of the nation."[141] The report failed to suggest what form that "multilateral framework" would take, or what a "growth pattern" capable of balancing economic and environmental concerns would look like. There was no easy answer to these questions, especially without engaging the "compensation" and "additionality" claims.

The debates over development greatly hampered both the spirit and the negotiations at Stockholm. "Hopes for global cooperation [were] premature," wrote a solemn David Brower in FOE's newsletter. "Fundamental differences between rich and poor, industrial and non-industrial countries, have been made too obvious for anyone to discuss ecological disruption or resource depletion, and make these differences a central feature of their analysis."[142] In the summer of 1972, the tensions that plagued the preparations for the conference remained unresolved.

### THE MEANING OF STOCKHOLM: THE LIMITS OF COMMON INTERESTS

Over a two-year period following Stockholm, Christian Herter, Jr., directed the U.S. efforts to shape the emerging UNEP. Congress reduced his initial $100 million request to $40 million to get the agency going, albeit with only $10 million committed for the first year. Although Train and Herter envisioned the United States as the leading donor country, by 1974 countries such as Japan and West Germany quickly outpaced U.S. contributions.[143] The United States and other developed nations wanted to situate the new environmental program's offices in Vienna, but the UNEP ultimately went to Nairobi, Kenya. Sierra Club officials had contacted the Kenyan delegation in Stockholm to pressure for the UNEP to be

---

[141] "United Nations Conference on the Human Environment: Report to the Senate," 8–10.

[142] David Brower, "After Stockholm, What Now?" *Not Man Apart*, Vol. 2, No. 7 (July 1972), 5.

[143] "The United Nations Environment Program Participation Act of 1973," Report No. 93–196. *Congressional Record* (Washington, DC: GPO, 1973). See also "Foreign Assistance and Related Agencies Appropriations for 1974," *Hearings before a Subcommittee of the Committee of Appropriations, House of Representatives, 93rd Congress, First Session* (Washington, DC: GPO, 1973), 1310–12.

independent of other UN agencies.[144] Kenya and other developed countries were more than happy to embrace the symbolic power of placing the new agency in the developing world. Herter ultimately acceded to LDC demands, and the UNEP became the first major specialized UN agency to reside in the Southern Hemisphere.[145] From its base in Nairobi, the UNEP quickly launched a number of important ecological surveys on topics such as disease epidemics, desertification, and population growth and became a meeting ground for a global network of environmental scientists and activists.[146] Small though it was, the UNEP nonetheless gave further institutional expression to the idea of crafting a global solution for global environmental problems.

The UNEP also came to symbolize the ongoing North-South tensions over the question of environmental protection. The Western powers, particularly the United States and Great Britain, viewed the UNEP as a relatively small research institute that could carry out significant surveys and monitor environmental changes in various regions across the globe. The developing nations, however, wanted to ensure that the UNEP spoke to their interests. It was clear to Western policy makers from the first meeting of the Governing Council that "the work of the UNEP was going to be as seriously influenced as other UN activities by the division between developing and developed worlds." As early as the fall of 1973, the UK's representatives worried that "matters of global and regional concern also contained many projects whose implementation would benefit only the interests of the developing world."[147] Even more troubling was the politicization of the organization. Having a built-in majority on the UNEP's Governing Council emboldened representatives from the Global South. Questions of "additionality" and "compensation" were not settled at Stockholm, but developing nations quickly sought to use the UNEP as a way to redress their ongoing concerns over those issues.

---

[144] Interview with Edgar Wayburn, "Global Activist and Elder Statesman of the Sierra Club: Alaska, International Conservation, National Parks and Protected Areas, 1980–1992," Sierra Club Oral History Series, Regional Oral History Office University of California, The Bancroft Library, Berkeley, California. [Online] Available: http://archive.org/stream/globalactivistoowaybrich/globalactivistoowaybrich_djvu.txt. Accessed January 12, 2012.

[145] "Developing Nations Stage Power Play at UN," *Los Angeles Times*, November 11, 1972, 5.

[146] "Etude Annuelle 1977–1978 par le Directeur Executif," *Programme des Nations Unies pour L'Environnement* (Nairobi: Printing and Packaging Corporation, Ltd., 1981).

[147] "Confidential Draft, United Nations Environment Programme – Future UK Policy," 1973. FCO 55/1007, NA-UK.

The other environmental programs created in the late 1960s and early 1970s continued to operate throughout the decade. The Committee on the Challenge of Modern Society pursued international research projects within NATO on a multilateral basis, much in the same way as the original surveys had done. In addition, it became an important forum for NATO members to explore energy issues, especially after the oil crisis.[148] The U.S.-U.S.S.R. Joint Committee on Environmental Protection, an important source of environmental research for both nations, also became an annual event through the end of the Cold War.[149]

Overall, though, the United States' commitment to international environmental programs waned. After his reelection in 1972, Nixon felt that his environmental efforts were not providing substantial political support for his administration nor taking much spotlight away from Vietnam. Therefore, he cut back on his earlier commitments.[150] "We are well on our way to winning the war with environmental degradation, well on our way to making peace with nature," Nixon told Congress in early 1973 amidst a deepening economic recession. Since this war was apparently being won, and since he wanted to cut federal spending (a campaign promise of 1972), Nixon quickly eviscerated the environmental bureaucracy he had created four years earlier.[151] The president moved further away from environmental issues following the OPEC embargo and energy crisis, the Watergate scandal, and Egypt and Syria's joint invasion of Israel.[152] Whereas in his first term Nixon initiated the CCMS, bilateral treaties with the U.S.S.R., and a leadership role at Stockholm, six months into his second term he put aside international environmental issues.

U.S. leadership also faded because of an absence of shared values with developing nations.[153] The initial success of programs such as the CCMS

[148] "Prepared remarks of the Honorable Russell E. Train Administrator, US EPA, For CCMS Round Table, Fall Plenary, October 22, 1974," box 43, Train Papers.
[149] Glenn E. Schweitzer, "Environmental Protection and Soviet-American Relations," in Jervis and Bialer, eds., *Soviet-American Relations After the Cold War*, 225–38.
[150] On Nixon's postelection decisions, see Hays, *Beauty, Health, and Permanence*, 57–8; Flippen, *Nixon and the Environment*, 188–9.
[151] Flippen, *Nixon and the Environment*, 188–91.
[152] Andrews, *Managing the Environment, Managing Ourselves*, chapter 15; Flippen, *Nixon and the Environment*, chapter 6; "Agriculture, Environmental, and Consumer Protection Appropriations for 1974," *Hearings before a Subcommittee of the Committee of Appropriations, House of Representatives, 93rd Congress, First Session* (Washington, DC: GPO, 1973), 8; Flippen, *Nixon and the Environment*, 204–5; Rothman, *Greening of a Nation?*, chapter 5.
[153] List and Rittberger, "Regime Theory and International Environmental Management," 91–7.

derived from the common interests among NATO nations who saw environmental policies as a way to revive fledgling institutions. These interests, however, were not shared by the developing nations. Leaders in the Global South viewed environmental protection through the lens of their aspirations for economic development and global power relations. Officials from Brazil and India, for example, wanted to address endemic poverty before the pollution problem. Nixon and Kissinger did not want to provide financial compensation or increase development expenditures.[154] The steadfast desire for national economic sovereignty and rapid development among governments in the Global South trumped the quixotic hopes of many in the Nixon administration that common interests might engender consensus.

## CONCLUSION: POST-CONFERENCE MOMENTUM FOR NGOS

Amid the feelings of disappointment that stemmed from Stockholm, officials in NGOs believed the conference created a foundation for future activism. Barbara Ward took over a small NGO called the International Institute for Environmental Affairs (IIEA). The IIEA had been founded by a wealthy Canadian, Robert Anderson, who, as chief executive of the Atlantic Richfield oil company, had an environmental awakening and wanted to study the effect his industry had on the global environment. Having worked closely with fellow Canadian Maurice Strong leading up the conference, Anderson took Strong's advice to ask Ward to lead the agency, as it sought to become more active internationally. She agreed, on the condition that the group could expand its mission and focus on international poverty. Under Ward's leadership, the group was renamed the International Institute for Environment and Development (IIED) and soon became a leading research institute for many of the issues she first publicized at Columbia and in Founex.[155]

Other groups broadened their objectives and expanded operations, too. David Brower's FOE received formal accreditation in 1973, and the American chapter soon stationed lobbyists at UN headquarters in New York.[156] He also persuaded the U.S. chapter to purchase a small building

---

[154] Rist, *The History of Development*, chapter 9.
[155] Satterthwaite, "Barbara Ward and the Origins of Sustainable Development," 14.
[156] Note from Steve O. (Ogilvy?) to DRB, "Proposing an FOE International Division," November 20, 1973, box 83, Brower Papers.

space near UNEP offices in Nairobi.[157] The IUCN redoubled its efforts to place ecology in the development process. Although it was lamentable that developing nations had "reacted violently" against "any inference that there should be a limit to growth, or any interference with their sovereignty," IUCN officials nonetheless looked forward to finding ways to "harness the energy and enthusiasm of NGOs to help in forwarding international environmental action."[158] Stockholm, despite its many disappointments, gave new momentum to many NGOs.

Environmentalists directed much of their post-Stockholm enthusiasm toward the UNEP. Having held parallel meetings in New York during an UN Economic and Social Council gathering and in Geneva during the first UNEP conference, various NGOs, including the WWF and FOEI, contributed funds to the construction of the Environment Liaison Centre (ELC) in Nairobi to work with the UNEP. Supported and staffed in its early years by environmentalists, the ELC soon had almost 200-member organizations and a distribution network of 4,000 NGOs for its quarterly bulletin. From its home base in Nairobi, the organization also communicated with over 2,000 environmental NGOs emerging in developing countries, seeking to induce policy changes at both an international and national level.[159]

In this process, the IUCN and the WWF culled close personal connections to important policy makers, and gradually worked their members into positions of power. Over the ensuing decade, many more NGOs cultivated such ties with governments. At the same time, the ELC and its constituent groups became leading forces actively working to mediate the growing North-South rift on environmental issues by enmeshing together local, national, and transnational groups.[160] Environmental degradation was a global problem; a decade after Stockholm, NGOs had established a network of institutions capable of addressing the problem in a truly global way.

Whereas in the 1950s and 1960s the environmental NGOs concerned with global development had struggled to convince leaders of developing countries to adopt environmental protection, in the years following

[157] "FOE named to US Commission to UNESCO," *Not Man Apart*, Vol. 2, No. 8 (August 1972), 2; Barbara Wesselman, "UN and FOE Open Nairobi Offices," *Not Man Apart*, Vol. 3, No. 12 (December 1973), 4.
[158] "IUCN Viewpoint, "IUCN Viewpoint: UN Conference on the Human Environment," *IUCN Bulletin*, Vol. 3, No. 7 (July 1972), 27–9.
[159] Morphet, "NGOs and the Environment," 126–7.
[160] Ibid., 127–8.

Stockholm many NGOs focused their activism on the sources of foreign aid and development assistance. In hoping to reshape development thought and policy in major corridors of power, activists seized on opportunities to play an increasingly active role in shaping U.S. foreign assistance policy, the World Bank's lending activities, and the UN's development programs. In this process, many questions emerged: How could and should environmental considerations be reconciled with developmental aspirations? How could major development agencies be made accountable for effects on the environment? And what could non-state actors do to pressure reticent states to take environmental protection more seriously? NGO efforts to answer these questions would spark many controversies, out of which would emerge a new understanding of both environmentalism and development policy.

# PART TWO

# REFORMS

# 4

## When Small Seemed Beautiful: NGOs, Appropriate Technology, and International Development in the 1970s

In 1973, a year after the Stockholm Conference, an influential and widely read book appeared in bookstores, the hands of youthful protestors, and the libraries of many environmentalists and development reformers. *Small Is Beautiful*, written by the economist Ernst Friedrich Schumacher, was a collection of essays that advocated for the decentralization of political power, participatory development planning, and economic localism. Schumacher had been born and raised in Germany, but worked professionally in the United Kingdom and as a consultant to multiple postcolonial nations in the 1940s, 1950s, and 1960s. His time in developing countries convinced him that mainstream development strategies – those that had prized rapid industrialization, vast engineering projects, and top-down decision making – were responsible for generating ecological devastation and social dislocation. He believed large-scale national development planning had sparked the many global problems Stockholm Conference attendees had identified. Over the 1960s and early 1970s, Schumacher argued in many forums that emphasizing local production for local needs should be the primary purpose of development and that redressing the overlapping environmental and social crises required a transition away from ambitious development schemes toward local empowerment. *Small Is Beautiful* presented Schumacher's peculiar strand of heterodox economic thinking for a wide audience. Published in the same year as the first global oil crisis, in the wake of the alarmist *Limits to Growth*, and amid a growing environmental movement that had proclaimed a global ecological crisis was underway, the book resonated with many readers.[1]

---

[1] E. F. Schumacher, *Small Is Beautiful: Economics as if People Mattered*, revised 1989 ed. (New York: Harper & Row Publishers, 1989).

Although reformers of all stripes found the book compelling, Schumacher's work especially captivated the environmental community. It harmonized with a major theme in environmentalists' critique of international development, one that centered on the use of technology in developing countries. As they endeavored to reconcile development with environmental concerns, many environmental activists focused on the role of technology in the development process. In postwar development planning and policies, many development experts believed that the application of advanced industrial technologies to the developing world would spark economic growth.[2] However, by the 1960s and 1970s, many environmentalists assailed development models that relied on such technology. Much like E. F. Schumacher, environmentalists pointed to the many large-scale, centralized technological projects – such as major dams, large irrigation systems, and vast electricity grids – that often led to environmental degradation, reduction of natural resource stocks, and social alienation. Many reformers argued that developers should replace capital-intensive, large-scale polluting technologies with small-scale, labor-intensive ones predicated on meeting local needs with local supplies. Building alongside and often upon Schumacher's thinking, this movement for reform, known at the time as the "intermediate technology," the "alternative technology," and most popularly, the "appropriate technology" (AT) movement, was a key component of the environmental critique of international development.[3]

[2] For works that address the relationship between culture, development, and the history of technology, see David E. Nye, *Technology Matters: Questions to Live With* (Cambridge: The MIT Press, 2007); Adas, *Machines as the Measure of Men*; Michael Adas, *Dominance by Design: Technological Imperatives and America's Civilizing Mission* (Cambridge: The Belknap Press of Harvard University Press, 2006); David Biggs, "Breaking from the Colonial Mold: Water Engineering and the Failure of Nation-Building in the Plain of Reeds, Vietnam," *Technology and Culture*, Vol. 49, No. 3 (July 2008), 599–623; Suzanne Moon, "Justice, Geography, and Steel: Technology and National Identity in Indonesia Industrialization," *Osiris*, Vol. 24 (2009), 253–77; Robert S. Anderson, Edwin Levy, and Barrie M. Morrison, *Rice Science and Development Politics* (Oxford: Clarendon Press, 1991); Ramachandra Guha, *The Unquiet Woods: Ecological Change and Peasant Resistance in the Himalaya* (Berkeley: University of California Press, 1989); Gabrielle Hecht, "Rupture-Talk in the Nuclear Age: Conjugating Colonial Power in Africa," *Social Studies of Science*, Vol. 32, No. 5–6 (Oct.–Dec. 2002), 691–727.

[3] I use the term "appropriate technology" as an umbrella term to contain a number of different reform movements that criticized the role of technology in the development process. In the 1960s, Schumacher and other scholars used the phrase "intermediate technology" to refer to technologies in the developing world that were neither wholly primitive nor the kind of heavy, advanced modern technologies that typified agricultural or industrial development among the wealthiest and most developed nations. By the

Advocates for appropriate technology saw the movement as a holistic initiative that encouraged societies to rethink how to ensure dignified and fulfilling work, how best to distribute political and social power, and how to build more sustainable relationships between humans and the natural world. They believed that it provided a means to meet local concerns, minimize environmental impacts, and avoid repeating the most harmful consequences of industrialization. While the AT movement was not solely about offering a less environmentally destructive means of satisfying material wants, the environmental component of the movement was among its most visible and significant. Well-known environmental leaders such as Barbara Ward and Russell Train celebrated the movement, and organizations such as Friends of the Earth (FOE) and the International Institute for Environment and Development (IIED) called for the use of small-scale, labor-intensive technologies in numerous publications.

Although many NGOs supported the movement, two groups – Volunteers in Technical Assistance (VITA) and the Intermediate Technology Development Group (ITDG) – played predominant roles in pressuring major institutions to adopt appropriate technologies in lending. These NGOs aggressively promoted local, needs-based technology organizations in the developing world and pressured donor governments to adopt small-scale technologies in their lending policies. While both grew slowly in the 1960s, by the mid-1970s, VITA and the ITDG became powerful interest groups capable of swaying both governmental and public opinion, and both won contracts and grants to establish their own AT projects in the developing world. The ITDG, founded by E. F. Schumacher to promote his ideas globally, established a wide-reaching network of engineers and activists that could lobby donor governments doling out aid, advise recipient governments deciding development strategies, and build up local, private capacity to carry out small-scale projects in local communities. In moving from academic and activist circles to major lending institutions, Schumacher and his acolytes showed that non-state actors could influence policy by building institutions with the credibility and clout to gain access to centers of power. By 1980,

mid-1970s, "intermediate" had fallen out of common parlance, as "appropriate technology" became the dominant phrase used by reformers. The "appropriate" moniker came to encapsulate other movements, as well. "Alternative" technologies came to be associated with the energy sector, particularly those energy technologies not based on fossil fuels. The term "indigenous technology," which referred to those tools based on local knowledge and habits (not Western science), gained popularity, too. Additionally, as this chapter makes clear, not all AT supporters were environmentalists. Likewise, not all environmentalists advocated on behalf of the AT movement, although many supported its aims.

appropriate technologies had become part of the lending activities of the
U.S. Agency for International Development (AID), the World Bank, and
the United Nations Development Programme (UNDP), with nearly 300
other different agencies, governmental and nongovernmental, offering
small-scale projects to developing nations.[4]

While the environmental benefits of small-scale technologies and participatory development often motivated AT advocates, the movement's
success depended on a series of contingent changes in the wider development community. Transformations in U.S. foreign aid policy in the wake
of the Vietnam War led to a "New Directions" policy that stressed minimal government commitment, greater funding for multilateral banks and
private enterprise, and increasing rural employment across the developing
world. Likewise, as lending agencies such as the World Bank redefined
the ultimate objective of development – from national economic growth
toward poverty reduction – new opportunities arose for alternative
methods of achieving these ends. Finally, scholars and leaders from the
Global South demanded development approaches that met "basic human
needs" such as food, shelter, and clean water for communities that had
been left behind during past development efforts. In all these instances, AT
provided a means for achieving these diverse goals.

As major institutions began to fund AT programs, the meaning and
ultimate purpose of small-scale technologies changed from the early 1970s
through the 1980s. AID's efforts abroad and those of a non-profit corporation created by Congress called Appropriate Technology International
(ATI) reveal the multiple meanings attached to the movement. Over the
course of the 1970s, in development circles the meaning of AT became
framed around small technologies' ability to relieve persistent unemployment, unlock entrepreneurial energies, and spur private enterprise as a new
means toward old objectives of economic growth. Its origins as a countercultural, environmental critique of industrial society fell from view.[5]
Charting the evolution of the small-scale technologies – from their rise as

---

[4] Nicolas Jéquier and Gerard Blanc, *The World of Appropriate Technology: A Quantitative
Analysis* (Paris: Development Centre of the Organisation for Economic Cooperation and
Development, 1983), 27.
[5] Scholars who have written on the history of AT have focused on it within the United States,
and they have presented AT as gaining brief popularity at home before quickly fading from
popularity. These works have overlooked the role of AT in international development
circles, where the use of appropriate technology was both more indelible and impactful.
See Carroll Pursell, "Presidential Address: The Rise and Fall of the Appropriate
Technology Movement in the United States, 1965–1985," *Technology and Culture*,
Vol. 34, No. 3 (July 1992), 629–37; Jordan Kleiman, *The Appropriate Technology*

a decentralized, countercultural prescription for the problems of industrial modernity to their celebration as a path toward individualized, market-based solutions to development quandaries – reveals that development institutions took hold of some important ideas originally animating the AT movement. However, they did so for very different reasons – and often with very different outcomes – than those for which environmentalists had argued.

## TAKE-OFFS AND TRANSFERS: THE ROLE OF TECHNOLOGY IN DEVELOPMENT, 1945–1970

In American popular culture, technology has been viewed as both a symbol of modernity and a catalyst for achieving material abundance.[6] In the years after World War II, many people celebrated the United States' technical expertise and lauded modern technology's capacity to satisfy both human needs and consumer desires. The United States had established a powerful matrix of academic expertise, government funding, and private enterprise. Intellectuals and policy makers believed that investing in new technologies was the major driving force behind American society's transition from a world of scarcity to one of abundance. Popular publications such as *Scientific American* and scholars such as Lewis Mumford venerated the use of new technologies to overcome material deprivation and enliven the human spirit.[7]

Development theorists, too, had long placed tremendous significance on technology. Karl Marx held that technological change drove the shift from one mode of production to another. Joseph Schumpeter regarded technological innovation as a key component of "creative destruction," or the prime mover behind the replacement of one economic order with another. In the postwar United States, many economists and social scientists, such as Joseph Kahl, Alex Inkeles, C. E. Black, and Daniel Lerner,

*Movement in American Political Culture*, (Ph.D. dissertation, University of Rochester, 2000); Thomas P. Hughes, *American Genesis: A Century of Invention and Technological Enthusiasm, 1870–1970* (New York: Viking, 1989), chapter 9; Langdon Winner, *The Whale and the Reactor: The Search for Limits in an Age of High Technology* (Chicago: University of Chicago Press, 1986); Kelvin W. Willoughby, *Technology Choice: A Critique of the Appropriate Technology Movement* (Boulder: Westview Press, 1990); Andrew G. Kirk, *Counterculture Green: The Whole Earth Catalog and American Environmentalism* (Lawrence: University of Kansas Press, 2007).

[6] Nye, *Technology Matters*; Adas, *Dominance by Design*; Pursell, "Presidential Address: The Rise and Fall of the Appropriate Technology Movement in the United States, 1965–1985."

[7] Hughes, *American Genesis*, chapters 8 and 9.

believed that a society's ability to dominate its environment through advanced technologies spurred the passage to modernity.[8]

Among postwar intellectuals, Walt Whitman Rostow exemplified the trend to stress the power of technology in the development process. Rostow, a preeminent development economist who served in varying capacities for both the Kennedy and Johnson administrations, placed technological change at the heart of the modernization process. Rostow argued that societies transition through various stages of economic growth, from a starting point in "traditional" or "pre-Newtonian" society endangered by persistent scarcity to a secure, constant state of high industrial output and mass consumption. The key transitional period for Rostow was the "take-off," a time of industrial expansion, widespread profit making, exploitation of natural resources, and revolutionary changes in agricultural productivity. Through analysis of case studies of Great Britain, the United States, and Canada, Rostow concluded that the adoption of new, large-scale technologies and investments in industry and agriculture, coupled with a political elite capable of guiding the transitional phase in the economy, generated rapid increases in productivity, wealth, and consumption.[9] Technologies made traditional societies modern, and Rostow and other modernization theorists in the United States and other advanced countries proposed "technocratically managed social and economic reform" to guide the use of new technologies and militate against radical, communistic modes of political organization. Rostow's arguments won favor in numerous policy circles and informed the thinking of mid-century development experts.[10]

Technology thus occupied an important place in postwar development policy. The transfer of "capital equipment," through direct bilateral assistance, specific grant programs, or through intermediary bodies such as corporations, was a founding component of the United Nations' first technical assistance programs.[11] Technology transfer was an important

---

[8] Elias H. Tuma, "Technology Transfer and Economic Development: Lessons of History," *The Journal of Developing Areas*, Vol. 21, No. 4 (July 1987), 403–38; Adas, *Machines as the Measure of Men*, 413–15.

[9] Rostow, *The Stages of Economic Growth*, 8.

[10] Quote from Gilman, *Mandarins of the Future*, 43. For contemporary works on the rise of technocracy, see Zbigniew Bzrezinski, *Between Two Ages: America's Role in a Technetronic Era* (New York: Viking Press, 1970); Daniel Bell, *The Coming of Post-Industrial Society: A Venture in Social Forecasting* (New York: Basic Books, Inc., 1973).

[11] P. Sinard to W. Rostow, "Technical Assistance and the Financing of Economic Development," March 19, 1949, G.X 26/1 "Economic Development Technical Assistance – Jacket 1," UNOG Registry Collection.

component of the technical assistance aspects of President Truman's Point IV program, and became a staple of U.S. foreign aid programs thereafter. And recipient leaders demanded big technologies, too. Leaders such as Jawaharlal Nehru and Kwame Nkrumah hailed large technologies as the catalysts of economic growth and symbols of national power and prestige.[12] Development theories rarely generate consistent support and widespread consensus, yet through the early 1960s elites in developing countries and policy makers in the West alike held a deep faith in the power of large-scale technologies to increase productivity, generate wealth, and overcome persistent material scarcity – in short, to remake societies for the better.

## TECHNOLOGY IN CRISIS: THE RISE OF APPROPRIATE TECHNOLOGY

Despite this academic and policy consensus, in the mid-1960s a small band of writers and cultural critics began to question the power of technologies to do social good. Leo Marx's 1964 *Machine in the Garden* exposed long-held tensions in American life between a pastoral ideal on the one hand, and the polluting, invasive technologies of industrial life on the other.[13] Jacques Ellul's 1964 tome *The Technological Society* identified the tendencies of technological systems to rationalize the world through increasingly complex bureaucracies and systems of control and argued that technological systems in both capitalist and socialistic systems posed threats to individual freedom.[14] Published in the same year, Herbert Marcuse's *One Dimensional Man* castigated pervasive and repressive technological systems swallowing individual freedom and alienating the human spirit.[15] Theodor Roszak's study of Western protest movements, *The Making of a Counter Culture*, argued that the youth movement sweeping the West was fundamentally a direct reaction to "technocracy."[16]

---

[12] See Chapter 1.

[13] Leo Marx, *The Machine in the Garden: Technology and the Pastoral Idea in America* (New York: Oxford University Press, 1964). See also Hughes, *American Genesis*, chapter 9; Kleiman, *The Appropriate Technology Movement in American Political Culture*.

[14] Jacques Ellul, *The Technological Society*, John Wilkinson, trans. (New York: Vintage Books, 1964).

[15] Herbert Marcuse, *One Dimensional Man: Studies in the Ideology of Advanced Industrial Society* (Boston: Beacon Press, 1964).

[16] Theodor Roszak, *The Making of a Counter Culture: Reflection on the Technocratic Society and Its Youthful Opposition* (Garden City, NY: Doubleday, 1969); Similar

Environmental writers echoed many of these themes, critiquing large-scale technologies and the political and economic systems that embraced them. Fears of nuclear disasters had worried Americans since the creation of the first atomic bombs. By the early 1960s, Rachel Carson's *Silent Spring* showed the unintentional consequences – often deadly – of human-kind's faith in technologies to alter endlessly the natural world for human ends.[17] Charles Reich's popular bestseller *The Greening of America* placed the rejection of existing technologies as central to countercultural and environmental sensibilities.[18] Prominent American ecologist Barry Commoner argued that advanced technology was the primary cause of environmental problems in his widely read 1971 book, *The Closing Circle*.[19] Within the international development community, Green Revolution seeds and plantations – the major technological innovation of the 1960s – generated criticism. No less a figure than World Bank President Robert McNamara worried about the costs of industrial, mono-culture agriculture that had blossomed over the 1960s. Monocultures invited disease, pests, and land loss, which together revealed to McNamara the "dangers and the frightful consequences to those hundreds of millions dependent on increased yields."[20] Technology, long seen a symbol of progress and the driving force behind the material abundance of liberal democratic society, was now being viewed by some observers as a threat to the underlying values those societies were supposed to nurture.[21]

Of these critics, E. F. Schumacher levied some of the most scathing attacks on large-scale technology transfers in the development process. In 1962, Schumacher returned home to Great Britain after serving as a consultant for the Burmese and Indian governments. Their drive for rapid industrialization and emphasis on success measured largely by aggregate economic statistics alarmed him. So too did the two nations' desire for

themes appear in Lynn White, Jr., "The Historical Roots of Our Ecological Crisis," *Science*, Vol. 155, No. 3767 (March 10, 1967), 1203–7.

[17] Rachel Carson, *Silent Spring* (Boston: Houghton Mifflin Company, 1962).

[18] Charles Reich, *The Greening of America: How the Youth Revolution Is Trying to Make America Livable* (New York: Random House, 1970).

[19] Barry Commoner, *The Closing Circle: Nature, Man, and Technology* (New York: Knopf, 1971).

[20] Robert McNamara to Russell Train, February 6, 1973, box 8, Russell E. Train Papers, Manuscript Division, Library of Congress. See also McNeil, *Something New Under the Sun*, 224–6.

[21] For a further elaboration on this point and on the relationship between environmentalism and AT in the United States, see Kleiman, *The Appropriate Technology Movement in American Political Culture*, chapter 3.

large-scale, invasive technologies, which seemed to impose on rural populations a disruptive vision of modernity designed by distant technocrats
ignorant of local culture. After his time in Burma, which Schumacher
called a "rewarding" experience, he noted in a personal letter to
Burmese official and future UN Secretary-General U Thant that there
seemed to be too many economic advisers from the West working on
surveys and consulting projects. Their theoretical and analytic level of
work was too far removed from the "actual doing" of development,
which for Schumacher needed to be closer to the peasantry and prospective workers whom development projects targeted.[22]

In addition, Schumacher expressed a disdain for large, centralized
development projects that were heavy on symbolism but weak on substance. Burma's government, for instance, had backed an ill-fated electrification scheme on the basis of lighting a different village each day.
Schumacher scoffed at the project. "Electrification must be justified by
something more than the mere love of electrification," he asserted while
arguing that the project simply replaced traditional, cheap oil lighting
with more costly electricity that required centralized oversight.[23] Working
as a consultant to India's government, Schumacher became fascinated
with Buddhist thought and Mahatma Gandhi. He searched for a new
way of spurring development that placed greater emphasis on ensuring
rural employment, dignifying work, and technologies that people could
use without relying distant technicians or a consistent influx of Western
money.[24]

Throughout the 1950s and 1960s, Schumacher traveled to many
other developing nations where he honed his thinking on the problems
afflicting contemporary development thought. In studying the problems
of Tanzania's development in the late 1960s, Schumacher began to
articulate a coherent critique of existing development models. "There
are no master-key solutions to the problem of healthy development,"
Schumacher wrote. "Gigantic schemes, whether in agriculture, industry,
communications, and even in education, may seem attractive in theory
but are invariably disastrous in practice."[25] The fundamental "error" of

[22] E. F. Schumacher to U Thant, March 29, 1955, box 1, E. F. Schumacher Papers, New
Economics Institute, Great Barrington, MA [hereinafter cited as Schumacher Papers].
[23] E. F. Schumacher to Unknown (Mr. Ahmed), August 29, 1955, box 1, Schumacher
Papers.
[24] Barbara Wood, *E.F. Schumacher: His Life and Thought* (New York: Harper & Row,
1984), chapter 22.
[25] "Confidential: Economic Development in Tanzania," by E. F. Schumacher, July 1968,
box 9, Schumacher Papers.

contemporary society, Schumacher had come to believe, was an exploitative "attitude toward nature" and the use of rapacious technologies that devastated the natural world. "Modern man," Schumacher explained, "does not experience himself as a part of nature but as an outside force destined to dominate and conquer it."[26] With "the world in a process of westernization" and elites in the developing world clamoring for the kind of wealth achieved by the North, Schumacher worried that leaders in the South might accept the same fallacious conclusions.[27] What the Global South countries needed were "intermediate" technologies based on local needs and using local supplies that local populations could choose and use to satisfy their most urgent requirements.

Schumacher's intermediate technology, soon thereafter subsumed under the banner of "appropriate technology," resonated with many prominent environmentalists. His thinking resembled many contemporary environmental critiques of modern society.[28] Participants at the groundbreaking 1968 conference on ecology and international development at the Airlie House in Virginia, for instance, disparaged the "careless" use of technologies by modern societies. Prominent American ecologist Barry Commoner argued that "the rescue rope offered to developing nations by modern science and technology is intrinsically unsound."[29] "Modern technologies, being massive and novel, inevitably intrude upon the natural environment on a large scale and in familiar ways," he proclaimed. Such objects crudely interfered with the complex dynamics of ecosystems.[30] Conferees castigated foreign aid policies that transferred technology suited for the temperate zones of the developed world, which tended to "fail operationally when imposed on alien, usually tropical environments" of developing nations.[31]

Other leading environmentalists widely embraced AT, too. Barbara Ward, a prominent economist and head of the influential International

---

[26] Schumacher, *Small Is Beautiful: Economics as if People Mattered*, revised 1989 ed., 13–18.

[27] Ibid.

[28] For example, Schumacher's thinking helped to popularize and give weight to those who ascribed to Stewart Brand's *Whole Earth Catalog*. On Brand's work and AT in American environmentalism, see Kirk, *Counterculture Green*.

[29] Barry Commoner, "On the Meaning of Ecological Failures in International Development," in M. Taghi Farvar and John P. Milton, eds., *The Careless Technology: Ecology and International Development* (Garden City, NY: The Natural History Press, 1972), xxiii.

[30] Ibid., xxv.

[31] M. Taghi Farvar and John P. Milton, "Foreword," in Farvar and Milton, eds., *The Careless Technology: Ecology and International Development*, xiii.

Institute for Environment and Development (IIED), celebrated the growing interest "the viability of small, decentralized, labor-intensive industrialization" as a means to avoid wide-scale ecological destruction.[32]
WWF-US president and former head of the CEQ and EPA Russell Train
argued that using small-scale technologies was necessary to conserve
natural resources.[33] Many environmentalists also questioned the values
inherent in a society of mass production and consumption over local
knowledge. As a member of Friends of the Earth International averred
in 1971 that the American "concept of progress denigrates the hand-
crafted outrigger canoe and exalts the factory-made fiberglass power-
boat," and believed that adopting small-scale, locally sourced
technologies could redress such assumptions.[34] The importance of
reforming the use of large-scale, environmentally destructive technologies
was a central concern for environmentalists at the 1972 UN Conference
on the Human Environment.[35]

In addition, the environmental movement saw Schumacher's work as
conceptual scaffolding to help build a broader solution for issues of
inequality and poverty as well as environmental devastation. On the surface, by replacing polluting, destructive technologies and empowering
poor populations through dignifying work, Schumacher's theories provided more space for individual and community uplift than earlier conservation arguments. AT seemed to emerge as a "synthesis" in the words of
one American community organizer and environmentalist. Schumacher's
work, he claimed, transcended "old concepts in the economics versus
environment dispute," because it allowed activists to support social justice
and environmental concerns "in the same breath without being denounced
as hopelessly idealistic or naïve."[36] Schumacher's rhetoric about community participation and local empowerment also resonated with environmentalists who, by the mid-1970s, were emphasizing the virtues of
community involvement and local self-determination in conservation.

[32] Barbara Ward, *Progress for a Small Planet* (New York: W.W. Norton & Company,
1979), 212. See also Barbara Ward, "Small Is Still Beautiful," *The Washington Post*,
October 2, 1977, 80.

[33] Russell Train, "Help for the Third World? Keep It Simple," *Los Angeles Times*,
December 16, 1976, D7.

[34] Robert Wenkam, "Economic Progress Versus Tradition," *Not Man Apart*, Vol. 1, No. 8
(August 1971), 8.

[35] "NGO Plenary Declaration," Reprinted in Special Issue: The Stockholm Conference, *Not
Man Apart*, Vol. 2, No. 7 (July 1972), 8–10.

[36] "High Technology: Is It Shifting into Low Gear?" *Conservation Letter* (October 1976), 3.
Viewed at the Wildlife Information Center, WWF-US, Washington, DC.

AT provided a way to tap local knowledge and needs, which many environmentalists believed would redound to the benefit of the natural world.

Schumacher derived as much inspiration from the environmental movement as the movement found in his own ideas. "Small-scale operations are always less likely to be harmful to the natural environment than large-scale ones," Schumacher concluded, "simply because their individual force is small in relation to the recuperative forces of nature."[37] To realize his aspirations for small-scale projects in development, Schumacher worked through much of the 1960s and 1970s to pressure major development bodies to implement his ideas.

### MAKING A MOVEMENT: VITA, THE ITDG, AND EARLY FORMS OF AT ADVOCACY

While it was not until the early 1970s that the AT movement developed coherence and theoretical weight, small-scale, labor-intensive technologies had been used in development policy in an ad hoc fashion for decades. Such technologies and localized technical assistance program were important aspects of early Point Four projects.[38] In the 1950s, philanthropic foundations such as the Rockefeller Foundation had funded "experimental" efforts in small-scale, alternative technologies, such as solar cookers, but only on a piecemeal basis.[39] In 1959, a group of engineers in upstate New York formed Volunteers for International Technical Assistance (VITA) to offer off-hours technical advice and pragmatic technical solutions to small-scale problems in the developing world. Over the course of its first few years, VITA built a network of volunteer experts to respond to mail inquiries from the developing world, eventually culling together some of their favorite hardware designs into a publication entitled *Village Technology Handbook.*[40]

---

[37] E. F. Schumacher, "The Economics of Permanence," essay submitted to a conference in New Delhi on "The Relevance of Gandhi to Our Times," 1970, box 1, Schumacher Papers; E. F. Schumacher, "The Environment," box 4, Schumacher Papers. Similar themes emerge in E. F. Schumacher, "Spaceship Earth – Questions of Growth," notes for an essay, box 1, Schumacher Papers.

[38] Stephen Macekura, "Point Four and the Crisis of U.S. Foreign Aid Policy in the 1970s," in Robert Devine, ed., *Harry S. Truman and Foreign Aid* (Kirksville, MO: Truman State University Press, 2015), 73–100.

[39] Ethan Barnaby Kapstein, "The Solar Cooker," *Technology and Culture*, Vol. 22, No. 1 (January 1981), 112–21.

[40] Bess Williamson, "Small-Scale Technology for the Developing World: Volunteers for International Technical Assistance, 1959–1971," *Comparative Technology Transfer and Society*, Vol. 6, No. 3 (December 2008), 239–40.

In these early years, VITA was small and staffed by enthusiasts. An informal group of fifteen founders expanded to eighty part-time volunteers by 1961. With steady work, it pulled in advocates from around the country. In 1965, a *Reader's Digest* article raised its profile, and by 1966 there were over 2,000 volunteers working for VITA. The organization developed informal ties with the U.S. government, primarily through AID and the Peace Corps. In 1965, nearly half of all VITA inquiries came from Peace Corps workers. Most VITA staffers worked from a professional ethos and personal desire to help build interesting and pragmatic tools, but it did not articulate a theoretical framework or galvanizing vision for its work.[41] A decade later, however, its scope and purpose changed dramatically.

As VITA volunteers sketched out designs, a more comprehensive approach for small-scale technologies was in the works across the Atlantic. Upon his return from his consulting trips to India in the early 1960s, Schumacher began to publicize his ideas about small-scale, rural development based on locally sourced technologies. Working primarily through the Overseas Development Institute (ODI), a British think tank funded by the Ford Foundation, Schumacher came into contact with many like-minded economists and development experts. Aided most closely by George McRobie, an old colleague and friend, and Julia Porter, a development expert, in May 1965 Schumacher founded the Intermediate Technology Development Group (ITDG) to promote AT in developing countries.[42]

In contrast to the engineer-tinkerers of VITA, the ITDG primarily sought to build up local capacity, the "software" side of the appropriate technology concept. Schumacher and his closest supporters – McRobie, Porter, British economic consultant Alfred Latham-Koenig, and Indian scientist Mansur Hoda – envisioned the group to fill the "gap in aid and development," what they claimed was "the virtual absence of organized, systematic efforts to provide the poor countries with a choice of low-cost, self-help technologies, adapted to meet their needs for labour-intensive and small-scale development." The ITDG sought to catalog, analyze, and distribute information about such technologies, and make them available, through the founders' personal connections, to relevant elites and managers in developing nations.[43]

[41]  Ibid., 242.
[42]  George McRobie, *Small Is Possible* (New York: Harper & Row Publishers, 1981), 22–5; Wood, *E.F. Schumacher*, chapter 17; "India Development Group, News Bulletin and Report, 1974," 2, box 5, Schumacher Papers.
[43]  E. F. Schumacher, "The Work of the Intermediate Technology Development Group in Africa," *International Labour Review*, Vol. 106 (1972), 76.

By 1969, the ITDG was beginning to grow. It started to build up AT programs in lending agencies and developing nations across the globe. This software building started with a series of design and construction workshops in Nigeria and Kenya in early 1970. The organization soon began funding experimental technologies in water purification, transport, and storage, as well as locally sourced agricultural implements, storage devices, and transportation devices in Zambia, Nigeria, and Tanzania. In 1970, Schumacher's group won grants from the International Labour Organization (ILO), the United Nations' Economic Commission for Africa (ECA), and the United Nations Industrial Development Organization (UNIDO) to fund engineering seminars, technical education in appropriate technologies, and entrepreneurial development. By 1972, the group was making efficient use of its £70,000 (British pounds) spent annually on field projects.[44] By the time *Small Is Beautiful* was published, the organization offered some concrete examples of how AT might be put into practice. As the organization was beginning to expand its operations in the early 1970s, a series of internal changes within the United States' foreign policy apparatus created an opportunity for the young NGO to promote AT in U.S. development policy.

### REFORMING DEVELOPMENT FROM WITHIN: "NEW DIRECTIONS" IN U.S. FOREIGN ASSISTANCE

In 1969, President Richard Nixon called for "New Directions" in U.S. foreign aid. He wanted to reform the means and ends of development assistance in the wake of the Vietnam imbroglio. In terms of the delivery of aid, Nixon said, "We ought to turn our foreign aid programs more in the direction of stimulating private enterprise."[45] As Nixon explained, the mixed record of development efforts in the 1960s made for difficult policy choices. "We need to understand much better than we do what, in fact, increases the appeal of Communism in particular countries and what drives nations closer to the Soviet Union or Communist China," the president claimed. However, Nixon also noted that he was "concerned about the tendency of our aid programs, and, indeed, of the activities of

---

[44] Ibid., 77–91.
[45] "Attachment, Memorandum from President Nixon to Secretary of State Rogers, Feb. 13, 1969," *FRUS, Vol. IV*, 253–4.

our personnel overseas, in general, to draw us into a deep involvement in the domestic politics of developing countries."[46]

"New Directions" signaled changes for the objects of development, not just the methods. A variety of internal reviews and presidential commissions recommended wholesale changes to foreign assistance, often noting how the rural sector had not experienced the kind of growth for which many theorists and policy makers had hoped. These reports noted how little assistance actually reached the most impoverished populations in the developing world.[47] A similar movement was underway within AID, spearheaded by its Nixon-appointed administrator, John Hannah. In 1971, Hannah ordered a comprehensive review of AID, which had become tied up in congressional debates over ending the Vietnam War. As a result of a series of internal discussions, AID devised a "sectoral strategy," reorienting its funding efforts toward reaching the poor, rural populations in the poorest nations. No longer would U.S. foreign assistance focus primarily on the controversial capital-intensive projects; instead, U.S. policy would now attempt to meet basic needs such as food, shelter, health, and education.[48] Such a focus could redress persistent rural

---

[46] "Letter from President Nixon to Secretary of State Rogers, Washington, April 12, 1969," *FRUS, 1969–1976, Vol. IV*, 259.

[47] Mark F. McGuire and Vernon W. Ruttan, *Lost Directions: U.S. Foreign Assistance Policy since New Directions*, Bulletin 89–5, Economic Development Center, University of Minnesota, 1989, 2; Rolf H. Sartorius and Vernon W. Ruttan, "The Source of the Basic Human Needs Mandate," *Journal of Developing Areas*, Vol. 23, No. 3 (April 1989), 332–7; "History of U.S. Economic Assistance Programs in Brief" in *Transition Briefing Book*, Staff Offices, Al McDonald Files, folder "Agency for International Development (AID) Transition Book 11/80," box 36, Jimmy Carter Presidential Library, Atlanta, GA [hereinafter cited as JCL]. In 1968, President Johnson appointed Cornell University President James A. Perkins to lead a committee that would recommend changes in U.S. foreign assistance programs. Although no new structural changes were present in the committee's conclusions, the Perkins Report called for increased focus on education and popular participation. A 1969 report by Nelson Rockefeller's Presidential Mission for the Western Hemisphere called for a reallocation of foreign assistance through multilateral and regional banks and greater private investment. Nixon reiterated the emphasis on banks and private capital in his 1970 Foreign Policy Report to Congress. In March 1970, the Peterson Task Force on International Development, run by Bank of America chairman Rudolph Peterson, called for an even more dramatic reorientation foreign assistance. The Peterson Report suggested that developing countries should take a greater role in determining the priorities of their assistance and that U.S. funding should be allocated in proportion to their own self-help efforts. The United States, then, could draw down its formal commitments while maintaining support for its allies and fostering closer ties between private enterprise and recipient governments.

[48] Congressional Research Service, "The New Directions Mandate and the Agency for International Development," in *AID's Administrative and Management Problems in Providing Foreign Economic Assistance*, Hearing before a Subcommittee of the

deprivation, and the administration recognized that funding education and local health were topics that Congress would be less likely to criticize.

After having his 1971 foreign aid request voted down by the Senate, Nixon supported the shift proposed by AID. It mirrored similar discussions between civil society groups and members of Congress who desired a change in U.S. international assistance. In addition, Hannah's new approach won the support of key members of the Overseas Development Council (ODC), an influential think tank, and the House Foreign Affairs Committee, and became law with the passage of the May 1973 Foreign Assistance Act.[49] With passage of the act, the new "sectoral strategy" redefined the targets of U.S. development aid.

Among other structural changes in the agency, New Directions also made good on Nixon's campaign promises about reducing AID's operating expenses and increasing the role of the private sector in foreign aid. Section 107, passed as part of New Directions as an amendment to the 1961 Foreign Assistance Act, included $32 million to support "centrally funded private and voluntary organization activities" to "strengthen the development role" of such organizations in carrying out the New Directions mandate.[50] AID officials believed that private voluntary organizations fit the new mandate particularly well, as they thought that NGOs had better experience working on the ground with the poorest communities, greater flexibility in their operations, and were more innovative in their approaches.[51] Under New Directions, AID offered direct

Committee of Government Operations, House of Representatives, 97th Congress, First Session, October 6, 1981 (Washington, DC: GPO, 1981), 109; "AID: The New Challenge, A Special Report of the Agency for International Development," 1975, box 16, FO3-2, Mutual Security, White House Central Files, Gerald Ford Presidential Library [hereinafter cited as GFL].

[49] The best overview of New Directions remains Vernon Ruttan, *United States Development Assistance Policy: The Domestic Politics of Foreign Aid* (Baltimore: The Johns Hopkins University Press, 1996), chapter 6. See also Ekbladh, *The Great American Mission*, 221–3.

[50] Agency for International Development, "Implementation of 'New Directions' in Development Assistance: Report to the Committee on International Relations on Implementation of Legislative Reforms in the Foreign Assistance Act of 1973" (Washington, DC: GPO, 1975), 22–3.

[51] AID officials used the category "Private and Voluntary Organization" to refer to any nonprofit (and thus tax-exempt) organization that provides charitable social services. In this sense, all NGOs are PVOs. In AID parlance during this era, PVOs referred to all private actors except for for-profit companies and universities, which had their own status in reporting. To avoid confusion, I try to minimize the use of the term "PVO" in this book, only employing it as a proper noun (in the case of AID's PVO Office) or when spoken by former AID officials. Rachel M. McCleary, *Global Compassion: Private and*

grants to private organizations to become development organizations themselves. Following the 1973 Act, NGOs would have "a greater responsibility in programming, management, and relationships with host governments and private institutions overseas."[52] New Directions altered the targets of foreign aid and the means of delivering assistance.

These legislative reforms had immediate effects on other fronts. Traditional bilateral assistance was on the wane. In its place came an increasing reliance on multilateral funding through the World Bank, a priority that Nixon and his advisors had pushed for, and to which Congress had agreed.[53] The bank itself was undergoing major structural changes in the early 1970s. Now headed by former U.S. Secretary of Defense Robert McNamara, the bank reoriented its funding strategies to emphasize poverty eradication. Rural development lending increased from 2.9 percent of total lending in 1969 to 11 percent in 1974. Agricultural projects increased from 12 percent in 1961–65 to 24 percent in 1973–74. At the same time, the share of money allocated for infrastructure projects fell from 55 percent in 1967 to 30 percent in 1977.[54] The changes within AID and the World Bank reflected a broader shift in the global development community toward helping the poorest populations with the poorest countries satisfy "basic human needs."[55] These

*Voluntary Organizations and U.S. Foreign Policy Since 1939* (Oxford: Oxford University Press, 2009), 174.

[52] Quoted in Judith W. Gilmore, *A.I.D.'s "New Directions" with Private and Voluntary Organizations*, Development Studies Program VI, USAID, March 11, 1977, 5–6. USAID Document Clearinghouse. [Online] Available: http://dec.usaid.gov/index.cfm. Accessed October 8, 2011. On the types of grants offered in the new policy, see McCleary, *Global Compassion*, 103–22. See also Judith Tendler, *Turning Private Voluntary Organizations into Development Agencies: Questions for Evaluation*, A.I.D. Program Evaluation Discussion Paper No. 12, USAID, April 1982. USAID Document Clearinghouse. [Online] Available: http://dec.usaid.gov/index.cfm. Accessed October 8, 2011.

[53] Hal Brands, "Economic Development and the Contours of U.S. Foreign Policy: The Nixon Administration's Approach to Latin America, 1969–1974," *Peace and Change*, Vol. 33, No. 2 (April 2008), 243–73; Ekbladh, *The Great American Mission*, 221–3.

[54] Statistics from Martha Finnemore, "Redefining Development at the World Bank," in Frederick Cooper and Randall Packard, *International Development and the Social Sciences: Essays on the History and Politics of Knowledge* (Berkeley: University of California Press, 1997), 217. See also Patrick Sharma, "The United States, the World Bank, and the Challenges of International Development in the 1970s," *Diplomatic History*, Vol. 37, No. 3 (June 2013), 572–604.

[55] The focus on rural development and poverty was a common theme in UN debates during the 1970s, too. "Interim Summary Report of the Study on Technical Cooperation and Rural Development," 1978, UNDP/PWG/98, G.X 26/1; "Economic Development Technical Assistance: General Correspondence and Documentation – Jacket 11," UNOG Registry Collection.

shifts augured well for AT advocates. McNamara wanted developing countries to employ technologies that would "advance their economic and social development without seriously offending their environment."[56]

In a very short amount of time U.S. development aid underwent tremendous change. Between 1967 and 1974, funds appropriated for U.S. foreign aid projects declined from $2.1 billion to $1.7 billion. In the process, AID cut its staff from 17,600 direct-hire American citizens and foreign nationals in 1968 to 9,400 in 1974. The organization emphasized using private organizations to carry out its new poverty-oriented projects. The number of private organizations receiving grants from AID rose rapidly, from 34 in 1970 to 70 in 1978 to 105 in 1981. The total amount granted to private groups for those same years reflected a similar increase from $106 million to $283 million to $462 million.[57] During the same period, the World Bank's loan commitments quadrupled from $1.1 billion to $4.3 billion, and its professional staff more than doubled from 734 to 1,752.[58] In the mid-1970s, the shape of development assistance was changing, and advocates for AT seized on opportunities presented by the transformation.

### NEW DIRECTIONS FOR PRIVATE ENTERPRISE: APPROPRIATE TECHNOLOGY INTERNATIONAL

Nonetheless, many of these reforms did not come quickly enough to please legislators. In July 1975, a young congressman from Maryland named Clarence Long spoke before the House Committee on International Relations to express his concerns about the state of foreign aid. Long, formerly a professor of economics at Johns Hopkins focusing in labor and unemployment, worried about the future of foreign aid and economic development. U.S. funding for development would likely continue to decline, he thought. He accused AID of not moving decisively to implement the New Directions changes and decried the "modest" progress resulting from the $90 billion spent on development aid during the previous decades. "No real priority," he explained, "has been given to helping the hundreds

---

[56] Robert McNamara to Russell Train, February 6, 1973, box 8, Train Papers.

[57] McCleary, *Global Compassion*, 104. The amounts cited are measured in 2005 U.S. dollars.

[58] Judith Tendler, *Inside Foreign Aid* (Baltimore: The Johns Hopkins University Press, 1975), 6.

of millions of small farmers improve their productivity per acre, and population increases have soaked up much of what growth occurred."[59] Vast rural parts of the globe were still facing endemic poverty.

To redress all these concerns, Long argued that AID should adopt appropriate technology as a way to achieve the objectives of the New Directions mandate. The congressman had been inspired by Schumacher's writings and the work the ITDG had been accomplishing around the world.[60] He saw appropriate technologies as a way to engage the poor, rural populations – the targets of AID's sectoral reforms – with reduced commitment from the federal government. Long argued that funding such projects would "initiate self-generating processes by which the people in developing countries produce the great mass of their own future capital, from their own labor and natural resources which in many cases are abundant."[61] He justified AT not on grounds of its environmental appeal, but rather on its promise to spur economic growth with less investment from the United States. Whereas Schumacher and his acolytes had seen small-scale technologies as a holistic solution to a worldwide ecological, social, economic, and political crisis, Long was one of many policy makers who saw such technologies primarily as a way to reduce persistent unemployment in the developing world.

Following the revived interest in using the private sector, Long called for a program "independent" of AID. It would receive federal money but exist outside formal management structures of federal agencies.[62] Assisting his effort was Edgar Owens, a career AID official who had grown frustrated with the agency's inefficiency and who had become enamored with appropriate technology.[63] Owens helped Long outline an experimental program, which quickly won support from others in Congress. The International Development and Food Assistance Act of 1975 allocated $20 million of section 107 for AID to organize an expanded and coordinated "private effort . . . to promote the development and dissemination of technologies

---

[59] International Development and Food Assistance Act of 1975, Hearings and Markup of the Committee on International Relations, House of Representatives (Washington, DC: GPO, 1976), 330–1.

[60] Nicholas Wade, "Congress Buys Small Is Beautiful," *Science*, Vol. 192, No. 4244 (June 11, 1976), 1086.

[61] International Development and Food Assistance Act of 1975, Hearings and Markup of the Committee on International Relations, House of Representatives, 331.

[62] Ibid.

[63] Ken Bode and Arpad Von Lazar, "Appropriate Technology: A New Theory Has Spawned a New Boondoggle," *The New Republic* (June 11, 1977), 12.

appropriate for developing countries."[64] Over the next year, AID officials, congressional staffers, and NGOs worked together to design the policy.[65] In particular, two groups were in a prime position to seize the opportunity offered by the new legislation: VITA and the ITDG.

VITA had undergone a major transformation over the preceding half-decade. In 1970, it abandoned its piecemeal, mail-order structure to become a more active lobbying group. Seeking to be closer to Washington, DC, the organization left its quaint home in New York and established headquarters in Mt. Ranier, Maryland. The move spurred a major shift in the organization's funding. In the late 1960s, it had earned a few contracts through Great Society money to test out pilot projects in blighted areas within the United States, although its focus generally stayed on voluntary international efforts. After its move to Washington, VITA hired Tom Fox, a former Peace Corps administrator with close ties to the development community, as its director. By 1970, VITA was receiving funds from eighteen different U.S. foundations and donations from thirty-eight corporations.[66] By 1975, it had a full-time headquarters staff of twenty and an annual budget of over $500,000, with many contracts coming from AID. After congressional hearings in the spring of 1976, it won a contract to survey existing programs and potential plans for future aid programs in Latin America.[67] AID also enlisted VITA to provide technical advice to its missions worldwide. By 1976, VITA had developed close personal and institutional ties with the government, leaving it well positioned to influence the direction of AID's new program.

Likewise, in the 1970s Schumacher's ITDG grew considerably. It won financial support from larger NGOs and philanthropic bodies, which enabled the organization to expand its global operations. Mansur Hoda, an ITDG cofounder, oversaw an AT organization in Varanasi, India, and the ITDG funded a similar center in Ghana. Schumacher led staffers on a

---

[64] "Appropriate Technology," *Hearings before the Subcommittee on Domestic and International Scientific Planning, Analysis, and Cooperation of the Committee on Science and Technology, U.S. House of Representatives*, 95th Congress, Second Session, July 25–27, 1978 (Washington, DC: GPO, 1978), 739.

[65] "Proposal for a program inappropriate technology, transmitted by the Agency for International Development, pursuant to Section 107 of the Foreign Assistance Act (rev. ed.)," *United States Agency for International Development*, 1977, 5–6, USAID Document Clearinghouse. [Online] Available: http://dec.usaid.gov/index.cfm. Accessed May 8, 2011.

[66] Letter from John Hannah to Gerald Ford, September 1, 1970, box 255, Agency Correspondence File, Gerald Ford Vice Presidential Papers, GFL.

[67] "Appropriate Technology for the Third World," *Science*, Vol. 188, No. 4192 (June 6, 1975), 1000.

trip to Pakistan in 1974, which led to an AT division in Pakistan's planning ministry.[68] The group also earned government support, receiving a four-year grant from Great Britain's Ministry of Overseas Development (ODM) to become, according to George McRobie, "an arm of the ODM in the field of small industry."[69] By 1975, the group employed a full-time staff of over forty people and an annual budget over $130,000, with about 60 percent of the money coming from the British government, 30 percent coming from foreign lending agencies and international institutions, and 10 percent from public donations.[70] Like VITA, the ITDG won an AID contract to survey potential projects in Africa and South Asia.[71] These NGOs were becoming increasingly interwoven with the government, both as interest groups shaping new legislation and as development agencies winning contracts to carry out the mandates they helped to craft.[72]

Schumacher himself visited the United States again in early 1977 to promote the ITDG and spread the gospel of small-scale technologies. On a 43-day, 12-state tour, Schumacher gave numerous talks and interviews about his philosophy. Alongside public events, Schumacher also met with numerous leaders. He talked with President Carter at the White House, and he spoke before Congress as part of a program called "Dialogs on America's Future."[73] While on Capitol Hill, Schumacher also helped to refine the new AT program under discussion with AID officials. The British economist met with members of Congress after hours, consulted various committee members on his ideas of technological change, and explained the ITDG's activities to staff members.[74] His theories had

[68] "Intermediate Technology Development Group, Ltd., The Chairman's Report, October 1, 1973–September 30, 1974," NA-UK, OD 63/60.

[69] George McRobie to Stuart Holland, June 28, 1974, NA-UK, OD 63/55.

[70] Kleiman, *The Appropriate Technology Movement in American Political Culture*, 101–2.

[71] "Foreign Assistance and Related Agencies Appropriations for 1977, Part 2: Economic Assistance," Hearings before a Subcommittee of the Committee of Appropriations, House of Representatives, 94th Congress, Second Session, April 2, 7, 1976 (Washington, DC: GPO, 1976), 383.

[72] On the growth of interest groups, see Theda Skocpol, "Government Activism and the Reorganization of American Civic Democracy," in Paul Pierson and Theda Skocpol, eds., *The Transformation of American Politics: Activist Government and the Rise of Conservatism* (Princeton: Princeton University Press, 2007).

[73] Senator Charles H. Percy to E. F. Schumacher, March 30, 1977, box 3, Schumacher Papers; Katherine P. Schirmer to E. F. Schumacher, March 29, 1977, box 3, Schumacher Papers; "Small Is Beautiful," March 2, 1977, *Congressional Record*, 95th Congress, First Session, 1977, Vol. 123, No. 36.

[74] Department of State, "Edited Transcript, November 17, 1976 Meeting, Preparation for 1979 UN Conference on Science and Technology for Development," 39, box 203, H. Guyford Stever Papers, GFL.

inspired the creation of AID's new program; the man himself helped determine the program's final shape.[75]

In their final proposal to Congress, AID officials asked for a new program called Appropriate Technology International (ATI). In line with the congressional mandate to emphasize the private sector, ATI was a nonprofit corporation. An independent board of directors oversaw its activities "to avoid the political and bureaucratic liabilities of direct government funding."[76] ATI gave grants directly to publicly backed groups, such as universities in developing nations, and it also contracted out to private businesses, individuals, or NGOs that produced small-scale technologies. The organization stressed the importance of capacity building, too. "Appropriate technology includes software as well as hardware," AID's proposal explained. The new organization would "assist developing countries strengthen their own capacities to develop, adapt and utilize appropriate technology."[77] Clarence Long, now on the House Committee for International Relations, and Committee Chairman Zablocki loved its design. ATI received the $20 million under section 107, with wide leeway to decide how to allocate the money. Edgar Owens, the AID official who had long advocated AT, took the lead in designing ATI.[78] By mid-1977, the corporation was operational, and appropriate technology had become a component of American foreign aid and established an exemplar of a public-private arrangement.[79]

Although the founding documents offered little in the way of environmental concerns, ATI won wide acclaim among prominent conservationists. Russell Train, who had left government to return to the private sector, explained, "We are learning that, with social as well as physical structures,

[75] Rep. Clement J. Zablocki, Chairman of the Committee on International Relations, claimed, "while we were drafting the proposal his presence was most helpful in alerting members to the issue of intermediate technology and his comments assisted us in structuring the program." "Quotes from the Press," *Appropriate Technology*, Vol. 4, No. 3 (November 1977), 4.

[76] Gilmore, *A.I.D.'s "New Directions" with Private and Voluntary Organizations*, 29, USAID Document Clearinghouse. [Online] Available: http://dec.usaid.gov/index.cfm. Accessed October 8, 2011.

[77] Quoted in "Proposal for a Program in Appropriate Technology," 9 and part II, 2, folder "Appropriate Technology, TA/AT, FY 77," box 58, RG 286, NARA II.

[78] "High Technology: Is It Shifting into Low Gear?" *Conservation Letter* (October 1976), 4. Viewed at the Wildlife Information Center, WWF-US, Washington, DC.

[79] "Project Description and Budget, Grant No. AID/DSAN-G-0047," June 15, 1978, USAID/Bureau for Science and Technology/Office of Forestry; Records Relating to Policy, Plans, and Programs, 1970–1981, folder "Appropriate Technology FY 78 FY 79," box 20, RG 286, NARA II.

we must build from the ground up, not from the top down. We must start where the people are, and with whatever resources, skills, and implements they have."[80] Barbara Ward, too, celebrated the organization, and commended the Americans for having "gone even further" than the British, Scandinavians, and international organizations in making small-scale technologies part of their lending process.[81] A few staffers of Ward's International Institute for Environment and Development (IIED) even met with ATI officials to discuss potential projects.[82]

However, by and large, AID maintained that the objectives of ATI had little to do with the environment, as officials focused instead on spurring growth in impoverished rural areas. "The main goals of our efforts," a 1977 overview of ATI said, "must be the creation of employment opportunities, increases in productivity, and improvement of personal income of those segments of LDC society that have not benefitted proportionately from previous development efforts." ATI would be less about challenging the presumptions of modernization than engineering economic growth in rural areas.[83] It soon began to give out contracts to American companies, small businesses in the Global South, and various NGOs to pursue these ends, although the growing emphasis on replicating private sector initiatives soon hampered the effectiveness of AT projects on the ground.

### THE CHALLENGES OF AT IN ACTION: SMALL-SCALE TECHNOLOGIES IN AFRICA

Africa received much of AID's and ATI's attention. By the mid-1970s, Africa garnered increasing interest among policy makers as the continent became a critical part of the global Cold War.[84] Despite decades of foreign

[80] Russell Train, "Help for the Third World? Keep It Simple," *Los Angeles Times*, December 16, 1976, D7.

[81] Barbara Ward, "Small Is Beautiful," *Los Angeles Times*, September 20, 1977, C7.

[82] Ted Owens, *Sustainable Development: A Research Action Program, A.T. International Progress Report*, September 1980, project Files Pertaining to Appropriate Technology (A.T.) International, folder "Workshop on Sustainable Development," box 5, RG 286, NARA II.

[83] The 1977 overview claimed that the "key question" was "whether any technology, old, new or modified, can be made more effective in achieving the aforementioned development goals." "Annual Budget Submission, FY1979, Appropriate Technology," Agency for International Development, 4, USAID Document Clearinghouse. [Online] Available: http://dec.usaid.gov/index.cfm. Accessed May 8, 2011.

[84] See, for instance, Odd Arne Westad, *The Global Cold War* (Cambridge: Cambridge University Press, 2005), chapters 6 and 7; Piero Gleijeses, *Conflicting Missions:*

aid, much of the continent remained extremely poor, with many countries struggling to develop as quickly as those in the Middle East, East Asia, and Latin America.[85] U.S. policy makers believed ATI would help carry out the New Directions mandate, win the support of local allies, and offer a new approach to development. Instead of helping recipient governments build capital-intensive dams or extensive railroad systems through direct bilateral assistance, the organization offered smaller, labor-intensive technologies in the hopes of nurturing small businesses and building up capacity for generating local economic growth.

ATI quickly began instituting a number of small-scale, environmentally conscious projects using the kind of groups the ITDG had helped to create.[86] In Lesotho, ATI offered $30,000 for a solar energy project. There local residents, under the guidance of indigenous NGOs, designed and constructed solar energy hardware and set up an extension service to facilitate implementation so the "software" side would not be overlooked. In Kenya, ATI covered the operating costs of quasi-governmental organization, with a $93,000 grant to fund start-up technology businesses. On a much smaller scale, it gave $9,000 to a Kenyan company to explore locally sourced charcoal production, and $3,000 to a project designed by Kenyatta University College to devise alternative roofs for homes in Kenyan villages.[87] By the summer of 1980, ATI had funded eighty-one projects in twenty-three developing countries by doling out contracts to various private groups to promote small-scale technologies.[88]

*Havana, Washington, and Africa, 1959–1976* (Chapel Hill: University of North Carolina Press, 2002); Melvyn P. Leffler, *For the Soul of Mankind: The United States, the Soviet Union, and the Cold War* (New York: Hill and Wang, 2007), chapter 4; McVety, *Enlightened Aid*, especially chapters 5–7.

[85] Agency for International Development, "reprinted speech on behalf of Stanley Scott's nomination as Assistant Administrator for Africa," November 10, 1975, Stanley S. Scott Papers, box 2, GFL.

[86] "Intermediate Technology (IT) Organizations in Africa and the Indian Sub-continent," Agency for International Development, 1976, 1, USAID Document Clearinghouse. [Online] Available: http://dec.usaid.gov/index.cfm. Accessed May 8, 2011.

[87] "AT International in Africa: An Evaluation of Projects in Lesotho, Swaziland, Malawi, and Kenya," 12, U.S. Agency for International Development, USAID Document Clearinghouse. [Online] Available: http://dec.usaid.gov/index.cfm. Accessed May 8, 2011. For a review of ATI's early activities, see Roger Moeller et al., "Report on the Current Status and Operations of A.T. International," July 24, 1979, USAID/Bureau for Science and Technology/Office of Forestry; Records Relating to Policy, Plans, and Programs, 1970–1981, folder "SCT Appropriate Technology – A.T. International [2 of 2]," box 17, RG 286, NARA II.

[88] "Action Memorandum for the Acting Assistant Administrator for Development Support," July 7, 1980, USAID/Bureau for Science and Technology/Office of Forestry;

At the same time, AID also incorporated small-scale technologies into its own lending activities, relying heavily on the private sector to carry out its new initiatives. Among others, VITA won a major contract to oversee all such projects in Guinea and another contract to develop and maintain a reference and information organization for AT activities.[89] Such contracts attested to the growing role NGOs played in carrying out the government's lending activities.[90] In total, between 1978 and 1980 AID and ATI awarded just under $1 million in contracts to VITA.[91] By the end of 1979, this infusion of funding allowed the group to consult on well over a hundred requests for advice on projects each month and to help establish seven research centers in the developing world.[92] For an organization that began as a small, off-hours assembly of tinkering engineers, the contracts showed just how intertwined VITA had become with the federal government.

Contractors played a crucial role in helping AID identify countries in the developing world to adopt small-scale technologies. Among a few others, Tanzania emerged as a willing partner to participate in AT projects. Although aid agencies and the Tanzanian government had had a tumultuous relationship during the 1960s, by the 1970s relations had warmed. Moreover, Julius Nyerere, still serving as the country's president, had long been an advocate of local, rural-oriented development programs, and the ITDG established a presence in the nation with his assent.[93]

Records Relating to Policy, Plans, and Programs, 1970–1981, folder "SCT Appropriate Technology – A.T. International [1 of 2]," box 17, RG 286, NARA II.

[89] "Final Report: Guinea Appropriate Technology Project," Submitted February 5, 1987, USAID Document Clearinghouse. [Online] Available: http://dec.usaid.gov/index.cfm. Accessed May 8, 2011; Letter from Michael Snyder, Grant Officer, AID to Henry Norman, Executive Director, VITA, "Grant No. AID/SOD/PDC-C-Ol49, February 26, 1979," "Project Data Sheet: A.T. International II," March 31, 1986, USAID Document Clearinghouse. [Online] Available: http://dec.usaid.gov/index.cfm. Accessed May 8, 2011.

[90] While running VITA, Tom Fox successfully lobbied Congress in 1977 for "a stronger and more centralized support system" for NGOs within AID. Shortly thereafter AID created the Bureau for Private Voluntary Organizations, where Fox later worked. "Foreign Assistance Authorization: International Development Assistance Act of 1977," Hearings before a Subcommittee on Foreign Assistance of the Committee on Foreign Relations, United States Senate, 95th Congress, First Session, March 23–25, 1977 (Washington, DC: GPO, 1977), 184.

[91] Delegate Briefing Book, Guyford Stever, UN Conference on Science and Technology for Development, August 20–31, 1979, 11, box 200, H. Guyford Stever Papers, GFL.

[92] "Agenda Paper for PRC Meeting, S&T and Development, July 13, 1979," 33. Jimmy Carter Presidential Library, RAC Project Number NLC 20-24-7-2-4.

[93] Julius Nyerere, "The Arusha Declaration: Socialism and Self-Reliance," January 29, 1967, reprinted in Julius Nyerere, *Freedom and Socialism: A Selection from Writings and Speeches, 1965–1967* (Dar es Salaam: Oxford University Press, 1968), 231–50;

However, after a decade of his *Ujamaa* programs for national self-sufficiency, Tanzania still ranked, according to the UN, as one of the twenty-five poorest nations in the world.[94] Nyerere needed outside help. During the 1970s, he found it through increasing ties to the ITDG, which visited the country many times, worked with international organizations to set up pilot AT programs, and funded small-scale businesses throughout the country.[95] Nyerere's own philosophy coupled with the legacy of the ITDG's early efforts made Tanzania a perfect place for AID's early programs in small-scale technologies.

In August 1978, a major increase in AT activities occurred when the Tanzanian government and AID signed an agreement for the "Arusha Planning and Village Development Project." A $14.6 million grant enabled local authorities in the Arusha region to build up local capacity for small-scale technology production.[96] For Nyerere, these efforts were critical steps to promote *Ujamaa* and spark the kind of economic growth he desired. For AID, the project represented much of the New Directions mandate in action, as it emphasized self-determination, bottom-up capacity building, and consideration of local ecological and cultural conditions. The agency contracted out responsibilities for most daily activities to a private firm, Development Alternatives, Inc. (DAI).[97] With the full participation of the Tanzanian government, DAI received responsibilities to carry out the initiatives required to build roads, facilitate local

---

Cranford Pratt, *The Critical Phase in Tanzania*; Andrew Coulson, *Tanzania*; Norman O'Neill, "Politics and Development Strategies in Tanzania," in Norman O'Neill and Kemal Mustafa, eds., *Capitalism, Socialism, and the Development Crisis in Tanzania*; 1–21; Yeager, *Tanzania: An African Experiment*. While AT advocates called for community participation and local choice, Nyerere's villagization required centralized, top-down control to spur development. See Scott, *Seeing Like a State*, chapter 7.

[94] "Agency for International Development: Introduction to the FY1974 Development Assistance Program Presentation to the Congress," box 136, Subject Files, Gerald R. Ford Vice Presidential Papers, GFL.

[95] E. F. Schumacher was invited to study Tanzania's development, and he authored a long report on how small-scale technologies could reduce rural poverty. E. F. Schumacher, "Confidential: Economic Development in Tanzania," July 1968, box 9, Schumacher Papers. On projects the ITDG funded, see McRobie, *Small Is Possible*, 238–40; Intermediate Technology Development Limited, Ltd., *Annual Report and Accounts for year ended 30th September 1976*, NA-UK, Records of the British Council [hereinafter cited as BW], 91/226; Intermediate Technology Development Group, Ltd., "Report on Development of Small-Scale Industries in Tanzania," May 1974, NA-UK, OD 63/55.

[96] "Experience with Regional Planning and Village Development in Arusha Region, Tanzania, Vol. I," 3, USAID Document Clearinghouse. [Online] Available: http://dec.usaid.gov/index.cfm. Accessed May 8, 2011.

[97] On the history of DAI, see *The First 40: A History of DAI* (Bethesda, MD: DAI, 2010).

industries, and procure and store commodities using appropriate technologies.[98]

The relationship soon ran into trouble, and bureaucratic problems undermined the technology's implementation. A series of errors in tracking expensive shipments, excessive use of fuel and local vehicles for personal purposes, and persistent "poor communication" by the contracted parties led American officials to "seriously question DAI's credibility" two years into the project. The private firm had to send in its president to Dar es Salaam to apologize to AID's Tanzanian office and "reestablish" a working relationship. After DAI's chief-of-party left, the relationship experienced a brief rapprochement. AID concluded nevertheless that "insufficient contractor overview" was a major problem for the organization.[99] In the end, even DAI acknowledged difficulties in the relationship and claimed "the many accomplishments of this project were the result of the efforts of the government and people of Tanzania."[100]

Throughout the early 1980s, AID struggled to manage ATI's diffuse efforts. Problems similar to those in Tanzania proliferated. A series of reports in the early 1980s detailed many instances of ATI's managerial and technical problems while focusing very little attention on the ecological and cultural consequences of the projects it financed. A 1982 report lauded the ability of private sector initiatives to spur entrepreneurial activity, but recommended that AID should "become more involved in ATI's efforts and provide a supportive environment for the private sector development efforts being funded and managed by ATI." ATI was ultimately limited because of its focus on the local, contingent, and private, with no mechanisms in place to build on or sustain its "successful" projects in any given locale – the kind of "national impact" that AID sought.[101] An evaluation of all the organization's worldwide efforts

[98] "Tanzania: Arusha Planning and Village Development Project, Vol. 1," AID Project Paper No. 621-0143, March 10, 1978, 2, USAID Document Clearinghouse. [Online] Available: http://dec.usaid.gov/index.cfm. Accessed May 8, 2011.

[99] "Arusha Planning and Village Development Project (No. 621-0143) Needs Increased Management Attention," Agency for International Development, August 20, 1982, USAID Document Clearinghouse. [Online] Available: http://dec.usaid.gov/index.cfm. Accessed May 8, 2011.

[100] Experience with Regional Planning and Village Development in Arusha Region, Tanzania, Vol. I, 3.

[101] "AT International in Africa: An Evaluation of Projects in Lesotho, Swaziland, Malawi, and Kenya," 55–62, U.S. Agency for International Development, USAID Document Clearinghouse. [Online] Available: http://dec.usaid.gov/index.cfm. Accessed May 8, 2011. These conclusions echoed concerns that AID officials had had dating back to 1978, along with larger institutional questions about the exact nature of the relationship

echoed such concerns. Without greater central oversight, the innovative program was just "an experiment without an extension mechanism."[102] The murky boundaries between administrative responsibilities also led to unforeseen problems. An audit revealed that ATI established "very lucrative" benefits for its employees along with high salaries for consultants, with the U.S. government left to foot the bill. The audit also suggested that ATI lacked quality project design, effective planning, and administrative oversight.[103] The experimental corporation, these reports all suggested, required greater central coordination and stronger management.

After the evaluations, AID and ATI officials agreed to a new cooperative agreement in 1983. While ATI retained its formal "management independence and operational autonomy and flexibility," the new accord brought with it "substantial AID involvement." AID gained new powers over the public corporation's project approval and authorization process, with greater oversight afforded to the agency's country missions in the developing world. ATI received an additional $23 million, supplemented three years later by an additional grant for $18 million. The reforms "encouraged" the organization to seek more external funds from other sources, but the multi-million dollar grants from the U.S. government kept it solvent during the 1980s.[104]

The new agreement coincided with a slight redirection in ATI's focus. By the mid-1980s, the organization became even less of a promoter of institution building and administrative capacity, the "software" that Schumacher and the ITDG had long stressed. ATI officials instead became enamored with the organization as emblematic of a "venture capital" model of aid.[105] In the early 1980s, the Reagan administration further

between AID and ATI. William Eilers to Henry Arnold, July 27, 1978, USAID/Bureau for Science and Technology/Office of Forestry; Records Relating to Policy, Plans, and Programs, 1970–1981, folder "Appropriate Technology FY 76, FY 77, FY 78 [2 of 3]," box 20, RG 286, NARA II.

[102] "Project Evaluation Summary: A.T. International," United States Agency for International Development, April 1982, i–v, USAID Document Clearinghouse. [Online] Available: http://dec.usaid.gov/index.cfm. Accessed May 8, 2011.

[103] USAID, Office of Audit, "Appropriate Technology, International," February 13, 1981, USAID/Bureau for Science and Technology/Office of Forestry; Records Relating to Policy, Plans, and Programs, 1970–1981, folder "A.T. International," box 16, RG 286, NARA II.

[104] "Project Data Sheet: A.T. International II," March 31, 1986, USAID Document Clearinghouse. [Online] Available: http://dec.usaid.gov/index.cfm. Accessed May 8, 2011.

[105] "Attachment A: Background," Appropriate Technology International, Quarterly Meeting of the Board of Trustees, Meeting Minutes. Project Files Pertaining to Appropriate Technology (A.T.) International, box 5, RG 286, NARA II; "Promoting Appropriate Technological Change in Small-Scale Enterprises: An Evaluation of

encouraged AID to channel its resources toward the private sectors of developing nations instead of their governments. Many in the administration saw ATI as a key element of this process.[106] This shift in purpose spurred more aggressive risk-taking and a greater focus on promoting entrepreneurial activity. Official documentation of the era rarely described small-scale technologies as a holistic approach to development that encouraged grassroots participation and ecological sensitivity. Rather, such tools became viewed solely as a way to spur private commercial enterprise in developing countries.

An example from Kenya illuminates this trend. In 1985, ATI doled out funds to three organizations to initiate production of fuel-efficient, ceramic jikos, wide stoves that originated in India but became commonplace in the broader Indian Ocean world. It directly financed a business association, KENGO (Kenyan Energy Non-Governmental Organizations), which in turn contracted to a local company, Miaki Jikos. Miaki Jikos oversaw the stove production, and worked closely with a third firm, Wagithuku and Associates, who received additional funds from ATI and assisted in the design and management of credit systems for the small manufacturers identified by Miaki Jikos.[107]

The project sought to commercialize and expand production of a highly regarded small-scale technology project AID had carried out over the previous half-decade. At the start of the 1980s, much of East and Central Africa faced what observers dubbed a woodfuel "crisis." Rampant deforestation and inefficient use of wood had greatly sapped a

Appropriate Technology International" (Washington, DC: Agency for International Development, 1986), v. Project Files Pertaining to Appropriate Technology (A.T.) International, folder PRE Project Files, FY94 AID Evaluation Special Study #45 Item No.: 07010 Permanent, box 6, RG 286, NARA II; "AT International: Annual Report 1990," 11, Project Files Pertaining to Appropriate Technology (A.T.) International, box 5, RG 286, NARA II.

[106] Agency for International Development, "Economic Growth and the Third World: A Report on the AID Private Enterprise Initiative" (Washington, DC: Agency for International Development, n.d.), 39–40, White House Office of Records Management, FG 342-03, Folder Case No. 342453 to Case No. 353048CU, George H. W. Bush Presidential Library [hereinafter cited as GBL]; "Promoting Appropriate Technological Change in Small-Scale Enterprises: An Evaluation of Appropriate Technology International" (Washington, DC: Agency for International Development, 1986), x. Project Files Pertaining to Appropriate Technology (A.T.) International, folder PRE Project Files, FY94 AID Evaluation Special Study #45 Item No.: 07010 Permanent, box 6, RG 286, NARA II.

[107] "Project Plan: Ceramic-Lined Jikos," 2–3. Project Files Pertaining to Appropriate Technology (A.T.) International, folder B12 Kenya Ceramic Lined Jikos PRAC 5/10/85, box 3, RG 286, NARA II.

major energy source (wood energy accounted for an estimated 70 percent of total household energy consumption in Kenya and up to 95 percent of total energy use in Tanzania).[108] AID created a program to build jikos that relied on local materials, local labor, and greatly conserved wood use. It was, in many ways, an archetypal project Schumacher would have had in mind. The ITDG, in fact, provided the design and testing for the jikos model that ultimately went into production.[109]

The jikos project succeeded insofar as it served the immediate purposes of its two main sponsors. For AID, the jikos successfully conserved energy and created a "self-sustaining production capability," a key tenet for the organization that was increasingly seeking to fund projects that were financially sustainable. Likewise, the project satisfied the main objectives of the Kenyan government to generate employment and income. It served the users, too, since the stoves reduced charcoal expenses, offered effective training courses and demonstration workshops that allowed people to decide whether the devices fit their needs, and were widely available through normal commercial channels. In this sense, the project made equally effective use of hardware and software.[110]

Not content to keep the project locally focused, AID officials hoped to use it as a springboard for similar stove-production businesses elsewhere. The one major outstanding issue, AID noted, was that the availability of the jikos remained "inadequate for the potential market both in Nairobi and elsewhere."[111] Although the project served the local needs of consumers in Nairobi, AID sought to commercialize it further. To do so, they turned to ATI to take over the project in 1985.

Under ATI's control, however, the project soon foundered. A number of "technical and management difficulties" scuttled the project from the start. The organizations tasked with carrying out the production of the stove – Miaki Jikos and Wagithuku Associates – proved to be unreliable. Of the nine grantees ATI had assisted in 1985, by mid-1986 two had not

---

[108] On the woodfuel crisis, see Phil O'Keefe, "Fuel for the People, Fuelwood in the Third World," *Ambio*, Vol. 12, No. 2 (1983), 115–17; Robin Mearns and Gerald Leach, *Energy for Livelihoods: Putting People Back into Africa's Woodfuel Crisis*, Gatekeeper Series No. 1 (London: International Institute for Environment and Development, 1989).

[109] Mike Jones, "Energy Efficient Stoves in East Africa: An Assessment of the Kenya Ceramic Jiko (Stove) Program," January 31, 1989, USAID Document Clearinghouse. [Online] Available: http://dec.usaid.gov/index.cfm. Accessed October 9, 2011.

[110] Eric Hyman, "The Experience with Improved Charcoal and Wood Stoves for Households and Institutions in Kenya," December 19, 1985, v. USAID Document Clearinghouse. [Online] Available: http://dec.usaid.gov/index.cfm. Accessed October 9, 2011.

[111] Jones, "Energy Efficient Stoves in East Africa," i–ii.

started production and three had gone out of business within four months. Only three remained operative after six months. Most of the producers receiving funds lacked the technical knowledge necessary to build the stoves, AID evaluators explained.[112] The emphasis on contracting out to local companies, many of which proved unable to replicate the stoves, prevented the technologies from being made in sufficient quantities and with satisfactory quality from the start.

Even more troubling, it was unclear future production was possible without an increase in technical knowledge. Evaluators noted that the basic problem of the project was "a scarcity of local technical and promotional capacity" that "results in the need to use entrepreneurs and producers as technical resources, which concomitantly produces both a conflict of interest and incompleteness and/or inadequacy of technical inputs."[113] It was difficult for local businesses to reproduce the stoves well, to disseminate information about them properly, and provide customer support. "The lack of sufficient local institutional and financial capability" to guide the production, implementation, and use of the stoves were the two most "severe constraints in the introduction of new technology," evaluators claimed.[114] Put another way, the project lacked adequate software. ATI officially suspended the project in mid-1986, and cancelled it shortly thereafter.[115] Although small-scale technologies had become a component of developing lending in U.S. assistance policy to Africa, faulty implementation and misguided emphasis on the ability of local entrepreneurs to replicate, commercialize, and greatly expand the production of such technologies threatened to undermine their potential ecological, economic, or social benefits.

### CONCLUSION: THE LEGACY AND LIMITS OF APPROPRIATE TECHNOLOGY

Between E. F. Schumacher's early critiques of large-scale technological systems and the evolution of ATI in the 1980s, appropriate technologies became a significant part of international development. Reformers such as Schumacher had believed that using appropriate technologies would inspire communities around the globe to rethink the ways in which they

---

[112] Mike Jones, "Energy Efficient Stoves in East Africa: An Assessment of the Kenya Ceramic Jiko (Stove) Program," 74–5.
[113] Ibid.
[114] Ibid., 85.
[115] Ibid., 74.

pursued economic growth and social transformation. The use of small-scale technologies symbolized the development lending communities' turn away from big, centralized infrastructure projects. Barbara Ward asserted that Schumacher's work in promoting this shift had "revolutionized the policies of international lending agencies and – though more slowly – of governments throughout the world."[116] Although hyperbolic, Ward's comment rightfully noted that small-scale technologies were a major component of the growing number of bottom-up, small-scale, basic needs strategies that prevailed in the development community during the 1970s. They were also a fixture of aid programs thereafter, and featured prominently in the revival of decentralized community development approaches of the 1990s and the wildly popular efforts to encourage small businesses through "micro-finance" during the 2000s.[117]

Despite the popularity of small-scale technologies in foreign aid, there were limitations on how effective such tools could be in reshaping the development process. Although a few developing countries, such as Tanzania, had warmly embraced AT, many leaders from the Global South still sought major, large-scale technologies geared toward national development premised on industrialization and worried that lending agencies would reduce their support for traditional technology transfers. Such fears became clear at the 1979 United Nations Conference on Science and Technology for Development. At the gathering, the Group of 77 (G-77) of developing countries "reacted negatively" to the U.S. delegation's emphasis on small-scale technologies, fearing that excessive sponsorship of small-scale technologies would keep them "backward."[118] Third World leaders, according to one observer, interpreted advocacy for AT as "an attempt by the western countries to undermine the industrial muscle" that Third World countries had sought. The G-77 supported the notion of increasing their capabilities to choose which technologies best served their needs, but they wanted to ensure that advanced industrial technologies were available on better terms and that they could build up their own national capacity for constructing such large-scale technologies.[119]

[116] Quoted in "Quotes from the Press," *Appropriate Technology*, Vol. 4, No. 3 (November 1977), 3.

[117] On the recent revival of interest in community-based development, see Immerwahr, *Quests for Community*, conclusion.

[118] "UNCSTD Resource Position Paper: Appropriate Technology," 1–4, box 201, Stever Papers, Ford Library.

[119] Anil Agarwal, "United Nations Conference on Science and Technology for Development (UNCSTD)," *Environmental Conservation*, Vol. 7, No. 1 (Spring 1980), 77.

The U.S. delegation to the conference responded by playing down the significance of small-scale technologies in the overall scheme of global development. U.S. delegates assured the G-77 that AT programs were only "an important element" of a broader development strategy, not replacements for older development models. They emphasized the "capital-saving" nature of such devices in the fields of agriculture, small industry, and energy.[120] In response, many developing countries acknowledged the possibility of using less costly technologies to help ease rural unemployment problems and increase agricultural production, but only if such tools did not impede their ability to pursue industrial growth or further the power of multinational corporations in the global market for technological goods. AT became only a small part of the conference, with few policy makers believing that it was a silver bullet capable of reinventing the development process or a comprehensive, holistic critique of modern industrial society, as its advocates had once hoped. It ended up as just another method to draw upon from the ever-growing pool of development approaches.[121]

The limitations of small technologies were also apparent in how foreign aid agencies came to rely on them as engines of economic growth, entrepreneurial activity, and commercial expansion. In a report commissioned by AID, the World Bank, and the OECD, George McRobie, Schumacher's close associate, and two colleagues stated that the movement had four basic aspects. AT was "by the people"; it was "location specific"; it was predicated on a "holistic" philosophy; and it was "futuristic" in the sense of prizing the sustainability of local communities well into future generations. In addition, AT had three clear goals: "environmental" (saving energy, reducing resource use, being "in harmony with local ecology"), "social" ("meeting basic human needs" and "giving power to the people"), and "economic" ("meeting local needs," "reducing economic inequality," and producing from local resources for local consumption).[122] In short, to its founders and environmental advocates the

[120] "UNCSTD Resource Position Paper: Appropriate Technology," 1–4, box 201, Stever Papers, Ford Library.

[121] Department of State telegram, "UN Conference on Science and Technology for Development (UNCSTD): Summary and Appraisal," October 1979, Stever Papers, box 201, GFL. On AT and the conference more broadly, see Romesh K. Diwan and Dennis Livingston, eds., *Alternative Development Strategies and Appropriate Technology: Science Policy for an Equitable World Order* (New York: Pergamon Press, 1979).

[122] George McRobie, William N. Ellis, Kenneth Darrow, and Frederick W. Smith, *Appropriate Technology Developments in the United States and Their Relevance to the Third World* (Paris: Development Centre of the Organisation for Economic Cooperation and Development, 1979), 5–7.

appropriate technology movement was about empowering communities to choose through representative organizations their own desired paths of development, and trusting that those choices, if based on the use of local resources, would lead to an ecologically sustainable way of life. Many environmentalists still share this view.[123]

The meaning that small-scale technologies had been given through ATI and AID, however, contrasted sharply with this holistic approach. Emphasis on project replication ("replicability," in ATI parlance) undermined the fact that being location-specific was what made such technologies appropriate in the first place. Commercialization sought profit making as much as satisfying specific community needs. Replication and commercialization both undermined the movement's emphasis on software – creating local institutions to guide the selection, adoption, and implementation of need-based technologies. AT advocates worried about this growing lack of emphasis on institution building in the mid-1980s.[124] Evaluations of ATI's overall performance also noted the trend. "The implementation of the replication strategy is a departure for ATI from its mandated style of responding to local needs," claimed evaluators. "The danger with new approach," the evaluators explained, "is its overemphasis on hardware elements . . . to the neglect of innovative soft technologies necessary for successful adoption and sustained utilization."[125] Without effective institutions to guide the choice and adoption of new technologies, ATI's efforts threatened to have little lasting or sustainable influence.

ATI faced limitations that derived from its institutional imperatives, as well. The need to give out grants, earn high returns, and satisfy the

---

[123] Most NGOs today have incorporated the principles of AT into their activities. The IUCN, for instance, has long stressed appropriate technology as a key component of how it tries to "harmonize environmental conservation with economic development." See, for instance, *IUCN Eighteenth General Assembly, Perth, Australia, 28 November–5 December 1990: Proceedings* (Morges, Switzerland: IUCN, 1990), 82–3. Bruce Rich, a leading environmental lawyer, celebrated ATI as an example of how development assistance should seek to empower the poor and conserve scarce environmental resources at the same time. "A Window into ATI," n.d. Project Files Pertaining to Appropriate Technology (A.T.) International, box 5, RG 286, NARA II.

[124] Nicholas Jéquier, "Appropriate Technology: The Challenge of the Next Generation," *Proceedings of the Royal Society of London. Series B, Biological Sciences*, Vol. 209, 1174 (July 28, 1980), 7–14.

[125] "Promoting Appropriate Technological Change in Small-Scale Enterprises: An Evaluation of Appropriate Technology International," H-4 (Washington, DC: Agency for International Development, 1986), v. Project Files Pertaining to Appropriate Technology (A.T.) International, folder PRE Project Files, FY94 AID Evaluation Special Study #45 Item No. 07010 Permanent, box 6, RG 286, NARA II.

objectives AID laid out in cooperative agreements contributed to the organization's need to focus on replication and commercialization. While serving on ATI's board of directors, Tom Fox, the former VITA director, argued that the organization's staffers had focused too much on replication to satisfy AID's shifting requirements. Fox warned that ATI had to resist the urge to "rush projects to contract" just to meet targeted objectives.[126] The very fact that the organization's directives came from Washington, and not local communities, also proved troublesome. ATI, two writers in *The New Republic* worried, ended up as just a "new boondoggle" for its advocates, not a method to revolutionize development.[127] Although the organization had been founded as an innovative institution supposedly free of bureaucratic red tape, its commercial motivations and government ties bound it as firmly to Washington, DC, as to its target communities in the developing world.

While major institutions used the idea of small-scale technologies in different ways than environmentalists had envisioned, NGOs promoting the tools did achieve closer connections to governing institutions as a result of their advocacy efforts. The use of small-scale technologies in U.S. development policy derived from key institutional developments – lobbying and contracting – as much as it did from intellectual shifts in thinking about the relationship between technology, environment, and development. This coevolution between NGOs and the state highlighted an important fact for activists looking to reshape development policy in other ways, too. The AT movement sought to reform development by challenging experts in lending institutions over the ways in which they conceptualized the role of technology in spurring economic and social change – or how development occurred on the ground. As some activists focused on technology, another set of NGOs challenged development agencies over whether to fund development projects at all. These groups hoped to make development agencies publicly accountable for their effects on the environment by dramatically reforming how projects were conceptualized, assessed, and funded in the first place.

---

[126] "Minutes of Quarterly Meeting of the Board of Trustees, September 11, 1985, Appropriate Technology International," in "Quarterly Meeting: ATI's Board of Trustees, December 17, 1985," 2. Project Files Pertaining to Appropriate Technology (A.T.) International, box 5, RG 286, NARA II.

[127] Bode and Von Lazar, "Appropriate Technology," 11–12. For other criticisms, see Witold Rybczysnki, *Paper Heroes: A Review of Appropriate Technology* (Garden City, NY: Anchor Books, 1980).

# 5

## Leveraging the Lenders: The Quest for Environmental Impact Statements in the United States and the World Bank

On September 29, 1986, two seasoned rock climbers affiliated with the Rainforest Action Network, an activist non-governmental organization (NGO) founded by firebrand activist Randy "Hurricane" Hayes, scaled the walls of a building adjacent to the World Bank and IMF offices in Washington, DC. As they neared the roof, they unfurled a giant banner emblazoned with the phrase "World Bank destroys tropical rain forests." The incident occurred amid a tense campaign against the World Bank that sought, among other demands, to make the organization produce detailed assessments of the environmental effects for each project it funded. While the bank was already required to do so, environmentalists charged that the reports had been weak, ineffective, or ignored. Activists argued that the bank needed to adopt stricter regulations and review procedures that would allow more thorough public oversight of its activities. Bank officials rejected the charges. They claimed that a more elaborate system of assessments would stifle the lending process and ultimately interfere with the right of countries receiving aid to pursue development on their own terms. "We're dealing with governments that are proud of their sovereignty," a bank spokesperson said in response to the protest banner. "What is a priority in Washington," he continued, was "not the case" in countries yearning for big projects to spur economic growth.[1] He implied that adopting robust review procedures for all projects would unjustly undermine other nations' sovereignty in the name of environmental imperatives defined by activists in the United States.

[1] Patrice Gaines-Carter, "Environmental Protest Reaches New Heights," *The Washington Post*, September 30, 1986, B3.

The protests against the World Bank over environmental assessments marked another significant reform effort by activists to reconcile environmental concerns with development practice. While promoting appropriate technologies represented one way that NGOs attempted to reform development policy, environmentalists also sought to alter how lending agencies funded projects in the first place. In particular, over the 1970s and 1980s a new generation of NGOs first pressured the U.S. government and then the World Bank to incorporate formal environmental reviews – particularly environmental impact statements (EIS) – in the project approval process.[2]

At first glance, the procedural shift generated by the presence of an environmental assessment may seem arcane, dryly technical, or insignificant. The EIS was a bureaucratic reform that required ecologists or other scientific authorities to review and assess the potential environmental impact of any proposed development project. In many instances, environmental reviews could not end a potentially damaging project, because policy makers often overrode or dismissed assessments altogether. However, officials within NGOs placed tremendous significance on this procedural reform, for two main reasons.

For one, the requirement to produce ecological knowledge about a proposed developed project marked a dramatic shift from past practice. NGO members had long protested how destructive development projects wreaked havoc on the natural world. Environmental protection was low on the list of priorities of development agencies and many national planning agencies alike. Injecting some degree of ecological knowledge into the process thus represented a tremendous check on the power of institutions and offered an alternative way of understanding the value of a development project. No longer assessed solely by how they met the political and economic needs of a nation, development projects, with an EIA attached, highlighted that economic development often came with unintended and potentially devastating ecological consequences. Development was often understood as encouraging endless economic growth; the EIS highlighted that there were necessary limitations to such growth, to alert developers of the potential pitfalls that resulted from the projects they funded.

Second, although policy makers often found ways to skirt environmental regulations, the presence of an EIA enabled NGOs to place an institutional

---

[2] There is distinction between an impact statement and impact assessment, which I explain later in this chapter. I use the phrase "environmental review" as an umbrella term for a formal process that identifies the environmental effects of development projects.

check on reticent agencies. Formal environmental reviews offered legal recourse for NGOs with experience and access to mount formal challenges against agencies that were unresponsive or outright dismissive of the new regulations. By the mid-1970s, newer NGOs that focused on litigation, such as the Environmental Defense Fund (EDF) and the Natural Resources Defense Council (NRDC), used their professional status and legal expertise to become influential interest groups of this type.[3] As public interest law firms, these groups were in a position, both institutionally and financially, to lobby major governing bodies to adopt environmental reviews. Likewise, they could sue agencies or exert political pressure through Congress if an institution failed to comply with these standards. By the 1970s, this "mandate and sue" style of governance, in which private organizations checked the power of public bodies by holding them accountable to narrow legal statutes, flourished in the environmental sector. New policies created new constituencies, and the National Environmental Policy Act (NEPA) opened up opportunities for NGOs to enforce environmental regulations through lawsuits.[4] Private environmental groups pressured the U.S. foreign policy apparatus and the World Bank by leveraging their technical knowledge, financial clout, and professional credibility to ensure that if these institutions willfully ignored environmental costs, they would face consequences for their inaction.

From the mid-1970s through the late 1980s, NGOs such as the EDF and the NRDC launched major campaigns against both the U.S. government's

---

[3] On professional environmental interest groups, see Gottlieb, *Forcing the Spring*, chapter 4; Dunlap; Ronald G. Shaiko, *Voices and Echoes for the Environment: Public Interest Representation in the 1990s and Beyond* (New York: Columbia University Press, 1999); Christopher J. Bosso, *Environment, Inc.: From Grassroots to Beltway* (Lawrence: University of Kansas Press, 2005).

[4] On this regulatory transformation, see, for instance, Shep Melnick, "From Tax-and-Spend to Mandate-and-Sue: Liberalism after the Great Society," in Sidney M. Milkis and Jerome M. Mileur, eds., *The Great Society and the High Tide of Liberalism* (Amherst: University of Massachusetts Press, 2005), 387–410; R. Shep Melnick, *Regulation and the Courts* (Washington, DC: Brookings Institution Press, 1983). For an excellent case study of the rise of public interest law firms and welfare policy, see Martha F. Davis, *Brutal Need: Lawyers and the Welfare Rights Movement, 1960–1973* (New Haven: Yale University Press, 1995). On the rise of such expert interest groups and federal governance, see Balogh, *Chain Reaction*. Political scientist Quinn Mulroy shows how the regulatory process developed in the late 1960s and 1970s relied on private litigators. Mulroy, *Public Regulation through Private Litigation*. See also Sean Farhang, *The Litigation State: Public Regulation and Private Lawsuits in the United States* (Princeton: Princeton University Press, 2010). On the legal innovations of NEPA, see Frederick R. Anderson and Robert H. Daniels, *NEPA in the Courts: A Legal Analysis of the National Environmental Policy Act* (Washington, DC: Resources for the Future, Inc., 1973).

foreign aid agencies and the World Bank. Working with allies from within the Council on Environmental Quality (CEQ), NGOs mounted successful litigation against the U.S. Agency for International Development (AID) and the Export-Import Bank. During these legal campaigns, they raised profound questions about the extraterritorial impact of domestic U.S. environmental law that led to a massive expansion of federal regulations on development lending and a concomitant rise in the use of private litigation to enforce the new rules. Likewise, by culling together support from sympathetic individuals within the bank's fledging environmental office and allies in Congress who could threaten funding for the bank, NGOs gained leverage to pressure bank officials to reform its entire lending process. By the time of the bank's major reorganization of the late 1980s, it was clear that American interest groups had reshaped the international institution. In both the AID and the World Bank cases, NGOs cultivated new paths to power.

Thus, the NGO campaigns were successful, insofar as they resulted in the U.S. government and the World Bank agreeing to reform their lending procedures by incorporating environmental concerns. In both cases, environmental activists raised profound questions about how far environmental standards set in the United States should interfere with national sovereignty, and whether unelected, non-state actors could shape how development institutions lent aid to recipient nations. The answers to such questions engendered great debate, and they still do. Rarely did these reforms spark a wider ecological ethos or appreciation for the significance of environmental protection. Development aspirations, by and large, continued to outpace environmental constraints. However, the EIA provided a new legal and political tool that allowed powerful NGOs to hamstring governing institutions from funding environmentally damaging development projects as easily as they had in earlier decades.

## THE ORIGINS OF IMPACT STATEMENTS

The origins of environmental impact statements lie in the experiences of Western environmentalists in the developing world. One of the earliest innovators of environmental review was an academic named Lynton Keith Caldwell. In 1954, Caldwell left his position as a professor of American politics at Syracuse University to take a job with the United Nations (UN) Technical Assistance Program. Over the next decade, he worked with the UN's development programs in Turkey and the Middle East. Through these experiences he came to realize that development projects too often resulted in debilitating and dangerous unintended consequences because of their neglect for environmental considerations. He eventually returned to the United States, bringing these insights to bear on his study of American politics. In 1963, he published an essay on the need for a comprehensive national policy to coordinate action on all activities that affected "the environment." His article proved influential, helping to create the subfield of environmental policy among political scientists.[5]

Caldwell quickly worked to translate his ideas into policy. In 1968, while consulting for the Senate Committee on Interior or Insular Affairs, he drafted a blueprint strategy for a national environmental program. Negotiating with supportive parties in Congress, Caldwell inserted his ideas into a bill. After extensive debates and hearing, Congress passed the bill in 1970 as the National Environmental Policy Act (NEPA). It was the most comprehensive set of environmental laws yet established anywhere in the world.[6]

One of the most important aspects of the new law was its mandate of formal environmental reviews. The law required all federal agencies that funded development projects to prepare two major types of review. First, agencies needed to produce an "environmental assessment" (EA) of a proposed project. If this initial assessment determined that the project under question might have a significant impact on the environment, the law required the agency to draft a much more thorough "environmental impact statement" (EIS). The purpose of the EIS was to identify the environmental costs of a project and propose less destructive alternatives. Crucially, NEPA required that before taking any action, an agency had to circulate the draft EIS for external review by "the public," broadly defined. This allowed for input and challenges by private citizens to discuss the potential impact of projects or propose alternatives.[7]

In practice, this stipulation enabled powerful NGOs to file lawsuits on behalf of the public interest to enforce regulations that the Environmental Protection Agency (EPA) or Council on Environmental Quality (CEQ)

---

[5] Lynton K. Caldwell, "Planned Control of the Biophysical Environment," CAG Occasional Paper, 1964, reprinted in Robert V. Bartlett and James N. Gladden, eds., *Environment as a Focus for Public Policy* (College Station: Texas A&M University Press, 1995), 55. See also Robertson, "'This Is the American Earth'," 581–3.

[6] On NEPA in general, see Andrews, *Managing the Environment, Managing Ourselves*, chapter 14; Lynton Keith Caldwell, *The National Environmental Policy Act: An Agenda for the Future* (Bloomington: Indiana University Press, 1998); Richard A. Liroff, *A National Policy for the Environment: NEPA and Its Aftermath* (Bloomington: Indiana University Press, 1976).

[7] Andrews, *Managing the Environment, Managing Ourselves*, 287–8.

could not do for lack of staffing, time, or financial resources. It thus gave to non-state actors a legal way to check the power of federal agencies. NEPA, in this sense, was transformative. No legislation had simultaneously opened the door for potential regulation through private litigation and mandated such open access and transparency on the government's decision-making process.[8] Eventually replicated in nearly a hundred countries, Caldwell claimed that it was probably "the most imitated U.S. law in history."[9]

NEPA generated a staggering amount of legal activity. In the law's first nine years, federal agencies prepared more than 11,000 impact statements. Over 1,000 were litigated to some extent. About 20 percent of agencies sued were enjoined by the courts, "normally to halt the action pending changes in the proposal or at least in the statement." By the late 1980s, the numbers of impact statements averaged about 4,000 to 5,000 each year, plus some 50,000 impact assessments, or preliminary reports, to determine whether or not to prepare a formal impact statement. NEPA was a bureaucratic revolution that gave private actors a prominent role in governing the environment.[10] Its focus on impact statement analysis likewise provided international NGOs with a powerful new tool to make lending agencies accountable for their effects on the environment.

## SHIFTING THE BURDEN OF PROOF

As Caldwell was formulating the ideas for the new law, international environmental NGOs were also beginning to laud such procedures as valuable tools to rein in international development practices. Decades of frustrated experience in the developing world had demonstrated the challenges of persuading young leaders in developing nations to resist the urge and desire to develop in destructive ways. Accordingly, many NGO

---

[8] Ibid.

[9] Caldwell, *The National Environmental Policy Act*, 98. Throughout the 1970s, the UN's Economic Commission for Europe (ECE) and the UNEP organized international efforts to standardize and measure the effectiveness of impact assessments. See Amasa S. Bishop to David A. Munro, December 29, 1976, G.X 34/26 "Co-operation between ECE and the United Nations Environment Programme (UNEP) – Jacket 2," UNOG Registry Collection. The UNEP published guidelines on impact assessments throughout the 1970s and 1980s. UNEP Governing Council, "Goals and Principles of Environmental Impact Assessment," 1987. So, too, did the IIED and the IUCN. John Horberry, *Environmental Guidelines Survey: An Analysis of Environmental Procedures and Guidelines Governing Development Aid* (Washington, DC, and London, UK: International Institute for Environment and Development, 1983).

[10] Andrews, *Managing the Environment, Managing Ourselves*, 287.

officials thought that reforming the major agencies that lent developmental aid would generate quicker and more lasting results.

Environmentalists mobilized around the issue of environmental review for development projects in the late 1960s. At the seminal 1968 conference on environment and development in Airlie House, Virginia, renowned American geographer Gilbert F. White highlighted the need to redress the "serious and general pattern of planning omissions" in development agencies, particularly the "nonexistent or inadequate techniques for ecological investigations," and helped generate consensus on the need for impact statements.[11] Shortly after the conference, the IUCN embraced the cause of promoting environmental review at its Tenth General Assembly meeting in New Delhi in late 1969 to ensure that development projects would be "planned in accordance with ecological principles."[12] A similar meeting, sponsored by the IUCN and the Conservation Foundation, followed in the Food and Agricultural Organization's (FAO) Rome office in the summer of 1970.[13] Participants at the Rome meeting tasked Raymond Dasmann, the IUCN's senior ecologist, to produce a guidebook for development planners. Drafted over the following two years with the aid of John Milton from the Conservation Foundation, Dasmann's book, entitled *Ecological Principles for Economic Development*, endorsed the use of formal environmental reviews.[14] Dasmann sought to "shift the burden of proof" from the environmentalists to the developers in order to

[11] Gilbert F. White, "Organizing Scientific Investigations to Deal with Environmental Impacts," in Farvar and P. Milton, eds., *The Careless Technology*, 915.

[12] Gerardo Budowski and Frank G. Nicholls, "Report on the Work of the Union Since the Tenth General Assembly," in *Proceedings: Eleventh General Assembly*, Banff, Alberta, Canada, 11–16 September 1971 1972, IUCN Publications New Series, Supplementary Paper No. 40E (Morges, Switzerland: IUCN, 1972), 96.

[13] "Ecology in Development Programmes: an IUCN Project," *IUCN Bulletin*, Vol. 2, No. 17 (October/December 1970), 141; International Union for the Conservation of Nature and Natural Resources and Conservation Foundation, "The Use of Ecological Principles in Economic Development Planning," Report of Working Group on Environmental Considerations in Development Projects, FAO Headquarters, Rome, Italy, September 24–25, 1970, i. IUCN Library.

[14] The project was funded by a $50,000 grant from the Swedish International Development Authority. "Swedish Agency Grants $50,000 to Support IUCN/Conservation Foundation Report," *IUCN Bulletin*, Vol. 3, No. 4 (April 1972), 15. Raymond F. Dasmann, John P. Milton, and Peter H. Freeman, *Ecological Principles for Economic Development* (London: John Wiley & Sons Ltd., 1973); D. Hackett, K. Hale, and K. Smith, "The Role of the Ecologist in Environmental Planning, Development and Management," a study for the Environmental Planning Commission of IUCN, December 1973, IUCN Library; *Annual Report of the International Union for the Conservation of Nature and Natural Resources for 1972* (Morges, Switzerland: IUCN), 14.

show that a development project would meet ecological criteria before moving forward.[15] IUCN and WWF officials followed up the release of Dasmann's book by holding multiple conferences "designed to lead to the formulation of practical guidelines" for states and international institutions to adopt impact statements in their planning.[16] If implemented, environmental reviews would become the primary mechanism to make development agencies incorporate ecological considerations in lending and thus to become accountable for their effects on the environment.

In the early years in which impact statements came to take hold in the environmental community, most development lenders adopted some form of formal review process, albeit slowly and reluctantly. AID, as a federal organization, agreed to take environmental factors into consideration for its larger capital and industrial projects, publishing a few short circulars to its missions on assessment guidelines in NEPA's wake. To oversee the process, the agency announced the creation of an "Environment and Development Committee" in May 1971.[17] AID officials, however, were hesitant to comply with NEPA's stringent requirements. They submitted a legal memo to Congress in May 1970, claiming that NEPA applied only to the environment "of the nation." In this interpretation, AID-funded projects abroad, save for major capital and industrial projects, would not require any review. Debates in Congress over the applicability of NEPA to extraterritorial programs and projects continued during 1971 and 1972, but with no resolution. AID had made a few minor changes, but by and large it positioned itself outside the bounds of NEPA and thus beyond environmental reviews.[18]

*[handwritten margin note: Does NEPA only apply to AID?]*

---

[15] Raymond Dasmann, "Beams and Motes," *IUCN Bulletin*, Vol. 4, No. 9 (September 1973), 37.

[16] Gerardo Budowski, "Should Ecology Conform to Politics?" *IUCN Bulletin*, Vol. 5, No. 12 (December 1974), 47. Prince Bernhard of the Netherlands, the nominal head of the WWF-International office, wrote to officials throughout the United Nations to "make provision for ecological validation of development projects." Prince Bernhard to Amasa Bishop, January 20, 1971, G.X 34/7 "Environment: Environmental Work Undertaken by Other Organizations – Jacket 1," UNOG Archives.

[17] In August 1970, Manual Circular 1221.2, entitled "Consideration of Environmental Aspects of U.S. Assisted Capital Projects" was issued, followed in September 1971 by Manual Circular 1214.1, "Procedures for Environmental Review of Capital Projects." U.S. AID, Environmental Procedures, 36 Fed. Reg. 22,686 (1971). AID's Committee on Environment and Development, established in May 1971, oversaw its response to NEPA.

[18] Legal Memorandum Prepared by the Office of the Legal Advisor, Department of State, 1970, in *Administration of the National Environmental Policy Act, Part 2, Appendix to Hearings before the Subcommittee on Fisheries and Wildlife Conservation* (Washington, DC: GPO, 1971), 548–57. "Environment and Development Committee Established by AID," Department of State *Bulletin*, August 9, 1971, 158; John Horberry, "The

In addition, the World Bank made changes in its lending policies at the same time. Alongside World Bank President Robert McNamara's initiative to focus bank activities on poverty alleviation, in 1970 the institution adopted many environmental reforms. McNamara announced that all projects would undergo an environmental review, and he established a new environmental office to oversee the process. Yet the changes had little effect. The environmental office lacked funds and personnel necessary to review the many projects in the bank's portfolio. Moreover, bank officials routinely dismissed environmental concerns, as they tended to maintain a hostile attitude toward the new office. By the mid-1970s it was clear that such changes would have a negligible effect on the actual functioning of the World Bank.[19]

In both institutions, reform efforts were largely cosmetic, poorly funded, or inadequately staffed. Early environmental reviews had minimal influence over lending policy. Yet NGOs kept close watch over implementation of new procedures. When governing organizations failed to comply, NGOs leapt into action with two elaborate campaigns, one against the U.S. government in the 1970s and the other against the World Bank in the 1980s.

## "LOWERING THE BOOM" ON AID

When NEPA went into effect, officials in the CEQ and in major environmental NGOs expected all federal agencies to produce impact assessments for the projects they funded. Many agencies, however, defied the new law.[20] Resistance was especially strong among agencies that focused on foreign affairs – AID, the Department of Defense (DOD), the State Department (DOS), and the Export-Import Bank (Eximbank). AID and the Eximbank were especially reluctant to adopt impact assessments for projects with an "extraterritorial" impact, or those pursued far beyond

Accountability of Development Assistance Agencies: The Case of Environmental Policy," *Ecology Law Quarterly*, Vol. 12 (1985), 840–1; Gary Igal Strausberg, "The National Environmental Policy Act and the Agency for International Development," *International Lawyer*, Vol. 7, No. 1 (1973), 53–5.

[19] Robert Wade, "Greening the Bank: The Struggle over the Environment, 1970–1995," in Devesh Kapur, John P. Lewis, and Richard Webb, eds., *The World Bank: Its First Half Century, Vol. 2: Perspectives* (Washington, DC: Brookings Institution Press, 1997), 611–734.

[20] See Matthew J. Lindstrom and Zachary A. Smith, *The National Environmental Policy Act: Judicial Misconstruction, Legislative Indifference, and Executive Neglect* (College Station, TX: Texas A&M University Press, 2001).

U.S. shores. It was unclear whether NEPA contained within it formal regulations for such activities. Many agencies assumed the law did not apply to projects with effects abroad. In addition, many agencies wanted to avoid the time and costs of preparing an environmental review for every project they funded and worried that adopting strict environmental regulations would hinder relations with foreign governments.[21]

AID officials, in particular, put up strong resistance to NEPA from the start. They worried that they lacked the staff to complete the reviews and expressed concern that finding contractors to complete impact statements would be expensive.[22] Bureaucrats within the agency also feared that recipient governments would balk at the new regulations, and one AID administrator noted that developing countries would view environmental regulations in foreign aid as "devices for imposing their own environmental protection standards" onto the Third World.[23] AID staffers stated that they intended to comply with NEPA for major capital projects, but maintained that "final decisions concerning [proposed] projects are not properly the responsibility of the United States, but of the requesting country or agency ... there is no intent to impose U.S. standards, priorities, or solutions on a foreign government through this procedure." They believed that the new procedures violated the national sovereignty of other countries. If the Indonesian government wanted to build a highway through a heavily forested area and if that construction project complied with domestic Indonesian law, then, officials reasoned, U.S. law was no longer applicable. To halt funding for a project in Indonesia would represent an unfair imposition of U.S. "standards" on a sovereign nation. AID officials held that NEPA only sought to protect the environment of the United States. Areas outside U.S. jurisdiction, they claimed, were not legally subject to the Act's guidelines.[24]

This interpretation rankled environmental NGOs. Officials from leading American NGOs, from the National Wildlife Federation (NWF) to the WWF to Friends of the Earth (FOE), published extensive materials on the issue and spoke before Congress demanding government-wide cooperation with the full extent of NEPA. By the early 1970s, it was becoming

---

[21] Caldwell, *The National Environmental Policy Act*, 100–3.
[22] James Fowler to Bill Parks, August 22, 1975, folder "Environment, TA/E FY 76," box 61, RG 286, NARA II.
[23] James R. Fowler, "Information Memorandum for the Deputy Administrator," May 3, 1973, folder "Environment, TA/E FY 76," box 61, RG 286, NARA II.
[24] Richard J. Tobin, "Pesticides, the Environment, and U.S. Foreign Assistance," *International Environmental Affairs*, Vol. 8, No. 3 (Summer 1996), 244–66.

increasingly clear that AID's efforts to incorporate environmental standards into its lending were far from what Ray Dasmann and Lynton Caldwell had envisioned. FOE officials lamented the agency's truculence. Writing in a 1971 newsletter, they complained that bill after bill and statement after statement contained "nothing to suggest that ecological reform is planned" in a serious way, "although the word 'environment' has been thrown in a couple times."[25] AID's commitment to environmental reform seemed specious.

Likewise, officials within the CEQ, many of whom were personally affiliated with leading environmental NGOs, also decried the lack of progress on environmental impact statements. In 1974, Lee Talbot, a former IUCN official working under Russell Train at the CEQ and who had been a major player in crafting the U.S. platform for the Stockholm Conference, was furious to find that not only had AID been slow to produce impact statements, but that the statements themselves were either inaccurate or so weak as to be practically useless. In the spring of 1974, an impact statement for a major infrastructure project in Indonesia – the Bogor Highway project – came across Talbot's desk. Although the document had been initially drafted in 1971, for unknown reasons it took three full years for it to reach the CEQ for review. "How is that this was done in 1971 and we did not get it until now?," Talbot wondered. Even more troubling was the content of the statement, which contained observations Talbot claimed to be "totally false." He acknowledged that the very existence of a statement was a step in the right direction, but AID's work was on the whole "pretty shallow and superficial." To combat the negligence, Talbot believed that the CEQ needed to "lower the boom on AID on this whole NEPA business."[26] Yet the CEQ did not have the time nor the resources to do so.

NGOs, however, did have such recourse available to them: an ability to force public bodies to comply with new regulations through the courts. While the IUCN and the WWF provided the intellectual inspiration for incorporating impact statements in development agencies, a new generation of environmental NGOs took the lead in pressuring U.S. foreign aid agencies to comply with American environmental law. Two groups in particular, the Environmental Defense Fund (EDF) and the National Resources Defense Council (NRDC), became significant players in this

[25] "Congressional Report," *Not Man Apart*, Vol. 1, No. 7 (July 1971), 6.
[26] Lee Talbot to John Busterud, April 1, 1974, "SCT 19, Environmental – Environmental Impact Statement (EIS)," Entry P88: Environmental Subject Files, Records of the Agency for International Development, box 3, RG 286, NARA II.

new area of organized political activity. The two organizations represented "a new phenomenon rapidly proliferating on the American
scene" – public interest law firms.[27]

Both groups focused on political advocacy and traditional legal services. Formed in 1966 by a handful of professional scientists and a young
lawyer to halt DDT spraying in parts of Long Island, the EDF focused on
litigation and public awareness campaigns. In its early years, the group
played an important role in shifting anti-DDT campaigns from Congress
to the courts. Funded initially by the Audubon Society and the
Conservation Foundation, by the end of the decade the group received a
grant from the Ford Foundation, achieved tax-exempt status, and established offices in New York, Berkeley, Denver, and Washington, DC.[28] The
NRDC was also set up in New York, by one group of lawyers seeking to
halt a hydropower project on the Hudson River and another group of
recent Yale Law School graduates. The group quickly focused on both
public advocacy and legal work.[29] The rise in federal regulations over
environmental issues in Nixon's first term ensured that both groups would
have plenty to do, and within a half decade of their creation these NGOs
became respected leaders in the field of environmental law.

Like-minded allies within federal agencies turned to such groups to
help enforce the new regulations. In particular, Russell Train, chairman of
the CEQ and a long-time member of numerous NGOs, saw the importance of nurturing such public-private partnerships. Following a flurry of
lawsuits, the Internal Revenue Service (IRS) moved in the spring of 1970
to suspend the tax-exempt status of groups such as the EDF and the
NRDC that had brought extensive lawsuits against the federal government.
Train leapt to their defense. In a personal letter to the IRS commissioner,
Train explained, "Private litigation before courts and administrative agencies has been and will continue to be an important environmental protection
technique supplementing and reinforcing Government environmental
protection programs." In particular, such NGOs had "strengthened and
accelerated the process of enforcement of antipollution laws ... identified
gaps in our regulatory procedures ... and brought before the courts the
public's interest in enforcement of such new governmental procedures as
the ... environmental impact statement requirement." If NGOs lost their

---

[27] IRS news release, October 9, 1970, in *Law and the Environment: Selected Materials on Tax Exempt Status and Public Interest Legislation* (Washington, DC: GPO, 1970).
[28] Bosso, *Environment, Inc.*, 42; Gottlieb, *Forcing the Spring*, 188–97. On the EDF and the anti-DDT campaigns, see Dunlap, *DDT: Scientists, Citizens, and Public Policy*, chapter 6.
[29] Bosso, *Environment, Inc.*, 43–54.

charitable contribution status to support the costs of litigating on behalf of the environment, Train worried, "this important private supplement to our governmental efforts would be seriously curtailed."[30]

The IRS ultimately relented, which opened the door for even more lawsuits and a formal legal challenge to AID's policies. Legal activity quickly focused on its support of dangerous pesticides.[31] Between the summer of 1969 and the summer of 1975, AID estimated that it had financed the purchase of more than $100 million worth of pesticides for use in more than twenty-five countries worldwide. While many of these pesticides had been banned for domestic use, the agency continued to support their purchase abroad. Officials maintained that NEPA did not require any formal assessment of the impact of such chemicals, since any restrictions of pesticide use in foreign countries would not significantly affect the United States' national environment and would represent an imposition of U.S. law onto a sovereign nation.[32]

In 1973, Russell Train wrote to AID administrator John A. Hannah to pressure his agency to provide a systematic review of its pesticide use. Train expressed frustration that the agency had yet to provide a single impact statement on the topic and that the agency was "becoming increasingly difficult to defend both to Congress and to the public."[33] More broadly, the CEQ had become frustrated with AID's repeated claims that NEPA had no jurisdiction over the projects it funded abroad. The agency was simply "not filing impact statements," and CEQ officials wanted "a determination be made whether A.I.D. should be required to file a statement or be excepted from the statutory requirements."[34] So the issue went to the courts.

[30] Russell Train to Randolph Thrower, September 30, 1970, in *Law and the Environment: Selected Materials on Tax Exempt Status and Public Interest Legislation* (Washington, DC: GPO, 1970).

[31] For an overview DDT's history and relationship to the global environment, see David Kinkela, *DDT and the American Century: Global Health, Environmental Politics, and the Pesticide that Changed the World* (Chapel Hill: The University of North Carolina Press, 2011).

[32] AID funded many different types of pesticides, including DDT, malathion, endrin, and heptachlor. Tobin, "Pesticides, the Environment, and U.S. Foreign Assistance," 249.

[33] Quoted in "International Application of NEPA: Environmentalists Challenge Pesticide Aid Program," *Environmental Law Reporter*, 5 ELR 10086 (June 1975).

[34] "Conversation with Council on Environmental Quality Staff," October 9, 1974, SCT 19, "Environmental – Environmental Impact Statement (EIS)," Entry P88: Environmental Subject Files, Records of the Agency for International Development, box 3, RG 286, NARA II.

On April 8, 1975, the EDF, the NRDC, the National Audubon Society, and the Sierra Club filed a joint lawsuit against AID over its pesticide program. Represented by Richard Frank and Eldon Greenberg, lawyers from the Center for Law and Social Policy (CLSP), another public interest law firm that had prepared a similar suit against the Department of Transportation, the suit quickly went to settlement talks. Seeking to avoid a lengthy court battle or punitive ruling, AID officials began negotiating a formal policy determination over the summer of 1975 with Frank and officials from the Department of Justice.[35] By August, AID agreed to produce an initial "assessment" for all activities. If that assessment indicated that a proposed activity "would significantly affect the environment of the United States or areas outside of any nation's jurisdiction," the agency would, "subject to foreign policy considerations," comply with NEPA in full and produce a formal impact statement. This stipulation gave AID staffers significant leeway to determine which projects moved from assessment to statement, and would be subject to public recourse. These officials maintained that the government would face "unique problems" for the conduct of foreign policy if it were "required to follow the NEPA impact statement procedures for all activities we sponsor, and particularly those which involve bilateral negotiations with sovereign states."[36] The statutory requirements seemed to imperil AID's ability to pursue its developmental objectives, and the settlement talks still left open the question of what to do about projects whose effects occurred under another nation's jurisdiction.

Richard Frank continued meeting with AID and Department of Justice officials throughout the early fall of 1975 to hammer out a more stringent set of regulations. By November, a full agreement had been crafted. It offered a compromise that forced AID to do an extensive review for its pesticide program and adopt new procedures. Under the new rule, AID would follow NEPA's basic two-step process. It would first file an assessment of whether a project would have "significant" environmental effects,

[35] "Memorandum to the Files – *EDF v. AID* – Settlement Talks," August 28, 1975, RG 1, Founder's Papers, Subgroup IV: Charles F. Wurster Papers, Series 10: Pesticides, box 5, USAID Pesticide Program, *EDF v. AID* Civil Action no. 75–0500 Settlement – Memoranda, 1975, Environmental Defense Fund Papers, Frank Melville Jr. Memorial Library, State University of New York–Stony Brook [hereinafter cited as EDF Papers].

[36] John A. Murphy to Russell W. Peterson, August 12, 1975, RG 1, Founder's Papers, Subgroup IV: Charles F. Wurster Papers, Series 10: Pesticides, box 5, USAID Pesticide Program, *EDF v. AID* Civil Action no. 75–0500 Settlement – Memoranda, 1975, EDF Papers.

and then submit a full impact statement if the proposed project would have an impact on the environment of the United States or the international commons. The assessment-statement division allowed for the agency to avoid an EIS for activities that did not have a "significant" environmental effect or that would seriously hamper its ability to conduct foreign policy. Nevertheless, the settlement reaffirmed that AID had to comply with NEPA. Both sides agreed on these terms. On December 5, 1975, the formal terms of the settlement were made public.[37]

In early 1976, AID began to work on formalizing its environmental procedures, which it eventually announced as "Regulation 216." Regulation 216 claimed that AID would review all projects with significant environmental effects and enshrined the assessment-EIS divide into agency practice.[38] Richard Frank proudly claimed that, as a result of the litigation, "U.S. Government financing of pesticide use abroad will, for the first time, be subjected to environmental analysis."[39] The NGOs considered the result a modest success. The work of the NRDC, the EDF, and others spurred AID to make reforms that they had previously showed no intention of doing. The power of private litigation mixed with support from key allies in government was apparent.

Despite the adoption of Regulation 216, there remained larger issues that worried some in the environmental community. For one, other foreign aid agencies still resisted the entire EIS process and the new guidelines were, in Richard Frank's words, "not very clear" for AID officers.[40] Furthermore, NGO officials wondered if the stipulation that allowed AID to skirt reviews when they would be detrimental to the conduct of foreign policy created too many loopholes. The settlement seemed to let AID off the hook for projects that affected "environments" other than those of the United States or the international commons. "We have to get that changed somewhat," Richard Frank said of the settlement's geographic stipulations, "so that, at the discretion of the Administrator, an

---

[37] Gary M. Ernsdorff, "The Agency for International Development and NEPA: A Duty Unfulfilled," *Washington Law Review*, Vol. 67, No. 133 (January 1992), 138–42.

[38] Tobin, "Pesticides, the Environment, and U.S. Foreign Assistance," 251.

[39] "Press Release – Government Agrees to Chang Pesticide Program," Center for Law and Social Policy, RG 1, Founder's Papers, Subgroup IV: Charles F. Wurster Papers, Series 10: Pesticides, box 5, USAID Pesticide Program, *EDF v. AID* Civil Action no. 75–0500 Settlement – Memoranda, 1975, EDF Papers.

[40] Richard A. Frank to Chap Barnes et al., March 22, 1976, RG 1, Founder's Papers, Subgroup IV: Charles F. Wurster Papers, Series 10: Pesticides, box 5, USAID Pesticide Program, *EDF v. AID* Civil Action no. 75–0500 Settlement – Memoranda, 1975, EDF Papers.

impact statement will also be prepared if the impact is in areas of unique cultural and natural heritage value or other aspects of the human environment."[41] In light of these deficiencies, NGOs pushed for even broader scope of NEPA's applicability and for increased accountability of federally funded development projects abroad.

## NEPA AND THE QUESTION OF EXTRATERRITORIALITY

Environmentalists' desire for wider application of extraterritoriality emerged in part because of their successful case against AID, but also because litigation campaigns were beginning to halt or slow potentially destructive development projects. One such legal success for NGOs came near the AID campaign's end. The case involved the construction of a new section of the Pan-American highway over the Darién Gap, a 100-mile long section of swampland and rain forest between Panama and Colombia. Both Panama and Colombia supported the project for the potential benefits that would follow from easier transportation across a treacherous area and for the symbolic value of completing the last section of the famed highway. The United States had funded the road's construction since the early 1970s, but environmentalists raised serious questions about its impact on the local ecosystems and the possibility that it might facilitate the flow of foot-and-mouth disease, an illness that greatly harmed livestock, from Colombia northward into countries from which it had been largely eradicated.[42] Although U.S. officials completed an initial impact assessment that allowed for construction to continue, the Sierra Club and three other NGOs sued them for an insufficient review. In the fall of 1975, a federal judge issued an injunction halting construction on the project while the Federal Highway Administration, the main agency behind funding and construction of the project, prepared a more comprehensive impact statement.[43] The environmental groups had succeeded in stopping a major development initiative until policy makers fully analyzed the project's ecological impact.

---

[41] Ibid.

[42] For a history of U.S. support for the project up to the late 1970s, see *Linking the Americas: Progress and Problems of the Darien Gap Highway*, Report by the Comptroller General of the United States, PSAD 78–65, February 23, 1978. Online [Available]: http://www.gao .gov/products/PSAD-78-65. Accessed March 11, 2014.

[43] *Sierra Club et al. v. Adams*, 578 F.2d 389 (U.S. App. D.C. 1978). Online [Available]: https:// law.resource.org/pub/us/case/reporter/F2/578/578.F2d.389.76-2158.html. Accessed March 11, 2014.

The Darién Gap case also exposed how the politics of sovereignty surrounding impact statements could upset leaders in other countries and frustrate U.S. officials. Colombian authorities were furious and "obviously disappointed" by the injunction. They claimed it was "highly discriminatory" against Colombia and worried about how long the impact statement might take to draft.[44] U.S. officials scrambled to respond. The Federal Highway Administration, working with a private company, crafted an initial impact statement in the summer of 1976, but the Sierra Club sued again claiming the new review was still insufficient. The Ford administration reiterated its commitment to the road and pressed the court to lift the injunction, but the presiding judge once again ruled in the Sierra Club's favor. U.S. diplomats made a series of overtures to Colombian and Panamanian officials asking for "understanding and patience" while they continued to wage legal battles and pursue lengthy environmental reviews.[45] NGO litigation had powerful consequences for U.S. foreign relations.

Amid these instances of successful NGO legal challenges, other foreign policy agencies continued to challenge the extraterritorial application of U.S. environmental law. As the AID case and the Darién Gap cases were being deliberated, serious questions arose over the status of the Export-Import Bank (Eximbank) and the projects it funded overseas.[46] NGOs believed the Eximbank was subject to the same sets of rules as any other federal agency. However, its officials were openly disregarding NEPA for the bank's nuclear power export program.[47] Eximbank officials held that the U.S. law did not apply to the "global environment," the same argument AID officials had made earlier. They argued further that including an impact statement for every project would impede the flow of American exports abroad while benefiting key U.S. competitors in Europe and

---

[44] U.S. Department of State Telegram 00245 Bogota, January 1976, State Department Telegrams, RG 59, General Records of the Department of State. Online [Available] http://aad.archives.gov/aad/series-description.jsp?s=4073. Accessed March 10, 2014.

[45] U.S. Department of State Telegram 063697, March 1977, State Department Telegrams, RG 59, General Records of the Department of State. Online [Available] http://aad.archives.gov/aad/series-description.jsp?s=4073. Accessed March 10, 2014.

[46] For a general history of the Eximbank, see William H. Becker and William M. McClenahan, *The Market, the State, and the Export-Import Bank, 1934–2000* (Cambridge: Cambridge University Press, 2003).

[47] The Sierra Club first brought suit against the Eximbank's program as part of a larger suit against the Atomic Energy Commission. John C. Pierce, "Exports and Environmental Responsibility: Applying NEPA to the Export-Import Bank," *Cornell International Law Journal*, Vol. 12, No. 247 (1979), 254–9.

Japan.[48] In a time of rising inflation and general economic stagnancy, Eximbank President William J. Casey and others explained, such actions would undermine American competitiveness in the global marketplace and exacerbate mounting economic problems at home. They claimed that since other nations chose to purchase goods supported by the Eximbank, it was incumbent on foreign nations, not the bank, to deal with the environmental consequences. Applying U.S. law to this end would be a violation of national sovereignty.[49] The NRDC and the Audubon Society filed suit against the Eximbank in January 1977, seeking a "declaratory judgment that NEPA applies with full force and effect to Eximbank." Unlike the AID case, bank officials showed little interest in negotiating new regulations.[50]

Upon Jimmy Carter's arrival in the White House, however, NGOs believed they had found an ally who could put to rest the ongoing bickering between themselves, the CEQ, and the Eximbank. Carter had culled close ties with the environmental community during his campaign, winning the support of many key NGOs and environmental leaders. The new president personally sympathized with much of the movement's goals, and his election brought with it new hopes within the community for an environmental revolution in Washington. Carter met frequently with environmental groups and had a personal rapport with key environmental leaders such as David Brower.[51] Carter even directed AID to begin funding programs abroad to conserve natural resources and strengthen environmental programs in the developing world.[52] In the spring of 1977,

---

[48] Stephen M. DuBrul, Jr., to John A. Busterud, November 19, 1976, folder "NEPA Guidelines (3)," box 11, RG 429, Records of Organizations in the Executive Office of the President, NARA II.

[49] Quoted in Edward Flattau, "Eximbank and the Environment," *The Free Lance-Star*, March 19, 1977, 19.

[50] John L. Moore to the President, December 6, 1977, folder WE November 1, 1977–December 31, 1977, box WE-2, Welfare, White House Central Files, JCL; Les Denend to Reginald Bartholomew, November 3, 1977, folder WE November 1, 1977–December 31, 1977, box WE-2, Welfare, White House Central Files, JCL.

[51] Memo, "Meeting with Major Environmental Groups," November 3, 1977, folder WE November 1, 1977–December 31, 1977, box WE-2, Welfare, White House Central Files, JCL. Jimmy Carter to David Brower, November 16, 1977, folder WE November 1, 1977–December 31, 1977, box WE-2, Welfare, White House Central Files, JCL.

[52] Thomas B. Stoel, Jr., S. Jacob Scherr, and Diana C. Crowley, "Environment, Natural Resources, and Development: The Role of the U.S. Agency for International Development," International Project, Natural Resources Defense Council, Inc., 1978, 5–6, USAID Document Clearinghouse. [Online] Available: http://dec.usaid.gov/index .cfm. Accessed January 4, 2012.

Carter issued an executive order authorizing the council to produce a set of binding regulations on the law's application abroad.[53]

The CEQ spent much of late 1977 preparing the new regulations. It pushed for a more robust determination than the AID settlement had offered. In the process, the agency had been emboldened by an influx of new officials, many of whom had worked for major environmental NGOs. For instance, James Gustave "Gus" Speth, one of the founders of the NRDC, joined the CEQ in 1977. Writing to White House officials in November 1977, Speth claimed that his agency "strongly reaffirm[ed]" its stance vis-à-vis the Eximbank. He asserted that the president's strong environmental views would help the CEQ make its case against reticent agencies.[54] Speth and other officials worked diligently to mobilize supporters from both inside and outside government.

The CEQ received encouragement from an unexpected source that December: AID. On December 9, AID administrator John Gilligan explained to CEQ head Charles Warren that the overall experience of AID's new regulations had been "a positive one." "The practical experience of A.I.D. has been that it is possible to undertake detailed environmental analyses of US-supported projects abroad," Gilligan claimed, and "the results obtained are useful to us, as well as to host country planners, in making project decisions." While Eximbank officials had claimed impact statements would create unnecessary costs, slow down an already sclerotic bureaucracy, and create economic problems with its allies abroad, none of these issues had been a "significant problem" for AID. Gilligan concluded that he had "no significant reservations about the preparation of environmental analyses for programs conducted abroad."[55] It was a remarkable change in tone from the start of the decade, and surely appreciated within the CEQ and environmental community.

In January 1978, with Gilligan's support, the CEQ released its new regulations. When it did so, controversy erupted. Although the new rules contained vague qualifications suggesting that agencies could opt out of impact statements that affected their ability to conduct foreign policy, the document stated clearly that NEPA did apply to the global commons,

[53] "Executive Order 11991, Environmental Impact Statements," May 24, 1977. [Online] Available: http://www.presidency.ucsb.edu/ws/index.php?pid=7580&st=&st1=#axzz1t YC172zQ. Accessed January 4, 2012.

[54] Gus Speth to Stuart Eizenstat, November 7, 1977, folder WE November 1, 1977–December 31, 1977, box WE-2, Welfare, White House Central Files, JCL.

[55] John Gilligan to Charles Warren, December 9, 1977, folder WE November 1, 1977–December 31, 1977, box WE-2, Welfare, White House Central Files, JCL.

Antarctica, and "one or more" foreign nations.[56] The CEQ came down in line with what environmental activists had been ~~pushing — total applicability~~ of NEPA abroad. In response, Eximbank officials balked at the new regulations. So, too, did officials from the State Department, Defense Department, Treasury Department, and many other agencies.[57]

The question of sovereignty stood at the heart of the debates. Deanne C. Siemer, the general counsel to the Department of Defense, worried that the regulations would hinder U.S. relations with other countries because foreign leaders might view the regulations as U.S. attempts at "meddling in the internal affairs of other nations" and violations of their sovereignty.[58] A CEQ official, by contrast, argued that the rules represented "respect for foreign sovereignty" because "other countries have a right to know whether U.S. activities in their countries might get them into serious health, safety, and environmental problems."[59] The CEQ convened a meeting with over a hundred officials from different agencies to discuss these differing views, along with whether and how to implement the new rules. The two sides failed to reach any consensus.[60] The foreign aid agencies staunchly resisted the new regulations, which they deemed too harsh, even punitive. CEQ officials hunkered down for a lengthy dispute.

By the spring of 1978, bureaucratic haggling and mid-level negotiations had percolated all the way up to the administration's most powerful figures, those who rarely dealt with environmental issue. Secretary of Defense Harold Brown wrote to National Security Advisor Zbigniew Brzezinski on May 9 to complain about the NEPA issue. "I am concerned by what I perceive to be a growing effort to extend mandatory environmental protections to United States government actions overseas," he wrote. He painted a bleak picture of diplomatic challenges and potential bureaucratic nightmares. "If this comes to pass, it will surely exacerbate our foreign relations as we try to impose our concepts of necessary environmental protections of other nations. Moreover, it will delay and

---

[56] Memorandum from Charles Warren to Heads of Agencies, January 11, 1978, folder FG 6–6, January 20, 1977–January 20, 1981, box FG-78, Federal Government-Organizations, White House Central Files, JCL.

[57] Mayer, *With the Stroke of a Pen*, 62.

[58] Deanne C. Siemer to Herbert Hansell, Robert Mundheim, C. L. Haslam, Anthony Lapham, and Warren Glick, April 25, 1978, Folder "NEPA: Eximbank," box 49, RG 429, NARA II.

[59] CEQ news release, April 6, 1978, folder "NEPA International (File 2) March 1978," box 50, RG 429, NARA II.

[60] Memo, Evening Report, Global Issues to Zbigniew Brzezinski, January 9, 1978, NLC-28-36-5-2-5, JCL.

disrupt our foreign programs as we wait for environmental impact statements to be drafted, endure public participation in the policy-making
process, and defend the inevitable lawsuits." Even the most important
aspects of U.S. foreign policy might be affected. "Arms transfers, U.S.
force relocations, and overseas military construction," Brown suggested,
"would probably be found to fall under these procedures."[61]

The debates drew in officials from agencies that rarely interacted with
one another, many of whom had little or no experience or interest in the
environment, which made consensus all the more elusive. Jessica
Tuchman Mathews of the National Security Council's Global Issues section attempted to craft a middle-ground position between the CEQ and
the more truculent agencies, but the dueling sides found little harmony
in the summer of 1978.[62] The ongoing conflict raised even basic questions
that at once seemed profound and absurd. An official from the DOD
wondered, only half-jokingly, if the new CEQ regulations would mean
that they would have to file an environmental impact statement before
declaring war.[63]

Debates heated up in June and July 1978. State Department officials
negotiated with the CEQ to water down its more stringent requirements.
Environmentalists fought back. In a letter signed by Russell Train (now
out of government and heading the World Wildlife Fund's office in
Washington) and leaders of the NRDC, the EDF, and other NGOs,
environmental groups pressured Carter to direct all agencies to comply
with NEPA. They worried that without clear guidelines from the administration or Congress, agencies would not comply or would continue to
abuse the environment.[64] Other NGOs, including Barbara Ward's
International Institute for Environment and Development (IIED), sent
similar letters of support.[65]

---

[61] Harold Brown to Zbigniew Brzezinski, May 9, 1978, folder WE May 1, 1978–May 31,
1978, box WE-2, Welfare, White House Central Files, JCL.

[62] Memo, Evening Report, Global Issues to Zbigniew Brzezinski, June 20, 1978, NLC-10-
12-6-3-8, JCL; Jessica Tuchman Mathews to Zbigniew Brzezinski, August 17, 1978,
folder HE 7, August 1, 1978–September 22, 1978, box HE-13, Federal Government-
Organizations, White House Central Files, JCL.

[63] Memo, Evening Report, Global Issues to Zbigniew Brzezinski, January 16, 1979,
NLC-10-17-6-31-2, JCL.

[64] Leonard C. Meeker and James N. Barnes to Jimmy Carter, July 21, 1978, folder WE August
1, 1978–September 30, 1978, box WE-2, Welfare, White House Central Files, JCL.

[65] Robert Stein to Jimmy Carter, August 17, 1978, folder HE 7, August 1, 1978–
September 22, 1978, box HE-13, Federal Government-Organizations, White House
Central Files, JCL.

The situation became more intense a month later, when environmentalists got hold of a draft order by the White House that attempted to tiptoe a middle line between the two sides. In another group letter, NGO officials noted that the draft order would not require "systematic environmental review of major federal actions abroad" and proclaimed that it was "distressing in its lack of commitment to the protection of the environment."[66] Through allies in the administration, word got to Carter's staff that the environmental community was feeling "seduced and abandoned" by the White House. Frustrated and bitter, they threatened to abandon formal support for him and mobilize around another candidate in the 1980 primary elections.[67] High-ranking congressional Democrats, such as Senator John Dingell, sided with the environmentalists and expressed frustration that Carter was dithering over whether to embrace their expansive reading of NEPA.[68]

Carter realized he had to bring some clarity to the issue. In meetings, though, he still seemed indecisive and often looked to Vice President Walter Mondale to play peacemaker among the competing agencies.[69] Advisors close to the president let him know that top-down action was necessary, unless Carter was willing to allow NGOs, through private litigation, to set the terms of the debate and the scope of NEPA. Robert Lipshutz, a lawyer from the Office of Legal Counsel, warned Carter in May 1978 that if the White House did not settle the question of extraterritoriality, "the courts will ultimately decide the issue." "There are two pending lawsuits that raise this issue," Lipshutz said in reference to the NRDC's cases, "and more can be expected."[70] Seeking to avoid congressional control over the issue and a flurry of future lawsuits, Carter resolved to take a firm stand through an executive order, although his drafts reflected a muddy middle road between the competing agencies.[71]

---

[66] James Barnes et al. to Jimmy Carter, August 11, 1978, folder HE 7, August 1, 1978–September 22, 1978, box HE-13, Federal Government-Organizations, White House Central Files, JCL.

[67] Phil Spector to Anne Wexler and Mike Chanin, August 17, 1978, folder WE August 1, 1978–September 30, 1978, box WE-2, Welfare, White House Central Files, JCL.

[68] John Dingell to Jimmy Carter, July 20, 1978, folder WE June 1, 1978–July 31, 1978, box WE-2, Welfare, White House Central Files, JCL.

[69] Memo, Evening Report, Global Issues to Zbigniew Brzezinski, September 6, 1978, NLC-10-14-7-22-4.

[70] Memo to Jimmy Carter from Robert Lipshutz, May 8, 1978, folder WE May 1, 1978–May 31, 1978, box WE-2, Welfare, White House Central Files, JCL.

[71] CEQ Chairman Charles Warren counted that Carter's draft order of August 1978 "went with CEQ 3 times, State 2 times, and [middle-ground language] 2 times" on the substantive issues. Mayer, *By the Stroke of a Pen*, 64–5.

Presidential action was a welcome development for many participants in the ongoing debates. By the early fall of 1978, all those involved yearned for a definitive answer from Carter. Gus Speth and others within the CEQ worked diligently with officials from other agencies to develop some kind of agreement over seemingly small procedural disputes, but to no avail.[72] The ongoing haggling over regulations left many officials exhausted. "I have never seen an issue consume so much time and effort when the result is so extremely small," wrote a staffer from the NSC to Zbigniew Brzezinski about the frustrating negotiations.[73] After months of debate, little had been resolved by agency officials.

On January 5, 1979, Carter issued a second executive order on NEPA. This time, the order mandated that all agencies must comply with the law, even those that funded projects with effects abroad. All agencies had to file assessments, and similar to the AID settlement, all except those projects most significant to the conduct of foreign policy would also require a formal impact assessment. The order required agencies to consider environmental effects in all areas, but produce formal impact statements only for the global commons and "especially significant" actions such as reactor sales or export of toxic chemicals.[74] That qualification represented an important compromise, leaving open the possibility for agencies such as the Eximbank to make arguments that its activities could be outside the scope of Carter's order. Still, the decision took a much stronger stance than most agencies would have liked. Indeed, it won the support of many environmentalists. The heads of the IUCN and the WWF-International wrote personally to Charles Warren, then the head of the CEQ, to celebrate Carter's "landmark" decision.[75]

Although ostensibly a final word on the issue, Carter's executive order contained loopholes and ambiguities to ensure future confusion and more litigation. Jessica Mathews, from the NSC's Global Issues desk, recognized this. Writing to Zbigniew Brzezinski, Mathews reflected, "With all the exemptions written into [the order], and the many opportunities for

[72] Gus Speth to Walter Mondale, August 29, 1978, folder HE 7, August 1, 1978–September 22, 1978, box HE-13, Federal Government-Organizations, White House Central Files, JCL.

[73] Memo, Evening Report, Global Issues to Zbigniew Brzezinski, September 6, 1978, NLC-10-14-7-22-4.

[74] Stu Eizenstat, Robert Lipshutz, and Margaret McKenna to the President, January 3, 1979, folder HE 7, September 3, 1978–January 31, 1979, box HE-13, Federal Government-Organizations, White House Central Files, JCL.

[75] John H. Loudon and Mohammed El-Kassas to Charles Warren, February 21, 1979, folder, HE 7, February 1, 1979–December 31, 1979, box HE-14, Federal Government-Organizations, White House Central Files, JCL.

case-by-case flexibility, the final result is pretty toothless. After all the hysterical fears that were raised ... during the eight-month debate on this issue, the final result is certainly one that will not damage our foreign policy interests – diplomatic, commercial, or military."[76]

Mathews's assessment proved prescient. Implementation of the order proved to be "uneven" in agencies, and neither subsequent administration's policies nor judicial decisions settled the fundamental issue of how far and to what extent NEPA extended beyond American shores.[77] A review from 1988 claimed that 20 percent of projects funded by AID in 1985 and 1986 alone had "unforeseen environmental impacts," most of which were "negative and were not adequately addressed."[78] Ultimately, Carter's new order reinforced the existing system that had been put in place with NEPA, and its vagueness and loopholes ensured that the extension of NEPA abroad would depend on fights waged by NGOs through the courts, after all.

Even with the procedures in place, many of the old problems with AID continued, although outside groups now had mechanisms to hold the agency accountable. For instance, from 1984 to 1987, AID officials sent approximately $1 million in aid to the government of Guatemala to eradicate the medfly, a small fruit fly known to cause extensive damage to agricultural crops. Guatemalan officials chose to use a potentially dangerous pesticide, malathion, as part of the operation. They sprayed it over vast stretches of territory, including villages, bodies of water, and in areas known to have endangered wildlife. The NRDC and the Sierra Club mounted a public campaign to draw attention to the controversy, highlighting the damage done to indigenous coffee growers and noting that AID officials were being slow to finish an environmental assessment. Before the groups could sue AID, Congress intervened and mandated a full environmental review.[79] Once AID completed the assessment and noted the harm it had done, officials discontinued the agency's role in

---

[76] Memo, Evening Report, Global Issues to Zbigniew Brzezinski, January 16, 1979, NLC-10-17-6-31-2, JCL.

[77] Mayer, *By the Stroke of a Pen*, 63; Therese M. Walsh, "Agency Responses to Executive Order 12,114: A Comparison and Implications," *Cornell International Law Journal*, Vol. 14, No. 2 (Summer 1981), 481–506.

[78] Siew Tuan Chew, "Environmental Assessments of Development Projects: A Preliminary Review of A.I.D.'s Experience," AID Evaluation Occasional Paper No. 17, June 1988, 15, USAID Documents Experience Clearinghouse. [Online] Available: http://dec.usaid.gov/index.cfm. Accessed June 19, 2012.

[79] Ward Sinclair, "Environmentalists Abuzz Over Fruit Fly Spraying," *The Washington Post*, October 16, 1987, A40.

the Guatemalan government's operation. Although this decision stopped further damage, AID's support for the project before the initial assessment had been completed brought both deleterious consequences to Guatemalan farmers and to the agency's public image.[80] The case highlighted the limitations of simply cutting off funding for development projects from the United States without sparking similar changes in the recipient country. Many early reviews of AID's new procedures revealed that most countries receiving aid still lacked effective environmental management practices or institutional capacity to implement more environmentally friendly development projects, regardless of the legal changes in the United States.[81]

Although situations such as the medfly incident would continue, the controversy over the extraterritorial application of NEPA proved an important milestone for many NGOs. Both the CEQ and the wider environmental community realized that they could rely on NGOs such as the NRDC to litigate their way toward compliance. If any federal agency sidestepped impact assessments in funding future development projects, groups such as the NRDC or the EDF would sue.[82] NGOs now felt inspired to confront an increasingly important institution in the development community: the World Bank.

## THE BATTLE FOR THE WORLD BANK

By the time the NGO campaign against the World Bank hit its high point in the mid-1980s, the bank had become synonymous with international development. This was not always so. Created during the Bretton Woods Conference as part of the institutional architecture for postwar global finance and monetary policy, the World Bank initially had very narrow

---

[80] Ernsdorff, "The Agency for International Development and NEPA: A Duty Unfulfilled," 147–8.

[81] Brian Johnson and Robert O. Blake, *The Environment and Bilateral Development Aid: The Environmental Policies, Programs and Performance of the Development Assistance Agencies of Canada, the Federal Republic of Germany, the Netherlands, Sweden, the United Kingdom and the United States* (Washington and London: International Institute for Environment and Development, 1979), 20–4, USAID Documents Experience Clearinghouse. [Online] Available: http://dec.usaid.gov/index.cfm. Accessed June 19, 2012.

[82] "No small percentage of our limited resources have been expended in invoking and defending this legislation," said John Adams of the NRDC. John H. Adams to Nicholas C. Yost, January 24, 1979, folder WE March 1, 1979–April 30, 1979, box WE-3, Welfare, White House Central Files, JCL.

aims.[83] During the immediate postwar years, the bank narrowly focused on providing loans to nations to help European recovery. In its first four years, 81 percent of its lending went to Europe. Over the 1950s and 1960s, the bank shifted dramatically toward funding economic development in the developing and postcolonial world. As part of this change, in 1960, it created the International Development Association (IDA) to provide long-term, low-interest loans to developing nations. Subsequently, Europe's share of total funding dropped to 20 percent for the 1950s and down further to 12 percent for the 1960s. This decline coincided with a rise in funding toward the developing world, particularly Asia and Latin America.[84] Sector targets shifted, too. Loans in the 1950s and 1960s focused heavily on infrastructure construction and industrial development; the 1960s and 1970s, by contrast, saw a rapid increase in funding toward rural development, agriculture, health, and poverty eradication.[85] The bank's purpose and focus shifted considerably over time.

Its status as a public institution, however, did not change. While the bank expanded its own bureaucracy over time and developed its own institutional imperatives, the fact that it remained bound to the dictates of its owners meant that powerful nations, particularly the United States, have been able to exert leverage over the bank through funding and the nomination of its president. These two salient features of the bank – its evolving purpose and its ties to the United States – proved significant for the NGOs that campaigned to alter the bank's lending practices in the 1980s.[86]

The campaign against the bank benefited from the small staff established by Robert McNamara. In 1970, McNamara hired James A. Lee, a respected epidemiologist, to serve as a consultant to the president and oversee the bank's new Office of Environmental Affairs (OEA), over a list of very prominent figures in the environmental movement including Barry

---

[83] Michele Alacevich, *The Political Economy of the World Bank: The Early Years* (Stanford: Stanford University Press, 2009).

[84] Devesh Kapur, John P. Lewis, and Richard Webb, *The World Bank: Its First Half Century, Vol. 1: History* (Washington, DC: Brookings Institution Press, 1997), 6–7. See also, in general, Edward S. Mason and Edward Asher, *The World Bank Since Bretton Woods* (Washington, DC: The Brookings Institution Press, 1973).

[85] See Sharma, "The United States, the World Bank, and the Challenges of International Development in the 1970s"; Kapur, Lewis, and Webb, *The World Bank: Its First Half Century, Vol. 1: History*, chapters 6 and 7.

[86] Kapur, Lewis, and Webb, *The World Bank: Its First Half Century, Vol. I: History*, 2–3 and chapter 18.

Commoner.[87] Lee's presence earned the bank high marks for having a distinguished scientific voice in an environmental position in an era when no other development agencies had done so.[88] Beneath the praise, there was also criticism over the bank's review process. Observers from the IIED noted that the existence of the bank's environmental measures should not "divert attention from how marginal they are in relation to total development efforts."[89] Although few outside observers recognized it at the time, James Lee's mandate was weak and his staff greatly undermanned. The OEA had only two full-time staffers besides Lee throughout most of the 1970s. Rather than systematically reviewing all major loan projects, Lee's office spent much of its early years responding to complaints, such as the placement of a power transmission line in a Tanzanian park.[90] More critically, environmental review came only at the tail end of the project cycle – the "appraisal" stage – at which point most of the groundwork for the program had already been done; the environmental review could do little to alter decisions over whether projects would be funded. Enforcement of environmental rules relied on the extent to which Lee and his two staffers could convince project teams to take environmental issues seriously.[91] Only 5 percent of projects reviewed in the first three years of Lee's tenure appeared serious enough to warrant outside consultation with experts.[92]

Furthermore, despite McNamara's open support for environmental reforms, internal resistance proved strong. Many groups within the bank disliked James Lee and found his advocacy for environmental issues

[87] *The World Bank and the World Environment* (Washington, DC: World Bank Group, September 1971), 6. [Online] Available: http://web.worldbank.org/WBSITE/EXTERNAL/ EXTABOUTUS/EXTARCHIVES/0,,contentMDK:22992993~pagePK:36726~piP K:437378~theSitePK:29506,00.html. Accessed May 13, 2012. See also Wade, "Greening the Bank," 618–21. James A. Lee, interview, World Bank Oral History Program, April 4, 1985, 3. [Online] Available: http://go.worldbank.org/QRKULSAFE0. Accessed January 24, 2012.

[88] Robert E. Stein and Brian Johnson, *Banking on the Biosphere? Environmental Procedures and Practices of Nine Multilateral Development Agencies* (Lexington, MA: D.C. Heath and Company, 1979), 11. In 1981, the Conservation Foundation even asked World Bank President A. W. "Tom" Clausen to give the Fairfield Osborn Memorial Lecture on behalf of the bank's environmental work. "World Bank Urges Conservation-Development Partnership," *IUCN Bulletin*, Vol. 13, Nos. 1–3 (January-March 1982), 23.

[89] Stein and Johnson, *Banking on the Biosphere*, 22.

[90] Lee, interview, World Bank Oral History Program, 3–4.

[91] Wade, "Greening the Bank," 627–30.

[92] Philippe Le Prestre, *The World Bank and the Environmental Challenge* (Selinsgrove: Susquehanna University Press, 1989), 29.

to be a "nuisance" that was "not taken too seriously."[93] Furthermore, Stein and Johnson noted that the bank's environmental performance was "properly bound ... by the priorities and proclivities of borrowing governments."[94] Put another way, leaders of developing nations could exert influence through voting rules to dismiss any environmental procedures they viewed as injurious to their economic interests. As was the case with AID, reluctant World Bank officials claimed that environmental review for projects in developing countries amounted to a violation of sovereignty. Influential intellectuals from the developing nations working at the bank, many of whom had pushed environmentalists to take developmental concerns seriously back at Founex in 1971, resisted environmental review, too.[95] When the bank and a coterie of other development organizations released a public statement in 1980 celebrating their environmental policies and procedures, it was more style than substance.[96]

The problems surrounding environmental review at the World Bank became clear in early 1983 over a proposed highway construction project in Brazil (Figure 6). The Polonoroeste project sought to connect the heavily populated south-central part of the country to the densely forested and sparsely populated northwest Amazon region. Brazil's military dictatorship, in the midst of a growing fiscal crisis and facing rampant inflation, saw the project as key to alleviating poverty in the region, a means for promoting regional economic growth, and an important developmental symbol for the regime. The bank offered to bankroll the Brazilian's government highway construction in exchange for the government agreeing to rehabilitate older agricultural areas, establish settlements for displaced persons, and create reserves and health care programs for the indigenous persons affected by the project. Although it quickly became a symbol of the bank's "unsustainable" development policies, it was

---

[93] Visvanathan Rajagopalan, interview, World Bank Oral History Program, 1993, 25. [Online] Available: http://go.worldbank.org/X4BGM4AT20. Accessed May 21, 2012.

[94] Stein and Johnson, *Banking on the Biosphere?*, 22.

[95] Wade, "Greening the Bank," 626; Le Prestre, *The World Bank and the Environmental Challenge*, 79; Mahbub ul Haq, "The Limits to Growth: A Critique," *Finance and Development*, Vol. 9, No. 4 (December 1972), 2–8.

[96] Bruce Rich stated as much in his opening statement to the June 1983 hearings. Statement of Bruce M. Rich in *Environmental Impact of Multilateral Development Bank-Funded Projects*, Hearings before the House Committee on Banking, Finance, and Urban Affairs, Subcommittee on International Development Institutions and Finance, 98th Congress, 1st Session, June 28–29, 1983 (Washington, DC: GPO, 1983), 51–4. See also Le Prestre, *The World Bank and the Environmental Challenge*, 135.

FIGURE 6: Map of Brazil, ca. 1981. The Polonoroeste project focused largely on the western regions of Rondonia and Mato Grosso. Courtesy of University of Texas Libraries.

conceived as a way to take ecological limitations and the rights of indigenous persons into account.[97]

---

[97] On the origins and development of the Polonoroeste project, see Wade, "The Greening of the Bank," 637–53.

The timing of the project was also noteworthy because it coincided with growing environmental and social justice movements within the Global South. In the 1940s and 1950s many developing nations often lacked thriving civil societies and expansive networks of activist NGOs. By the early 1980s, however, many nations held local, homegrown movements that agitated against extractive industries, overbearing governments, and multinational corporations that endangered local communities and ecosystems. The most notable case, the Chipko movement, emerged in northern India during the 1970s when a group of villagers stopped a timber-harvesting operation by threatening to tie themselves to trees about to be taken down.[98]

Over time, other such movements would grow to represent what intellectuals from the Global South defined as an "environmentalism of the poor" to contrast with Western environmentalism. Western views of environmental protection, they charged, originated only after material abundance had been achieved; concerns over building large national parks absent human beings and managing game reserves for leisurely hunting took hold only after basic needs had been met. The poor, by contrast, often lived closely to the natural world, and their survival often depended on their ability to work intimately within it and respect ecological limits. Although they strove to overcome persistent scarcities through development, they also nurtured a deep care and concern for the world around them and wished to see it protected. Movements similar to Chipko flourished in Brazil, particularly among villagers in the Amazon who began mobilizing against infrastructure projects, deforestation, and forced relocation schemes in the 1970s and early 1980s. In a few years, these protestors would become important players in the campaign against the bank's support for the Polonoroeste project.[99]

The Polonoroeste project, after all, worried many environmental observers because of its likely ecological consequences, its effect on local indigenous people, and the Brazilian government's steadfast commitment to seeing it completed. Robert Goodland, the bank's resident tropical ecologist and the third person added to Lee's OEA, raised concerns on the first fact-finding mission sent to the region in late 1979. Goodland

[handwritten margin note: a retort to Western ideas that indigenous people are not interested in caring for the land]

---

[98] Guha, *The Unquiet Woods.*

[99] Guha and Juan Martinez-Alier, *Varieties of Environmentalism;* Juan Martinez-Alier, *The Environmentalism of the Poor: A Study of Ecological Conflicts and Valuation* (New Delhi: Oxford University Press, 2005); Kathryn Hochstetler and Margaret E. Keck, *Greening Brazil: Environmental Activism in State and Society* (Durham: Duke University Press, 2007).

argued that any project that cleared forests on the scale proposed by Polonoroeste would expose fragile soils and upset the local ecosystem. Goodland believed that systematic reviews of the project vis-à-vis other alternative agriculture programs were necessary. However, the head of the Brazil country program, with the support of other influential bank officials, began disbursements for the project over Goodland's critiques, believing (quite rightfully) that Brazilian government officials had no interest in delaying the project or choosing alternative sites. While bank officials recognized that Polonoroeste would have tremendous consequences for indigenous persons living in the area, they also recognized that the Brazilian government contained within it a diverse and powerful array of interests that had little desire to protect the environment or the native populations. The decision to move forward with Polonoroeste was not driven by official negligence so much as a respect for the sovereignty and wishes of the Brazilian government.[100]

Nonetheless, when the NGO campaign began, reformers placed blame squarely on the bank, rather than the Brazilian government. Although the campaign eventually turned into a large-scale grassroots mobilization, it began as a small lobbying effort by a handful of elite, highly respected lawyers and officials from three of the most respected U.S. environmental groups: the NRDC, the Environmental Policy Institute (EPI), and the National Wildlife Federation (NWF).[101] Within these organizations, a handful of skilled lawyers led the way: Thomas Stoel, Jr. and Bruce Rich of the NRDC, Brent Blackwelder of the EPI, and Barbara Bramble of the NWF.[102] Although McNamara had retired in 1981 and passed the reins of the bank over to A. W. "Tom" Clausen, the former CEO of Bank of America, these individuals, through their institutional connections to prominent U.S. congressmen and Treasury Department officials, were able to maintain constant contact with high-level bank officials. They sought to use the leverage they had to push the bank to "apply to the bank measures that they had previously pressed USAID to adopt."[103]

To spur these reforms, NGO leaders turned to Congress in early 1983. Their timing was propitious. In 1983 Congress held hearings over its

---

[100] Wade, "The Greening of the Bank," 643.

[101] The EPI was created as a spinoff of Friends of the Earth's Washington, DC, office in 1972, amid David Brower's and others' push for a stronger lobbying and political presence in Washington, DC. See Gottlieb, *Forcing the Spring*, 198–9.

[102] Bruce Rich spoke at the hearings in June 1983 as a consultant to the Sierra Club's International Program, but soon joined the NRDC.

[103] Le Prestre, *The World Bank and the Environmental Challenge*, 190.

replenishment to the bank's International Development Association (IDA) amid a debilitating, global debt crisis that had struck many developing countries.[104] When Mexico defaulted on its debt repayments in 1982, it raised international attention on the staggering debt many developing nations had accumulated. Private lending dried up almost overnight. Nations across the world struggled to pay back what they owed. In response, the bank itself took a greater role in disbursing loans to encourage recovery in debt-strapped nations, usually through the "structural adjustment" of domestic economies to cut public programs and produce more exports. The bank felt more pressure to loan than ever before. With debt repayments coming in slowly, it needed more capital to do so. Bank officials viewed IDA replenishment with tremendous urgency.[105]

In this context, Bruce Rich, Barbara Bramble, and Brent Blackwelder spoke in late June at a special congressional hearing on the multilateral development banks' effects on the environment.[106] Over the two days they detailed the myriad ways in which projects funded by multilateral development banks had damaged fragile ecosystems and displaced indigenous peoples throughout the developing world. They made specific references to both Polonoroeste and the large Sardar Sarovar dam-building project along the Narmada River in India, which had come to represent the two main symbols of destructive bank-funded projects.[107]

In particular, Rich, Bramble, and Blackwelder focused on the inadequacy of World Bank policies and procedures, particularly the absence of satisfactory and timely impact statements in the lending process. While John Horberry of the IUCN acknowledged the institutional and economic challenges the bank faced at the time, he called for the bank to improve its assessment process to allow project staff to "ask the right questions at the

[104] Every three years, the question of IDA funding comes before Congress. While the bank gets support from numerous governments, the U.S. maintains a preponderant role in this regard. For example, U.S. annual payments in the 1980s to the IDA varied, but the U.S. share of the group hovered generally around 25 percent. Catherine Gwin, "U.S. Relations with the World Bank, 1945–1992," in Kapur, Lewis, and Webb, eds., *The World Bank: Its First Half Century, Vol. 2: Perspectives*, 238.

[105] On the technical aspects of the debt crisis and the ways in which it stoked fears within the bank of an ongoing "negative net transfer" problem, see Bruce Rich, *Mortgaging the Earth: The World Bank, Environmental Impoverishment, and the Crisis of Development* (Boston: Beacon Press, 1994), 78–80.

[106] Rich spoke on behalf of the NRDC as well as Friends of the Earth, the Sierra Club, the WWF-US, the Izaak Walton League of America, and the National Audubon Society. *Environmental Impact of Multilateral Development Bank-Funded Projects*, 54–5.

[107] Wade, "Greening the Bank," 664.

right time."[108] Others were less circumspect. Bruce Rich stated bluntly that although the bank had prepared a series of guidelines for impact statements, there were "no procedures and mandatory regulations to insure their systematic use and early integration into project design."[109] He and the other representatives presented a list of demands to Congress: to add an environmental representative to the National Advisory Council for International Monetary and Financial Policies (a group established at the Bretton Woods Conference to review loan projects); to pressure national executive directors of the bank to adopt new impact assessment regulations and vote down any project that would result in "unnecessary and unacceptable environmental destruction"; and to organize an in-depth study on what kinds of impact assessment guidelines the bank should adopt. It was an ambitious agenda. Seeking more information on the topic and interested in the bank's response, the congressmen requested the Treasury Department to forward the NGOs' written statement to the bank.[110]

World Bank officials did not anticipate that Congress would take NGO concerns so seriously, and they scrambled to respond. James Burnham, the U.S. executive director to the bank, asked James Lee to address the criticisms.[111] Lee's superiors agreed that he was the most appropriate figure for the task, as he was one of a handful of people in the bank with a meaningful understanding its environmental procedures.[112] While Lee's final report reiterated much of what bank officials had said in the past and acknowledged bank deficiencies in some aspects of its environmental record, it offered little in the way of new recommendations.[113] Lee was careful to inform his superiors of the bank that it was unlikely to deter future lobbying efforts from the NGOs. He urged officials to take their concerns seriously. "The political importance of these organizations cannot be overemphasized," Lee wrote in his memo to senior bank staff.

---

[108] Statement of John Horberry in *Environmental Impact of Multilateral Development Bank-Funded Projects*, 28.

[109] Statement of Bruce M. Rich in ibid., 52.

[110] Ibid., 54.

[111] James Burnham to James Lee, July 19, 1983, "Clausen Papers – Alphabetical Files – Environment, Population and Natural Resources – Meeting 1984-03," World Bank Archives [hereinafter cited as WBA], World Bank Group, Washington, DC.

[112] James Lee to V. Rajagopalan, July 20, 1983, "Clausen Papers – Alphabetical Files – Environment, Population and Natural Resources – Meeting 1984-03," WBA.

[113] James A. Lee to Thomas Blinkhorn, January 11, 1984, "Clausen Papers – Alphabetical Files – Environment, Population and Natural Resources – Meeting 1984-03," WBA; Wade, "Greening the Bank," 660; Rich, *Mortgaging the Earth*, 117–19.

"As friends and supporters of the work of the bank, their views and recommendations are deserving of serious consideration at the highest management levels."[114] With the IDA replenishment decision looming in the summer of 1984, Lee's plea struck a powerful chord within the bank.

Indeed, shortly after the formal issuance of the bank's rebuttal in January 1984, Stoel, Rich, Bramble, and Blackwelder began corresponding and meeting with upper-level bank officials. In large part, this stemmed from the dissatisfaction NGOs felt about the bank's handling of the questions raised over Polonoroeste. "We are gravely disappointed and profoundly disturbed by the evasive, unconstructive, reactive tone and content of the World Bank's response," Thomas Stoel explained to a sympathetic member of the House Subcommittee.[115] Tom Clausen agreed to meet with the NGO representatives in late February 1984 in order to hear their grievances and work toward a solution. With more congressional hearings looming over the coming months, the NGOs had put the bank on the defensive.

In this process, individuals within the bank helped NGOs develop their public campaign. James Lee had long been affiliated with many NGOs.[116] Analysts of the bank noted that Lee's OEA – renamed the Office of Environmental and Scientific Affairs (OESA) – had come to work with external NGOs to mobilize support for their own frustrations.[117] Anonymous officials sympathetic to Lee's situation and frustrated by the bank's intransigence allowed NGO officials to enter offices after hours to collect evidence on how loan projects often generated deleterious unintended ecological consequences with inadequate – or nonexistent – environmental reviews.[118]

This confluence of internal and external pressure deeply distressed bank officials. With regard to Lee, bank officials felt almost paranoid about information he could be leaking to NGOs. Speaking of the NGOs,

[114] Memo, "Response of the World Bank – 1983 Congressional Hearings on the Environmental Activities of the Multilateral Banks," February 22, 1984, "Clausen Papers – Alphabetical Files – Environment, Population and Natural Resources – Meeting 1984-03," WBA.

[115] Letter Thomas B. Stoel, Jr., et al. to Jerry Patterson (Subcommittee on IDIF), February 15, 1984, "Clausen Papers – Alphabetical Files – Environment, Population and Natural Resources – Meeting 1984-03," WBA.

[116] Jay D. Hair to A. W. Clausen, June 8, 1982, "Clausen Papers – General Correspondence – Correspondence 02 (1982)," WBA.

[117] Le Prestre, *The World Bank and the Environmental Challenge*, 106.

[118] Robert Wade notes that "internal leaks" provided a key source of information on the destructiveness of bank-funded projects. Wade, "Greening the Bank," 661.

J. William Stanton, a counselor to the bank president, told Clausen, "I think they have an ally in our Jim Lee."[119] No longer just a nuisance to reluctant bank staffers, Lee, it seemed to some in upper management, now posed a threat to the public credibility of the bank and a key figure in the NGO campaign.

Most worrisome to bank officials was the potential of the NGO campaign to fuel rising anti-aid sentiment on Capitol Hill and within the White House. Shortly after the inauguration of Ronald Reagan, foreign aid emerged as a target for budget hawks seeking to curtail U.S. spending. Some in the administration and many conservative Republicans in Congress viewed the World Bank as "merely a world-wide welfare fund." William Stanton worried that the NGOs would further encourage such rhetoric. "They play a very dangerous game and this should be pointed out to them," he said of the NGOs.[120] Foreign aid was a target for the administration's rhetorical and budgetary attacks on liberal internationalism. The bank's funding was in jeopardy, and the NGO campaign risked further enflaming the parochial, anti-foreign sentiment of conservative politicians and officials within the Reagan administration.[121]

In this fraught and tense environment, NGO leaders met with Clausen and upper-level bank staff in late February 1984. Stoel, Rich, Bramble, Blackwelder, and a few others sat down to reiterate the many complaints that had first aired back in June 1983. They claimed that new procedures were necessary to require universal impact statements earlier in the lending cycle; Lee's office needed more qualified staffers with backgrounds in ecology; and that the bank should more effectively integrate basic conservation principles in its natural resource management policy. Clausen accepted the criticisms, but claimed he faced both institutional and political constraints. After all, he and his colleagues explained, the project staff, not Lee's office, had ultimate power in determining projects.

---

[119] J. William Stanton to A. W. Clausen, February 23, 1984, "Clausen Papers – Alphabetical Files – Environment, Population and Natural Resources – Meeting 1984-03," WBA.

[120] Peter Riddleberger to A. W. Clausen, July 14, 1981, Clausen Files – "Clausen's U.S. Congress Correspondence – 11/80–12/81," WBA.

[121] The critiques of the World Bank and foreign aid in general were part and parcel of a larger set of criticisms about the role of the state and state planning in economic development. On this topic in the late 1970s and 1980s, see Latham, *The Right Kind of Revolution*, 175–82; Ekbladh, *The Great American Mission*, 259–64. For a broad overview of many criticisms of state-led development at the time, see Deepak Lal, *The Poverty of "Development Economics"* (London: The Institute for Economic Affairs, 1983).

He pleaded with the NGOs not to give fuel to the anti-aid fire smoldering in Washington. Rather than voicing their opposition to Congress, Clausen asked that NGOs speak directly with bank officials to air their grievances.[122]

The bank responded in the late spring of 1984 with new regulations, which won support from key environmental figures. Amid other guidelines that would limit the bank's ability to support environmentally destructive projects, the new regulations asserted that the bank would not fund any project that would "severely harm or create irreversible environmental deterioration ... without mitigatory [sic] measures acceptable to the bank."[123] Russell Train, now working at the head of the WWF-US office, wrote a personal note to Tom Clausen congratulating him on the new restrictions. He reiterated this over lunch in Clausen's office with the bank president and Prince Philip, who was still the nominal head of the WWF-International. Yet Train worried about next steps. He was "extremely interested in the plans" for the implementation of the new guidelines.[124] To this end, he even offered to help the bank put the new procedures into practice by offering trained scientists affiliated with the WWF to serve as environmental consultants in the research and writing of future impact statements.[125] Train did not see his organization or other like-minded groups as a destructive force toward the bank; rather, they just wanted the bank to live up to its own standards.

Others within the NGO campaign, by contrast, felt that the regulations were taking too long to implement or were just a symbolic gesture. Indeed, it was still up to project officers and their superiors, not James Lee's office, to incorporate environmental considerations, and most officials showed little interest in doing so.[126] In addition, challenges persisted within recipient nations. Many elites from recipient countries, particularly leading officials within the Brazilian government, balked at the idea that external funding for their development projects might get cut off. Over the mid-1980s environmental protests against the bank provoked a

---

[122] "Mr. Clausen's Meeting with Representatives of Environmental and Population Groups," "Clausen Papers – Alphabetical Files – Environment, Population and Natural Resources – Meeting 1984-03," WBA.

[123] OMS 2.36, quoted in Wade, "Greening the Bank," 634.

[124] Russell Train to A. W. Clausen, June 15, 1984; Prince Philip to A. W. Clausen, June 8, 1984, "Clausen Papers – General Correspondence – Correspondence 02 (1982)," WBA.

[125] Russell Train to A. W. Clausen, November 1, 1984, "Clausen Papers – General Correspondence – Correspondence 05 (1984 – July–December)," WBA.

[126] Wade, "Greening the Bank," 635.

defiant nationalist backlash among Brazil's ruling class.[127] In this context, some NGOs began to redouble their efforts against the bank.

In pushing to achieve greater accountability of the bank, NGOs were able to draw from a new set of allies – the growing grassroots activist community in Brazil. In the early 1980s, environmental and indigenous rights activism became much more widespread in the country, as repression of social movements eased somewhat and a growing number of reformers came to sympathize with the environmental critiques of Brazil's development model.[128] NGO officials in the United States leapt at the chance to tap into this growing network. At a special hearing on the Polonoroeste project, José Lutzenberger, a prominent Brazilian activist, highlighted the highway's deleterious impact on local people and ecosystems. Lutzenberger charged in a prepared statement that the Polonoroeste project had sparked "uncontrolled" development and "devastation of the forest."[129] Furthermore, he testified that World Bank officials had "not yet listened to Brazilian environmentalists" who had researched alternatives to the costly project.[130] Broadcast on television in Brazil and the United States, the hearing drew widespread attention to tropical deforestation and the bank's history of support for large-scale development.

Building on Lutzenberger's testimony, sympathetic congressmen and NGO officials increased their activity against the bank. The chairman of the House committee wrote to U.S. Treasury Secretary Donald Regan urging him confront the bank about the project, whereas Bruce Rich penned a letter to Tom Clausen that echoed Lutzenberger's testimony that he published in the *New York Times* against Clausen's wishes.[131] In response, the bank sent a letter back to Rich explaining that the project had been "carefully planned," and most importantly, long approved by Brazilian authorities.[132] The letter made clear that there was little Clausen could or would do.

[127] Andrew Hurrell, "Brazil and the International Politics of Amazonian Deforestation," in Hurrell and Kingsbury, *The International Politics of the Environment*, 403–9.

[128] Hochstetler and Keck, *Greening Brazil*, 32.

[129] "Tropical Forest Development Projects: Status of Environmental and Agricultural Research," *Hearings before the Subcommittee on Natural Resources, Agriculture Research and Environment of the Committee on Science and Technology, House of Representatives, 98th Congress, Second Session* (Washington, DC: GPO, 1985), 18.

[130] Ibid., 14.

[131] Eric Eckholm, "World Bank Urged to Halt Aid to Brazil for Amazon Development," *New York Times*, October 17, 1984, A17.

[132] Roberto Gonzalez Confino to Bruce Rich, November 7, 1984, quoted in Wade, "Greening the Bank," 663.

The response infuriated Rich. Frustrated and seeking to exert more pressure against the bank, he turned to an unlikely ally: a conservative Republican senator from Wisconsin, Robert W. Kasten, Jr. Kasten had a personal interest in environmental issues, and he recognized his constituency valued them, as well (he had replaced Gaylord Nelson, the godfather of Earth Day, in the Senate). He was also a member of the anti-aid constituency on Capitol Hill, looking for a pretext to cut funding for the World Bank. He had, in fact, met with Clausen earlier in the decade to explain congressional intransigence over foreign aid support.[133] While many worried about building a coalition with Kasten, Bruce Rich saw only the upsides. In his own history of the campaign against the bank, Rich claimed that the senator's multiple motives "made the threat [to cut funding] all the more effective." Kasten wrote letters to Tom Clausen and Don Regan, putting the bank, once again, on the defensive.[134]

Over the rest of 1984 and throughout 1985, the campaign against the World Bank heated up. In December 1984, Congress approved a laundry list of bank reforms written by NGO members. Clausen met with Kasten and environmental NGOs in May 1985 to discuss the letters. Thereafter, Ernest Stern, the bank's senior vice president for operations, sent a note of response that overstated the bank's past work and left Rich and other NGOs feeling as though they were being brushed aside. At the same time, other large infrastructure projects drew increased concern.[135] Rich lashed out at bank officials over a loan for a transportation project in Indonesia "beset with enormous social and environmental risks" even greater than those associated with Polonoroeste.[136] In November 1985, Brent Blackwelder brought up again the environmental destruction associated with the Sardar Sarovar dam in India, which was slowly coming to stand alongside Polonoroeste as a major symbol of development gone awry.[137] More NGOs and protestors got on board, coming in droves to bash the bank, including many from Brazil.[138] In 1986, Stephan Schwartzman, an anthropologist and friend of Bruce Rich, published a

[133] M. P. Benjenk to A.W. Clausen, July 14, 1982, Clausen Files – "Clausen's U.S. Congress Correspondence – April 1982–December 1982," WBA.

[134] Rich, *Mortgaging the Earth*, 125.

[135] Wade, "Greening the Bank," 662–3.

[136] Bruce Rich et al. to A. W. Clausen, June 10, 1985, "Clausen Papers – National Resource Defense Council – Sierra Club Correspondence – Correspondence 01," WBA.

[137] Brent Blackwelder to A. W. Clausen, November 6, 1985, "Clausen Papers – General Correspondence – Correspondence 07 (1985 – September–December)," WBA.

[138] Rich, *Mortgaging the Earth*, 128–30.

full-color book exposing the ill effects of past bank projects – replete with images of imperiled wildlife, endangered indigenous peoples, and ravaged landscapes – entitled *Bankrolling Disasters*.[139]

As the campaign burgeoned, divisions emerged among the NGOs involved. Bruce Rich's passionate but often-aggressive style helped draw attention to the cause and build a grassroots campaign. It contrasted with the more reserved and deliberative style of other groups who had sought to maintain close ties with bank personnel. IIED officials stressed the "practical difficulties" the bank faced over the moral outrage that came through in public presentations. Brian Walker, the president of the IIED, told Clausen as much. Sending the bank president a copy of special issue of the *Ecologist* magazine deploring the bank, Walker explained that the IIED was "again defending the bank's efforts" and tried to tone down the criticisms launched from the environmental community. He added that the bank needed to make reforms because his organization was "putting [its] reputation on the line" on behalf of the bank.[140] As Walker's letter made clear, although the outcome of the NGO campaign remained uncertain in 1985, it was evident that Rich's style of protest – public denunciations, hyperbolic rhetoric – was beginning to dominate.

The campaign reflected this hostile tone as it intensified in 1986. Major newspapers and publications focused on the story of the NGO campaign against the bank, and began to draw national public attention toward the Polonoroeste and Narmada projects.[141] Furthermore, at the September 1986 annual meeting for the World Bank and the IMF, groups of NGOs put on an "alternative" gathering that resembled the many gatherings outside the 1972 Stockholm meeting. While Rich, Bramble, Stoel, and others continued their dialogue with upper-level bank officials, grassroots activists paraded around Washington, DC, with colorful protest banners. As the meeting opened, activists from the Rainforest Action Network climbed up the nearby office building to display the "World Bank destroys tropical rain forests" banner.[142]

---

[139] Stephan Schwartzman, *Bankrolling Disasters: International Development Banks and the Global Environment* (Washington, DC: Sierra Club, 1986).

[140] Brian W. Walker to A. W. Clausen, June 3, 1985, "Clausen Papers – General Correspondence – Correspondence 06 (1985 – January–August)," WBA.

[141] The *New York Times* and the *Washington Post*, in particular, covered the campaign against the bank.

[142] Patrice Gaines-Carter, "Environmental Protest Reaches New Heights," *The Washington Post*, September 30, 1986, B3.

Amid this increasing fanfare, the NGO campaign soon achieved key victories, although their successes came from two unexpected sources. First came a shift in strategy at the Treasury Department. In September 1985, as the global debt crisis deepened, new Treasury Secretary James Baker launched a new plan – the "Baker plan" – to relieve the debt burden by greatly increasing World Bank loans to struggling countries. Whereas the Reagan administration had been hostile toward the bank and ambivalent toward NGO overtures, Baker believed that a major infusion of capital from Congress to the bank was necessary to implement his plan. He also recognized that the plan would be nearly impossible to implement with both anti-aid Republicans and environmentally minded Democrats opposing the World Bank in Congress. Baker immediately began to pressure officials to clean up the bank's environmental record. In June 1986, he convinced the U.S. executive director to vote down a loan for a 25-dam hydropower project in Brazil on environmental grounds – it was the first time any member of the bank voted against a loan for environmental reasons.[143] Over the next few years, Baker consistently pressed bank officials to clean up their environmental record and to reach out in a "more systematic" way to environmental NGOs.[144] Unexpectedly, the NGOs had stumbled into a powerful and respected ally.

A second boon to the NGO campaign came from a change in leadership at the top of the bank. In 1986, Clausen stepped down. Barber Conable, a veteran congressman with no previous experience in international affairs or financial management, took command. Conable, a well-respected legislator in Washington, recognized the public relations nightmare facing the bank and the importance of getting Congress on board for future replenishments. Most importantly, he was sympathetic to environmental causes, even more so than McNamara had been. Conable made it his personal priority both to support the Baker plan and to oversee a major overhaul of the bank's environmental practices.[145]

In early 1987, Conable worked with bank staffers to devise a complete reorganization of the entire organization that included a vast expansion of

[143] Wade, "Greening the Bank," 670; Rich, *Mortgaging the Earth*, 137.
[144] "Restricted Session of the Joint Ministerial Committee of the Boards of Governors of the Bank and the Fund on the Transfer of Real Resources to Developing Countries," April 10, 1987, "Development Committee, Meeting No. 31, Verbatim, April 10, 1987," WBA.
[145] Ernest Stern, interview, World Bank Oral History Program, January 5, 1995, 51. Online [Available] http://go.worldbank.org/QTZ3Y8B1U0. Accessed May 21, 2012. See also Wade, "Greening the Bank," 672.

the bank's environmental offices. On May 5, 1987, Conable spoke before the World Resources Institute, an NGO that had been founded by Gus Speth and Jessica Mathews, both of whom, incidentally, had been involved in the debates over NEPA's extraterritorial application (Speth at the CEQ, Mathews at the NSC). There, Conable shocked his audience. "We are creating a top-level Environment Department to help set the direction of Bank policy, planning, and research work," he announced. The new department, he explained, would "take the lead in developing strategies to integrate environmental considerations in our overall lending and policy activities." Conable looked over his rapt audience and called for greater cooperation with NGOs. "We need your advice, your expertise, your influence, and your imagination," Conable explained, "to make the urgent work of environmental protection a coordinated campaign for a safer, richer, healthier world."[146] NGOs celebrated the address.

Unlike past declarations that took years to implement, Conable acted quickly. He established a central Environment Department as well as four Regional Environment Divisions (REDs) to provide research, consultations, and assistance to country departments. The REDs not only reviewed projects for the environmental quality, but also had formal "sign-off authority" on projects that "greatly enhanced their ability to influence lending."[147] By the end of 1987, there were fifty full-time environmental posts in the World Bank, ten times the number of positions that existed in 1986.[148]

The changes did not end there. The main NGOs behind the original campaign – plus the Environmental Defense Fund (EDF), where Bruce Rich now worked – appreciated Conable's institution building but still worried that impact assessments were inadequate. They turned once again to Congress, working with a new ally in California Representative Nancy Pelosi, who eventually put an amendment to the *International Development and Finance Act of 1989* that required the U.S. executive director to propose procedures for "systematic environmental assessment of development projects" according to guidelines that the UNEP had crafted with a handful of NGOs.[149] Officials from REDs within the bank began crafting new assessment guidelines during the spring of

---

[146] Barber Conable, "Address to the World Resources Institute," May 5, 1987 in *The Conable Years at the World Bank: Major Policy Addresses of Barber B. Conable, 1986–91* (Washington, DC: The World Bank, 1991), 21–9.

[147] Wade, "Greening the Bank," 674.

[148] Ibid., 675.

[149] Gwin, "U.S. Relations with the World Bank, 1945–1992," 241.

1989. After extensive internal debates, new procedures were announced in late 1989 as a formal Operational Directive.[150]

The new regulations marked a tremendous shift in bank policy. The revised rules moved up the environmental review process in the loan cycle, a complaint of NGOs that had dated back to the late 1970s. In addition, the regulations created new mechanisms for public disclosure. The bank was now required to show the review process to "borrower and affected groups and local NGOs."[151] Critically, too, for the first time all environmental assessments would have to be disclosed to executive directors, which bucked a long history of support for confidentiality of borrower-country documents. In effect this allowed for executive directors to release further the documents to interested and qualified parties, such as NGOs. These reforms allowed for NGOs to gain access to internal bank documents and pressure it to halt loans to sovereign nations on the basis of their environmental activities. In so doing, NGOs became a permanent fixture in monitoring and indirectly enforcing the bank's environmental policy.

This fact did not sit well with some in the bank, who complained that NGOs had become too powerful. As one member of the Development Committee explained, "NGOs have the proverbial privilege of power without responsibility. When the chips are down, it is not they who answer; it is we who are to answer for the problems that we are facing."[152] Fearing that environmental procedures would hamper developing nations' desire for economic growth, such officials complained that now the bank had given in far too much to NGO demands. It was clear to many that a handful of American NGOs had exerted tremendous influence over a major international institution.

These changes also generated frustration among leaders in recipient countries who scoffed at the thought that environmentalists in the United States could shape how and to what extent the World Bank lent money for their own nation's development program. Brazilian officials, in particular, viewed the reforms as impositions on their country's right to development. Brazil's military dictatorship had officially ended under a negotiated

---

[150] "Development Committee Meeting – April 15, 1988, Environment and Development: Implementing the World Bank's New Policies," February 22, 1988, 6–7, Development Committee, folder "Environment. 1986–1987," WBA.

[151] OD, 4.01, para. 21, quoted in Wade, "Greening the Bank," 686.

[152] "Restricted Session of the Joint Ministerial Committee of the Boards of Governors of the bank and the Fund on the Transfer of Real Resources to Developing Countries," April 10, 1987, "Development Committee, Meeting No. 31, Verbatim, April 10, 1987," WBA.

transition in 1985, but the new democratically elected government sought rapid economic growth to overcome widespread fiscal problems and rampant inflation. Leading officials subsequently framed environmentalism in terms of imperialism, often criticizing Western environmentalists for impairing Brazil's right to pursue economic growth in language highly reminiscent of the Stockholm Conference. Following the passage of the new regulations, Brazilian President José Sarney explained in March 1989 that Brazil would not "accept the developed world's manipulation of the ecology issue to restrict Latin America's autonomy and progress." Foreign Minster Abreu Sodré agreed. "Brazil does not want to transform itself into an ecological reserve for humanity," he proclaimed in the same month. "Our greatest duty," Sodré added, "is with our economic development." Although the Sarney administration began to introduce environmental reforms into the government during its tenure and the murder of rural activist Chico Mendes generated even greater international attention on Brazil's destruction of the Amazon region, Brazilian officials still resisted the bank's new environmental regulations. They believed the bank's new rules had gone too far, impinging on Brazil's national sovereignty by creating a powerful check on the nation's ability to gain financial support for its development projects.[153]

While the bank's reforms did not radically alter the Brazilian government's economic plans, changes made during the 1980s proved to have far more significant effects than earlier initiatives and empowered NGOs to have a more active role in bank practices than ever before. It took a few years for the Environment Department to fill the new positions with experts in ecology and natural resources, rather than economists. However, the department greatly reduced earlier staffing shortages and ensured that the review process, slow though it was, would take place.[154] Although it also took a few years for all the new regulations to be implemented, and although project staff still had preponderant power in determining initial projects and final loan disbursements, NGO pressure and Conable's reforms had created sufficient institutional momentum to ensure that the bank would be accountable for its effects on the environment.

The creation of an Inspection Panel in 1993 further strengthened NGO influence on the bank. Amid Conable's restructuring, debates had continued over the status of the Sardar Sarovar dam in India (Figure 7).

---

[153] Officials quoted in Hurrell, "Brazil and the International Politics of Amazonian Deforestation," 405.
[154] Rajagopalan, interview, World Bank Oral History Program, 1993, 27.

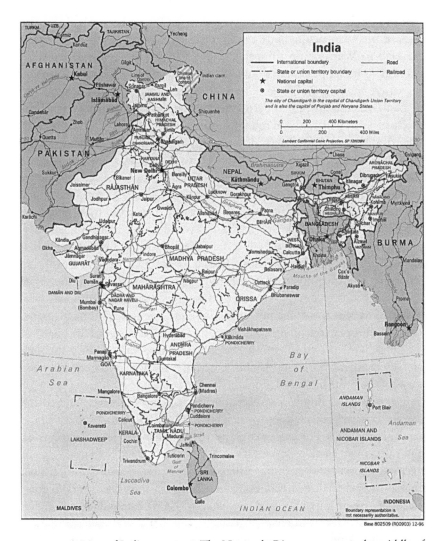

FIGURE 7: Map of India, ca. 1996. The Narmada River cuts across the middle of the country, from the Arabian Sea north of Mumbai to the center of the subcontinent. Courtesy of University of Texas Libraries.

As U.S. activists waged their campaign against the bank in Washington, a groundswell of opposition to Sardar Sarovar emerged in India. Spearheaded by the activist Medha Patkar, indigenous Indian groups protested the dam's overall economic viability, its ecological consequences, and the Indian government's village resettlement and relocation plans. By the early 1990s, Patkar and other protestors had drawn international attention to the project. As José Lutzenberger had done as part of his advocacy against the Polonoroeste project in Brazil, Patkar traveled to Washington to speak before Congress. The extensive local protests in India, punctuated by widespread marches and hunger strikes, increased pressure on the bank to alter its lending policies once again.[155]

Bank officials agreed to perform a formal, independent review of the entire project, which, when released in June 1992, demonstrated management mishaps and fueled NGO concerns for more transparency in the loan disbursement process.[156] Various activists testified before Congress that same month, demanding that it withhold further IDA replenishment unless the bank established an "Independent Appeals Commission" for indigenous or international NGOs to bring complaints over proposed projects before the bank.[157] In late 1993 and 1994, bank officials discussed, debated, and ultimately established a formal Inspection Panel, through which concerned parties could challenge proposed bank projects. Independent of bank management, the panel represented a compromise between NGOs pushing for greater transparency and bank officials who hesitated to cede too much power to non-bank members. While the panel had no authority to stop projects itself, it reported directly to the board of directors, and provided another venue for non-state actors, through increased bureaucratic and legalistic activity, to slow and even alter the way in which the bank functioned.[158]

The NGOs' ability to pressure the World Bank ultimately stalled the Sardar Sarovar project, about which environmentalists had spoken in the same breath as the Polonoroeste project since the mid-1980s. In late 1992 and early 1993, bank representatives haggled with the Indian government over the project's status. Indian officials, who had steered the country on a course of financial and economic liberalization and had sparked high national growth rates, refused to give in to NGO demands to terminate construction. Many echoed the frustrated sentiments of Brazilian officials, fearing that American activists would exercise preponderant influence in defining the shape and content of aid to India. A bank representative paraphrased one close participant from the Indian government as saying,

---

[155] Patrick McCully, *Silenced Rivers: The Ecology and Politics of Large Dams* (London: Zed Books, 2001), 301–6.

[156] Ibrahim F. I. Shihata, *The World Bank Inspection Panel*, 12–13.

[157] Ibid., 26–7. The NRDC had long pushed for such an appeal mechanism. See Eric Christensen, *Green Appeal: A Proposal for an Environmental Commission of Enquiry at the World Bank* (Washington, DC: NRDC, 1990).

[158] Shihata, *The World Bank Inspection Panel*, chapter 2.

"Damn the NGOs, we are not going to submit to crybabies, we will continue to build the dam." However, high-level bank officials convinced Indian leaders to do so, for the sake of an upcoming debate over IDA replenishment. The bank's vice president for South Asia put the matter bluntly: "Either we cancel," he told Indian officials, "or you tell us you will not submit requests for disbursements." In the end, the Indian government capitulated and stopped asking the bank for support. Domestic NGOs in India even got Indian officials to halt construction altogether while drafting new resettlement schemes.[159] Concerns that NGO activity would spur Congress to halt IDA replenishment again led bank officials to alter their lending practices in ways they would not otherwise. While debates between NGOs and bank officials continued over which projects the bank should support, the creation of the Inspection Panel provided an avenue for NGOs to slow the process of loans and disbursements before development projects such as Sardar Sarovar could begin, ensuring private actors an influential place in the functioning of the World Bank.

### CONCLUSION: ENVIRONMENTAL NGOS AND PRIVATE POWER FOR PUBLIC ENDS

Although the conflict with the World Bank garnered headlines around environmental impact statements in the late 1980s, it was in fact at the tail end of a much longer historical process by environmentalists to make all development agencies accountable by incorporating some kind of procedural environmental review by experts. From the 1960s through the high-profile cases in the World Bank, NGOs waged extensive legal and political campaigns that attempted to change the way the world's most important development lenders – the United States and the World Bank – could allocate funding for potentially destructive development projects. Environmental review was one way that development could be made more accountable.

The evolution of impact assessment and statement guidelines, however, unfolded in a fraught, contested, and uneven way. While the review process ended up making development agencies more accountable for their effects on the environment, it was not because officials within those agencies began making better decisions as soon as new procedures were put into place. Rather, the impact assessment–statement process

[159] Wade, "Greening the Bank," 705–6.

opened up a new means for NGOs to hold agencies accountable for failing to adopt the full impact assessment procedures. It was through the courts of law, congressional mandates, and public pressure that accountability came into being. The use of impact statements was only possible with NGOs providing a kind of private governance, leveraging their expertise of environmental law and culling close ties with advocates in government – often the CEQ – to pressure other federal agencies to comply. For all the talk of making these institutions more accountable and transparent to the public, in practice, "the public" had come to signify those NGOs capable of exercising legal authority and political influence.

In the end, the accountability achieved relied on what had become by the 1980s an increasingly antiquated notion: a separation between the concepts of "environmental protection" and "development." The procedural requirements of the EIA required officials to separate environment and development. NGOs, in turn, served as countervailing political forces to governing bodies. Yet as NGOs campaigned for environmental review, a different intellectual process was taking place within the environmental and development community. This process sought to convince policy makers that development would be more effective if environmental constraints were integral to, not separate from, development objectives. This move toward the concept of "sustainable development" planning sought to integrate ecological thinking into development thinking, so that projects would be ecologically sensitive from their inception.

# 6

## Conservation for Development: The *World Conservation Strategy* and the Rise of Sustainable Development Planning

In September 1975, the International Union for the Conservation of Nature (IUCN) met for their Thirteenth General Assembly in Kinshasa, Zaire. The meeting was fraught with tensions. For one, the event host, Zaire's dictatorial leader Mobutu Seso Seko, had armed guards patrol meetings and often made quick, unexpected schedule changes that left participants nervous and aggravated. More deeply, however, conflicts within the organization that had been simmering for years finally erupted. The IUCN had spent the past two decades trying to make the case for environmental protection as countries pursued economic development, often defining the two concepts as irreconcilable. By the mid-1970s, some officials had begun to wonder whether it would be more desirable and effective for nations to fold conservation principles into their development planning from the start – to emphasize "conservation's value as an instrument for sound development everywhere" as the IUCN's 1974 annual report suggested.[1] Yet others remained skeptical of making such a shift, believing that the organization should hew closely to their older focus on species and landscape protection. In Kinshasa, debates over how to define the organization's purpose exacerbated anxieties over other issues – such as whether the IUCN was becoming too bureaucratic and whether it had forged too many ties with the UN system – and deeply frustrated participants. The meeting, later dubbed the "Night of the Long Knives," ended with a "bad-tempered" session of the group's executive board, a dramatic

---

[1] *IUCN Yearbook 1974: Annual Report of the International Union for the Conservation of Nature and Natural Resources for 1974*, 13, IUCN Library.

overhaul in the group's leadership, and widespread confusion, uncertainty, and anger among its members.[2]

The Kinshasa meeting and the many similar debates over the direction of environmental activism attested to the fact that the IUCN and many other environmental non-governmental organizations (NGOs) were at a crossroads in the 1970s. Activists could celebrate movements pushing to rethink development, such as the appropriate technology movement, and growing awareness of the need for accountability mechanisms, such as impact statements, to rein in development lenders. Yet the desire for economic development continued to captivate leaders across the world, and many nations still resisted comprehensive environmental protection policies. Powerful questions hung over the purpose of environmental NGOs toward the Global South: How could groups such as the IUCN convince leaders in developing countries to include conservation in their development strategies? And to what extent should activists place conservation in service of economic objectives?

Over the 1970s and 1980s, the IUCN and a few other NGOs sought to answer these questions by offering a new approach for how nations should and could craft development plans and manage natural resources. By the mid-1980s, their efforts resulted in a concept called "sustainable development," which purported to have bridged old divisions between economic growth and ecological limits. Both environmental and economic objectives could be achieved, environmentalists argued, if all nations revised how they planned for economic growth by basing development models on ecological principles. Reforming the foundations of development planning represented another way in which environmentalists sought to reconcile tensions between economic development and environmental protection.

The idea of sustainable development arose from two critiques of development planning – an environmental critique and the "basic human needs" critique. In the postwar years, many developing nations created national development plans that often ignored environmental considerations, which they believed would compromise economic growth. By the 1960s, environmentalists rallied against such plans because they had depleted natural resources, generated pollution, and imperiled wild flora and fauna. At the same time, countries of the Global South faced extensive poverty, poor health conditions, and fragile economies subject to the vicissitudes of global finance, trade, and aid. Amid the environmental

[2] Holdgate, *The Green Web*, 125–9.

criticism of development planning, reformers from the developing world critiqued the same plans for neglecting the basic human needs of the poor and demanded "alternative" approaches.[3]

These two critiques slowly merged in the 1970s through a small, transnational network of leading environmentalists and influential development experts. Spearheaded by key environmentalists such as Maurice Strong, Barbara Ward, David Munro, Ray Dasmann, and Lee Talbot, this network gradually developed an alternative approach to planning that sought to redress poverty and environmental degradation. The approach, which they termed "sustainable development," emerged as officials in the IUCN and the World Wildlife Fund (WWF) worked with the United Nations Environment Programme (UNEP) to craft the *World Conservation Strategy*. These groups hoped that the *World Conservation Strategy* would create environmental guidelines that all nations could follow. Initiated during the IUCN's internal debates during the mid-1970s and finished in 1980, the document outlined basic principles for managing ecosystems. It allowed for economic growth to continue, so long as development plans ensured the protection of genetic diversity, prevented the eradication of species within a given ecosystem, and did not outstrip the regenerative capacities of natural systems. If nations followed these broad suggestions, the crafters of the guidebook argued that nations could achieve short-term economic needs without eroding the ecological conditions on which material abundance depended in the long run.[4]

Reframing conservation to serve development purposes proved to be a contentious process. The institutional ties forged between environmental groups and development experts, along with intellectual shifts within leading NGOs, sparked dramatic conflicts within the environmental community. These tensions erupted at the IUCN's 1975 General Assembly meeting in Kinshasa, Zaire, and reappeared through early drafts of the *World Conservation Strategy*. After a series of deliberations on the purpose of conservation, the IUCN redoubled its commitment to

---

[3] On the rise of "alternative development" and the basic human needs approach to development, see Nemchenok, *A Dialogue of Power* and Rist, *The History of Development*, chapter 9. While the alternative development reformers had many diverse objectives, they shared a concern for redressing poverty, protecting individual human needs, overcoming the legacies of colonialism, and drawing global attention to North-South socioeconomic conflict. Specifically, they advocated major increases in foreign aid and technology transfers, global standards for price floors on commodities, regulation of transnational corporations, and guaranteed access to markets of OECD members.

[4] *World Conservation Strategy: Living Resource Conservation for Sustainable Development* (IUCN-WWF-UNEP, 1980).

frame conservation in terms of development in the late 1970s. Officials rebranded the organization's purpose to suggest that conservation needed to alleviate poverty, improve public heath, and redress global inequality. The *World Conservation Strategy* mirrored the changes occurring within environmental groups. By the end of the decade, many environmentalists had gradually come to embrace the alternative development paradigm.[5]

Sustainable development in national planning, however, proved easier to imagine than to implement. Zambia, one of the first nations to craft national plans based on the *World Conservation Strategy*, demonstrated just how difficult the creation and implementation of a national strategy could be. NGO officials learned that reorienting an entire national economy along ecologically sustainable lines needed more than just good science. Sustainable development planning in Zambia and the rest of the developing world required unwavering political commitment from national leaders, substantial institutional change, and extensive financial support from the developed world. As it had been in the early 1970s, in the 1990s the future of environmental protection in the developing world was inextricably bound to the foreign aid policies of the developed countries.

By the 1980s, sustainable development became detached from its roots as a way to connect environmentalism with alternative, reformist development approaches premised on poverty eradication and community participation. As the phrase became more popular, sustainable development (and later, "sustainability") became much more capacious and used as shorthand for making vague linkages between the environment and development. The most popular text for drawing public attention to the phrase, the 1987 Brundtland Commission report, highlighted the multigenerational, long-term justifications for environmental protection alongside the social justice and socioeconomic equality elements.[6] Over time, in popular discourse the focus on equity for future generations came to overshadow the extent to which the environmentalists who had first supported the sustainable development idea had stressed the need to redress present-day inequalities as a necessary step in realizing effective environmental protection. Thus, as many NGOs began to reconcile long-standing tensions between environmental protection and demands of social and economic justice emanating from the Global South, they lost

[5] On environmentalists' general embrace of liberal development, see Bernstein, *The Compromise of Liberal Environmentalism*. For a very brief overview of the WCS, see John C. McCormick, "The Origins of the World Conservation Strategy," *Environmental Review*, Vol. 10, No. 3 (Autumn 1986), 177–87.

[6] *Our Common Future* (Oxford: Oxford University Press, 1987).

control of the sustainability discourse as the concept became associated with a variety of different definitions having little to do with its original purpose.

In 1970, French development economist Ignacy Sachs began to explore how developing nations could pursue economic growth while minimizing environmental damage. In the past, leaders in developing nations had interpreted environmental regulations as costly additions to existing economic programs and growth models. Sachs thought these concerns could be redressed by designing plans that made environmental conservation a fundamental component of planning, rather than a corrective to plans that had gone awry. "Environmental control should be fit into development plans to a much larger extent than hitherto," Sachs argued in an early paper.[7] Working with Maurice Strong, over the ensuing years Sachs developed a new approach to economic growth, which he called "ecodevelopment."[8]

The ecodevelopment concept married a concern for an equitable distribution of resources and satisfaction of basic needs with a desire to limit pollution and ensure long-term ecosystem health. Ecodevelopment emphasized decentralized and participatory planning, elimination of poverty, appropriate technologies, self-reliance, and judicious husbandry of natural resources.[9] If planners incorporated these components into their economic strategies, Sachs believed, they could still achieve material abundance and economic growth while avoiding the catastrophic missteps associated with rapid industrialization and urbanization.[10]

---

[7] Ignacy Sachs, "Employment Potential of Environmental Control Works in Less Developed Countries – notes for a research project," June 26, 1970, G.X 34/7 "Environment: Environmental Work Undertaken by Other Organizations – Jacket 1," UNOG Registry Collection; Ignacy Sachs to Ben Reiner, October 2, 1970, ibid.

[8] "Ecodevelopment: A Definition," *Ambio*, Vol. 8, No. 2/3 (1979), 113.

[9] Ibid.

[10] B. Gosovic to Maurice Strong, September 19, 1978, folder 979, box 103, V. UNEP, Maurice F. Strong Papers, Environmental Science and Public Policy Archives, Harvard University, Cambridge, MA [hereinafter cited as Strong papers]. Under Strong's direction, the UNEP produced a major research paper on the subject that it released in early 1976. "Ecodevelopment," January 15, 1976, UNEP/GC/80. Viewed in G.X 34/26 "Co-operation between ECE and the United Nations Environment Programme (UNEP) – Jacket 2," UNOG Registry Collection.

Ecodevelopment gained traction during a series of international conferences in the early 1970s. Barbara Ward, director of the International Institute for Environment and Development (IIED), brought together Sachs and other development and environmental experts at two symposiums in 1970 and 1971.[11] Enthusiastic about these exchanges, Maurice Strong, then the executive director of the Stockholm Conference, and Ward convened a major gathering in Founex, Switzerland, in the spring of 1971. They invited the developing world's leading experts associated with "alternative development" paradigms, such as Sachs, Mahbub ul Haq, Gamani Corea, Enrique Iglesias, and Samir Amin. They hoped to mollify the concerns of developing countries in the lead-up to the Stockholm Conference by creating a policy framework that linked issues of poverty eradication, public health, and environmental degradation.[12] Even a few policy makers took notice of the new concept. Speaking to the UN about the "interlocking" problems of development and environment in advance of the Stockholm gathering, U.S. Ambassador George H. W. Bush proclaimed, "Perhaps we are moving toward a new science of 'eco-development,' which will combine the values of economics and ecology and will make it forever unnecessary to choose between the curse of poverty and the curse of pollution."[13] The idea was gaining support.

The network of experts behind ecodevelopment quickly organized more meetings to grapple with its meaning and implications for policy. In October 1974, Ward convened a follow-up in Cocoyoc, Mexico, dubbed "Founex II."[14] The meeting came a few months after the developing countries had put forth a declaration at the UN General Assembly for a "New International Economic Order" (NIEO) that called for restructuring the global economy along more equitable lines to support the needs of the Global South. The Cocoyoc meeting captured much of the spirit animating the NIEO and sought to bridge it with the growing

---

[11] Satterthwaite, *Barbara Ward and the Origins of Sustainable Development*, 43; Ward, Runnalls, and D'Anjou, eds., *The Widening Gap.*

[12] Maurice Strong, "Stockholm: The founding of IIED," in Nigel Cross, ed., *Evidence for Hope: The Search for Sustainable Development* (London: Earthscan Publications Ltd., 2003), 21–23; "Development and Environment: Founex, Switzerland, June 4–12, 1971," (Mouton, France: École Pratique des Hautes Études, 1971), 125–8; Frederic Lapeyre, "Transcript of Interview of Ignacy Sachs," May 9, 2000, United Nations Intellectual History Project, *The Graduate School and University Center, City University of New York*, 36–9, oral history in author's possession.

[13] "George Bush, U.S. Representative to UN, "Environment and Development: The Interlocking Problems," July 5, 1971, Department of State *Bulletin*, 21–2.

[14] Nemchenok, *A Dialogue of Power*, chapter 2, 62–5.

interest in ecodevelopment. In the gathering's summary declaration, Ward articulated the emerging synthesis between environmental and development concerns. She called for a new international system "capable of meeting the 'inner limits' of basic human needs for all the world's people and of doing so without violating the 'outer limits' of the planet's resources and environment." Furthermore she claimed, "The road forward does not lie through the despair of doom-watching nor through the easy optimism of successive technological fixes. It lies through a careful and dispassionate assessment of the 'outer limits,' through cooperative search for ways to achieve the 'inner limits' of fundamental human rights, through the building of social structures to express those rights, and through all the patient work of devising techniques and styles of development which enhance and preserve our planetary inheritance."[15] Ward stitched together environmental protection, alternative development strategies, and the need for socioeconomic equality between North and South. Her work also inspired more expert gatherings to discuss crosscutting issues related to environmental protection, poverty, and inequality.[16]

Alongside Ward's efforts, environmental NGOs also began to rethink development planning. In the early 1970s, the IUCN funded and coordinated multiple conferences designed to derive ecological guidelines for developers across the world. Their efforts resulted in a 1973 book, *Ecological Principles for Economic Development*, written by IUCN biologist Ray Dasmann and Conservation Foundation official John Milton. The book proposed to reorient national planning around the regenerative capacities of ecosystems, offering specific strategies for managing humid tropical lands, pastoral lands in semiarid regions, and river basins. In addition, the authors listed a series of general ecological principles for development experts to follow. "Lack of consideration for the ecological realities of an environment can doom development efforts, with consequent waste of money and impairment in the condition of life," they wrote. Like Barbara Ward, they hoped that the injection of ecological knowledge into development plans could satisfy "human needs and

---

[15] "The Cocoyoc Declaration," *International Organization*, Vol. 29, No. 3 (Summer 1975), 896.

[16] William Clark, "Paper to the Board and Council of IIED on the Role of IIED," June 1983, folder 2389, box 253, VII IIED Correspondence London, Strong Papers. The main conferences, held under UN auspices but often organized with substantial NGO support, were on population (1974), food (1974), human settlements (1976), and science and technology (1979). As with the Stockholm Conference, Barbara Ward even prepared guidebooks for the latter two meetings *The Home of Man* (New York: W.W. Norton and Co., 1976) and *Progress for a Small Planet* (New York: W.W. Norton and Co., 1979).

aspirations" of the present and contribute "to the stability and productivity of the planet" in the long term.[17]

Through these gatherings and publications in the early 1970s, a few important themes emerged. Officials such as Ward and Strong came to believe that while greater coordination and cooperation between NGOs and governing bodies was necessary, it was also important to carve out a transnational space in which experts could meet, discuss, and deliberate global issues. They recognized that gatherings focused around leading nations, such as the 1972 Stockholm Conference, had failed to organize effective global cooperation. Ward, Strong, Sachs, and their colleagues wanted to change state policies worldwide, but they believed they first needed to craft their own institutional arrangements to discuss new ideas through a process that was not bound by parochial, national interests.[18] They were also beginning to embrace the development community as a partner in shaping the international environmental agenda. For much of the mid-1970s, officials in leading NGOs built on these efforts, as they nurtured new institutional relationships and revised their basic assumptions about resource use and development planning.

## MAURICE STRONG, THE UNEP, AND NEW INSTITUTIONAL RELATIONSHIPS

In this process of engaging the development community, the UNEP played a key role. In part, this derived from the influence developing countries had achieved within the UN system. Their voting majority in the UN General Assembly gave them enough leverage to have the new agency headquartered in Nairobi. It was the first UN agency based in the Third World. Developing countries, who also had a built-in majority on the UNEP Governing Council, used the organization to voice their desire for additional financial support to fund environmental programs and frame environmental discussions around themes of poverty and inequality. Although many UN officials envisioned it as an apolitical, technocratic organization, after the UNEP Governing Council's first session in 1973, it

---

[17] Dasmann, Milton, and Freeman, *Ecological Principles for Economic Development*, 1–2; "Ecology in Development Programmes: an IUCN Project," *IUCN Bulletin*, Vol. 2, No. 17 (October/December 1970), 141; D. Hackett, K. Hale, and K. Smith, "The Role of the Ecologist in Environmental Planning, Development and Management," a study for the Environmental Planning Commission of IUCN, December 1973, IUCN Library.

[18] Ward dedicated much of her energies during the 1970s to nurturing this network. Mahbub ul Haq to Barbara Ward, November 8, 1976, box 3, Ward Papers.

"became clear that the work of UNEP was going to be as seriously influenced as other UN activities by the division between developing and developed worlds."[19]

When Maurice Strong took over as executive director of the UNEP in 1974, he used the agency as a venue for bringing together environmentalists and representatives from the developing world. As a friend of leading environmentalists, a respected development expert, and an ally of many Global South elites, Strong positioned himself as a mediator between these groups. From his arrival in Nairobi, Strong envisioned the UNEP as a "catalyst, initiator, and coordinator" for tackling issues of environment and development, particularly in the developing world.[20] He encouraged environmentalists to work with developing nations seeking technical support, sending the likes of the IUCN's Kai Curry-Lindahl to work as a consultant on many issues.[21] Through the mid-1970s, the UNEP hosted a number of regional conferences in the developing world, which brought together development economists, ecologists, and officials from national planning ministries to "show environment as a dimension of development."[22]

Strong also hoped to strengthen ties between environmental NGOs and the UN system by encouraging officials to work in both worlds. "I am convinced," he wrote in 1973, "that effective environmental action depends on a much closer and more cooperative relationship between the inter-governmental and non-governmental institutions that has yet been experienced, at least internationally."[23] Under Strong's guidance, from the mid-1970s many officials cycled between NGOs and the UNEP. For instance, David Munro, a high-ranking UNEP official during the mid-1970s, became IUCN's executive director in 1978. Peter Thacher, an American diplomat who had assisted Strong during the Stockholm proceedings, served as executive director of the UNEP in the late 1970s before working for various environmental NGOs in the 1980s. Strong

---

[19] "United Nations Environment Programme – Future UK Policy," December 1973, NA-UK, FCO 55/1007.
[20] "Remarks by Maurice Strong, Executive Director, UNEP to the UNA of Great Britain and Northern Ireland," July 22, 1975, folder C. 1246, Scott Papers.
[21] Kai Curry-Lindahl to Robert Hunter, December 22, 1976, folder 978, box 103, V. UNEP, Strong Papers.
[22] "Ad Hoc Expert Group Meeting on Alternative Patterns of Development and Life Styles for Africa, Nairobi, March, 23–25, 1977," G.X 34/42 UNEP/ECE Conference on Alternative Lifestyles and Development, UNOG.
[23] Maurice Strong to Robert O. Anderson, January 12, 1973, box 73, V. IIED 73–74, Strong Papers.

himself moved between the different organizations. In addition to his role with UNEP, he held key positions within the IUCN, sat on the Executive Council of the WWF, and unofficially advised the IIED throughout the 1970s.[24]

Under Strong's direction, the UNEP also provided critical financial support to key NGOs during 1970s, which proved particularly important as many groups struggled to secure funding due to "donor fatigue" amid global economic instability and waning excitement for environmental causes. In the early 1970s, Strong personally lobbied Ford Foundation officials to support the IIED and the IUCN; when philanthropic support fell short, the UNEP stepped in. In late 1973, it began to deliver financial support, in the form of grants to cover operating expenses and new initiatives, to help the IIED.[25] Strong also set up a system of grants to cover the IUCN's basic operating costs. In early 1974, the UNEP offered the organization $1 million in general support, with another $1.5 million set aside for 1975.[26] Just a few years later, such support counted for over 40 percent of IUCN's total income.[27] The UNEP's funding played a "major role" to help "rehabilitate" the IUCN during the 1970s.[28]

The relationship between the UNEP and leading environmental groups was a boon for all involved. By funding respected environmental groups, the UNEP developed ties to a community of scientific experts that bolstered its credibility. The IUCN received badly needed funding for its basic programs, and it found new connections that enabled officials to engage directly with experts from the developing world. In turn, a well-funded IUCN greatly helped its other main funding source: the WWF. With the new arrangement in place, the WWF could broaden its activities to other areas, and its ancillary ties to the UN system afforded it some cover from criticisms that it was still too narrowly focused on species protection. UNEP support enabled these NGOs to expand their international conservation activities.[29]

---

[24] McCormick, *The Global Environmental Movement*, 125–6.

[25] "The Position of the International Institute for Environment and Development in Mid-October 1973," box 73, V. IIED 73–74, Strong Papers.

[26] "Decisions of UNEP Governing Council," *IUCN Bulletin*, Vol. 5, No. 4 (April 1974), 13–14.

[27] "WWF and UNEP funding," Agenda Paper UC.77/3, October 1977, box 80, V. IUCN Meetings, Strong Papers.

[28] Maurice Strong to Marshall Robinson, February 28, 1978, box 64, V. Ford Foundation, Strong Papers.

[29] "13th (Extraordinary) General Assembly, Geneva, Switzerland: Progress Report on the Strategy and its Component Programmes," Agenda Paper GA.77/3, 1977, folder 730, box 76, IUCN, Strong Papers.

Of all these changes, the new connections were particularly significant for the IUCN. Its long list of affiliated experts made it the central hub for disbursing environmental knowledge to governments and international institutions. It had established its scientific bona fides and earned considerable clout on issues such as endangered species monitoring. However, throughout the 1970s, critics from the developing world increasingly assailed the organization. They argued that the organization's professionalization had increased the power of a small technocratic elite based in Switzerland at the expense of broader participation from its national chapters. IUCN members from Kenya lambasted the organization for failing to provide enough information on its changing activities.[30] The Kenyans reiterated an older criticism that the organization was "overly European" in character, with too many leaders drawn from the United States and Western Europe.[31] As a result, the Kenyans felt as though they had "no participation" in the IUCN outside the triennial General Assembly meetings, and no way to shape the organization's activities. These criticisms reminded leading NGO officials of the extent to which developed nations felt marginalized and threatened by leading environmentalists.

By working in closer connection with the UNEP, IUCN officials had the opportunity to redress these objections by incorporating more of the concerns of developing nations into their overall strategy. Over the 1970s, the institutional connections enabled officials in environmental groups with the financial support, intellectual networks, and experiences to rethink old assumptions about the relationship between environmental protection and economic development.

### REVISING OLD ASSUMPTIONS, MAKING NEW CLAIMS

Through their experiences and exchanges with the development community, NGO leaders slowly began to adopt a more holistic approach to conservation during the 1970s. Barbara Ward positioned the IIED to pursue "the integrative aspects of international environmental programmes."

[30] "Report by Kasainga Mulwa on 12th General Assembly and 13th Technical Meeting of IUCN," Archival records from Department of Wildlife Conservation and Management and tourism-Environmental Planning Division (Government of Kenya), [hereinafter cited as KW] 5/23 International Conservation of Nature (IUCN) 1975, Kenyan National Archives [hereinafter cited as KNA], Nairobi, Kenya.

[31] "Issues to be Considered by Delegates to the IUCN General Assembly at Zaire," KW 5/23, IUCN-1975, KNA.

Although she told Maurice Strong that she did not believe "any one body is trying to persuade the pure conservationists to see the slum child as an endangered species," she thought that her organization needed to play a "catalytic" role in bringing together conservationists, development experts, and UN officials to focus on how conservation might aid reformers in the developing world. Under Ward's guidance the IIED began to organize expert meetings and publish books, pamphlets, and guidebooks toward this end.[32]

Along similar lines, the IUCN began to reframe conservation as a tool to pursue economic development. Beginning in 1972, the organization made "conservation *for* development" a key theme of its activities.[33] Earlier the organization had often made declarations about "conservation and development," but now the change in preposition signified its efforts to incorporate conservation into development planning. "No great foresight is required to see that unless conservation and by this we mean, broadly, the *rational* use of natural resources leading to improved *quality* of life – is made an integral part of all planning for the future, chances are there will be little left to conserve," editors of the IUCN's newsletter claimed.[34]

By the end of 1974, IUCN President Gerardo Budowski acknowledged the extent to which his organization had also begun to wrestle with the need to focus on eradicating poverty along with nature protection. He wondered whether "ecology should conform to politics." Acknowledging the concerns of developing nations, Budowski lamented the "poor distribution of wealth and other inequalities" worldwide. There was, he claimed, "no question of global inequities .... But ecological realties must also be faced at the same time, and action to correct the grave imbalances between human populations, resources and environment must go hand in hand with struggles against the injustices of social and economic systems." He hoped to frame the environment and development debate around the differences between short-term fixes and long-term ecological planning. Like many others, he was beginning to think along the same lines as Ward and Strong.[35] A year after Budowski's article, IUCN official Robert Allen castigated environmentalists for their

[32] Barbara Ward to Maurice Strong, February 14, 1974, box 73, V. IIED 73–74, Strong Papers.

[33] *Eleventh General Assembly: Proceedings* (Morges, Switzerland: IUCN, 1972). [Online] Available: http://www.iucn.org/knowledge/publications_doc/publications/. Accessed November 14, 2011.

[34] "Conservation for Development," *IUCN Bulletin*, Vol. 3, No. 10. (1972), 43.

[35] Gerardo Budowski, "Should Ecology Conform to Politics?" *IUCN Bulletin*, Vol. 5, No. 12 (December 1974), 44–5.

"political agoraphobia" for an unwillingness to negotiate and compromise with decision makers, especially those from the developing world.[36]

This desire to incorporate the concerns of the developing world mirrored a broader intellectual project about the relationship between local peoples and the management of national parks and protected areas. In particular, Ray Dasmann, the IUCN's senior ecologist, began to prod leading conservation organizations to place a greater emphasis on the participation of indigenous peoples and rural communities in the management of protected spaces. Dasmann broached a controversial topic; conservationists had long supported the forcible expulsion of such people from parks and reserves.[37] In the early 1970s, Dasmann gradually rethought this relationship as he worked with Maurice Strong's network of experts.[38] After engaging in a variety of UNEP seminars and meeting with development experts such as Ignacy Sachs and the Nigerian intellectual Jimoh Omo-Fadaka, Dasmann concluded that development *and* environmental protection efforts "must be directed to meeting the basic needs of the poorest people before paying attention to the wants of the elite."[39] He also admired and hoped to build on the work of economist E. F. Schumacher and biologist Barry Commoner, both of whom had offered forceful criticisms of the large-scale technological systems that had come to define how societies pursued economic development.[40]

By the mid-1970s, Dasmann had developed powerful critiques of leading NGOs. In 1973 and 1974, he chided the IUCN for ignoring local self-determination and for rejecting participatory planning.[41] "Attempts to solve" conservation problems "at a global, or even national level," he claimed, "often strike far from the mark, because they fail to take into account the attitudes or motivations of the people concerned." He further castigated conservationists for their poor treatment of indigenous people. Dasmann drew a distinction between "ecosystem people," indigenous persons who lived directly off the land, and "biosphere people," who

---

[36] Robert Allen, "Conservation for Decision-Makers: Decisions for Conservationists," *IUCN Bulletin*, Vol. 6, No. 5 (May 1975), 17.

[37] See Chapter 2 of this book; Dowie, *Conservation Refugees*.

[38] Stephen Macekura, "The Limits of Global Community: The Nixon Administration and Global Environmental Politics," *Cold War History*, Vol. 11, No. 4 (2011), 489–518.

[39] Dasmann, *Called by the Wild*, 178–9.

[40] "Raymond F. Dasmann: A Life in Conservation Biology," University of Santa Cruz Library, 49. [Online] Available: http://library.ucsc.edu/reg-hist/dasmann. Accessed February 7, 2012.

[41] Raymond Dasmann, "Sanctuaries for Life Styles," *IUCN Bulletin*, Vol. 4, No. 8 (August 1973), 29.

lived at a distance from the land and lived a polluting lifestyle. The "ecosystem people," he argued, were not the irrational resource wasters but constituted societies with an intimate knowledge of biophysical limits and natural cycles. The greatest threat to conservation came from the "biosphere people" – Westerners with profligate lifestyles. He criticized the environmental movement for its past impositions on indigenous populations, particularly those in Africa who had long been marginalized from their ancestral homelands. "If we were to enquire when nature conservation in Africa was most effective," the answer would be "long before the words 'nature conservation' were ever spoken," he claimed.[42]

Over the next few years, Dasmann spread his message through many venues. He reiterated the ecosystem-biosphere people dichotomy in a lengthy article for *The Ecologist*.[43] At the WWF's Fourth International Conference in 1976, Dasmann asserted that for those in the developing world, there was "no way out through following the development patterns advocated by the industrialized world." Rather, the developing world needed to rely on "using sources available locally to build self-sustaining local economies" and "drawing on their own traditions and cultural patterns to learn how" to do so.[44] Dasmann's support of "ecosystem people" coupled with his critique of existing development approaches amounted to a forceful argument against top-down methods of park management and development planning. For organizations with a long history of casting aside indigenous persons on behalf of a vision of a wilderness absent human beings, it was a remarkable transformation. Aided by later shifts in ecological science that reinforced Dasmann's political claims, within a few years many other influential IUCN officials accepted his basic arguments.[45]

---

[42] Raymond F. Dasmann, "Lifestyles and Nature Conservation," *Oryx*, Vol. XIII, No. 3 (February 1976), 281–2.

[43] Raymond Dasmann, "National Parks, Nature Conservation, and 'Future Primitive,'" *The Ecologist*, Vol. 6, No. 5 (June 1976), 164–7; Raymond Dasmann, unpublished oral history, 114–15; Raymond F. Dasmann, "The Relationship Between Protected Areas and Indigenous Peoples," in Jeffrey A. McNeely and Kenton R. Miller, eds., *National Parks, Conservation, and Development: The Role of Protected Areas in Sustaining Society* (Washington, DC: The Smithsonian Institution Press, 1984), 667–71.

[44] James N. Glass, ed., "This Fragile Earth: Toward Strategies for Survival," Report on the Fourth International Congress of the World Wildlife Fund, November 28 to December 1, 1976, 64. Viewed at the Wildlife Information Center, World Wildlife Fund-United States, Washington, DC.

[45] Robert Allen, "Sustainable Development and Cultural Diversity – Two Sides of the Same Coin," *IUCN Bulletin*, Vol. 6, No. 4 (April 1975), 13. By the late 1970s and early 1980s, ecologists and biologists had begun to rethink many basic assumptions about the inherent stability and invariable succession of undisturbed ecosystems toward a climax community or steady state. By the late 1970s, however, research had begun to critique such

Alongside this participatory vision of planning and management, many environmental NGOs increasingly broadened the scope of their activities beyond parks, species, or ecosystem protection. The IIED established a new focus on urban pollution and poverty under the moniker of "human settlements."[46] The IUCN, the WWF, the IIED, and many other NGOs took interest in energy use and sources.[47] The groups also adopted a broader focus on ecological areas that cut across national lines, particularly around deforestation in tropical rain forests and desertification in East Africa.[48] The IIED, the IUCN, and the WWF had begun to tackle a much wider variety of issues than they had at the start of the decade.

In all of these cases – suggesting that conservation should redress poverty, adopting a more participatory vision of conservation, and increasingly dealing with urban areas and root causes – NGOs rethought the relationship between conservation and development planning. In each instance, they increasingly brought concerns of developing nations into their own thinking. This process, however, sparked tensions within and among leading NGOs. A major identity crisis soon emerged for these organizations, which, after all, had been created largely to protect the environment from human use. The simmering conflicts erupted in September 1975, when IUCN members met for the Thirteenth General Assembly in Kinshasa, Zaire.

## INSTITUTIONAL CONFLICT AND VARIETIES
## OF CONSERVATION

In many ways, the Kinshasa gathering marked a transitional moment for the IUCN. The new ideas that had been developing over the previous years came to dominate the conference. Members from developing

notions and show that biological diversity actually depends on some degree of disturbance. For an overview of disturbance theory and the evolution of American ecological science, see, for instance, S. T. A. Pickett and P.S. White, eds., *The Ecology of Natural Disturbance and Patch Dynamics* (Orlando: Academic Press, Inc., 1985); Frank Benjamin Golley, *A History of the Ecosystem Concept in Ecology: More Than the Sum of Its Parts* (New Haven: Yale University Press, 1993); Sharon E. Kingsland, *The Evolution of American Ecology, 1890–2000* (Baltimore: The Johns Hopkins University Press, 2005). I thank Ed Russell and Leif Frederickson for alerting me to this literature.

[46] David Satterthwaite, "Setting an Urban Agenda: Human Settlements and IIED-América Latina," in Cross, ed., *Evidence for Hope*, 122–46.

[47] "Energy and Conservation," *IUCN Bulletin*, Vol. 5, No. 6 (June 1974), 14; Gerald Leach, "The Energy Programme," in Cross, ed., *Evidence for Hope*, 96–107.

[48] Duncan Poore, "Saving Tropical Rain Forests," *IUCN Bulletin*, Vol. 5, No. 8 (August 1974), 29.

nations expressed concerns about representation and participation in IUCN activities, similar to those Kenyan members had expressed.[49] Ray Dasmann spoke before the General Assembly about indigenous rights, and won support for a resolution acknowledging the importance of indigenous ways of life in the management of protected areas. Duncan Poore, a British botanist serving as one of the organization's chief scientists in Switzerland, prepared a new program for the organization to place more emphasis on Strong's ecodevelopment concept. Mobutu Seso Seko, Zaire's president and conference host, talked frequently about the need to focus on city planning and other urban issues.[50]

Amid these changes, members worried that the organization had lost sight of its original purpose. IUCN Director-General Gerardo Budowski recalled complaints from the "preservationists" in the organization who detested the shift away from narrowly protecting natural landscapes and endangered species. A few key donors and representatives from national chapters grumbled about the close connections the organization had developed with the UNEP. The growing expenses of the headquarters staff in Switzerland also upset many members, who "did not want IUCN to become a bureaucracy" that made top-down decisions from afar. They worried that the IUCN was neglecting its initial goal of building networks of conservation experts, and instead mimicking a UN agency or development advocacy group. Questions arose over financing, too. Rumors circulated that the organization's increased spending on its central staff and worldwide activities had outpaced the UNEP contributions, causing the IUCN to fall, once again, into the red.[51]

As such grievances and complaints circulated among participants, a series of bizarre and unanticipated events exacerbated the situation. Hosted in one of Mobutu's palatial compounds, IUCN officials envisioned the conference as a symbol to show their commitment to strengthening ties with developing nations. Leaning heavily on the dictator for

---

[49] Patricia Rambach, "Report on 12th General Assembly of IUCN," October 7, 1975, carton 3–38 International Union on Conservation of Nature, 1972–80, Sierra Club International Program Records, BANC MSS 71/290c, [hereinafter cited as Sierra Club International Program Records], The Bancroft Library, University of California, Berkeley.

[50] "Conservation Resolutions," in *Twelfth General Assembly: Proceedings* (Morges, Switzerland: IUCN, 1976), 153–54; 166; 217–22 [Online] Available: http://www.iucn .org/knowledge/publications_doc/publications/. Accessed November 14, 2011.

[51] Holdgate, *The Green Web*, 125–7; Rambach, "Report on 12th General Assembly of IUCN," carton 3–38 International Union on Conservation of Nature, 1972–80, Sierra Club International Program Records.

accommodations, however, proved troublesome. Many conferees felt uncomfortable around the swarms of Mobutu's special troops parading about the grounds with full armor and automatic weapons. Mobutu also derailed a planned field trip to a high elevation national park when he made available only two aircraft for the trip, which provided enough space for only the VIPs and upper-level management. Conservation luminaries, such as the WWF's Peter Scott, fumed when told their wives and families would be unable to attend. Even worse, as the two planes experienced a lengthy delay on their return from the park, a group of officials upset by Budowski's handling of the budget "mutinied" and demanded that Budowski promise not to run for reelection. By all accounts, the meeting was a disaster. Words such as "bleak," "sad," "confused," and "scared" peppered the recollections of the group's leading officials.[52]

While the Kinshasa meeting left the organization with tremendous uncertainty, subsequent changes in leadership brought stability and reinforced the "conservation for development" message. Budowski agreed to let his term expire without reelection, and in his place Duncan Poore, the advocate for ecodevelopment, took over as acting director-general. In 1977, David Munro, a close friend of Maurice Strong's and former UNEP official, won the support of many high-level officials in the organization and became permanent director-general. Lee Talbot, who oversaw a committee on budgetary and organizational matters after Kinshasa, ascended up the leadership ladder. He became an important voice for promoting the "conservation for development" message, as well. Munro engineered an extension of UNEP's contract and an added injection of funds from the WWF around the same time generally quelled concerns over finance.[53] Within a couple years after the Kinshasa debacle, changes in leadership had ensured that the organization would continue down that same path for years to come. IUCN official Robert Allen declared that the focus on how to "integrate conservation programmes with development" was the most important outcome of Kinshasa.[54]

Munro and Talbot prodded the organization to adopt "conservation for development" as an organizing theme for all of its activities in 1977 and 1978. "A significant portion of IUCN's conceptual work is, now,

[52] Holdgate, *The Green Web*, 126–7.
[53] "WWF and UNEP Funding," Agenda Paper UC.77/3, October 1977, box 80, V. IUCN Meetings, Strong Papers.
[54] Robert Allen, "Conservation and Development: A Betrothal," *New Scientist*, September 22, 1975, 692.

concerned with the contribution that ecology should make to economic development," claimed an internal report.[55] Maurice Strong became chairman of the IUCN Bureau, the equivalent of a board of directors. Strong pushed the organization to strengthen its ties to the developing world by encouraging fellowships granted to scientists and development experts from developing nations and facilitating more conversations with UNEP staff and representatives.[56] In a UNEP-IUCN joint meeting in early 1977 attended by Munro, Poore, Dasmann, and Allen, IUCN officials redefined the organization's purpose as "the promotion of world conservation action covering particularly species and habitats as an integral part of plans for social and economic development." At the same gathering, the UNEP offered to extend its financial support for another four years.[57]

As the IUCN redefined its purpose, Russell Train, a friend of many IUCN officials, adopted similar ideas for the WWF's office in the United States (WWF-US). Train had left government in 1975, to return to work with environmental advocacy groups. He spent much of 1977 as a special fellow to the IIED, where he nurtured a friendship with Barbara Ward and became acquainted with her network.[58] In 1978, he took the opportunity to lead the WWF-US, which was growing increasingly wealthy. There, Train adopted a "systems approach" to planning for the organization that placed its species-protection campaigns in the broader context of development policies.[59] "It is essential," Train said, "that those of us who care about wildlife be sensitive to the fact that over much of the globe, particularly in less developed areas, there can be no long-term future for wildlife unless human problems such as malnutrition and over-crowding are effectively addressed."[60] He helped to engineer a shift in the organization along the lines of what the IUCN had been pursuing.

[55] "13th (Extraordinary) General Assembly, Geneva, Switzerland: Progress Report on the Strategy and Its Component Programmes," Agenda Paper GA.77/3, 1977, folder 730, box 76, IUCN, Strong Papers.

[56] David Munro to Maurice F. Strong, October 1, 1977, folder 752, box 78, V. IUCN 1976, Strong Papers.

[57] "Minutes of Meeting UNEP – IUCN Held at IUCN Headquarters, Morges," January 13–14, 1977, folder 746, box 78, V. IUCN 1977, Strong Papers.

[58] Barbara Ward to Russell Train, January 23, 1978, box 2, Ward Papers.

[59] Barbara Ward referred to this approach by the phrase "you can't save the animals one by one," Barbara Ward to Maurice Strong, January 24, 1978, box 75, V. IIED 1977–78, Strong Papers.

[60] "WWF-US Press Release," March 8, 1978, box 115, WWF/1978 January–April, Strong Papers.

Train's actions conflicted with the European elite who still ran the WWF's international secretariat out of Switzerland. Early in his tenure, Train effectively severed ties with the international secretariat. In what some called a "Monroe Doctrine" for conservation, the two organizations accepted a de facto split in responsibilities. The WWF-US organized its own campaigns and projects in the Western hemisphere, while the international secretariat oversaw efforts for the rest of the world. Train's WWF-US essentially became a distinct NGO.[61]

Deeper tensions lurked beneath Train's administrative maneuver. While the IIED, the IUCN, and now the WWF-US embraced the conservation for development idea, the WWF international office was far less sanguine about the concept. Its hesitancy reflected that many of its influential leaders, members, and donors preferred to focus narrowly on wildlife protection. Guy Mountfort, one of the WWF's founders and a close associate of Julian Huxley, expressed "serious doubts" over Maurice Strong's suggestion that the WWF make organization-wide reforms similar to those of the IUCN.[62] Charles de Haes, the WWF's director-general, acknowledged that fund-raising demands from those affiliated with the development community had pushed the organization to address "the problems of human population increase, of high technology agriculture, of industrialization and urbanization, of pollution, of misuse and waste of resources and energy, of famine and of poverty." Yet he also claimed many members of the board of trustees hoped to limit the organization's objective to "saving species."[63]

It was clear that de Haes did not desire the kind of organization-wide transformation that Ward, Strong, Talbot, Munro, and Train had engineered. "If solutions to these problems can be found WWF's aims will be more easily achieved, for it is clear that the conservation of nature cannot be dealt with in isolation from the human condition," he told Maurice Strong. "But in view of the limited funds at present available, WWF's priority projects are for the most part, though not exclusively,

---

[61] Raymond Bonner, *At The Hand of Man: Peril and Hope for Africa's Wildlife* (New York: Alfred A. Knopf, 1993), 67–71. The IUCN was also in constant tension with the leadership of WWF-International during this time over personnel and financing issues. See Jon Tinker, "IUCN: Crisis and Opportunity," *New Scientist*, May 13, 1976, 349–50. "Minutes of Meeting UNEP – IUCN Held at IUCN Headquarters, Morges," January 13–14,1977, folder 746, box 78, V. IUCN 1977, Strong Papers.

[62] Guy Mountfort to Exco Members, September 3, 1977, box 115, WWF/1977 September–October, Strong Papers.

[63] Charles de Haes to All Exco Members, December 21, 1977, box 115, WWF/1978 January–April, Strong Papers.

FIGURE 8: The WWF had long attracted criticism of being elitist from within and outside the environmental community, particularly for the organization's focus on protecting individual species over more holistic approaches. Those divisions only became more apparent during the debates over environmental NGOs' relationship to development in the 1970s and 1980s. The charges of elitism were not lost on WWF members themselves. The top of this photograph, from Russell Train's papers, reads, "WWF an elitist organization? Why in the world would you say that?" From left to right: Prince Philip, president of WWF-International, Russell E. Train, William K. Reilly, president of WWF-US, and in the background, Lord Buxon, British politician. At the home of Augustus Busch, ca. 1984. Courtesy of Russell Train Papers, Manuscript Division, Library of Congress.

directed towards animals, plants, and their wild habitat, and the promotion of public awareness of the immediate dangers that threaten nature."[64] Whereas the IUCN, the IIED, and the WWF-US embraced new approaches and strategies, the WWF still cleaved to older imperatives (Figure 8).

While debates over the purpose of conservation continued between NGOs, the IUCN completed its acceptance of the new approach. At the

---

[64] Charles de Haes to Maurice Strong, June 7, 1977, box 114, WWF/1977 June, Strong Papers.

1978 General Assembly, the organization announced that its primary focus over the coming years would be on the *World Conservation Strategy*, to publicize the conservation for development idea to a global audience. One reporter called it a "radical change in the world conservation movement," because of the IUCN's new emphasis on "the needs of the Third World."[65] In 1979, Talbot spoke before the WWF's Executive Committee to announce the formal reorganization of the IUCN's priorities. He described how his organization had struggled in the past to make its cause relevant to the societies they had hoped to reform. "By reacting to perceived problems – which almost always are the result of human actions – conservationists have been seen to be opposed to development or to human welfare," he asserted. No longer would this be the case. The IUCN would henceforth set itself up to protect nature by redressing those "human problems" that endangered the natural world in the first place. An important conceptual shift had occurred, although Talbot hinted at the practicality of such change. "Development in the broad sense will proceed," he admitted, "so the challenge is to guide it along ecologically responsible directions."[66]

By the end of the 1970s, then, ideas about placing conservation in the service of meeting human needs and alternative approaches to economic development had moved from the fringes of a few expert meetings to become the guiding framework for the IUCN. The significance of this shift was clear. "The age of wise and benign Northerners telling good little Southerners what to do is over," Barbara Ward told Maurice Strong in 1978.[67] Such realizations set the stage for the drafting of the *World Conservation Strategy*.

## CONSERVATION FOR DEVELOPMENT: THE WORLD CONSERVATION STRATEGY

The desire for a global strategy for conservation had been identified in 1975, but it did not get off the ground until 1978. Maurice Strong and other officials had discussed a desire to craft a strategy that was global in scope and all nations could apply back in the mid-1970s. The incidents at Kinshasa and the ongoing internal struggles within the IUCN had hampered any follow-up. By 1977, IUCN officials returned to it, and

[65] Jon Tinker, "Comment," *New Scientist*, October 12, 1978, 90.
[66] "Executive Report" March 1, 1979, folder 1102, box 116, WWF/1979, Strong Papers.
[67] Barbara Ward to Maurice Strong, January 24, 1978, box 75, V. IIED 1977–78, Strong Papers.

they won support from both the UNEP and the WWF.[68] IUCN Senior Policy Advisor Robert Allen, who had authored multiple essays and books on international conservation, took up the job of drafting the first version.[69]

The crafting of the strategy mirrored the debates happening inside the IUCN. Robert Allen declared, "The aim of the strategy is ... to develop policies and outline programmes of action to maintain the potential of wild plants and animals of the ecosystems of which they are part to meet changing human needs." It attempted to balance the concerns of those who still believed in the preservationist orientation and those who championed the "conservation for development" concept.[70]

Allen's first draft, however, was ambiguous, clumsy, and ultimately ineffective. He wrote, "It would silence a frequent criticism if it were to be made quite explicit that ecosystem conservation must be carried out within the framework of environmental policies which work towards the elimination of social and economic injustices and which strive to raise the level of well-being of all mankind. Indeed, ecosystem conservation, properly pursued, should make an important contribution to that end."[71] Yet there was little elaboration on that point, and the rest of the document proceeded to show basic strategies for ecosystem management with little discussion of how they could serve human needs.

Allen's halfhearted embrace of the "conservation for development" message appalled many environmentalists who read the first draft. Although Allen made a rhetorical gesture toward the development community, Lee Talbot lamented that the first draft amounted to "basically a wildlife conservation textbook."[72] Sierra Club official Patricia Scharlin explained, "The draft does not yet come to grips with ... the place of conservation in the global development process ... and the place of people as part of ecosystems. With regard to the latter point, there still remains the old conservationist point of view that man must control nature." She continued, "There is still too much emphasis on protection of specific areas or species and not enough focus on the part conservation plays" in

[68] The revival of interest for the WCS arose, in part, as a way for the UNEP to justify its extensive aid to environmental NGOs. Holdgate, *The Green Web*, 120.

[69] "Robert Allen," carton 8–11 World Conservation Strategy, 1979–80, Sierra Club International Program Records.

[70] "First Draft of A World Conservation Strategy," January 1978, 1, IUCN Library.

[71] Ibid., 3.

[72] Lee Talbot, "The World Conservation Strategy," in Francis R. Thobideau and Hermann H. Field, eds., *Sustaining Tomorrow: A Strategy for World Conservation* (Hanover, NH: University Press of New England, 1984), 15.

developing nations. She even suggested the IUCN go further to help the developing nations' push for the NIEO and global socioeconomic justice.[73] Others agreed. "If we are to win the battle for environmental protection in the developing world," National Resources Defense Council (NRDC) official Thomas Stoel, Jr., told Robert Allen, "environmental protection almost by definition must become an aspect of the development process."[74] Various African officials echoed these opinions, claiming that the strategy should not "just focus on nature" and include more specific strategies for redressing poverty.[75]

While these officials argued the document was far too narrow, others felt that it had, in fact, gone too far to accept the concerns of developing nations. The same debates that had pervaded the IUCN's acceptance of the conservation for development message resurfaced during the drafting of the *World Conservation Strategy*. "Conservation's job is not to accommodate development," explained one WWF official in a letter to Robert Allen. In particular, Allen needed to show more concrete strategies for "sane development" on the basis of "preservation of [biological] resources." The official also claimed that the strategy should be more than a reflection of "IUCN's plans for itself, nor solely defined by what UNEP is requiring of IUCN."[76]

While ambiguity of Allen's draft led to widely differing criticisms from the environmental community, UNEP officials unequivocally rejected it for not sufficiently addressing the developmental aspirations of the Global South. Upon seeing a draft, one official exclaimed, "This things stinks! It is dyed-in-the-wool preservationism." Reuben Olembo, a UNEP official who had been working to popularize the old ecodevelopment concept, wrote directly to the IUCN expressing similar dismay.[77] In a comprehensive evaluation of the early drafting process, Thomas Power, a consultant

[73] Patricia Scharlin to Robert Allen, April 7, 1978, carton 8–10 World Conservation Strategy, 1979, Sierra Club International Program Records.

[74] Thomas Stoel, Jr., "General Comments on First Draft of IUCN World Conservation Strategy," April 1978 in Thomas Stoel, Jr. to Robert Allen, March 30, 1978, carton 4–17 World Conservation Strategy, 1978, Sierra Club International Program Records.

[75] Holdgate, *The Green Web*, 150.

[76] Thomas Lovejoy to Robert Allen, June 1, 1978, carton 8–10 World Conservation Strategy, 1979, Sierra Club International Program Records; Jorge Morello and Thomas F. Power, Jr., "Evaluation of Projects Contracted for Execution to the International Union for Conservation of Nature and Natural Resources as a Supporting Organization," May 11, 1979, folder 555, box 58, Peter S. Thacher Collection, Part I, 1960–1996, Environmental Science and Public Policy Archives, Harvard University, Cambridge, MA [hereinafter cited as Thacher Papers, Part I].

[77] Holdgate, *The Green Web*, 151.

hired to analyze the draft for the UNEP, found it "regrettable and ironic" that the draft had "failed" to integrate developmental concerns when the IUCN itself had changed its own program to accommodate the developing world.[78]

As the major funding source for the project, the UNEP used its considerable leverage to shape the final document, and the IUCN went to great lengths to align the strategy with its partners' concerns. Discussions between Power, the UNEP staff, and the IUCN resulted in Allen rewriting multiple chapters.[79] Shortly after hearing the third round of criticisms, Robert Allen flew to Nairobi from Switzerland to meet with Olembo and other staff members. After a series of discussions, Allen concluded, "The strategy had to be put in the context of development for it to be taken seriously. . . . It had to cover what development was, and how conservation furthered it." With help from Olembo and David Munro, Allen rounded the last draft into form in late 1979 and early 1980.[80] Officials finally completed the strategy for international release in March 1980. The tumult of the drafting process was not lost on NGO officials. "The very existence of this strategy might be viewed as something of a miracle," remarked Russell Train.[81]

In its final iteration, the *World Conservation Strategy* offered general principles that could be applied to development to incorporate environmental concerns. It outlined three principles to guide all development plans: maintain essential ecological processes and life-support systems; preserve genetic diversity within the world's ecosystems; and ensure the sustainable utilization of species in ecosystems. If done so, planners could gear their economic policies toward satisfying basic needs without destroying the resource base on which development depended. The document referred to this compromise as a model for "sustainable development."[82]

The document also revealed striking evidence of the extent to which the IUCN officials had accommodated developmental aspirations. In general, it called for the "need for global strategies both for development and for

---

[78] Thomas F. Power, Jr., to Mostafa K. Tolba, May 17, 1979, folder 229, box 25, Thacher Papers, Part I.

[79] Holdgate, *The Green Web*, 151.

[80] Ibid.

[81] Joanne Omang, "Conservation Strategy Mapped by 30 Nations," *The Washington Post*, March 6, 1980, A13.

[82] The desire to mix the necessity of meeting human needs and managing resources in line with ecological principles appeared in the title for the first section of the strategy: "living resource conservation for sustainable development." *World Conservation Strategy*, 7.

the conservation of nature."[83] The guidebook also claimed that "humanity's relationship with the biosphere . . . will continue to deteriorate until a new international economic order is achieved, a new environmental ethic adopted, human populations stabilize, and sustainable modes of development become the rule rather than the exception." Thus, amid older environmental ideas, the document explicitly endorsed the developing nations' push for global socioeconomic reform as a fundamental tenet of conservation. Furthermore, the document declared that conservationists had actually encouraged the incompatibility of environmental protection and development by "too often resisting all development." Alongside sections on managing various ecosystems, it also included numerous mentions of poverty eradication, an entire chapter on local participation in conservation activities, and various other aspects of "people-centered development."[84] The final document would have stunned many conservationists just decades earlier.

In 1980, many in the environmental and development community celebrated the strategy. Mark Halle, an official who worked with the UNEP, the WWF, and the IUCN, hailed the new document for bringing "conservation solidly into the mainstream of social and economic development." Because it also reconciled environmentalists to framing their work within the developmental needs of the poorest nations, he also called the document "the most significant advance in conservation" since the birth of modern environmentalism a few decades earlier.[85] Quite apart from the first draft, Lee Talbot looked positively on the final version as a "consensus between the practitioners of conservation and development."[86]

IUCN officials released the strategy with much fanfare on March 6, 1980. The IUCN convened a public launch, in which the organization announced it was distributing a condensed pack of materials especially designed for policy makers in national governments and international institutions around the world. It also organized national launch parties in countries where the organization had influential allies; Russell Train and Robert McNamara hosted the strategy's release party in the United States, and Peter Scott from the WWF oversaw a series of similar

---

83 Ibid., i.
84 *World Conservation Strategy*, part 1. On poverty, see pages 7–8: on participation, see pages 33–4; on conservation serving people-centered development, see 33–6.
85 Mark Halle, "The World Conservation Strategy – An Historical Perspective," September 30, 1984, folder 979, box 103, Thacher Papers, Part I.
86 Talbot, "The World Conservation Strategy," 14.

celebratory events in the United Kingdom.[87] The UNEP General Council presented the strategy at its annual session to "very positive reception."[88] The launch attracted worldwide attention from major media sources in the developed and developing world, in nations such as United States, China, and Kenya.[89]

While the publication of the document was an important milestone, NGO officials recognized that tremendous work remained to put its ideas into policy. To encourage implementation in developing nations, the IUCN established, with financial support from the UNEP, the Conservation for Development Centre (CDC). Spearheaded by Maurice Strong, the new organization provided consultative services to governments that wanted to adopt the *World Conservation Strategy* and for development assistance agencies that wanted to fund projects in line with the strategy's principles.[90] Over the next decade, however, officials in the IUCN and the CDC struggled to implement the strategy's principles in nations and foreign aid agencies.

## THE CHALLENGES OF IMPLEMENTING THE WORLD CONSERVATION STRATEGY

Zambia was one of the first nations to pursue a national conservation strategy, but only because the country faced a dire economic crisis in the early 1980s. For years, Zambia had organized its entire economy around copper mining. By the mid-1970s, a staggering 95 percent of its foreign exchange earnings came from copper exports. Global instability in commodity prices during the 1970s sharply reduced the nation's income, and Zambia plunged into a balance-of-payments crisis. More troubling for the nation, the burgeoning microelectronic revolution caused copper prices

---

[87] "World Conservation Strategy: The Public Launch," First Memorandum, folder C.1138, Scott Papers; "World Conservation Strategy: Launch of the Americas from the Hall of the Americas," carton 8–11 World Conservation Strategy, 1979–80, Sierra Club International Program Records.

[88] Memo to David Munro, April 26, 1980, folder 168, box 18, Thacher Papers, Part I.

[89] "Environmental Consciousness-Raising," *The Washington Post*, March 10, 1980, A26; John Yemma, "Making Resources an Economic Global Priority," *Christian Science Monitor*, March 6, 1980, 4; "East Africa: In Brief; Kenya's Interest in Conservation," *BBC Summary of World Broadcasts*, March 8, 1980; "Other Reports; Environmental Protection Month," ibid., March 15, 1980.

[90] Brian Johnson to Arthur Norman, Maurice Strong, Max Nicholson, and Lee Talbot, March 21, 1980, folder 2386, box 253, VII IIED Correspondence London, Strong Papers; Lee Talbot to Terry Lisniewski, March 23, 1981, folder 2415, box 256, VII IUCN Correspondence, Strong Papers.

to plummet further in the early 1980s. The price fluctuations exposed profound fiscal problems. Zambia, like many developing nations, had borrowed heavily from commercial banks to fund its efforts at industrial development. When the global debt crisis struck in 1982, Zambia found itself among the most troubled nations. By 1984, Zambia held $3.5 billion in debt (with a GDP of $2.7 billion), and it was paying out over 60 percent of its foreign exchanges to service those obligations. By 1986, interest on the debt alone amounted to 40 percent of the government's entire budget.[91] Without a stable source of foreign exchange earnings and burdened with staggering debt, Zambia's leaders faced daunting choices.

Zambia President Kenneth Kaunda, who had ruled the country since independence in 1964, hoped to reorganize the entire economy by moving away from mining and toward agricultural production. With the focus on copper, rural development had been largely neglected.[92] With only 6 million inhabitants and a territory larger than France, however, Zambia seemed ripe for widespread agricultural production.[93] Yet even the small agricultural programs the country had pursued were floundering. Analysts of Zambia suggested that environmental problems seriously hampered the country's agricultural efforts. A 1982 report claimed that soil erosion was a particular problem, with observers estimating that the country may have been losing over 3 million tons of topsoil annually. Seeing an opportunity to make use of the nation's largely untapped land, Kaunda approached the IUCN about crafting a national conservation strategy. With his country shackled with crippling debt and no longer able to rely on copper exports to spark recovery, desperation, rather than a newfound environmental ethos, drove his pursuit of a conservation strategy (Figure 9).[94]

Nonetheless, the IUCN welcomed the opportunity to put the *World Conservation Strategy* into action. In 1982 and 1983, the organization sent two expert missions to Zambia to begin discussing a strategy with

---

[91] John Clark and Caroline Allison, *Zambia: Debt and Poverty* (Oxford: Oxfam, 1989), 11–13. For a history of the copper industry in Zambia, see Chukwuma F. Obidegwu and Mudziviri Nziramasanga, *Copper and Zambia: An Econometric Analysis* (Lexington, MA: Lexington Books, 1981), chapter 1. For a very general overview of Zambia's political evolution, see Bizeck Jube Phiri, *A Political History of Zambia: From Colonial Rule to the Third Republic, 1890–2001* (Trenton, NJ: Africa World Press, Inc., 2006).

[92] "The Start of a Zambian NCS," *World Conservation Strategy in Action* (June 1984), 2, IUCN Library.

[93] "Zambia," *World Conservation Strategy in Action* (March 1984), 4, IUCN Library.

[94] "Draft Environmental Profile of Zambia," March 1982, iii, USAID Document Clearinghouse. [Online] Available: http://dec.usaid.gov/index.cfm. Accessed July 31, 2012.

FIGURE 9: Map of Zambia, ca. 1988. Courtesy of University of Texas Libraries.

government officials. After Zambian officials agreed to the general outline of a report, the IUCN obtained a few small grants from Sweden and Holland's foreign aid agencies to draft a full strategy.[95] In 1984, the CDC sent one of its consultants, Stephen M. J. Bass, to Zambia. Over that spring and summer, Bass worked with Kaunda and other high-level

[95] J. K. Rennie, "National Conservation Strategies: An Individual's Overview," November 1984, 27, folder 974, box 102, Thacher Papers, Part I.

Zambia officials to outline the contours of national plan in accordance with the *World Conservation Strategy*'s principles. Kaunda expressed rhetorical support for the strategy. "We in Africa have come to appreciate that protection of our continent's environment should be a priority," he claimed. "It would be folly to think of development without considering the environmental basis on which it depends."[96] After holding a national convention on the strategy that July, Kaunda and his administration seemed "ready to adopt some of its ideas" into policy.[97] The IUCN was hopeful of its prospects, and it launched a national newsletter, drafted press releases, circulated posters, and organized an exhibit at Zambia's National Agricultural Show to promote the strategy.[98]

Many problems bedeviled the strategy's implementation from the start. Limited donor funds reduced the planning process to seven months. Bass admitted that this was enough time to produce a "practical strategy," but he lamented that he had skipped over many opportunities for more detailed analysis of Zambia's agriculture and did not have enough time to tailor the strategy to specific capabilities of existing government departments. The Zambian government also lacked any environmental agencies; Bass had to scramble with Zambian officials to create the first executive-level environmental department. These institutional shortcomings led to confusion over whom, exactly, would implement and enforce the strategy. Likewise, in the political process of negotiating the strategy, which involved Bass and Kaunda's administration, the "narrowest issue of conservation for development ended up dominating."[99] Officials glossed over topics such as preserving biological diversity for its own sake (focusing on wildlife solely as a source of meat production), which rankled some environmentalists back in Europe and the United States.[100] Finally, although the *World Conservation Strategy* placed heavy emphasis on local participation in planning, Zambia's strategy lacked any public engagement; even its national parliament was kept out of the loop. Financial and time constraints, on top of Kaunda's one-party rule, ensured that the crafting of the strategy was far from a participatory process.

[96] "The Start of a Zambian NCS," *World Conservation Strategy in Action* (June 1984), 1, IUCN Library.

[97] "Zambia," *World Conservation Strategy in Action* (March 1985), 5, IUCN Library.

[98] Rennie, "National Conservation Strategies: An Individual's Overview," 28.

[99] Stephen M. J. Bass, "National Conservation Strategy: Zambia," in Czech Conroy and Miles Litvinoff, eds., *The Greening of Aid: Sustainable Livelihoods in Practice* (London: Earthscan Publications, Ltd., 1988), 188.

[100] Quoted in Robert Prescott Allen, "National Conservation Strategies and Biodiversity" (December 1986), IUCN Library.

Rather, Bass claimed it was "essentially a technocratic exercise" in top-down development planning.[101]

Above all, there was a fundamental problem that militated against full implementation: insufficient funding. Reorienting an economy that had been dependent on mining a single commodity for decades into a diverse and ecologically sustainable agricultural producer was a very expensive proposition. Small grants had made possible the crafting of the strategy, but much more money would be required to see it through. Nations such as Zambia faced "a very real need for additional support" to finance environmental planning. Such funds were not forthcoming, at least not to the extent needed for full adoption of the strategy. Although many aid agencies were increasing their support for environmental projects by the 1980s, Bass noted that the strategy had to compete for funds with short-term projects designed to generate foreign exchange, to finance debt repayments, and to provide relief for disasters – projects donors were more likely to support.[102] In addition, the strategy failed to attract any governmental or private investment within the country. The few components of the strategy that did get implemented came largely through sympathetic environmental groups such as the Wildlife Conservation Society of Zambia, an elite organization run largely by foreigners.[103] The strategy "never fully became part of the five-year planning process," Bass admitted.[104]

Over the following years, the Ministry of Lands and Natural Resources, the lead agency in the drafting process, continued to champion the strategy with limited success. Without the strategy serving as an overall framework for managing the development process, Zambia's shift to agriculture devolved into a series of uncoordinated, often experimental projects led by foreign donors and environmental groups attempting to promoted new "integrated" development and conservation

---

[101] Steve Bass and Lubinda Aongola, "Case Studies of Zambia's Environmental Mainstreaming Experience," in Lubinda Aongola et al., *Creating and Protecting Zambia's Wealth: Experience and Next Steps in Environmental Mainstreaming* (London: International Institute for Environment and Development, 2009), 21.

[102] Bass, "National Conservation Strategy: Zambia," 190–1.

[103] The Wildlife Conservation Society, chaired by HRH Charles, Prince of Wales, resembled many older colonial wildlife organizations. After touring Zambia in 1984, Prince Charles offered a £15,000 donation for environmental education through conservation clubs his society had created, but little substantive support for reorienting the economy or meeting basic needs of the population. "The Start of a Zambian NCS," *World Conservation Strategy in Action* (June 1984), 3, IUCN Library.

[104] Bass and Aongola, "Case Studies of Zambia's Environmental Mainstreaming Experience," 21.

projects.[105] It took well over a decade from its inception before Zambia began, slowly, to implement some of the guidelines. Zambia only created national institutions with the legal and political authority necessary to enforce environmental regulations in 1992.[106] The national strategy may well have provided for an ecologically sustainable economy. However, it was not sustainable in a short-term fiscal sense.

Recognizing the depth of financial problems afflicting countries such as Zambia, NGOs hoped to encourage greater foreign assistance to offset the costs of implementing national strategies. While the CDC primarily offered expert guidance to nations crafting their own strategies, IUCN officials also envisioned it as a "broker" between the environmental community and foreign aid agencies. In 1982, CDC officials, working with Maurice Strong and David Runnalls of the IIED, approached AID about a possible partnership to design and implement sustainable natural resource management programs across the world.[107]

AID, after all, had started funding environmental projects a few years earlier. As a corollary to their campaign for impact assessments, environmental NGOs had successfully lobbied Congress to mandate that agency do so in 1977.[108] Soon thereafter, AID began writing "environmental profiles" of all nations that received aid, although it still lacked qualified ecologists and general knowledge about conservation practices. Struggling to fulfill their congressional mandate and deepen their environmental programs, AID officials responded positively to Runnalls's approach.[109] In August 1982, AID signed a cooperative agreement with

[105] For an example of one such isolated development project, see Carla Wainwright and Walter Wehrmeyer, "Success in Integrating Conservation and Development? A Study from Zambia," *World Development*, Vol. 26, No. 6 (1998), 933–44.

[106] Ibid., 22–3; Kjetil Børhaug, "From Policy Guidelines to Problem Solving: A Critical Assessment of the National Conservation Strategies of Botswana and Zambia," Working Paper, Chr. Michelsen Institute, 1993, 7–18. See "Interview: Caring for the Future," September 12, 2011. [Online] Available: http://www.capacity.org/capacity/opencms/en/topics/change-facilitation/caring-into-the-future.html. Accessed August 4, 2012.

[107] "World Conservation Strategy: A Follow-up Report," folder 2396, box 253, VII WWF Board, Strong Papers. IIED and IUCN formed a "Joint Environmental Service" to facilitate this process.

[108] Thomas B. Stoel, Jr., S. Jacob Scherr, and Diana C. Crowley, "Environment, Natural Resources, and Development: The Role of the U.S. Agency for International Development," International Project, Natural Resources Defense Council, Inc., 1978, i–iii. USAID Document Clearinghouse. [Online] Available: http://dec.usaid.gov/index.cfm. Accessed January 4, 2012.

[109] "Project Data Sheet: Environmental Planning Management," 1984, 7, USAID Document Clearinghouse. [Online] Available: http://dec.usaid.gov/index.cfm. Accessed August 4, 2012.

the IIED to provide general technical assistance for environmental programs. IIED, in turn, contracted out to the CDC, and by 1983 advisers from the two groups used U.S. government funds to craft conservation strategies for Sri Lanka, Nepal, and the Philippines.[110]

These institutional ties allowed NGOs to pursue more conservation strategies, although it was still unclear to what extent implementation would follow. The initial seven-figure grants to the IIED were enough to fund the creation of strategies, but developing nations required far more financial support to ensure implementation, enforcement, and continual adaptation of conservation principles in resource management programs. When the first cooperative agreement expired in 1989, AID and NGO officials agreed on another one. This time around, however, officials recognized that far more external aid was necessary to do anything more than draft broad strategies. Accordingly, the "principal focus" of the new agreement was on funding institutional capacity in developing nations, with a particular emphasis on host country "institutional ownership of the [natural resource management] processes and public participation at the grassroots level" in development planning. The new agreement was an important start, but it also underscored the fact that far more assistance than they could provide was necessary to make the strategies into operational development plans.[111]

Cases such as Zambia and other efforts to craft national strategies worldwide thus demonstrated that the fate of the *World Conservation Strategy* as an actual policy framework depended on the extent to which its designers could find extensive funds to pay for its adoption and implementation. The IUCN frequently encouraged its member nations to craft strategies throughout the 1980s.[112] Many received help from the IUCN, the CDC, or the IIED – or some combination – to draft plans, strategies, or profiles.[113] Yet until there emerged clear and consistent answers

[110] "Mid-Term Evaluation: Environmental Planning and Management, April 1984," iii, USAID Document Clearinghouse. [Online] Available: http://dec.usaid.gov/index.cfm. Accessed August 4, 2012. David Runnalls to Maurice Strong, May 6, 1983, folder 2392, box 253, VII IIED Correspondence Washington, Strong Papers.

[111] "Report: Environmental Planning and Management (EPM)," July 1991, 61, USAID Document Clearinghouse. [Online] Available: http://dec.usaid.gov/index.cfm. Accessed August 4, 2012.

[112] A. K. Chebukaka to Director for National Environment & Human Settlements, July 23, 1985, archival records from Ministry of Environment and Natural Resources, Headquarters (Government of Kenya) 7/24, KNA.

[113] Conservation for Development Centre, "Tanzania: Natural Resources Expertise Profile," December 1986, IUCN Library; Conservation for Development Centre, "Kenya: Natural Resources Expertise Profile: Revised Edition," January 1986, IUCN

to questions of funding, any national strategy based on the *World Conservation Strategy* was bound to languish.

## A NEW DISCOURSE: THE SUSTAINABILITY MOMENT

While the *World Conservation Strategy* ran into problems in the policy realm, it had a far greater influence on the discourse surrounding international development. After its publication, talk of sustainable development proliferated. The IUCN released numerous publications related to the strategy, and rephrased much of its programming to include use of "sustainable development."[114] The sustainability discourse predominated in discussions surrounding the ten-year follow-up to Stockholm held in Nairobi in 1982.[115] The World Bank began using the term by the mid-1980s.[116] Sustainable development was a major theme of the Global 2000 Report in the United States, which had been commissioned by President Carter in 1977 and was the closest the United States came to drafting a national conservation strategy. Although the Reagan administration quickly shelved the document and dismissed its findings, many environmentalists held it as a seminal declaration that explained the necessity for programs of sustainable development.[117] In all these cases, sustainable development became a common phrase to describe how development concerns could take in environmental ideas, and vice versa.

Talk of sustainable development became truly dominant in global development discourse following the work of the UN's World

Library; Conservation for Development Centre, "Draft Proposal: Preparation of the National Conservation Strategy for Kenya," May 1987, IUCN Library.

[114] Lee Talbot to Terry Lisniewski, March 23, 1981, folder 2414, box 256, VII IUCN Correspondence, Strong Papers.

[115] "Nairobi Declaration," May 1982. Online [Available] http://www.unep.org/Law/PDF/NairobiDeclaration1982.pdf. Accessed August 28, 2012.

[116] "World Bank Urges Conservation-Development Partnership," *IUCN Bulletin*, Vol. 13, Nos. 1–3 (January–March 1982), 23; A. W. Clausen, "Sustainable Development: The Global Imperative," 1981. [Online] Available: http://documents.worldbank.org/curated/en/1981/11/15532206/sustainable-development-global-imperative-fairfield-osborn-memorial-lecture-w-clausen-president-world-bank. Accessed August 28, 2012; "World Bank Procedures for Integrating Environmental Issues into Country Strategies," October 19, 1987, DC_Environment. 1987–1990, World Bank Archives; "Environment, Growth, and Development," paper prepared by World Bank staff for consideration by the Development Committee, March 1987, folder 1034, box 108, Thacher Papers, Part I.

[117] "Minutes, Cabinet Council of Natural Resources and Environment, March 25, 1983," Randall E. Davis Files, box 4, OA 12582, CCNRE: March 25, 1983 – CM 200 Global Issues, CM 121 Coal Slurry and CM 049 Clean Air (Acid Rain), Ronald Reagan Presidential Library, Simi Valley, CA [hereinafter cited as Reagan Library].

Commission on Environment and Development, better known as the Brundtland Commission. Chaired by Norwegian Prime Minister Gro Harlem Brundtland, the group formed in 1983 to build on the conceptual work done by the *World Conservation Strategy* and offer more practical suggestions for how nations might adopt its guidelines. Between 1985 and 1987, the commission supported dozens of surveys, reports, and meetings. While Brundtland nominally chaired the commission, its members – led by Maurice Strong and Canadian environmentalist Jim MacNeill – did much of the legwork. Many officials affiliated with NGOs, particularly the IIED, also helped to shape the report's content.[118]

The commission's final report, entitled *Our Common Future*, appeared in 1987. It stressed the need to strengthen environmental institutions in developing nations; increase funding for the UNEP; and deepen connections between policy makers and NGOs. It thus reiterated many ideas that the *World Conservation Strategy* had supported. It defined sustainable development as the need "to ensure that [development] meets the needs of the present without compromising the ability of future generations to meet their own needs." In essence, the Brundtland Commission culled together earlier ideas – from Strong and Sachs's ecodevelopment concept, to Ward's notion of inner and outer limits, to the *World Conservation Strategy* – to emphasize both contemporary short-term socioeconomic equality and long-term intergenerational environmental equality.[119]

Following the Brundtland report, the concept of "sustainable development" and the discourse of "sustainability" became wildly popular worldwide. Many nations, including the United States, endorsed the report's definition of sustainable development and national leaders began speaking in the language of sustainability.[120] In 1990, the G-7 nations announced at their annual economic summit that sustainable development should be

---

[118] Brian W. Walker, "Time for Change: IIED, 1984–1990," in Cross, ed., "Evidence for Hope," 35. For a detailed history of the Brundtland Commission, see Iris Borowy, *Defining Sustainable Development for Our Common Future: A History of the World Commission on Environment and Development (Brundtland Commission)* (London: Routledge, 2014).

[119] Report of the World Commission on Environment and Development, A/RES/42/187, December 11, 1987. [Online] Available: http://www.un.org/documents/ga/res/42/ares42-187.htm/. Accessed August 15, 2012.

[120] The administration endorsed the concept in the most general sense, but "refrained from any broad endorsement" of the report, and thus its specific policy suggestions. "Points to be Made: Environment," addendum to letter Jerry W. Leach to Colin L. Powell, March 31, 1988, "Environment – Ozone & Acid Rain [1]," box 92365, Tyrus Cobbs Files, Reagan Library.

the target for all national government worldwide.[121] Other institutions embraced the new phrase, as well. In higher education, for example, a group of thirty-one university leaders from fifteen nations signed an agreement in 1990 that committed their universities to pursuing sustainability.[122] As a result of this proliferation of sustainable development rhetoric, a journalist for the *Times* claimed that the Brundtland report demarcated a major turning point in the history of international politics because it "may well have marked the point where politicians began to take notice, in a systematic way, of the environment as a problem" across the entire world.[123] By the twenty-first century, sustainability became a "core organizing principle" for institutions and individuals alike and a "master term" that resonated across the world.[124]

However, for all its use, the sustainable development idea also invited attacks for its broadness. Almost as soon as the Brundtland report came out, the meaning of sustainability became muddled as debates emerged between various experts over whether environmental protection was truly compatible with economic growth and market-based development approaches. Over the course of the 1970s, this debate had focused on questions of resource exhaustion and population growth. Biologist Paul Ehrlich suggested that runaway population growth in the Global South would lead to a Malthusian food crisis; economist Julian Simon optimistically predicted that technological innovation would cure any ills. Ehrlich's thinking came to symbolize the ecological limits to economic growth and demanded a need for regulations to rein in development, whereas Simon's arguments fueled skepticism of government intervention and nurtured faith in market forces and technological innovation to overcome any environmental problems.[125] Although many environmentalists favored Ehrlich's stress of regulations, by the 1980s Simon's arguments resonated with many leaders and laypeople alike as market-based solutions to social, economic, and environmental problems grew in popularity.

[121] "Paris Economic Summit: Economic Declaration," July 16, 1989, *Public Papers of the President*, 1989–93. [Online] Available: http://www.presidency.ucsb.edu/ws/index.php?pid=17300&st=sustainable&st1=. Accessed January 13, 2014.

[122] Yates, "Abundance on Trial," 11.

[123] Michael McCarthy, "Dawning of a 'Green Age' Shatters Old Certainties," *The Times*, December 29, 1989.

[124] Yates, "Abundance on Trial," 12, 1.

[125] Paul Sabin, *The Bet: Paul Ehrlich, Julian Simon, and Our Gamble Over the Earth's Future* (New Haven: Yale University Press, 2013).

In turn, advocates for sustained economic growth, minimal regulations, free trade, and privatization seized on the sustainability phrase to emphasize a need to *sustain* development. Advocates for freer markets, from the editorial authors of *The Economist* magazine to the top officials at the IMF and the World Bank to leading multinational corporations, endorsed the concept of sustainable development, but did so by stressing that free markets and liberalized trade were the best tools to reconcile economic growth and environmental protection.[126] This rhetoric and thinking became popular in the international development community, as many prominent development economists called for minimizing the role of the state in development planning and attention and support for the NIEO faded amid strong resistance from the United States and leading European nations.[127] Unmoored from its roots in the *World Conservation Strategy*, by the end of the 1980s the sustainable development phrase thus came to mean different things to different people – a trait that would soon become very evident at the 1992 Rio Earth Summit. The phrase became associated with definitions for which its original crafters did not intend, and many people from outside environmental community infused the phrase with an optimism about the dynamism of markets and technological innovations to suggest that humankind could continue pursuing economic growth without radical policy change or much sacrifice.

In the global diffusion of sustainable development as a phrase, concept, and model for developers and environmentalists to pursue, questions of environment and development became fixed around the notion that environmental protection measures needed to serve economic development. Environmental protection initiatives, the new thinking went, had to promote local participation, the satisfaction of basic needs, and the eradication of poverty. In short, as the *World Conservation Strategy* and Brundtland report had stressed, themes of alternative development approaches of the 1970s had thus become mainstream by the 1980s.[128] As the phrase came to hold many different definitions in rhetoric across world, the work of the IUCN, the IIED, the WWF, and the UNEP over

---

[126] For more on the connections between sustainable development and the rising valorization of market forces in the 1980s and 1990s, see Bernstein, *The Compromise of Liberal Environmentalism*, 70–83.

[127] Borowy, *Defining Sustainable Development for Our Common Future*, 42–9; Prashad, *The Poorer Nations*, chapter 1.

[128] Robin Clarke and Lloyd Timberlake, *Stockholm Plus Ten: Promises, Promises? The Decade Since the 1972 UN Environment Conference* (London: Earthscan, 1982), 58–62.

the 1970s ensured that going into the future, conservation would be *for* development.

The rise of sustainable development discourse and thinking marked an important shift in the history of international development and environmentalism. In the 1950s and 1960s, environmental activists foundered in their attempts to promote environmental protection in the developing countries because they failed to address adequately the needs, desires, and preferences of leaders, intellectuals, and local communities alike. These tensions spilled over into the fractious debates surrounding the Stockholm Conference, as environmental protection became explicitly bound up in the Global South's desire for economic development on its own terms. From the early 1970s, though, a transnational network of development experts and environmental activists engaged in an intellectual project to rethink the relationship between economic growth and environmentalism. Influential leaders in this group, particularly Maurice Strong and Barbara Ward, brought together unofficial representatives of the development and conservation communities who hoped to reform existing development policies. The transnational character of this movement was significant; these activists believed existing institutional arrangements were insufficient to redress truly global problems. International gatherings such as Founex provided a way for experts to discuss issues that affected all people, and they offered environmentalists the opportunity to interact with leading voices from the developing world. This process of transnational debate greatly shaped the contours of the *World Conservation Strategy*, which in turn provided a model for future global initiatives such as the Brundtland Commission.

Such engagement was particularly important for officials associated within the WWF and the IUCN, which, as they crafted the document, also reoriented their own organizational focus. The handful of NGO officials who worked directly with leaders in the developing world, particularly Maurice Strong, David Munro, Lee Talbot, and Robert Allen of the IUCN, brought their experiences and ideas to bear on the content of the sustainable development approach. Sustainable development signaled an important phrase for the development community's acceptance of environmental limitations to economic growth. It also exposed a deep and profound shift in the way major environmental NGOs understood themselves and their relationship to the development community and developing world. The concept of sustainable development was as much about incorporating developmental aspirations into environmentalism as it was about including insights from environmentalism into development thought. Many activists, leaders, and scholars criticized the concept of sustainable development for its vagueness, and many worried that the concept gave tacit approval for economic growth to continue.[129] The environmental community's embrace of developing nations' right to economic development helps to explain how and why the phrase came to hold many different meanings.

While this process rankled many in the conservation community who feared that leading NGOs were losing their true focus and purpose, it did provide remarkable institutional support for environmentalists to keep their organizations solvent. Put simply, the UNEP sustained the IUCN during difficult times. Likewise, the strategy came shortly after major developing agencies in Sweden, Canada, and the United States began funding environmental activities, and thus many NGOs positioned themselves to earn contracts to help shape "sustainable" development plans. Through its agreement with AID, for instance, the IIED was "strengthened as a major international private sector organization which can offer developmentally relevant advice on environmental problems."[130] Framing conservation in the language of development helped NGOs achieve greater gains than before, as environmental officials became more amenable to dialogue and cooperation with the development community.

Despite these changes, questions remained about how to implement sustainable development planning. Speaking on the twentieth anniversary of the WWF's creation in 1981, Max Nicholson, who had been at Julian Huxley's side at the organization's founding, celebrated the *World Conservation Strategy* as an emblem of how far the conservation

---

[129] On criticisms of sustainable development from various angles – for its lack of conceptual clarity, that it justifies continued patterns of exploitation, or that it legitimizes existing power relationships, see Lele, "Sustainable Development: A Critical Review"; Escobar, *Encountering Development*, chapter 5; Radkau, *Nature and Power*, 280–330; Wolfgang Sachs, *Planet Dialectics: Explorations in Environment and Development* (London: Zed Books, 1999); and Rist, *The History of Development*, chapter 10. For an insightful overview of such criticisms, see Robinson, "Squaring the Circle?"; Joshua J. Yates, "Abundance on Trial: The Cultural Significance of 'Sustainability,'" *The Hedgehog Review*, Vol. 14, No. 2 (Summer 2012), 8–25.

[130] "Project Data Sheet: Environmental Planning & Management," 1985, 19, USAID Document Clearinghouse. [Online] Available: http://dec.usaid.gov/index.cfm. Accessed August 4, 2012.

movement had come. He lauded the movement's willingness to seek alliances with the "hitherto uncooperative and discordant movement for development in the Third World." However, he also recognized that conceptual and rhetorical advances had outpaced implementation of conservation programs in the developing world. Despite the many "well-meaning declarations of intent" from leaders from the Global South about the sustainable development idea, Nicholson worried that the rhetoric had raised expectations among his colleagues to unwarranted degree. "There is no evidence," he said that the developing world was willing to commit to – and pay for – changes "necessary to reduce, let alone eliminate, the massive harm which it is still inflicting on the environment."[131]

Nicholson's call for caution was astute. As efforts to implement the guidebook through national strategies showed, true policy commitment to follow its principles required greater financial and institutional support. NGOs came to realize this, as did government leaders. Thus, as preparations began in the mid-1980s for the milestone two-decade follow-up to the Stockholm Conference, dubbed the Rio Earth Summit, two old ideas resurfaced: additional resources to help developing nations pay for new environmental institutions ("additionality") and compensation for lost revenues during the process of reorienting their economies.

As had been the case in Stockholm, in Rio discussions of environmental accords hinged on questions of foreign aid, international development, and North-South financial relations. Leading up to the conference, environmentalists were optimistic that the discourse of sustainability had given new legitimacy to environmental protection in the developing world, but unsure about whether the idea would translate to new policies and changes on the ground. Many questions beguiled them. What kinds of resources would powerful nations, such as the United States and those in Western Europe, commit to aid developing nations? How much sovereignty would developing nations accede in response to pressing global issues, particularly the realization of global climate change? Would the collapse of the Soviet Union and end of the Cold War – which occurred as preparations for Rio were underway – lead to greater cooperation between nations? Or would older socioeconomic and political divisions prove far too intractable to change in such short time?

---

[131] Max Nicholson, "The First World Conservation Lecture," *The Environmentalist*, Vol. 1, No. 2 (Summer 1981), 114.

# PART THREE

# PERSISTENT PROBLEMS

# 7

# The Persistence of Old Problems: The Politics of Environment and Development at the Rio Earth Summit

Standing before exasperated delegates on June 12, 1992, at the United Nations Conference on Environment and Development (UNCED) in Rio de Janeiro, President George H. W. Bush spoke in vague terms. "We believe that the road to Rio must point toward both environmental protection and economic growth, environment and development," the president proclaimed. "By now it's clear: To sustain development, we must protect the environment. And to protect the environment, we must sustain development."[1]

President Bush's words left many onlookers baffled. On the one hand, Bush spoke the language of sustainability, noting the interrelationship between economic development and environmental protection. Soon after his speech, the president signed the conference's formal declaration, which proclaimed "sustainable development" as the discursive framework for the United Nations' development policies. He acknowledged the need to integrate environmental protection into all economic development policies. On the other hand, President Bush did not attempt to describe exactly how that process would occur. He also rejected many of the formal conventions on the table in Rio. The president refused to sign a treaty on biodiversity protection, and he only agreed to support an agreement on global climate change that came without any binding stipulations. Although the president had accepted the necessity of crafting environmentally friendly approaches

[1] George H. W. Bush, "Address to the United Nations Conference on Environment and Development in Rio de Janeiro, Brazil," June 12, 1992. [Online] Available: http://bushlibrary.tamu.edu/research/public_papers.php?id=4417&year=&month. Accessed December 28, 2009.

to development, it was clear that full cooperation and significant concrete measures remained out of reach.

The gulf between the president's rhetoric and actions revealed two salient aspects of how the relationship between environmentalism and economic development had evolved over the previous decades. As President Bush's speech indicated, the conference legitimized the use of sustainability rhetoric to acknowledge the link between environmental protection and economic development, which major environmental non-governmental organizations (NGOs) had been promoting for over a decade. In the immediate aftermath of World War II, many policy makers conceived of environmental protection and economic policy as separate policy domains; by 1992, every government leader acknowledged the interconnectedness of the two concepts and every leader spoke of "sustainable development." In some respects, NGOs such as the International Union for the Conservation of Nature (IUCN) and the World Wildlife Fund (WWF) had succeeded beyond their expectations in popularizing the sustainability concept.[2]

Despite this rhetorical shift, the Rio Conference also highlighted a decades-long continuity in the international politics of environment protection. As had been the case for decades, the question of "additionality," whether the industrialized nations would commit to new and additional resource transfers to fund environmental protection programs in the developing world, dominated discussions over international environmental accords. In the years before the Rio Conference, many environmental NGOs had helped to demonstrate the tremendous ecological and economic threats posed to the developing world by trends such as desertification, species loss, deforestation, and global climate change. Developing countries organized again through the Group of 77 (G-77), although the organization carried less influence than it did in the 1970s as Third World activism and support for the New International Economic Order had waned considerably by the 1980s.[3] G-77 countries recognized these threats but resisted binding environmental accords that did not also

---

[2] The leading accounts of the Rio Earth Summit, which have been written by participants, journalists, or political scientists, all acknowledge this basic fact. See Engfeldt, *From Stockholm to Johannesburg and Beyond*; Hopgood, *American Foreign Environmental Policy and the Power of the State*; Philip Shabecoff, *A New Name for Peace: International Environmentalism, Sustainable Development, and Democracy* (Hanover: University Press of New England, 1996).

[3] Vanessa Ogle, "State Rights against Private Capital: The "New International Economic Order" and "The Struggle over Aid, Trade, and Investment, 1962–1981," *Humanity*, Vol. 5, No. 2 (Summer 2014), 211–34.

include increased foreign aid transfers and more favorable terms for technology transfer. Many key environmentalists, including the Rio Conference's General-Secretary Maurice Strong, had come to sympathize with the G-77 position and demand additionality as a sine qua non of any major agreement in Rio, too. Most industrialized nations, however, once again rejected any substantial increases in direct resource transfers.

In particular, the United States' resistance to additionality scuttled negotiations in the lead-up to Rio. The Bush administration was willing to give explicit rhetorical support to most environmental issues, but it was unwilling to incur substantial additional financial obligations vis-à-vis the developing countries. The administration often couched their position – which resembled Nixon and Kissinger's stance at the Stockholm Conference – in a pro-market rhetoric that demonized any new regulations. Since the 1970s, a "culture of faith in the market" suffused American life, as the private sector and market forces became viewed as the ideal tools for pursuing economic development and much else.[4] Bush administration officials consistently lauded the power of market principles to solve environmental problems, frequently invoking arguments about the logic of incentives, the virtues of cost-benefit analysis, and the perils of increased government regulation. The Bush administration, in turn, rejected any international agreements – such as the treaty over climate change – that called for binding regulations or a major increase in foreign aid flows.

---

[4] The phrase comes from Thomas Borstelmann, *The 1970s: A New Global History from Civil Rights to Economic Inequality* (Princeton: Princeton University Press, 2012), 5. On the rise of market fundamentalism, see also Daniel Yergin and Joseph Stanislaw, *The Commanding Heights: The Battle for the World Economy* (New York: Free Press, 1998); Daniel T. Rodgers, *Age of Fracture* (Cambridge: The Belknap Press of Harvard University Press, 2011); Mark Mazower, *Governing the World: The History of an Idea* (New York: The Penguin Press, 2012), chapter 12; Daniel Stedman Jones, *Masters of the Universe: Hayek, Friedman, and the Birth of Neoliberal Politics* (Princeton: Princeton University Press, 2012). This faith in market-based solutions also appeared in international development circles in the 1980s with the "Washington Consensus" policies that focused on liberalizing trade, sound monetary policy, cutting back the public sector. See, for instance, John Williamson, "Democracy and the Washington Consensus," *World Development*, Vol. 21 (1993), 1329–36; Philip Arestis, "Washington Consensus and Financial Liberalization," *Journal of Post Keynesian Economics*, Vol. 27, No. 2 (Winter, 2004–2005); Narcís Serra and Joseph E. Stiglitz, eds., *The Washington Consensus Reconsidered: Towards a New Global Governance* (New York: Oxford University Press, 2008); Eklbadh, *The Great American Mission*, chapter 8. On the broader global shift toward the market, see Mazower, *Governing the World*, chapter 12. On the growing consensus around market-based solutions for international environmental issues during the late 1980s, see Bernstein, *The Compromise of Liberal Environmentalism*, 70–83.

Moreover, many Bush administration officials believed that the end of the Cold War revealed that any kind of centralized or extensive regulatory system could not and would not ameliorate social, political, or even environmental problems. Although many observers hoped that the end of the Cold War would signify a new era of international cooperation over international environmental matters, in practice the collapse of the "second world" reinforced the belief of Bush administration officials that freer trade and fewer regulations, not more foreign aid, would best redress international environmental problems. In spite of the shifting international system, comprehensive and concrete measures at the Rio gathering in 1992 proved elusive because of many of the same tensions that had beguiled participants at the 1972 Stockholm Conference. As was the case in Stockholm, environmental protection in the developing world foundered in discussions over North-South economic relations.

In the end, the debates over additionality also exposed the weakness of the new sustainability discourse. Robert Allen and the IUCN officials who crafted the *World Conservation Strategy* had learned that defining sustainable development was a contentious process. Once in the mainstream of development discourse, the phrase became even more ambiguous. Already by the time of the conference, astute observers noted that the phrase had acquired over forty different definitions.[5] Environmentalists, policy makers, and industry leaders often interpreted the phrase quite differently. For some, it was a rich concept that signaled a new ethic and responsibility toward the natural world and a need for global socioeconomic equality; for others, it was a hollow slogan that amounted to little more than "green-washing" of existing development practices. What few questioned, however, was that the concept sanctioned continued economic growth and placed environmental protection in the service of economic development, as President Bush had noted in his June 12th speech to the Rio delegations. The Stockholm Conference had left many environmentalists feeling enthusiastic about the possibility for future reform. The disconnect between the sustainability discourse and the absence of sufficient cooperation over additionality after the Rio meeting left the environmental community far more uneasy and uncertain about the future.

---

[5] Steven Bernstein also notes that the Rio Declaration "does not even attempt a consensus definition." Bernstein, *The Compromise of Liberal Environmentalism*, 5. Bernstein draws his number from the "gallery of definitions" provided in David Pearce, Anil Markandya, and Edward Barbier, *Blueprint for a Green Economy* (London: Earthscan Publications Ltd., 1989), 173–85.

## THE GLOBAL ENVIRONMENT IN THE 1980S:
### THE BACKGROUND TO RIO

The idea for a major twenty-year follow-up conference to Stockholm came largely from Maurice Strong. In October 1986, Strong visited Sweden to meet with former officials who had been instrumental in setting up the original UN environmental gathering. Strong informed them of his work with the Brundtland Commission. He wanted the Brundtland Commission's report to receive widespread attention, and he also hoped that a major international conference could pressure major states to adopt its guidelines. Recent efforts to implement the "sustainable development" approach to planning in the developing world disappointed Strong and many other activists in the environmental community. The *World Conservation Strategy*, for instance, generated positive reviews as a general guide but had yet to be implemented systematically at the national level. Likewise, the formal ten-year follow-up to Stockholm, a gathering of the UNEP General Council in Nairobi in 1982, generated little fanfare outside the environmental community and UN system. Strong believed that only another international conference like Stockholm could make meaningful steps to ensure the Brundtland Commission's report would not meet a similar fate to the *World Conservation Strategy*.[6]

Strong also recognized the importance of "additionality" and personally sympathized with the ongoing economic and fiscal challenges afflicting the developing world. He had nurtured close ties with leaders and intellectuals from the Global South, and his experiences in reshaping many environmental NGOs during the 1970s had been spurred by his desire for environmentalists to pay greater attention to problems such as poverty and inequality. Strong believed that "industrialized and developing countries would have to change the way they deal with each other," for the *World Conservation Strategy*'s sustainable development method of planning to take hold.[7]

Strong's desire to implement sustainable development practices and redress economic imbalances appeared increasingly urgent in the mid-1980s. When Strong and his Swedish colleagues met for lunch in September 1986, in Washington, DC, environmentalists protested the World Bank's support for destructive development programs in Brazil and India. The crushing burden of the global debt crisis, coupled with

---

[6] Engfeldt, *From Stockholm to Johannesburg and Beyond*, 114–17; Strong, *Where on Earth Are We Going?*, 194–5.

[7] Strong, *Where on Earth Are We Going?*, 205.

structural adjustment policies premised on export-led recovery, spurred many developing nations to pursue strategies that raise short-term revenues at the expense of long-term planning. Tropical deforestation and growing desertification, in particular, became major global problems.[8] Such trends seemed all the more worrisome in light of the emerging scientific research on "biodiversity," which suggested that species loss greatly harmed the ecosystems and the ecological processes that supported life on earth.[9] Finally, a series of horrific disasters around large industrial sites – such as the Union Carbide factory in Bhopal, India, and the Chernobyl nuclear power plant in the Soviet Union – offered stark warnings of unheeded development.[10]

Most troubling of all, new scientific research over the previous decade had revealed that industrial development had profoundly altered the planet's life support systems. The ozone layer of the atmosphere had been torn apart, leaving a gaping hole over Antarctica. Acid rain, toxic precipitation caused by industrial emissions of sulfur dioxide and nitrogen oxide, corroded the built and natural environment alike and imperiled human health across the globe. Worse still, the global climate appeared to be warming, driven in part by carbon emissions stemming from growing reliance on fossil fuels as a cheap energy source for economic development worldwide. Global climate change threatened every natural system of the planet and posed human society with unknown and unprecedented risks. These were all truly global problems for which there was little in the way of institutional or political precedents to manage.[11] The combination of

---

[8] NGOs had taken an interest in deforestation in the tropics as a major issue in the 1970s, and many began to link its spread to the debt crisis by the early 1980s. Barbara J. Bramble and Tom Plant, "Third World Debt and Natural Resources Conservation," carton 15–18 Debt for Nature Swaps, July-December, 1989, Sierra Club International Program Records; "Debt-for-Nature Swaps: A New Conservation Tool," *World Wildlife Fund Letter*, Vol. 1, No. 1 (1988); "Commentary," *Conservation Foundation Letter*, January–February 1986, 2.

[9] See Jane Guyer and Paul Richards, "The Invention of Biodiversity: Social Perspectives on the Management of Biological Variety in Africa," *Africa: Journal of the International African Institute*, Vol. 66, No. 1 (1996), 1–13. The IUCN and the WWF had begun promoting the term in the 1970s, and formalized a definition at the 1982 World Congress on National Parks. Bruce A. Wilcox, "In Situ Conservation of Genetic Resources: Determinants of Minimum Area Requirements," in McNeely and Miller, eds., *National Parks, Conservation, and Development: The Role of Protected Areas in Sustaining Society*, 639–47.

[10] Shabecoff, *A New Name for Peace*, 55.

[11] On the ozone, see Edward Parson, "Protecting the Ozone Layer" in Peter M. Haas, Robert O. Keohane, and Marc A. Levy, eds., *Institutions for the Earth: Sources of Effective International Environmental Protection* (Cambridge: The MIT Press, 1993),

ongoing environmental destruction and these new threats amounted to "an emerging global crisis," claimed the IUCN.[12]

Strong and his Swedish colleagues believed these problems all required global cooperation and immediate action. In September 1987 Swedish delegates to the UN put forth a proposal at the UN General Assembly to host a twenty-year follow-up to Stockholm that would identify frameworks for both national and international action to promote "sustainable development" as the Brundtland Commission had defined it.[13] In planning the conference, Strong identified six key goals for the conference: the drafting of an "Earth Charter," inspired in part by a follow-up under way to the *World Conservation Strategy*; the drafting of "Agenda 21," a follow-up to Stockholm's Action Plan that would lay out a strategy for all nations achieving "sustainable development" models of planning; formal institutions to oversee Agenda 21; financial agreements to fund Agenda 21; discussion over rules for technology transfers; and conventions on climate change and the protection of biological diversity (which later grew to include conventions on forest protection and desertification).[14] The questions of North-South resource transfers underscored each goal. The outcome of the conference, Strong admitted, depended on the North's willingness to commit greater resources to the South. On these issues, he believed, "The North [had] to budge."[15]

Strong's framing of the conference along these lines ensured that the 1992 meeting would be dominated by many of the same economic and political questions that had shaped the Stockholm gathering. Brazil, the nation that had taken so central a role in articulating these points in 1972, reemerged through the G-77 as the leading voice over international economic issues in 1987. Although Sweden initially offered to host the 1992 gathering, Brazil, with G-77 backing, countered. As a result, when the UN finally agreed to host the conference in December 1989, Rio de Janeiro,

---

27–74; on acid rain, see Marc A. Levy, "European Acid Rain: The Power of Tote-Board Diplomacy," in Haas, Keohane, and Levy, eds., *Institutions for the Earth*, 75–132; on climate change, see Spencer Weart, *The Discovery of Global Warming* (Cambridge: Harvard University Press, 2003).

[12] *Director General's Report on the Activities of the Union Since the 16th Session of the IUCN General Assembly in November 1984 to May 1985*, May 1985, iii. IUCN Library, Gland Switzerland.

[13] Strong, *Where on Earth Are We Going?*, 195–6.

[14] Engfeldt, *From Stockholm to Johannesburg and Beyond*, 144.

[15] Ross Howard, "Earth Summit: North Is North, South Is South, Will Ever the Twain Meet?" *The Globe and Mail*, August 24, 1991.

not Stockholm, won the right to host the conference.[16] The choice to host the gathering in the developing world held great symbolic power. If the negotiations at Rio were going to generate meaningful action on environmental issues, participants would first have to make concrete agreements on issues of international development and financial assistance.

## ENVIRONMENTALISM IN THE LEAD-UP TO RIO

While the North-South conflict loomed over the Rio preparations, NGOs had many reasons to be hopeful at the start of the negotiating process. NGOs had generated many important institutional responses to the environmental threats of the 1980s. For instance, the IUCN took a leading role in shaping international action over biodiversity protection. The organization's transition to the "conservation *for* development" message in the 1970s led it to adopt the language of biodiversity as a more politically palatable alternative to older notions of national park and protected area policies. In 1982, at the Third World Conference on National Parks held in Bali, Indonesia, IUCN officials working on protected areas positioned themselves to focus on "sustainable resource management and sustainable wildlife use," rather than older preservationist notions. Following the meeting, IUCN officials working with the groups' Environmental Law Centre began to draft a possible international convention on biodiversity protection based on the need to "conserve biodiversity at the genetic, species and ecosystem levels" and including "a funding mechanism to alleviate the inequality of the conservation burden between the North and the South." In the mid-1980s, the IUCN collaborated with the World Resources Institute, the UNEP, the World Bank, and other international institutions to produce a series of influential publications on biodiversity.[17] Many NGOs also participated in innovative "debt-for-nature" swaps to purchase developing nations' debt in exchange for the expansion of domestic environmental programs.[18]

---

[16] Ibid.

[17] See Jeffrey A. McNeely, "Conserving Biological Diversity: A Decision-Maker's Guide," *IUCN Bulletin*, Vol. 20, N. 4–6 (April/June 1989), 6–7; Martin Holdgate, *The Green Web: A Union for World Conservation* (London: Earthscan Publications, Ltd., 1999), 214. The IIED took a major interest in sustainable tropical forest management, with its program led by two veterans of the WCS drafting and implementation process – Duncan Poore and Stephen Bass. See Duncan Poore and Stephen Bass, "Forestry and land use," in Cross, ed., *Evidence for Hope*, 77–95.

[18] On debt-for-nature swaps, see Cord Jakobeit, "Nonstate Actors Leading the Way: Debt-for-Nature Swaps," in Robert O. Keohane and Marc A. Levy, eds., *Institutions for*

Similarly, the IUCN and the WWF assumed a leading role to organize political action over tropical forest protection. The World Wildlife Fund, Friends of the Earth, the Rainforest Action Network, and many other NGOs initiated major fund-raising campaigns and organized boycotts designed to draw attention to tropical deforestation. NGOs such as the International Institute for Environment and Development (IIED) and the IUCN worked to pressure states to enforce international agreements over forestry use.[19] The IUCN also began a tropical forest research initiative and formed a new wing of its organization to focus on deforestation. Working with the UNEP, the IUCN folded in many concerns from developing nations and adopted a focus on resource transfers in their forest program, in a process that mirrored what had occurred in drafting the *World Conservation Strategy*. Throughout the 1980s, many other NGOs popularized the notion of tropical deforestation during the campaign against the World Bank.[20]

In addition to this international activism, at Rio NGOs had more formal opportunities to participate in conference preparations than they had at Stockholm. Maurice Strong's position of leadership gave the most influential organizations – particularly the IUCN – an access point to shape the secretariat and the conference agenda.[21] National delegations also allowed NGOs to participate in formal preparatory committees on a much wider scale than had been the case in Stockholm.[22]

The IUCN and the WWF nurtured close relationships between their own high-level officials and the U.S. government. President Reagan had frustrated many environmentalists by filling key regulatory positions in

---

*Environmental Aid: Pitfalls and Promise* (Cambridge: the MIT Press, 1996), 127–66. For a recent legal review that covers much of the legal and political science literature on the swaps, see Jared E. Knicley, "Debt, Nature, and Indigenous Rights: Twenty-Five Years of Debt-for-Nature Evolution," *Harvard Environmental Law Review*, Vol. 36, No. 1 (2012), 80–122.

[19] In particular, the IIED worked to generate compliance of the International Tropical Timber Agreement, a 1983 international agreement adopted by a few dozen states under the auspices of the UNCTAD. Poore and Bass, "Forestry and Land Use," 83–6. See also Richard G. Tarasofsky, ed., *Assessing the International Forest Regime*, IUCN Environmental Policy and Law Paper No. 37, 1999.

[20] Holdgate, *The Green Web*, 161, 185.

[21] Ibid., 215. Strong also tasked allies in the NGO community to organize a parallel conference akin to the forums held at Stockholm. Strong, *Where on Earth Are We Going?*, 204–5.

[22] "Decisions by Nairobi Meeting of the UNCED Preparatory Committee Regarding Arrangements for NGO Participation in UNCED Participatory Process," folder 428, box 46, Thacher Papers, Part I.

his administration with people antagonistic toward the environmental movement and regulation, and during his tenure, the United States, once a leader in international environmental politics during the Nixon years, became the world's most powerful opponent to major international accords.[23] By contrast, the election of George H. W. Bush opened up the opportunity for "envirocrats" to cycle between the leading NGOs and the new administration.[24] Bush appointed many former NGO officials to key positions in government. Curtis Bohlen of the WWF-US became the assistant secretary of state for Oceans and International Environmental and Scientific Affairs; William Reilly, also from the WWF-US, became the administrator of the Environmental Protection Agency (EPA); and Michael Deland, the head of the Council of Environmental Quality (CEQ) under Bush, had many close friends in the environmental community and provided leading NGOs with another ally in government.[25]

Beyond these opportunities for political influence, environmentalists believed that rapid changes in international politics might encourage greater cooperation on environmental issues. By mid-1990, when preparations for Rio began in earnest, the international system was in flux. Many of the key nations and regions that had defined the Cold War were undergoing a remarkable transformation. The Soviet Union was on the brink of collapse; Eastern Europe had left the Soviet empire; Germany was in the process of reunification; India and China were beginning to liberalize their economies. A "new world order," as President Bush called it, appeared on the horizon. Environmentalists, journalists, and other observers all hoped that a new spirit of cooperation would emerge in the wake of the global ideological conflict. The IUCN sought to encourage cooperation with the former Soviet bloc.[26] "The prospects for peace and international co-operation," wrote one journalist in early 1990, "appear as great as they have been at any time in this savage century."[27] Many others recognized that greater U.S. engagement with international institutions and greater commitment to international accords was critical to avoid creating future tensions between nations or slipping into "an

---

[23] Andrews, *Managing the Environment, Managing Ourselves*, 330.

[24] Gottlieb, *Forcing the Spring*, chapter 4.

[25] Peter Thacher to Donna Wise, April 9, 1990, folder 428, box 46, Thacher Papers, Part I; Philip Shabecoff, "Bush Expected to Name Conservationist to a Top Environmental Post," *The New York Times*, December 23, 1989, A16.

[26] Jan Cerovsky, "IUCN and Eastern Europe: An End to Isolation," *IUCN Bulletin*, Vol. 21, No. 4 (December 1990), 27.

[27] "The Dawn of a Brave New World?," *The Globe and Mail*, January 1, 1990.

environmental Cold War" between the North and South over questions of aid and sovereignty.[28]

Environmentalists looked hopefully on Rio because major international agreements over environmental issues seemed to be proliferating. European countries, for instance, had shown a willingness to create, sign, and implement binding international agreements. All major European states (except the United Kingdom) agreed to a major 1987 agreement on the reduction of sulfur emissions to curb acid rain.[29] Likewise, every major industrialized nation eventually signed the Montreal Protocol of 1987, which required nations to phase out chemicals that depleted the ozone layer and contribute to a shared fund to help defray the costs of poorer countries' efforts to minimize the use of such products.[30]

Excitement that the Rio Conference might produce significant treaties also emerged from an unexpected source in late 1989: the World Bank. In September, France's finance minister, Pierre Bérégovoy, proposed the creation of a centralized fund to provide additional financing to developing nations for "global" environmental issues. The World Bank had just begun its massive reorganization to focus on global environmental issues, and the bank staff saw the Global Environmental Facility (GEF) as a tool to help carry out their new mandate. Likewise, Bérégovoy had been told by French delegates to the Intergovernmental Panel on Climate Change (IPCC), the body tasked with exploring and drafting an international climate convention, that without any mechanism for additionality, developing nations would reject any climate change agreement. In response, he proposed that the bank use its new emphasis and funding to create a voluntary fund from which developing nations could draw as they created new programs and mechanisms to fight major issues of global significance. Bérégovoy stated that France was prepared to offer $100 million (U.S. dollars) to fund the first three years. West Germany, which had perhaps the strongest domestic environmental constituency of any Western nation, immediately announced its support for the initiative.[31]

---

[28] Paul Shrivastava, "Environmental Cold War," *The Christian Science Monitor*, May 16, 1991, 19; Alice M. Rivlin, "New World, New Dangers," *The Washington Post*, April 10, 1990, A23.

[29] The verbose title of the agreement is "Protocol to the 1979 Convention on Long-Range Transboundary Air Pollution on the Reduction of Sulphur Emissions or Their Transboundary Fluxes by at Least 30%."

[30] Parson, "Protecting the Ozone Layer," in Haas, Keohane, and Levy, eds., *Institutions for the Earth*, 27–74.

[31] "Funding for the Global Environment," March 26, 1990, folder 1000, box 105, Thacher Papers, Part I; "Funding for the Global Environment," April 10, 1990, folder 1000,

The supporters behind the GEF, as the fund came to be called, believed it could resolve old divisions over additionality. Developing countries, through the G-77 and through most every other international venue available to them, demanded such additional resource transfers for decades to cover the costly switch to environmental protection. The *World Conservation Strategy* had shown a way toward creating an ecologically sustainable economy, but its limited implementation revealed that the transition phase to such a system would be extremely expensive. Maurice Strong told World Bank President Barber Conable that the GEF and donor nation contributions to it would be "important factors in meeting developing country requirements for 'additionality'" in the lead-up to the UNCED.[32] All of Maurice Strong's initiatives hinged in one way or another on additionality; thus, some accord on resource transfers from North to South was necessary for the conference's success. The GEF figured to be a foundational part of any Rio agreement.[33]

In short, there were many reasons for environmentalists to be hopeful that the Rio Conference might lead to global cooperation on major international initiatives. However, their hopes quickly faded. In the lead-up to Rio, clear divisions soon emerged between the most powerful and important developed country, the United States, and the developing nations.

## THE UNITED STATES AND THE RIO PROCESS

Although it later developed a reputation for being obstructionistic and antagonistic toward environmental issues, in 1989 and 1990 the Bush administration appeared as though it would support major international environmental initiatives. While Ronald Reagan often decried environmentalists, George H. W. Bush had long supported the movement. He had served as the U.S. ambassador to the United Nations during the Stockholm Conference and worked closely with Russell Train and the rest of the American delegation. Bush maintained a friendship with Train through the years, and he stayed informed about pressing environmental issues such as climate change through the 1980s by turning to Train for

box 105, Thacher Papers, Part I; "Statement by GEF Participants on the Future Evolution of the Global Environmental Facility," May 4, 1992, folder 1000, box 105, Thacher Papers, Part I.

[32] Maurice Strong to Barber Conable, April 5, 1990, DC "Environment. 1987–1990," WBA.

[33] Strong, *Where on Earth Are We Going?*, 205.

information and advice. Even during the low point of the environmental community's relationship with the Reagan administration in the early 1980s, Bush cultivated personal ties with key environmental leaders; he invited the WWF-US senior staff and board members to the vice presidential mansion for cocktails before the group's annual board dinner.[34] Likewise, Bush often publicly proclaimed his support for the environment, declaring "I'm an environmentalist" on the campaign trail in 1988.[35]

As president, Bush followed up such declarations with key personnel decisions and major policy initiatives. With Bush's nominal support behind them, William Reilly, Curtis Bohlen, and Michael Deland pursued international cooperation over issues such as the biodiversity treaty, tropical forest protection, debt-for-nature swaps, and climate change.[36] Early in his term, Bush also showed a willingness to pursue domestic legislation, such as the 1990 revision to the Clean Air Act.[37]

The Bush administration nominally supported cooperation on environmental issues because key officials saw agreements over such problems as part of a larger foreign policy strategy. In general, with the Cold War ending and the global strategic landscape rapidly shifting, the administration hoped to enmesh all nations in institutional webs through regimes, alliances, and agreements that promoted openness and interconnection.[38] Cooperation over environmental issues, alongside narcotics trafficking and space exploration, represented areas of "growing global importance" in the administration's 1990 *National Security Strategy Statement*.[39]

---

[34] Russell E. Train, *Politics, Pollution, and Pandas: An Environmental Memoir* (Washington: Island Press, 2003), 267–71.

[35] Presidential Candidates Debates, "Presidential Debate at the University of California in Los Angeles," October 13, 1988. Online by Gerhard Peters and John T. Woolley, The American Presidency Project. [Online] Available: http://www.presidency.ucsb.edu/ws/?pid=29412. Accessed September 10, 2014.

[36] Philip Shabecoff, "Bush Expected to Name Conservationist to a Top Environmental Post," *The New York Times*, December 23, 1989, A16; Hopgood, *American Foreign Environmental Policy and the Power of the State*, 129–30.

[37] Keith Schneider, "The Environmental Impact of President Bush," *The New York Times*, August 25, 1991, D4.

[38] Robert B. Zoellick, "An Architecture of U.S. Strategy After the Cold War," in Melvyn P. Leffler and Jeffrey W. Legro, eds., *In Uncertain Times: American Foreign Policy after the Berlin Wall and 9/11* (Ithaca: Cornell University Press, 2011), 26–42.

[39] *National Security Strategy of the United States*, March 1990, 18. [Online] Available: http://bushlibrary.tamu.edu/research/pdfs/national_security_strategy_90.pdf. Accessed November 28, 2012.

Yet for all the rhetoric about supporting environmental issues, the Bush administration's commitment to market-based solutions to environmental problems constrained its policy making.[40] From the late 1970s onward, a growing faith in the market as the primary solution to social, economic, and even thorny political problems suffused American life.[41] Following the economic difficulties of the 1970s – and particularly the challenges posed by rising inflation and stagnant economic growth – policy makers turned to policies that favored monetarism in fiscal matters, free trade regimes, privatization, and deregulation. The deregulation of major industries that had begun in the 1970s led many by the late 1980s to believe that strong regulation distorted incentives, created sclerotic bureaucracies, and ultimately stifled individual choice in favor of narrow special interests. These economic policies reflected the broader political culture, as politicians and conservative intellectuals came to lionize the power of free markets to generate prosperity and ensure individual liberty. President Reagan's rhetoric exemplified the trend. Simplistic statements such as "government is not the solution to our problem; government is the problem" encouraged wider public skepticism toward the ways in which government had been historically used to structure markets and protect capitalism.[42] Many European nations, particularly the United Kingdom under Margaret Thatcher's leadership, and development experts embraced similar ideologies and the rhetorical support for market forces and market friendly policies in the 1980s.[43]

The Bush administration followed the Reagan administration's general policy approach. In general, President Bush proclaimed his economic goals included the pursuit of policies designed to minimize inflation, encourage free trade and open markets, and "avoid unnecessary regulation and design necessary regulatory programs to harness market

[40] On the tensions between Bush's various advisors, see Hopgood, *American Foreign Environmental Policy and the Power of the State*, 156–8; Keith Schneider, "The Environmental Impact of President Bush," *The New York Times*, August 25, 1991, D4. There was also debate within the administration over whether to focus on one specific gas such as carbon dioxide or to pursue a more comprehensive program aimed at reducing all gasses known to contribute to global warming. David Victor to C. Boyden Gray, "Re: Comprehensive approaches to greenhouse policy," folder – Global Climate Change – General [3], box 9, White House Counsel's Office, Jeffrey Holmstead Files, George H. W. Bush Presidential Library, College Station, TX [hereinafter cited as BPL].

[41] Borstelmann, *The 1970s*, 5.

[42] Reagan quoted in Ronald Reagan, Inaugural Address, January 20, 1981. [Online] Available: http://www.reagan.utexas.edu/archives/speeches/1981/12081a.htm. Accessed January 21, 2013.

[43] Mazower, *Governing the World*, chapter 12.

forces."[44] Although Bush generally avoided controversial rhetoric and dogmatic ideological positions, many of his closest advisors – such as Presidential Chief of Staff John Sununu, Vice President Dan Quayle, and Vice Presidential Chief of Staff Bill Kristol – adopted an aggressive free-market stance.[45] Quayle's "Council on Competitiveness," in particular, advocated for dramatic decreases in federal regulation.[46]

In international environmental policy, the administration believed that government should structure markets and give incentives to encourage private investment for environmentally beneficial projects. Accordingly, the administration resisted any global agreements or regulations that established binding rules or constrained national decision making. The 1990 Clean Air Act revisions, for instance, established an emissions permit trading scheme that sidestepped formal regulatory caps on emissions by constructing a market to buy and sell permits to pollute.[47] At the very start of the Rio preparations, the administration made it clear to other delegations that it would seek to be "innovative in our approach to sustainable development." By this, the administration meant primarily "providing market-based incentives, eliminating structural impediments, and ending international trade practices that distort global markets" to solve environmental problems.[48] Quayle's Council on Competitiveness also monitored deliberations over major environmental accords to block any new regulations being discussed, particularly those in the biodiversity treaty.[49] All the while, President Bush and officials from his administration frequently used the term "sustainable development" to emphasize their commitment to market-based mechanisms as solutions to environmental problems, which reinforced the trend of deploying the phrase in a

---

[44] George Bush: "Message to Congress Transmitting the Economic Report of the President," February 6, 1990. [Online] Available: http://www.presidency.ucsb.edu/ws/index.php?pid=99388&st=Bush&st1=free+markets. Accessed January 21, 2013.

[45] On Bush's rhetorical caution and leadership style, see Jeffrey Engel, "A Better World ... But Don't Get Carried Away: The Foreign Policy of George H. W. Bush Twenty Years On," *Diplomatic History*, Vol. 34, No. 1 (January 2010), 25–46.

[46] Michael Ross, "Quayle's Competitiveness Council Comes Under Fire," *Los Angeles Times*, December 9, 1991.

[47] Officials in the Reagan administration had favored market-based systems of emissions credit trading over formal regulations in debates over acid rain in the early to mid-1980s. Naomi Oreskes and Erik M. Conway, *Merchants of Doubt: How a Handful of Scientists Obscured the Truth on Issues from Tobacco Smoke to Global Warming* (New York: Bloomsbury Press, 2010), chapter 3.

[48] "Press Release: Statement by Ambassador Jonathan Moore," March 8, 1990, folder 429, box 46, Thacher Papers, Part I.

[49] Hopgood, *American Foreign Environmental Policy and the Power of the State*, 171–4.

very different way than the authors of the *World Conservation Strategy* and the Brundtland report had intended.

More than just rhetoric, the administration's commitment to market-based solutions meant that it would resist any binding regulations discussed in Rio about resources and in the proposed treaties over climate change, tropical forest protection, and biodiversity. The administration's position appeared particularly strong amid a growing feeling among policy makers, intellectuals, and the general public that the ending of the Cold War had vindicated liberal capitalism. This feeling did not signify a total disregard for the state in structuring economic policy; rather it seemed to reinforce prevailing opinions in the late 1980s about the need to avoid, to the greatest extent possible, centralized control, compulsory regulations, and discriminatory trade practices. Even the UN's General Assembly acknowledged in a special 1990 session the importance of pursuing liberal notions of economic growth in light of communism's collapse.[50] Officials throughout the administration backed such notions, with even the former environmentalists favoring market-based solutions over extensive new regulations. Speaking about the update to the Clean Air Act, William Reilly proclaimed that "market mechanisms" were the key element to "arrange, in effect, a marriage between the environment and the economy."[51] Throughout the Rio process, the administration echoed these sentiments, as they frequently expressed an unwillingness to incur new regulatory commitments or increase of existing federal spending to international initiatives. The administration was thus open to international cooperation over environmental issues, but it would only pursue a very narrow type of agreement. In turn, the Bush administration's commitment to market-based solutions had another immediate consequence in early negotiations over the Rio Conference. It greatly fueled developing countries' growing skepticism and fears over the entire process.

## THE DEVELOPING COUNTRIES IN THE LEAD-UP TO RIO

While the solidarity sought by developing nations during the 1970s had unraveled considerably over the late 1980s, the Rio Earth Summit very

[50] Paul Lewis, "Rich and Poor Lands Agree on Path to Economic Growth," *The New York Times*, May 2, 1990.

[51] William K. Reilly, "The New Environmentalism: Ecology and the Economy," Detroit Economic Club, April 30, 1990, folder "Economics and the Environment," White House Counsel's Office, Jeffrey Holmstead Files, Environmental Subject Files, BPL.

much represented a last gasp for the G-77. Significant divisions within the G-77 had become apparent during the 1980s. Splits emerged between the newly wealthy East Asian "tigers"; between OPEC and non-OPEC countries; and between those who had certain resource endowments, such as Brazil's and India's forests, and those smaller countries without such resource reserves.[52] Nevertheless, from the first General Assembly hearings over the proposed conference in 1987, the G-77 mounted a collective defense of their interests loosely tied together around a series of issues: more favorable terms in technology transfer, absolute defense of resource sovereignty, a formal proclamation from the UN conference to enshrine a "right" of the South to develop, a demand for all developed nations to meet the now decades-old commitment of 7 percent GDP in foreign aid, and the need for additional financial support above and beyond existing aid channels to fund environmental protection policies, broadly defined, in the developing world.[53]

The concept of "sustainable development," as articulated in the *World Conservation Strategy* and the Brundtland report, had explicitly endorsed these views, but the evolving meaning of the phrase obscured these origins. Many developing countries still felt the old concerns of the New International Economic Order had not been sufficiently addressed in actual policy, and the broader issue of North-South socioeconomic equality still had to be addressed before comprehensive environmental agreements were put in place. Questions of sovereignty persisted, too. The debt crisis still devastated much of the Global South, wreaking havoc on national economies. Environmental protection in any form seemed to developing nations as a threat to their ability to develop as they saw fit. Representatives for the G-77 made their stance clear in meetings in advance at the first preparatory committee meeting in the summer of 1990, with nations such as India scuttling early treaty discussions over any clauses that could be construed as undermining national sovereignty.[54] As a result of North-South conflicts at the meeting, Maurice Strong claimed it was a "very unruly, divisive, frustrating operation."[55]

---

[52] Clyde Singer, "Narrowing the Gap," *The Globe and Mail*, April 26, 1990. On the decline of Third World activism, see Mark T. Berger, "After the Third World?: History, Destiny, and the Fate of Third Worldism," *Third World Quarterly*, Vol. 25, No. 1 (2004), 9–39.

[53] Engfeldt, *From Stockholm to Johannesburg and Beyond*, 116.

[54] Mukund Govind Rajan, *Global Environmental Politics: India and the North-South Politics of Global Environmental Issues* (Delhi: Oxford University Press, 1997), 203.

[55] Shabecoff, *A New Name for Peace*, 132–4; Engfeldt, *From Stockholm to Johannesburg and Beyond*, 139–43.

The G-77 also rebuked the United States' suggestion of using market-based solutions to solve problems such as reducing carbon emissions to avert climate change. In preparatory discussion, U.S. officials learned that Brazil, India, and other developing countries were "hostile to the market-place permit concept ... because of suspicions that the U.S. and other developed countries would use their economic leverage to transfer emissions reductions obligations to LDCs in ways which would interfere with their development," claimed one U.S. diplomat. Moreover, U.S. officials also believed that "the LDCs already perceive the global climate issues as giving them new leverage to pursue their historical North-South agenda; U.S. sponsorship of a emissions trading approach is unlikely to discourage them."[56] Accordingly, by early 1990 the United States already was approaching developing nations with considerable skepticism.

North-South fissures impeded discussions over most other issues, too. This was particularly true for the biodiversity treaty. The biodiversity treaty attempted to integrate existing treaties related to species protection, such as the Convention on the Trade in Endangered Species, into a much broader agreement over species protection and guidelines for resource use. The United States had long supported such a comprehensive approach to issues of biodiversity, and William Reilly and other key officials voiced support for the treaty early on in the negotiating process.[57]

Leading developing countries, by contrast, used the treaty as a way to contest the North over the increasingly lucrative biotechnology industry. During the 1980s, U.S. pharmaceutical companies benefited greatly from U.S. patent law that allowed corporations to visit remote locations in the Global South – particularly rain forests in Brazil and India – and identify plant species with potential agricultural, industrial, or medical uses. Under existing U.S. law, such companies could receive exclusive intellectual property rights to their "discoveries" and profit greatly by repackaging them as commodities. Unsurprisingly, developing countries balked at this, claiming a financial stake in natural resources located in their soil. The United States and many of its European allies, however, maintained the right of Northern corporations to claim legal ownership over their medicinal discoveries as the outcome of free enterprise. Already by the late 1980s the United States threatened India with trade sanctions over the

---

[56] William A. Nitze to Alan Kreczko, December 11, 1989, folder "Climate Change, General 2," box 9, White House Counsel Files, Jeffrey Holmstead Files, BPL.

[57] William K. Reilly, "Reflections on the Earth Summit," July 15, 1992, "FOIA – 2005 – 0336F – Bromley – UNCED 1," BPL.

Indian government's unwillingness to adopt existing patent standards in such cases.[58]

Thus, developing countries hoped to use the biodiversity treaty as a way to redress what they saw as an unfair infringement on their sovereignty. The G-77 demanded that the treaty "commit the industrialized countries to ensuring that companies taking advantage of developing countries genetic resources shared their profits equitably and gave the source countries access to technologies developed from those resources."[59] Agreeing to do so would place strict regulations on private investment and exploration, compromising what the United States interpreted as the free flow of private capital and businesses across borders. As with the issue of additionality and climate change negotiations, the developing nations saw the biodiversity treaty as a tool of exerting what little leverage they had at Rio. By the time the first preparatory committee meeting took place in March 1990, the conflict over the developing nations' quest for development and environmental protection threatened to undermine all major agreements on the docket for Rio.

## THE ROCKY ROAD TO RIO: DIPLOMATIC STALEMATES IN 1990 AND 1991

Beginning with an organizational gathering in March 1990, negotiations for Rio moved along three separate tracks. First, there were four formal preparatory committee meetings led by Maurice Strong and Tommy Koh, a respected lawyer and diplomat from Singapore, who served as the chairman of the Main Committee. The preparatory committees split into various working groups that met periodically to discuss the biodiversity and forest protection treaties, as well as the drafting of Agenda 21, agreements over additionality, and potential institutional follow-ups to the conference. Second, climate change negotiations, held through the IPCC, took place at a separate series of conferences. Finally, there was the public posturing and private diplomacy that occurred independent of any formal diplomatic channels, but nonetheless shaped public perceptions of the conference, and, in the weeks just before the meeting, eventually dominated the headlines.

[58] Rajan, *Global Environmental Politics*, chapter 7; Hopgood, *American Foreign Environmental Policy and the Power of the State*, 168–77.
[59] Quoted in Hopgood, *American Foreign Environmental Policy and the Power of the State*, 170.

Over the first two preparatory committees, the United States and developing countries reiterated their main points of contention vis-à-vis one another. At Maurice Strong's urging, additionality quickly dominated the discussion at the first prep meeting. "The key issue," Strong announced at the opening of the organizational meeting in March 1990, "was to give the developing countries access to the new technologies they needed and to additional resources to integrate the environmental dimension into their national development activities."[60] Strong claimed that additionality was "no mere political slogan." The concept, he said, reflected the "stark reality that however much developing nations may recognize that investment in sustainable development makes sense in terms of their long-term economic and environmental interests, they simply cannot afford the additional funds this will require in the short term." Strong identified the GEF as a potential source of funding for additionality, but called on all developed nations to increase direct financial transfers to developing countries.[61]

By framing the first preparatory meeting in this way, Strong sparked immediate conflict between the United States and the developing world. At the March meeting, U.S. representatives lambasted the calls for resource transfers and instead reiterated the importance of minimizing trade barriers, ending subsidies in the developing world, and promoting market-based solutions, such as permit trading schemes, to solve major problems. The G-77, for its part, took Strong's rhetoric and ran with it. They spent most of the spring and summer months inserting calls for additional financial resource transfers into the working papers for every major working group.[62] This led to an immediate stalemate in the talks. "Despite the fact that the development/environment relationship is being acknowledged on the conceptual level," Strong lamented, "there has been little real progress in giving effect to it in the ongoing processes of economic and sectoral policy and decision making."[63] Others shared Strong's frustration. In the summer of 1990, Peter Thacher, Strong's old colleague from the UNEP, cautioned Strong that "it would be difficult if not

---

[60] "Press Briefing by the Secretary-General of Conference on Environment and Development," March 5, 1990, folder 430, box 46, Thacher Papers, Part I.

[61] "Remarks by Maurice Strong at the Opening of First Meeting of the Preparatory Committee for the 1992 United Nations Conference on Environment and Development," March 5, 1990, folder 435, box 47, Thacher Papers, Part I.

[62] "Working Group 1, September 24, 1990," box 52, folder 489, Thacher Papers, Part I.

[63] "Press Briefing by the Secretary-General of Conference on Environment and Development," March 5, 1990, box 46, folder 430, Thacher Papers, Part I.

impossible" to complete any agreement under negotiation with "anything more than pious good wishes."[64]

As negotiations stalled, an unexpected event in early August 1990 threatened to derail the conference altogether. While delegates prepared to head to Nairobi for the first official preparatory committee meeting, on August 2 Iraq bombed and subsequently invaded Kuwait. The ensuing Gulf War had two major effects on the Rio proceedings. For one, the event focused high-level attention away from the conference. While the post–Cold War period had appeared initially to allow leaders to put greater emphasis on "non-traditional" security issues such as the environment, the war shattered such illusions. Second, the invasion sparked tremendous instability in global oil prices. The volatility struck the United States particularly hard. Oil prices rose, consumer confidence decreased at home, and an economic downturn already underway worsened. By the fall of 1990, the United States' economy fell into a recession, one that threatened to spread to Western Europe, as well. It seemed global economic circumstances "became a serious brake," in the words of one Swedish diplomat, on any industrialized nations' willingness to negotiate any major new commitment of additionality.[65] The United States was already antagonistic to the additionality idea; the recession only reinforced its position.

Throughout 1991, discussions dragged along slowly. The exact nature of an agreement over forest protection remained murky, as did the components of the proposed biodiversity treaty. In both cases, the G-77 redoubled their demands that additionality was the sine qua non of any agreement. Malaysian delegates made this case most forcefully at the second preparatory committee in the spring of 1991, where they demanded that the Northern industrialized nations had to pay for any Southern forest protection agreement.[66] At the same meeting, Kofi Awoonor, Ghana's ambassador and a representative for the G-77, gave a similar speech to all delegates. He argued that unless Northern nations committed to redressing global economic imbalances, the Global South would resist any accords over global environmental problems.[67] By the spring of 1991, one observer noted that the constant posturing and dramatic rhetoric made the

---

[64] P. S. Thacher to M. S. Strong, July 19, 1990, box 47, folder 435, Thacher Papers, Part I.

[65] Engfeldt, *From Stockholm to Johannesburg and Beyond*, 143.

[66] Langston James Goree VI, "Electronic Briefing Note Number 6," March 25, 1991, box 47, folder 439, Thacher Papers, Part I.

[67] Martin Khor Kok Peng, "North-South relations revisited in light of UNCED," August 1991, box 53, folder 501, Thacher Papers, Part I; Shabecoff, *A New Name for Peace*, 135.

preparatory committees over forests and biodiversity seem less formal negotiations than "kabuki-like theater."[68]

Likewise, the climate change negotiations stalled over questions of additionality and emissions regulations. President Bush believed "actions to slow global warming should be taken now," but did not want to make any binding commitments. Key conservative figures in the administration, such as Chief of Staff John Sununu, pressed for him to tow a hard line on the agreements.[69] "The United States insists on reviewing funding for justification and effectiveness," explained one internal administration memo. "We will not legally bind ourselves to a financial obligation that is uncertain in scope and devoid of specifics."[70]

The administration's stance contrasted with European Community (EC) members and Japan, who generally favored timetables and a hard cap on emissions. The United States' unwillingness to define clear a time-table was thus "viewed as inadequate by both the environmental commu-nity and the rest of the OECD nations." In addition, the United States' steadfast position threatened to undermine alternatives, such as its own counterproposals for market-based systems. "Developing countries as well as much of Europe (and most American environmentalists) may object to international emissions trading proposals as long as they appear to be a dodge to displace reductions from U.S. sources to other nations," one advisor cautioned.[71]

Amid frustrations over the United States' unwillingness to agree to additionality or to accept a binding timeline for emissions reductions, Maurice Strong further fueled discontent in August 1991. In an interview, Strong claimed that to achieve true sustainable development – having all nations reorient their national economies along the lines of the Brundtland Commission report – it was necessary to generate approxi-mately $125 billion in additional resource transfers from North to South. Although Strong later backtracked from the statement, his words rankled many U.S. and European officials while seemingly opening the door for the G-77 to double down in negotiations.[72]

---

[68] Langston James Goree VI, "Electronic Briefing Note Number 6," March 25, 1991, box 47, folder 439, Thacher Papers, Part I.

[69] Hopgood, *American Foreign Environmental Policy and the Power of the State*, 156–60.

[70] "Questions and Answers on U.S. Views on Global Climate Change," Folder: Environment: UNCED [2 of 3], Council of Economic Advisers, David Bradford Files, BPL.

[71] "White House/Global Warming Position," December 23, 1991, Folder: "Environment – Bush Administration," White House Counsel Files, Jeffrey Holmstead Files, BPL.

[72] Paul Lewis, "U.N. Seeks Third-World Ecology Aid," *The New York Times*, March 2, 1992, A3.

Throughout these debates, NGOs found little success in bridging the gap between nations. Emulating his efforts at Founex in 1971, in 1991 Strong organized a series of informal gatherings where experts could meet to discuss the pertinent issues in a forum less susceptible to the histrionics of conference preparatory gatherings. Unlike Founex, these events generated little consensus and did not spark the same degree of momentum and excitement as the original gathering.[73] Many NGOs perceived that the conflict over additionality had elicited political divisions far too intractable for them – or anyone – to overcome. "By linking these two (environmental issues and economic development) and persuading governments to treat the meeting as a summit, Maurice Strong raised the ante considerably," said David Runnalls, Barbara Ward's former assistant and long-time official in the IIED. "And so far," he added, "the omens are not promising."[74]

The major NGOs had focused their efforts along two tracks that helped shape the conference agenda but did little to sway negotiations during the preparatory commissions. Groups such as the IUCN wrote major scientific papers on the issues in question. Amid the stalemate over financing, the quality of the scientific findings mattered little. Other groups maintained close contact with Maurice Strong, such as the World Resource Institute, a rapidly growing and influential U.S. organization led by Peter Thacher. Yet with the seemingly intractable conflict between the United States and the G-77, these close personal connections to Strong and the secretariat carried little weight. Finally, although the WWF and the IUCN had been able to place several of their officials onto national delegations (as they had in Stockholm), many other NGOs felt as though major states either ignored or rejected their input altogether.[75] By the summer of 1991, many NGOs found themselves "reverting to their traditional lobbying outside the official events" of the conference.[76]

Internal divisions bedeviled the broader NGO community, too. Although the leading international activist groups had hoped to use Rio as a platform to organize a global network of activists capable of exerting

---

[73] Many NGO officials ran into difficulties securing sufficient funding for such gatherings, too. P. S. Thacher to Mohamed El-Ashry and Gus Speth, October 17, 1990, box 47, folder 434, Thacher Papers, Part I.

[74] Ross Howard, "Earth Summit: North is North, South is South, Will Ever the Twain Meet?" *The Globe and Mail*, August 24, 1991.

[75] Langston James Goree VI "Electronic Briefing Note Number 4," March 22, 1991, box 47, folder 439, Thacher Papers, Part I.

[76] Peter Gorrie, "Eco-summit Losing Lustre," *Toronto Star*, July 23, 1991.

collective leverage over the conference, North-South fissures emerged within the environmental community. A variety of environmentalists formed the International Facilitating Committee (IFC) to organize the Global Forum, a separate NGO conference to take place alongside the main conference at Rio that would welcome NGOs from across the world. In March 1991, however, Southern NGOs decided to boycott the IFC over "a lack of democratic processes" within the IFC. The group, they claimed, reflected narrow Northern environmentalist interests and thus smacked of "NGO neo-colonialism" that disempowered, among others, local Brazilian grassroots groups.[77] Already by 1991, it seemed that NGO activities at Rio would resemble the diverse and disparate protesting that had taken place in the gatherings around Stockholm twenty years earlier. As the conference neared, both international negotiations and transnational activism faltered.

## THE GEF, INSTITUTIONAL CONTROL, AND THE ONGOING ADDITIONALITY PROBLEM

By 1991, the one major hope for an agreement over additionality, the World Bank's GEF, also became a source of frustration. The United States displayed an unwillingness to support its growth. After an initial donation from France, the World Bank quickly formed a pilot program for the new fund in which developing countries applied for cofinanced concessionary grants to support projects that sought to mitigate "global" problems such as climate change. While most leading industrialized nations supported the pilot program's expansion, the United States resisted. Bush administration representatives told World Bank officials that the GEF was moving too quickly and offering too many loans with loose criteria. U.S. officials also worried that widespread support for the GEF would fuel developing nations' arguments that greater additionality was a necessary component of any global treaty.[78]

In addition, the GEF faced critical challenges from the Global South. For developing nations, their position derived from questions of control.

---

[77] Langston James Goree VI, "Electronic Briefing Note Number 6," March 25, 1991, box 47, folder 439, Thacher Papers, Part I.

[78] "Statement by Kenneth Piddington," Meeting on Funding for the Global Environment, March 15, 1990, box 105, folder 1002, Thacher Papers, Part I; "U.S. Views, Global Environmental Facility Participants' Meeting, May 1–2, 1991," box 105, folder 1002, Thacher Papers, Part I.

While a consortium of World Bank, UNDP, and UNEP officials nominally governed the GEF, in practice the World Bank itself managed day-to-day operations.[79] Many developing nations, including the large influential countries such as Brazil and India, remained locked in ongoing struggles with the bank over the new "green conditionality" for loans on development projects. Ceding control to allocate additional resources to bank officials and governmental representatives from developed countries was unpalatable. Their concerns only intensified in early 1992 when a leaked memo by Larry Summers, the World Bank's chief economist, suggested that it was economically sound for developed nations to export toxic waste and polluting industries to developing countries. Although Summers insisted the memo was sarcastic, many developing nations interpreted it as dismissive, sinister, and emblematic of the bank staff's collective callousness.[80]

Many NGOs also expressed concern over the GEF. Given the slow pace with which the World Bank had begun implementing its environmental reforms, many veterans from the impact statement campaign of the 1980s saw the GEF as a ruse for a development lender looking to improve its public image. Bruce Rich, the lawyer who had spearheaded much of the action against the bank in the 1980s, called the GEF a "green fig leaf." The GEF, he argued, was "merely a smokescreen diverting attention away from the need to make the bank's overall annual lending" more supportive of environmental causes.[81] Likewise, many NGO officials criticized the closed-door pilot program, which shut out the NGO community from deliberations and seemed to indicate that the bank, as it had before the 1980s, was making important decisions without any "public" participation or external accountability.[82]

Despite the frustrations surrounding the GEF, for a brief moment in the spring of 1992, the organization recaptured the hopes of many Rio participants when the United States made an unexpected change in its policy. In February 1992, the Bush administration made a surprising move, agreeing to give $50 million to the GEF pilot program. The administration also made a tentative commitment to offer $25 million in new

---

[79] Turan S. Kivanc, "Report on the Discussion Notes," June 22, 1990, DC Environment. 1987–1990, WBA.

[80] John Vidal, "A Gaffe over the GEF," *The Guardian*, February 14, 1992.

[81] Carey French, "Report on the Environment: World Bank Comes Clean," *The Globe and Mail*, June 2, 1992.

[82] David Reed, "The Global Environmental Facility and Non-Governmental Organizations," *American University International Law Review*, Vol. 9, Issue 1 (1993), 204–6.

grants and loans to developing nations to pursue alternative energy sources as part of an effort to generate consensus over a climate agreement, albeit one without binding emissions caps or timetables. It seemed, on the surface, to be an important shift.[83]

While the Bush administration presented the donation as a beneficent concession to developing nations, strategic calculations lurked behind the gesture. By the spring of 1992, a number of important critics assailed the administration for its handling of the Rio negotiations. For one, powerful conservative and industry lobbyists pressured the administration to avoid binding commitments and any new international bureaucracy at the Earth Summit "in view of the lessons of central planning from Eastern Europe."[84] On the other side, pro-environmental legislators, particularly Senators Al Gore and John Chafee, expressed their dissatisfaction over the United States' intransigence over biodiversity and climate change. Democrats in the House of Representatives also pursued legislation that would commit the United States to a hard cap on carbon emissions and a timetable for reductions, an effort that culminated in Representative Henry Waxman's climate protection bill in the early spring of 1992.[85] Bush administration officials worried that such domestic initiatives would undercut diplomatic negotiations and undermine their hard-line stance on the climate bill. With the presidential election looming in November, key Democratic leaders, particularly Senator Gore, also began making speeches in key states, such as Florida. Bush and his cabinet saw support for the GEF in part as a way to undercut the domestic political criticism that stemmed from its handling of the Rio negotiations – supporting the climate change negotiations by offering a modicum of funding but without committing to any firm timetables for reducing greenhouse gas emissions.[86]

[83] Michael Weisskopf, "U.S. to Give Third World Environmental Aid," *The Washington Post*, February 27, 1992.

[84] Some industry leaders encouraged Bush to attend, such as Enron executive Kenneth Lay, although they wanted Bush to defend only nonbinding agreements and "market-based" solutions. Conservative activists were generally more skeptical. In a letter to the president signed by conservative activists such as Phyllis Schlafly, Grover Norquist, and Paul Weyrich, Fred Smith of the Competitive Enterprise Institute called the UNCED a form of "ecological imperialism" by the UN to "centralize control" of global environmental and economic resources. Fred L. Smith, Jr., to George Bush, April 7, 1992, Kenneth Lay, Enron Corporation to George Bush, April 3, 1992, Folder: Case No. 320455CU to Case No. 325581SS, WHORM FO006-16, BPL.

[85] Hopgood, *American Foreign Environmental Policy and the Power of the State*, 164–5.

[86] William K. Stevens, "U.S. to Pledge Aid to Fight Warming," *The New York Times*, February 27, 1992, A14.

Moreover, backing the GEF gave the Bush administration a way to support additionality in principle without making other substantial foreign aid increases. The donation offered a talking point for officials to suggest the United States had offered a major concession vis-à-vis the developing world; U.S. officials claimed that their support for the GEF "underscored" their "commitment to environmentally sustainable development."[87] However, by ceding additional resource transfers through the World Bank, the administration could direct their allocation. Institutional control was key; the United States maintained preponderant control over World Bank voting and could thus greatly shape the course of GEF funding. In essence, the United States turned to the GEF for the same reasons that NGOs and developing nations distrusted it. Once the United States declared it would donate to the fund, administration officials identified it as the only mechanism for additionality, declaring that "virtually all items being considered in the UNCED context should be funded by GEF to the extent they are funded" at all.[88] In other words, the Bush administration firmly drew a line on additionality that ended at the fund and subsequently used the donation to justify its resistance to any further accommodations toward the G-77.

In the end, the $50 million was not nearly enough to provide even a start for the kind of additional resources that developing nations desired. The United States steadfastly maintained its resistance to the idea of raising its official assistance to 0.7 percent of national income, which developing nations had demanded since the start of negotiations. Although Strong had suggested that as much as $125 billion in annual resource transfers were necessary for successful reorientation of national economies along "sustainable" lines, and although developing nations called for a "green fund" managed independently, the United States, fresh off its commitment to the GEF, balked at that as well.[89]

Uncertainty loomed as the conference neared in April and May 1992. The climate change discussions reached a low point in the spring of 1992 when the United States convinced the British to pull their support for an emission cap. The British quickly began lobbying other European nations to do the same, which caused confusion and discord among the European

[87] "Note for General Scowcroft: Draft UNCED Fact Sheets," May 27, 1992, Folder: UNCED [OA/ID FO1319] [3 of 4], Nicholas Rostow Files, National Security Council, BPL.

[88] Bob Grady to Mike Young and Bob Zoellick, March 6, 1992, Folder: Environment: UNCED [3 of 3], David Bradford Files, Council of Economic Advisers, BPL.

[89] Shabecoff, *A New Name for Peace*, 153.

Community (EC) nations.[90] Likewise, the biodiversity treaty seemed on the brink of total collapse in May. Developing nations inserted provisions about intellectual property, causing a furor among U.S. negotiators.[91] The administration worried about the "tragic flaw" of Article 16 in the treaty text, a clear statement crafted by developing nations to give them total sovereignty over their own natural resources (and retain the right to trump existing patent law on new scientific "discoveries"). Conservatives in the Bush administration – particularly those affiliated with Vice President Quayle's Council on Competitiveness – mobilized against signing the treaty on such grounds. On May 29, the State Department published a press release declaring that the United States "does not and cannot sign" an agreement that was so "fundamentally flawed." A public relations nightmare ensued as journalists, environmentalists, and officials from many other nations ridiculed the Bush administration for publicly declaring that they would not sign the treaty at Rio. The U.S. decision to back out and publicly announce its position was, according to CEQ Director Michael Deland, "an absolute disaster."[92]

Meanwhile, the additionality question hamstrung other discussions. Talks for an agreement over forest protection broke down at the final preparatory committee meeting. A group of American NGOs "hijacked" a reception for U.S. negotiators, demanding that "the voices of environmental victims and the poor be heard!" Likewise, while most of Agenda 21, Strong's signature document for the conference, had been hammered out in negotiations, the chapter on additional financing proved intractable. In one speech Curtis Bohlen acknowledged that additional financing would be necessary. He also reiterated that the private sector should be the key vehicle to deliver such resources and once again reiterated that the United States would not increase its overall aid to 0.7 percent of GNP.[93] When representatives from the United States and Europe rebuffed the developing nations' call for a "green fund" of additional resources outside the GEF, the G-77 walked out of the Rio negotiations altogether.[94] Maurice Strong and Tommy Koh worked diligently to facilitate a more

[90] Clayton Yeutter to Chris Sheehan, Environment: UNCED [1 of 3], David Bradford Files, Council of Economic Advisers, BPL.
[91] Jane Perlez, "Environmentalists Accuse U.S. of Trying to Weaken Global Treaty," *The New York Times*, May 19, 1992.
[92] Hopgood, *American Foreign Environmental Policy and the Power of the State*, 172–6.
[93] Quoted in Hopgood, *American Foreign Environmental Policy and the Power of the State*, 149–52.
[94] Lawrence E. Susskind, *Environmental Diplomacy: Negotiating More Effective Global Agreements* (New York: Oxford University Press, 1994), 38–9.

substantive debate, but the best they could achieve were guarantees from all nations to continue discussions in Brazil.[95] Less than a month before the conference, consensus on the three major issues in question – biodiversity, climate change, and additionality – seemed out of reach.

As negotiations at the final preparatory meeting in May halted, the entire conference threatened to become a farce when public debate turned to a seemingly trivial question – whether Bush himself would actually attend. Administration officials worried that a public appearance in Rio would leave the president open to all sorts of criticism from NGOs, the Global South, European allies, and even Al Gore (who was attending as a special representative of the U.S. Senate). The press, environmentalists, and political opponents lambasted Bush on this matter during the spring of 1992. Media mogul and wilderness enthusiast Ted Turner launched a national media blitz to pressure the president to attend.[96] Lobbyists and influential figures in American politics weighed in, all demanding the president's attendance.[97] After much internal deliberation with his cabinet, Bush agreed to attend only three weeks before the conference began. The president's dithering sparked even more criticism. Al Gore spoke out against the administration's "policy of photo opportunities and symbols instead of real commitments," and Arkansas governor and likely Democratic presidential nominee Bill Clinton criticized Bush for his prevarications. Against the backdrop of the administration's intransigence in negotiations, the president appeared indecisive and opportunistic. Few saw his decision to attend as a grand gesture for cooperation or a symbol of genuine concern for the environment.[98]

## "STANDING ALONE": THE RIO EARTH SUMMIT AND GROWING U.S. ISOLATION

Bush's choice to appear at Rio even troubled some within his administration, as the timing of his decision generated tremendous confusion and

---

[95] Engfeldt, *From Stockholm to Johannesburg and Beyond*, 148–52.

[96] Nancy G. Maynard to Dorrance Smith, March 25, 1992, FOIA – 2005 – 0336F – Bromley – UNCED 1, BPL.

[97] See, for instance, Kenneth Lay to George Bush, April 3, 1992, Folder: Case No. 320455CU to Case No. 325581SS, WHORM FO006-16, BPL. Conservative activists, by contrast, pressured the president to stay at home. See, for instance, Fred L. Smith, Jr., to George Bush, April 7, 1992, Kenneth Lay, Enron Corporation to George Bush, April 3, 1992, Folder: Case No. 320455CU to Case No. 325581SS, WHORM FO006-16, BPL.

[98] "Bush Plans to Join Other Leaders at Earth Summit in Brazil in June," *New York Times*, May 13, 1992, A8.

chaos within the U.S. government. The president announced his decision on May 13; with the conference set to begin just three weeks later, the administration scrambled to reorganize its delegation to account for the president's inclusion. Moreover, the late decision meant that White House staff and Bush's inner circle became much more familiar with the conference's key documents, particularly Agenda 21, which had to date been negotiated by mid-level State Department and EPA officials such as Curtis Bohlen and William Reilly. At the last minute, Clayton Yeutter, a former head of the Republican National Committee and a counselor to President Bush, attempted to reorganize the entire delegation to encourage more White House participation, only deciding who would actually attend three days before the conference began. Bohlen and Reilly, who had been the nominal head of the U.S. delegation, felt assailed by Yeutter's eleventh-hour mingling. "You can't imagine what a frustrating experience it was," Bohlen recalled.[99]

The administration launched a last-ditch effort to reclaim goodwill by announcing its own international initiative on forest protection, but to no avail. It was clear from the events in May that there would not be any formal treaty on forest protection signed at Rio. Hoping to curb domestic criticism and make a few headlines, the president announced on June 2 that he would propose an extra $150 million in U.S. aid to nations to help fund reforestation projects if they did so through "market-based" mechanisms. "Centralized funds are the typical answer to global environmental protection," an internal administration memo suggested with regard to earlier efforts at tropical forest protection, "but they mean central planning, high administrative costs, little concern for cost-effectiveness, and arbitrarily large payments ... from the [United States]."[100] The "Forests for the Future Initiative," the administration figured, would present a different way forward. However, many viewed the offer as cynical and doubted that the administration would follow through with the commitment. Analysts who parsed through the president's short speech on the initiative noted that the proposal would not preserve or protect uncut forests, just help rebuild those that developing nations chose to cut down. Environmentalists decried the initiative,

---

[99] Quoted in Hopgood, *American Foreign Environmental Policy and the Power of the State*, 187.

[100] "Points on Renewing Our Call for a Market-based Global Forests Agreement," Folder: UNCED [OA/ID FO1319] [4 of 4], Nicholas Rostow Files, National Security Council, BPL.

saying Bush had "sabotaged" and "recklessly undermined" the Earth Summit with such a feckless, last-minute gesture.[101]

Shortly after the conference began, another diplomatic debacle reinforced the negative perceptions of the United States. Prior to leaving for Rio, Yeutter had secretly given Reilly instructions to reopen talks with the G-77 over the biodiversity treaty, to see if the developing nations would soften the language and thus allow the administration to sign. On June 5, Reilly wrote a memo back to the administration that Brazil was willing to try to "fix" the treaty in a last-ditch attempt to get the United States to sign. Yeutter and the rest of the White House staff chose, ultimately, not to move forward with the negotiations. Reilly's memo leaked to the *New York Times*, angering President Bush, embarrassing Reilly and the delegation, and ending any hope of the United States signing the treaty. Reilly fell between a rock and a hard place. Although the memo revealed him as an active force for compromise within an otherwise truculent administration, a group of influential NGOs demanded Reilly's resignation over his inability to shift the president's position. The Reilly memo controversy pervaded much of the media's coverage of the conference and reinforced the perception that the United States had little interest in pursuing genuine cooperation.[102] According to Germany's environment minister, it was as if a "fear of a new Communism hidden behind ecology" had swept through the White House.[103]

As public attention focused on the growing isolation of the United States, negotiators met in closed-door meetings to salvage as much as possible. Spurred on by a determined Maurice Strong and Tommy Koh, representatives from national delegations worked late into the night to hammer out the final language of Agenda 21. The G-77 eventually dropped their call for a "green fund," which helped secure final agreement of the major language of the agreement. Yet absent a firm commitment on funding sources, all the treaties and conventions, including Agenda 21, were left without any clear mechanism for support. Of the wealthiest countries, only France ultimately agreed to commit to the 0.7 percent of national income in aid that the G-77 demanded. The French commitment, it turned out, proved specious; a few years after

---

[101] "North-South Sniping Threat to Key Accords," *The Advertiser*, June 4, 1991.
[102] Hopgood, *American Foreign Environmental Policy and the Power of the State*, 186–91; Ronald A. Taylor, "Chief of EPA Stung by Rio Rift," *The Washington Times*, A1.
[103] Paul Lewis, "U.S. at the Earth Summit: Isolated and Challenged," June 10, 1992, A8.

the conference their actual contribution declined precipitously.[104] Elsewhere, negotiators hammered out the final language of the biodiversity and climate change conventions, both of which had been considerably weakened by a lack of U.S. support. Meanwhile, NGO pageantry fueled excitement outside the walls of the main conference, but left little imprint on actual proceedings. One IUCN member called the Global Forum, the chief NGO event, a "dazzling and confusing spectacle" that was "chaotic and often flaky."[105] By the second week, the participants' focus turned once again to the United States' delegation, and in particular to President Bush's impending arrival.

The president's appearance came not with a bang, but a whimper. Bush flew to Brazil with his eyes firmly fixed on electoral politics at home. Bush and his advisers had decided that a hard line stance against the Rio Conference would help stave off the conservative insurgency led by Texas billionaire Ross Perot, who was surging in the polls in May and June. Standing outside Air Force One before he left, Bush declared, "I am determined to protect the environment." He quickly qualified that claim by adding, "I am determined to protect the American taxpayer. The days of the open cheque-book are over." When, exactly, the "cheque-book" had ever been open for major international environmental issues was unclear. Bush's increasingly defiant rhetoric meant the president would attend the conference in a defensive posture.[106]

Once in Rio, Bush unsuccessfully attempted to generate support for his administration's positions. He held a brief and unproductive meeting with representatives from leading American NGOs, who expressed their displeasure with the administration's stance.[107] The president also found little sympathy from other delegations. When explaining his decision not to sign the biodiversity treaty, Bush proclaimed he was "standing alone on

---

[104] Nicholas Schoon, "The Earth Summit: Plan of Action Agreed But Who Pays?," *The Independent*, June 15, 1992; *Earth Negotiations Bulletin*, Daily Issue No. 12, June 13, 1992. [Online] Available: http://www.iisd.ca/vol01/. Accessed October 16, 2012. France's contributions declined annually from 1994 to 2001. On Official Development Assistance (ODA) data, see the UN table on ODA as a percentage of gross national income (GNI). Online [Available]: http://mdgs.un.org/unsd/mdg/Series Detail.aspx?srid=568. Accessed December 2, 2012.

[105] Mark Halle, "A Dazzling and Confusing Spectacle," *IUCN Bulletin*, Vol. 21, No. 3 (September 1990), 20; Shabecoff, *A New Name for Peace*, 170-1.

[106] Hopgood, *American Foreign Environmental Policy and the Power of the State*, 193.

[107] "The Daily Diary of President Bush," Folder: 6/12/92, White House Office of Appointments and Scheduling, Presidential Daily Diary, box 103, BPL; Hopgood, *American Foreign Environmental Policy and the Power of the State*, 197-8.

principle." Yet the president's words, according to one analyst, were met with "little applause and some chuckling from delegates."[108] Bush further invoked the Cold War to justify his unwillingness to adopt binding regulations or hard timetables on carbon emissions. He told those who wanted "state control to protect the environment" to "go to Eastern Europe, where the poisoned bodies of children now pay for the sins of fallen dictators, and only the new breeze of freedom is allowing for cleanup."[109] In front of exasperated delegates angry at the United States' intransigence, Bush's words generated little enthusiasm for the power of market forces to solve environmental problems.

Environmentalists, unsurprisingly, assailed the president for his posturing. "At this point," claimed one environmentalist on June 13, "George Bush calling himself the environmental president is like Saddam Hussein calling himself a friend of the Kurds." Al Gore intensified his criticism of the president and the administration. "Saving the Earth's environment is the most important consideration in the post–Cold War world," Gore claimed, but the Bush administration had "failed to provide the necessary leadership."[110] Bush's staff wrote to many leaders of American NGOs, including the president's old friend Russell Train, after the conference explaining his decision to reject the biodiversity treaty and avoid binding agreements over climate change. However, their efforts fell on deaf ears.[111]

The Rio Conference did generate consensus on a few key documents and established important institutional mechanisms for future negotiations. After lengthy discussions and debates, all parties signed Agenda 21. All countries also agreed to a general, nonbinding statement about

---

[108] Al Gore rallied against the administration's posturing, which reportedly impressed prospective Democratic presidential nominee Bill Clinton back home. Gore and Chafee made a last-ditch effort in May to pressure the administration to sign, but to no avail. John Chafee and Al Gore to George Bush, May 13, 1992, Folder: Case No. 327559CU to Case No. 328354, BPL; Brent Scowcroft to Al Gore, June 23, 1992, Folder: Case No. 327559CU to Case No. 328354, BPL; Hopgood, *American Foreign Environmental Policy and the Power of the State*, 199.

[109] George H. W. Bush, "Address to the United Nations Conference on Environment and Development in Rio de Janeiro, Brazil," June, 12, 1992. [Online] http://bushlibrary.tamu.edu/research/public_papers.php?id=4417&year=&month. Accessed December 28, 2009.

[110] "Jeers Greet Bush at Summit," *The Globe and Mail*, June 13, 1992.

[111] Philip Brady [assistant to the president and staff secretary] to Mike Deland, June 15, 1992, Folder 086027SS – 106475, WHORM Subject File – FG342-03, BPL. Bush's letters went to Train and the leaders of the National Resources Defense Council, the Environmental Defense Fund, and Conservation International.

ED NATIONS CONFERENCE ON
RONMENT AND DEVELOPMENT
o de Janeiro 3–14 June 1992

FIGURE 10: Maurice Strong (second from left) speaks at the Earth Summit's opening, June 3, 1992. Seated left to right are Nitin Desai, Deputy Secretary-General of the Conference; Strong; UN Secretary-General Boutros-Ghali; Brazil President Fernando Collor de Mello; and Miles Stoby, Secretary of the Conference. Courtesy of UN Photo Library.

financing after the United States won the softest language imaginable used to discuss foreign aid (the industrialized nations, the statement said, would agree to "reaffirmation" of 0.7 percent as a general "target"). Conferees also agreed to sign the Framework Convention on Climate Change, which included no binding timetables or targets and which essentially punted substantive negotiations to future conferences. The biodiversity treaty won almost unanimous support, as well; the United States was the only country not to sign it (Figure 10).[112]

In the end, the gathering bequeathed a legacy of uncertainty. Whereas Stockholm appeared as the start of an exciting process to all involved, Rio left many participants and observers wondering what would happen next. IUCN Director-General Martin Holdgate claimed the Earth Summit "left a mountain of problems untackled" and that many "fundamental

---

[112] Engfeldt, *From Stockholm to Johannesburg and Beyond*, 197–9. For an overview of all outcomes, see Peter M. Haas, Marc A. Levy, and Edward A. Parson, "Appraising the Earth Summit: How Should We Judge UNCED's Success?" *Environment*, Vol. 34, No. 8 (October 1992), 6–33.

FIGURE 11: President George H. W. Bush and his wife, Barbara, add their names to the "Earth Pledge" wall during the Earth Summit, even though those who signed the wall had pledged "to act to the best of my ability to help make the Earth a secure and hospitable home for present and future generations." Courtesy of George H. W. Bush Presidential Library.

questions were side-stepped."[113] Although there would surely be follow-up conferences, domestic legislative initiatives, and a plethora of public statements, the North-South stalemate made future agreement seem remote. The language of "sustainable development" had offered legitimacy to the notion that environmental and development issues were interlinked. Yet the phrase was amorphous enough to trigger perceptions of development as a right and environmental protection as a form of political coercion. Deep political and economic divisions scuttled the conference's major initiatives, particularly the biodiversity treaty and the watered-down climate agreement. Absent a substantial agreement on international financing beyond the GEF and without the world's most powerful nation on board for major treaties, the Rio Earth Summit rightfully left many participants and observers more frustrated than hopeful (Figure 11).[114]

[113] Martin Holdgate, "Questions about Rio," *IUCN Bulletin*, Vol. 21, No. 3 (September 1992), 2.
[114] John Vidal, "Vested Interests Come Out on Top," *Guardian Weekly*, June 21, 1992.

## "BITTER FARE FOR HOPEFUL PARTICIPANTS":
### THE MEANING OF RIO

On July 15, 1992, William Reilly penned a mournful reflection on the Earth Summit to all his employees at the EPA. The Rio Conference had left Reilly frustrated, with two pressing questions on his mind. First, he wondered, "Why was so little asked of the developing countries?" To Reilly, the "lessons of Eastern Europe" were clear – democracy and free markets brought greater prosperity than any other system, and the world had entered "a new era where trade, not aid, will provide needed resources" for environmental protection. Developing countries, he believed, had yet to draw the same conclusions. He thought that after the Cold War, with "traditional security and strategic claims" on the wane, the Global South had constructed a "new rationale for demanding concessions from richer countries."[115] Environmental issues, he implied, had become a new feature in North-South politics.

Impassioned though they were, his reflections skirted over the tumultuous history surrounding the global politics of environment and development. It was inaccurate to suggest that the end of the Cold War had completely reshaped the international politics of development or that it had newly inspired leaders from developing countries to seek concessions from the developed world. Rather, the Global South had made similar arguments for decades. Such debates had scuttled cooperation at Stockholm, and they persisted at Rio because they hinged on powerful questions over the right of all nations to define development on their own terms, the ability pursue their own paths to achieve it, and who should and would pay the costs of global environmental protection. For the developing countries, environmental protection, in 1992 as it was in 1972, was inextricably tied to questions of justice, power, and equality.

The other question that bedeviled Reilly was why the United States had played "such a low-key defensive game in preparing for Rio." He charged the administration for failing to take initiative on the major aspects of the conference. The Bush administration had "assigned a low priority to the negotiations of the biodiversity treaty, were slow to engage the climate issue, were last to commit our President to attend Rio . . . [and] committed few resources." All of this contributed to the "negative feelings toward the United States."[116] Reilly's words marked a common refrain. Many

---

[115] William K. Reilly, "Reflections on the Earth Summit," July 15, 1992, "FOIA – 2005 – 0336F – Bromley – UNCED 1," BPL.
[116] Ibid.

participants felt frustrated by the United States' intransigence over funding and struggled to explain why the negotiating process had been so laborious and wearisome. At the end of the conference, with an eye toward the United States, Maurice Strong claimed that "never had the rich felt so poor," as if to blame the stalemate on the recession.[117]

Contrary to Reilly's and Strong's suggestions, the tensions that erupted in the lead-up to Rio could not just be blamed on hasty preparations or the economic downturn. Once Strong had made additionality the sine qua non of any agreement at Rio, the success of any agreement depended on whether the United States would support a major resource transfer to the developing countries. There is little evidence to suggest that the Bush administration would have agreed to substantial additionality even had the president committed himself to attend earlier or the recession not occurred. Already by 1989 the United States made it clear it would not commit any significant, long-term additional resource transfers; aside from its brief gesture toward the GEF and the last-minute forests initiative, no greater "additionality" ever materialized. The Bush administration's position hamstrung U.S. negotiators much in the same way that Nixon and Kissinger's early decision to avoid any increase of development financing left the U.S. delegation to the Stockholm Conference feeling incapable of addressing the developing nations' concerns. The Bush administration's rhetoric that valorized market-based solutions reinforced the United States' long-standing unwillingness to increase its financial commitment to the Global South.

In the end, both of Reilly's questions stemmed from the realization that international environmental protection treaties could not escape the nettlesome questions of international power relations, inequities in the global economy, and international development and foreign aid policies. "The Earth Summit was originally supposed to be about the environment, as was the 1972 U.N. ecology conference in Stockholm," wrote one reflective journalist, "but the development issues got on board with equal footing."[118] Without greater agreement on those development issues, "comprehensive" environmental protection regimes remained elusive.

This fact was not lost on many NGOs, either. Over the previous two decades, many of them had come to sympathize strongly with the developing countries and with their claims about economic inequality. The same journalist noted that while many NGO forums contained

---

[117] Engfeldt, *From Stockholm to Johannesburg and Beyond*, 143.
[118] Joel Achenbach, "The Browning of Ecology," *Washington Post*, June 8, 1992, C1.

discussions over biodiversity and climate change, at root the NGOs were "wrapped up in social and economic issues."[119] Additionality was the most important issue discussed in Rio. "Finance," claimed David Runnalls, Barbara Ward's old colleague from the IIED, was where Rio had been "truly disappointing." He explained, "All countries have been prepared to admit the relationship between poverty and environmental degradation. Few were prepared to accept the financial challenges. Even after putting the best possible interpretation on the leaders' speeches, I find it difficult to come up with more than US\$2–3 billion per year in new and additional resources for sustainable development."[120] Mark Halle, who had been instrumental in attempting to implement the *World Conservation Strategy* for the IUCN, agreed. Nations pledged only a "small fraction of the minimum amount" of additional transfers necessary. Future prospects looked dim. "Everyone knew," he said, "that if financial commitments were not made at Rio, they are unlikely to be made when the pressure is off." He struck a sorrowful tone. "If money is the proof of the pudding served at Rio, the Earth Summit provided only bitter fare for hopeful participants."[121]

NGOs thus found themselves oscillating between optimism and frustration. They could still feel optimistic because in the twenty years since Stockholm they put international environmental issues on the agenda. They had also succeeded in creating piecemeal reforms – substituting different types of technologies based on local needs, procedural reforms in lending that allowed for legal and political challenges, and new models for development planning that sanctioned development, but sought to bound economic growth within the limits of a given ecosystem. However, nagging frustrations reined in such hopes. The financing and cooperation necessary to sustain a comprehensive agreement to redress climate change remained out of reach. So too did a global shift in values. The leaders of developing nations, although now speaking the language of "sustainable development," interpreted the concept as an acknowledgment of their right to pursue poverty alleviation and economic growth and still viewed major environmental agreements with tremendous skepticism. Leaders in the United States used the phrase, too, but did not follow through with financial commitments necessary to enable the kind of

[119] Ibid.
[120] David Runnalls, "A Duty to Hope," *IUCN Bulletin*, Vol. 21, No. 3 (September 1992), 19–20.
[121] Mark Halle, "Bitter Fare," *IUCN Bulletin*, Vol. 21, No. 3 (September 1992), 22.

North-South equality that the original advocates of the "sustainable development" idea thought was a precondition to the concept's realization. Despite the decades of remarkable institutional and intellectual transformations by leading NGOs, the ongoing struggle to establish deep and lasting international cooperation to counter climate change and other forms of environmental destruction left many in the environmental community to ponder an uncertain and worrisome future.

## CODA: THE ROCKY ROAD FROM RIO

In the years following the Rio Earth Summit, environmentalists' concerns over the lack of international cooperation around major issues only deepened. For a brief moment after the election of Bill Clinton in November 1992, it appeared that the United States might assume a leadership role in encouraging international cooperation. Its efforts ended with disappointment, too. Vice President Gore took a leading role in the UN's Commission on Sustainable Development, the body tasked with overseeing the follow-up to Rio and the future of Agenda 21. Additionally, less than six months after taking office, President Clinton announced that the United States would sign the biodiversity treaty in June 1993.[122] Yet the Commission on Sustainable Development had no formal authority to oversee Agenda 21's implementation, and it foundered as time passed. Domestic politics undermined the biodiversity treaty, because the Senate never ratified the agreement. To this day, the United States remains a nonparty to the treaty.

International negotiations over climate change followed a similar trajectory of initial hopes meeting long-term disappointment. The Intergovernmental Panel on Climate Change continued to hold talks over a binding international agreement on carbon emissions after the Rio gathering. At the second Conference of the Parties in 1996, the Clinton administration agreed to develop legally binding targets for emission reductions based on 1990 levels. A year later, at the third Conference of the Parties in Kyoto, Japan, the negotiations led to a formal agreement called the Kyoto Protocol. In its draft form, the deal obligated the industrialized nations, through a binding agreement, to reduce their emission by an average of 6 to 8 percent below 1990 levels by 2012. The agreement was

---

[122] William K. Stevens, "Gore Promises U.S. Leadership on Sustainable Development Path," *New York Times*, June 15, 1993, C4.

set to become operational when ratified by at least fifty-five countries representing at least 55 percent of total emissions. Compromises between negotiators from the Clinton administration and the Global South established some loopholes that allowed countries to meet their requirements slowly or through special schemes. Participating countries would be allowed to count offsetting "sinks" that were believed to reduce the ecological impact of emissions, and the agreement sanctioned emissions trading for countries to achieve some amount of their required reductions.[123]

As with earlier talks, though, domestic and international political disputes undercut the final protocol agreement. Days before President Clinton endorsed the Kyoto Protocol, the U.S. Senate unanimously approved the Byrd–Hagel resolution. The resolution stated that the United States would not honor any agreement to cut its own emissions unless "the protocol or other agreement also mandates new specific scheduled commitments to limit or reduce greenhouse gas emissions for Developing Country Parties within the same compliance period."[124] This stipulation signified that the Senate would not approve the Protocol, since it had been designed with differing responsibilities for "developed" and "developing" countries. Moreover, during negotiations over the protocol, Chinese and Indian officials balked at the notion of committing their countries to any agreement that called for limits on carbon emissions without resource transfers to accompany it. China's right to pursue economic growth on its own terms, one of its chief diplomats explained, was "a matter of human rights" that could not be trumped by any ecological imperative.[125] Relations between the United States and the Global South, and in particular, questions of financing and foreign aid, continued to hamper negotiations.

---

[123] Andrews, *Managing the Environment, Managing Ourselves*, 357.

[124] The text of the resolution is available online: http://www.nationalcenter.org/KyotoSenate. html. On climate negotiations from Kyoto to the present, see Henrik Selin and Stacy D. VanDeveer, "Global Climate Change: Kyoto and Beyond," in Norman J. Vig and Michael E. Kraft, eds., *Environmental Policy: New Directions for the Twenty-First Century*, 7th ed. (Washington, DC: CQ Press, 2010), 265–85. On NGOs and the Kyoto Protocol, see Michele M. Betsill, "Environmental NGOs and the Kyoto Protocol Negotiations: 1995 to 1997," in Michele M. Betsill and Elisabeth Corell, eds., *NGO Diplomacy: The Influence of Nongovernmental Organizations in International Environmental Negotiations* (Cambridge: The MIT Press, 2008), 43–66. On the mechanics of the protocol, see Michael Grubb with Christiaan Vrolijk and Duncan Brack, *The Kyoto Protocol: A Guide and Assessment* (London: Royal Institute of International Affairs, 1999).

[125] Joby Warrick, "Climate Pact Rescued in Final Hours; Turbulence Pervaded First Round of Greenhouse Gas Talks," *The Washington Post*, December 13, 1997, A01.

A comprehensive and binding global agreement to redress climate change became even more difficult to achieve during the administration of George W. Bush. Although the Clinton administration had supported the nonbinding protocol, Bush refused even to engage in formal talks over an international convention on climate change. Shortly after the president's inauguration in early 2001, his administration formally pulled out of negotiations altogether because negotiators would not agree to bind developing countries to curb their greenhouse gas emissions and for fear that a new agreement would impair U.S. economic growth.[126] The Bush administration even went as far as to question the widely accepted scientific evidence that climate change even existed. For example, a formal Environmental Protection Agency report on the U.S. environment did not even contain a section on global warming because the White House refused to approve any report that did not include language suggesting "greater uncertainty about [global warming] than the consensus of the scientific community." The administration did support "voluntary" efforts by countries to reduce their carbon emissions, but rejected out of hand any approach with binding or even specific commitments.[127]

Spearheaded by the European Union, other countries did commit to the Kyoto Protocol, although problems remained beyond the Bush administration's rejection of international environmental politics. In July 2001, after the United States had left negotiations, a reconvened Conference of Parties stitched together a compromise that brought the Kyoto Protocol into force. A total of 157 governments, including all major industrial countries except the United States and Australia, signed the protocol. It became operational in 2005.[128] However, unresolved tensions percolated over financing for the agreement between the EU nations and Japan on one side, and rising powers such as India and China and many other developing countries on the other. Save for a few exceptions, foreign aid levels fell well short of the targets established back at the Earth Summit. Many countries in the Global South, even if far less unified as a bloc than in prior decades, remained frustrated at the lack of compensatory aid coming their way. According to one Swedish diplomat, "the problem of

---

[126] "Bush Pulls U.S. Out of Kyoto Talks," *The Boston Globe*, March 29, 2001; Edmund L. Andrews, "Bush Angers Europe by Eroding Pact on Warming," *The New York Times*, April 1, 2001, A3.

[127] Andrews, *Managing the Environment, Managing Ourselves*, 381–6.

[128] Ibid., 386.

how to break out of the North-South impasse remained the challenge in the UN process" of negotiating a global agreement.[129]

⌈North-South politics continued to bedevil negotiators even after the United States recommitted to international environmental politics following the election of Barack Obama⌉ In meetings over the follow-up to the Kyoto Protocol in Copenhagen in 2009, negotiators entertained the idea of once and for all abolishing the distinction between "developed" and "developing" nations in a new agreement designed to overcome past disagreements. Yet the talks quickly unraveled. President Obama "hinted" that Chinese intransigence was to blame for the inability of all nations to commit to a new framework for redressing climate change. Furthermore, the G-77 nations balked at eliminating the "developed" versus "developing" distinction, viewing such a move as "an attempt by the rich world to wriggle out of its responsibility for climate change." They further criticized the Obama administration for coming to the table with a commitment of reducing emissions by only 4 percent on 1990 levels. The Copenhagen meeting ended in frustration once again; national leaders stressed the importance of "sustainable development" but did not agree to any mechanisms that would force a reduction of carbon emissions. The final accord represented, in the words of the G-77's chief negotiator, "the lowest level of ambition you can imagine."[130] Even with increasing scientific evidence about the dire consequences of climate change in the future and present day, a binding agreement over carbon emissions involving all countries remained elusive.[131]

Two decades after the creation of the Intergovernmental Panel on Climate Change, then, political differences continued to scuttle cooperation. In the few years leading up to the Rio Earth Summit, serious tensions emerged over the costs and consequences of a binding agreement to confront global climate change. Those conflicts remained powerful in the years that followed. In Obama's second term, environmentalists pointed to declining costs of alternative energy and domestic initiatives as promising if insufficient tools for combating climate change.[132] Still, a

---

[129] Engfeldt, *From Stockholm to Johannesburg and Beyond*, 203–4.

[130] John Vidal, Allegra Stratton, and Suzanne Goldenberg, "Low Targets, Goals Dropped: Copenhagen Ends in Failure," *The Guardian*, December 19, 2009, 1.

[131] Intergovernmental Panel on Climate Change. IPCC press release, 2013/20/PR. September 27, 2013.

[132] Jeff Goodell, "Obama's Last Shot," *Rolling Stone*, April 23, 2014. [Online] Available: http://m.rollingstone.com/politics/news/obamas-last-shot-20140423 Accessed 24 April 2014.

measure with the political force and symbolic power as a binding global accord remained out of reach. In the absence of a comprehensive agreement on carbon emissions, efforts to reconcile global ecological imperatives with aspirations of economic growth would continue to have to come through other means: through voluntary reforms at the local, regional, or national level, or, more likely, through the continued efforts of committed NGOs to reshape development policies and approaches around the world.

# CONCLUSION

# The Growth and Limits of NGOs

In 2003, Sebastian Mallaby, a veteran reporter for the *Washington Post*, visited Uganda. Development experts were celebrating the country as a success story because it had slashed its poverty rate by approximately 40 percent during the 1990s while many of its neighbors languished. Mallaby wanted to understand the changes. He also hoped to explore why, in spite of the rapid growth rates, some of Uganda's most important regions still faced endemic poverty. In particular, he wanted to see a region that for decades had captured the minds of many Westerners, particularly environmentalists – the impoverished area around the proposed Bujagali dam. The dam had been held up by many conservationists as an alternative to Uganda's proposed dam at Murchison Falls in the 1960s; only Idi Amin's last-second political maneuvering had spared Murchison. Decades of instability had plagued the country, though, and the Bujagali dam had yet to be built. Nearly fifty years after conservationists such as Julian Huxley, Peter Scott, and Russell Train had become preoccupied with Uganda's dams, Mallaby found himself similarly inspired.[1]

Mallaby's visit to East Africa, however, came after environmentalists had won a major victory in Uganda. In the 1960s, Western activists went to East Africa and experienced tremendous difficulties to halt the construction of Uganda's dams. In 2003, they were in the midst of a successful yearlong campaign that had blocked financing for the Bujagali project. In need of a World Bank loan to pursue the project, the Ugandan government had been stymied by a group of American non-governmental

[1] Sebastian Mallaby, "NGOs: Fighting Poverty, Hurting the Poor," *Foreign Policy*, No. 144 (September–October 2004), 50–8.

organizations (NGOs) that had held up the loan in the bank's environmental review process. The International Rivers Network (IRN), a group based in Berkeley, California, had mobilized against the dam. They claimed that likely long-term social and environmental damage would undermine any short-term economic benefits.

The Ugandan government saw the project in a much different light. Ugandan officials believed the dam would spark an economic transformation in the region by providing electricity to impoverished villages. The tensions between Uganda's governing elite, the small NGO half a world away, and the struggling villagers caught in between perplexed Mallaby. "Was the NGO movement acting as a civilized check on industrialization, standing up for millions of poor people whose views the World Bank ignored?" he wondered. "Or was it retarding the battle against poverty by withholding electricity that would fuel economic growth, ultimately benefiting poor citizens?"[2]

Mallaby decided upon the latter. After interviewing local Ugandans who favored the dam for the economic windfall it would bring, Mallaby penned an article for *Foreign Policy* magazine. He argued that Western environmental NGOs, given their clout at international development institutions such as the World Bank, had become too powerful. The Bujagali story was "a tragedy for Uganda," Mallaby wrote. "Clinics and factories are being deprived of electricity by Californians," he asserted. Distant and aloof, the activists cleaved to abstract principles designed to "save the earth," when in reality they denied other governments the right to pursue the projects they wanted or allow local people the right to choose their own paths out of poverty. Mallaby's article appeared as a ferocious attack upon the entire NGO community.[3]

Many NGO officials fired back. Mark Halle, the former International Union for the Conservation of Nature (IUCN) official who had worked closely with Maurice Strong to implement the *World Conservation Strategy*, complained that Mallaby's essay was "curiously one-sided and superficial."[4] Jim MacNeill, Strong's close associate and the former leader of the Brundtland Commission, called the article a blatant "polemic" that was far more "disappointing" than revelatory. Bruce Rich, the lead NGO lawyer during congressional hearings against the World Bank in the 1980s, charged Mallaby with writing a "misinformed and illogical

[2] Ibid., 51–2.
[3] Ibid., 52.
[4] Mark Halle, "Letter to the Editor of *Foreign Policy*," 2004. [Online] Available: http://www
.iisd.org/publications/pub.aspx?id=668. Accessed December 26, 2012.

screed."[5] All three accused Mallaby of grossly oversimplifying the relationship between NGOs, development lenders, and developing countries.

The sharply defensive tone of their responses revealed how fiercely Mallaby's criticisms had stung the NGO community. An article such as Mallaby's would certainly upset donors, and that alone would cause consternation among NGOs. However, the piece struck deeper. It offered an opportunity to reflect on the many consequences of the environmental movement's evolution. Over the many years since Train's and Huxley's early trips to Africa, NGOs had grown tremendously in size, scope, and influence. The IUCN and the World Wildlife Fund (WWF) had been formed by amateur elites with small budgets and a very narrow focus; five decades later, a journalist could write an article arguing that professional, wealthy, and politically connected NGOs held too much influence in shaping flows of international development aid. NGOs' evolution throughout the latter half of the twentieth century evoked many vexing questions. What were the results of their five decades of transnational activism? What had NGOs accomplished, and what major challenges around the world still stood before them? How had NGO activism evolved over the years, and to what extent had it deviated from its original purpose? How should environmentalists understand the nature of their growth and the limits of their influence? These questions all mattered greatly, because they reflected upon NGOs' legitimacy, purpose, and power.

## LEGITIMACY

First and foremost, by the 1990s NGOs faced questions about legitimacy. In his Bujagali example, Mallaby argued that the International Rivers Network purported to represent the interests of the poor and to protect the natural world in Uganda. In practice, though, their resistance to the dam only perpetuated poverty by denying electricity that local people desired. Similarly, he claimed that NGOs had become influential special interest groups that co-opted elected officials for their own benefit. He charged NGOs with using the World Bank's Inspection Panel – the review body formed at the end of the NGO campaign against the bank in the early 1990s and which Jim MacNeill had led in the 1990s – with favoring

---

[5] MacNeill and Rich quoted in "Dammed Project," *Foreign Policy*, No. 145 (November–December 2004), 6–10.

activists over the bank's staff by blocking a loan for a wide-scale resettlement scheme in Qinghai, China, which would have moved some 58,000 farmers to more productive agricultural land. In Mallaby's description of the Bujagali and Qinghai projects, a clear pattern emerged: NGOs decided to mobilize against a development project, successfully convinced key officials to resist the project or used some elaborate legal mechanism to block the project's funding, and ultimately imperiled the people in the developing world whom the project purported to help. All of this occurred, his article implied, without any accountability or questioning of the NGOs' legitimacy to do so in the first place.[6]

Behind Mallaby's critiques lurked some truth. Over the previous four decades, NGOs reshaped development policy in part by aggrandizing their own political influence vis-à-vis major institutions. In pushing for appropriate technology funding in USAID, NGOs seized on a moment of crisis in U.S. foreign aid policy to lobby sympathetic congressmen for more money, then positioned their institutions as development organizations capable of receiving the grants to carry out projects in the field. Working so closely with the government posed challenges for reformers. Government officials viewed appropriate technologies far more narrowly than did the movement's leaders, who had understood the tools as part of a larger critique of industrial, mass society. In practice, appropriate technology programs often lacked the reformer's holistic approach and instead stressed far more traditional objectives of spurring economic growth in lagging sectors. Likewise, in successfully forcing USAID and the World Bank to follow formal environmental review procedures, NGOs used litigation campaigns and public pressure through Congress to engineer a new mode of private accountability for public institutions. Although NGOs provided a new mechanism to make lending agencies accountable for how their loans altered the environment, the NGOs themselves often stood in as "the public" or acted on behalf of the common interest.[7] In turn, the reforms raised new questions about how representative NGOs were, the nature of special interests in international development, and the general difficulties of defining a set of ethical

---

[6] Mallaby, "NGOs," 53–5.

[7] This is not to suggest that all NGO officials or activists claimed that they were representing people in the developing world; most NGO officials would reject such claims. Rather, as institutions NGOs had come to stand in as a proxy for "the public" as countervailing forces against large governing institutions and the governments of developing countries.

standards and means of accountability to assess and manage powerful non-state actors.[8]

Questions of legitimacy came not only from external observers like Mallaby, but from within the environmental community itself. Throughout NGOs' broad efforts to reform development policy, tensions emerged within the environmental community on a number of fronts: between those with close ties to centers of power and those focused on radical campaigning; between those from Western Europe and the United States and between people from the developing world; between those who focused narrowly on species protection and those who sought to include poverty eradication and social justice into their activism. In Mallaby's piece, he further fueled these debates by decrying the more "radical" NGOs that rarely compromised in contrast to the "grown-up groups," such as the World Wildlife Fund, which "may accept your olive branch."[9]

Such criticisms resonated in part because they came at a time when many NGOs were posing questions about how strategic partnerships with government and industry affected their own legitimacy within the movement. Formerly aggressively independent and primarily grassroots groups such as Greenpeace had by the late 1990s chosen to partner with major corporations, for instance. These partnerships raised questions of purity and purpose within the larger environmental community that had been gestating for some time. Greenpeace, in fact, followed the lead of the WWF, which for years had positioned itself as industry-friendly, and like the IUCN, had been afforded a privileged status in government advising, international conferences, and corporate partnerships.[10] David

---

[8] On accountability of NGOs, see, for instance, Steve Charnovitz, "Accountability of Nongovernmental Organisations (NGOs) in Global Governance," The George Washington University Law School Public Law and Legal Theory Working Paper No. 145 (2005); Kenneth Anderson, "What NGO Accountability Means – and Does Not Mean," *American Journal of International Law*, Vol. 103, No. 1 (2009), 170–8; Paul Wapner, "Defending Accountability in NGOs," *Chicago Journal of International Law*, Vol. 3 No. 1 (2002), 197–205; Lisa Jordan and Peter van Tujil, eds., *NGO Accountability: Politics, Principles, and Innovations* (Sterling, VA: Earthscan, 2006). On questions of NGOs and the ethical dimensions of their work, see Jennifer Rubenstein, *Between Samaritans and States: The Political Ethics of Humanitarian INGOs* (New York, Oxford University Press, 2015).

[9] Bruce Rich, in particular, took umbrage with this statement. "Dammed Project," 9–10.

[10] See for instance, Alana Conner and Keith Epstein, "Harnessing Purity and Pragmatism," *Stanford Social Innovation Review*, Vol. 5, No. 4 (Fall 2007), 61–5; Andrew J. Hoffman, "Shades of Green," *Stanford Social Innovation Review*, Vol. 7, No. 1 (Spring 2009), 40–9; Ida E. Berger, Peggy E. Cunningham, and Minette E. Drumwright, "Social Alliances: Company/Nonprofit Collaboration," *California Management Review*, Vol. 47, No. 1 (Fall 2004), 58–90. I thank Allison Elias for directing me toward these

Brower, who left the Sierra Club to form the more grassroots Friends of the Earth in the late 1960s, had half-jokingly lambasted the WWF for this during the Stockholm Conference when WWF officials had been granted special access on national delegations and important roles in the conference itself.

The question of how closely to work with governments and how to stay pure as a social or reform movement confronts any activist group.[11] There was no clear answer to this for any leading environmental NGOs, although accommodation and close ties with states had led to greater influence and put many NGOs on more stable financial footing. Above all, the very fact of those questions attested to how broad, diverse, and complicated the environmental movement had become – to the point where talking about a single "global environmental movement" was simply untenable.[12] Over a long fifty-year process, NGOs created ways to make major development institutions accountable for their effects on the environment. In the process, they raised questions about the legitimacy of NGOs to stand in for the public interest, to determine who constituted "the public," and whether certain forms of activism were more legitimate than others.

### PURPOSE

Questions over NGO legitimacy also raised a similarly perplexing set of questions about the purpose of environmental protection in the developing world. Mallaby's article, for instance, touched on a larger debate about environmentalists' ultimate aims that had been going on for decades. In his piece, he portrayed environmentalists as antagonistic toward all major development projects. "Have my critics ever favored the construction of a large dam?" he wondered in a rebuttal to Bruce Rich and Jim MacNeill, as if to paint activists as inherently hostile to social and economic change.[13] Mallaby's depiction, however, was not accurate.

articles. The corporate alliances have sparked fierce internal debates within NGOs, particularly the IUCN. See Holdgate, *The Green Web*, 221–2.

[11] There is no shortage of literature on this point from activists and from scholars of social movements. A key foundational text that prized the more radical tactics and helped to shape the ongoing debate about compromise and activity in electoral politics is Francis Fox-Piven and Richard A. Cloward, *Poor People's Movements: Why They Succeed, How They Fail* (New York: Vintage Books, 1979).

[12] On the diversity of alliances and allegiances for the IUCN alone, see Holdgate, *The Green Web*, 253–4.

[13] "Dammed Project," 10.

Over the previous fifty years, many environmental NGOs had revised their own missions to accommodate the basic concerns of developing nations by making issues of poverty, health, and urbanization central to their agenda. This shift, in turn, created some confusion within the activist community over what was the ultimate purpose of environmental protection.

By the twentieth century's end, many NGOs still struggled to reconcile their environmental or scientific objectives with the newfound emphasis on socioeconomic and political goals. For instance, the IUCN's controversial decisions in the 1970s to remake its own program around the "sustainable development" theme still resonated in the 1990s and early 2000s. Although the follow-up to the *World Conservation Strategy*, entitled *Caring for the Earth*, reiterated the older document's basic message, it still engendered opposition. According to IUCN Director-General Martin Holdgate, General Assembly meetings in the 1990s still devolved into conflicts over the "longest-running saga," namely the "balance to be struck between nature protection and sustainable development." IUCN board meetings still experienced the same tensions that had existed in the 1970s. Officials still argued over whether to admit members who supported indigenous hunting of animals, even if such acts were "strictly sustainable."[14] Likewise, by the 1990s the WWF adopted a new focus on local participation and "people-centered" conservation in the management of protected areas, in sharp contrast to their longer history of supporting conservation and preservation programs predicated on marginalizing the role and rights of indigenous groups. Early evaluations of the WWF's new approaches, however, highlighted ongoing challenges of reconciling traditional organizational priorities (preservation and protection) with the ideological commitments. The WWF had "begun using the language of participation and people-centered processes," noted one evaluator. Yet it had done so "without significant organisational change and realignments of political, scientific and bureaucratic powers" necessary to implement such approaches in policy.[15]

Reconciling environmental protection with economic development proved just as difficult to manage in international treaties as it did among NGOs. Throughout the 1990s and 2000s, the political right of developing countries to pursue national economic development remained one of the primary issues over the stillborn international

[14] Holdgate, *The Green Web*, 221.
[15] Jeanrenaud, *People-Oriented Approaches in Global Conservation*, viii.

climate treaty. Even though President Bill Clinton publicly endorsed the Kyoto Protocol – a step toward making a binding climate change agreement with hard-cap timetables – the U.S. Senate unanimously approved the Byrd–Hagel resolution, which was premised on the notion that developing nations and developed nations needed to share equally in cutting global emissions. Developing countries resisted those arguments in Kyoto and in subsequent meetings, frequently claiming that increased foreign aid financing for environmental protection was a necessary part of any agreement.

As the debates at Stockholm and Rio had shown, the fate of environmental protection in the developing world required that developed countries first contend with the Global South's demands for increased financial transfers. The ongoing stalemate over a climate change agreement illuminates the inability of both the developed and developing worlds to cooperate over questions of foreign aid levels and international developmental policy. Some scholars have even begun to question whether to continue pursuing a treaty at all, given the continued frustration and disappointment over the stalled talks.[16] NGOs had offered approaches for developing nations to pursue development in a "sustainable" way. Nevertheless, achieving sustainable development still requires expensive economic transformations that also require substantial changes in the wealthy countries' foreign aid policies.

Through the 1990s, then, key questions over the purpose of conservation and its relationship to economic development in the developing world remained unanswered. Ongoing disputes over development projects like the Bujagali dam exposed a lingering ambivalence and uncertainty in the environmental community over the purpose of environmental protection and its relationship to economic development. Would pragmatic accommodation to development experts and the developing world dilute the environmental movement's purpose? How far should environmental NGOs go to embrace their newer objectives, like poverty eradication, when the projects designed to alleviate poverty still threatened the natural world in the long term? Should NGOs still employ the phrase "sustainable development" when its breadth and vagueness has opened it up to misinterpretations and meanings far removed from what its progenitors had in mind? And to what degree should environmental NGOs sympathize

---

[16] Robert Keohane and David G. Victor, "The Regime Complex for Climate Change," *Perspectives on Politics*, Vol. 9, No. 1 (March 2011), 7–23.

with developing nations' demands for more extensive aid and resource transfers?

The concept of "sustainable development" had come to signify that development and environmental protection were inextricably intertwined. Although Mallaby established stark divide between protecting nature and eliminating poverty, many NGOs had wrestled with the connections between the two goals for decades. Sustainability, however, offered little clarity for priorities moving forward. The sustainable development concept justified a vast range of attitudes, values, and decisions. Advocates for market-based approaches to economic development used it while shunning any additional environmental regulations or checks on economic growth, just as environmentalists deployed the phrase to suggest that natural limits should bound any development plan. Moreover, implementing the original sustainable development plans outlined by the *World Conservation Strategy* required a dramatic increase in resource transfers to the Global South and reforms of the entire global economy – changes in policy that NGOs alone could never achieve. Although Mallaby's article suggested that NGOs could halt individual development projects by holding up funding, the challenges of implementing NGOs' original definition of sustainable development revealed much more pervasive limitations on their power and influence.

### POWER

The questions of legitimacy and purpose ultimately mattered, after all, because they reflected on questions of power. From the 1940s through the 1990s, NGOs grew from marginal actors to major players in international politics. This trend was not lost on many observers in the 1990s. Writing in *Foreign Affairs* in 1997, Jessica Mathews, a senior fellow at the Council on Foreign Relations, identified a "novel redistribution of power" taking place. "The steady concentration of power in the hands of states that began in 1648 with the Peace of Westphalia is over, at least for a while," Mathews claimed. Nations were in a process of "sharing powers" with businesses, international organizations, and NGOs. For Mathews, NGOs were of particular importance. She counted millions of NGOs across the world, "from the tiniest village association to influential but modestly funded international groups." NGOs, Mathews noted, could accomplish much. They could generate new ideas, shape and implement major policies at the national level, monitor international agreements, and change norms and institutions in the global arena.[17]

Mathews wrote from a position of experience, as her own career highlighted many of the themes she laid out. She had been the National Security Council's liaison during the debates within the U.S. government over the "extraterritoriality" of environmental impact statements, when she witnessed first hand how a legal initiative from a small NGO could reshape government policy. A few years later, Mathews cofounded the World Resources Institute, which by the mid-1990s had become one of the most influential environmental NGOs.[18] From there, she joined the Council of Foreign Relations as a Fellow for a brief time before moving on to her current role as president of the Carnegie Endowment for International Peace, one of the largest and most important foreign policy think tanks. Like many of her generation, Mathews moved between the government and the nonprofit sector, with her professional status conferring greater legitimacy upon the NGOs with whom she worked.

In addition, there was a great deal of evidence available to support Mathews's claims in her *Foreign Affairs* article. By the 1990s NGOs had grown more powerful in terms of their ability to shape development policy of major lending institutions. They had become wealthy enough to mobilize political support to spark new policy initiatives, such as the appropriate technology movement. They also transformed into important sources of environmental expertise, capable of shaping the agenda for major international conferences. They helped to author major environmental laws, won positions both on national delegations and within government departments to adopt and enforce those laws, and became public interest law firms that could use litigation to enforce the law's implementation. As Mallaby's article also showed, they had created sophisticated ways of checking the ability of the world's most prominent development organization – the World Bank – to allocate funding. Likewise, NGOs reformed the discourse around development toward talk of sustainability, helped to provide new models and norms for development planning, and in a few instances helped to reshape national environmental institutions along the guidelines they had set in documents such as the *World Conservation Strategy*.

---

[17] Jessica T. Mathews, "Power Shift," *Foreign Affairs*, Vol. 76, No. 1 (January/February 1997), 50–66.

[18] Mathews cofounded the group with James Gustav Speth, who had worked for the CEQ under the Carter administration and played a key role in drafting the Global 2000 report.

In the process, environmental NGOs coevolved with the U.S. government, the World Bank, and the United Nations to refashion the relationship between those institutions and the activist community. The appropriate technology movement revealed how NGOs could seize on shifts in government policy toward privatization and effectively lobby politicians to create new policies and earn contracts to carry out projects on the ground. The campaigns for environmental review demonstrated how NGOs could use public pressure and private litigation to reshape how the U.S. government and the World Bank lent development aid. The process of writing the *World Conservation Strategy* showed how NGOs could, through personal connections and financial ties, help to define the purpose of the UNEP but also, in turn, have their own ideas altered by the UNEP's network of experts. In all these instances, NGOs revised the ways in which development institutions conceptualized, carried out, and assessed foreign aid programs.

Despite these institutional innovations, there remained important limits to non-state actors' power. Over the course of the twentieth century, transnational and international organizations had chipped away at the underlying world order of nation-states – the world order that had legitimized decolonization and had so concerned Huxley and other environmentalists. However, their reforms came less from minimizing state power than from strategically coevolving with government institutions. After all, nation-states remained remarkably robust through the entire period, especially at the highest levels of leadership.

The enduring strength of nationalism and national politics appeared vividly during negotiations for an international, binding climate change agreement. The power of national leaders was one lesson that many took from the Rio Conference. One country, the United States, had scuttled many of the conference's main agreements. The developing nations had organized their opposition around the notion that every nation had a fundamental right to self-determine its own economic future. NGOs found few sympathetic figures in the Bush administration or in Congress to support massive resource transfers to developing nations. Although the Global Environmental Facility provided basic financing for major environmental protection projects in the developing world, it lacked the capacity and funds to support sustainable development as Maurice Strong and other environmentalists had envisioned. NGOs had reshaped development assistance policies. Yet they still encountered tremendous difficulties in changing the hearts and minds of key leaders and national elites, especially with regard to substantial increases in foreign aid or direct resource transfers. Deep and lasting international cooperation over climate change remained elusive because national elites still chose to assign priority to national economic goals and political objectives over environmental imperatives.

Moreover, NGOs' success in reshaping the lenders of development aid did not translate to similar successes in keeping national leaders in the developing world from pursuing large development projects on their own. Such intransigence was apparent among the leaders in Uganda and China who Mallaby wrote about in his article. International NGOs and NGOs in the United States generally achieved more influence over the institutions that lent development aid than they did over the leaders and elites in the developing world who received it. For countries across the world, development – as both a symbolic and concrete process of change – remained inextricably bound to nationalist projects. For all his evidence about NGOs' power over the World Bank, Mallaby also incidentally cited a key limitation, as well. Although environmental groups held up financing for the Qinghai resettlement scheme, the Chinese government ultimately pulled its request from the bank and pursued the project on its own without external funding. Absent an equally strong domestic civil society to resist the project in China, there was little international groups could do to alter the Chinese government's path of action.[19] After all, they had focused their attention on the World Bank and other lenders of development assistance in part because NGOs' influence remained so limited elsewhere.

\* \* \*

From Russell Train's and Julian Huxley's first trips to Africa in the 1950s through Mallaby's article five decades later, environmentalists grappled with the concepts of growth and limits. At root, environmental reformers believed that there were environmental limits to economic growth. Their efforts to reshape international development policy derived from this basic belief, as they hoped to prevent past destructive patterns of development from continuing into the future.

Environmentalists also confronted with the growth of their NGOs and the limits of their influence. NGOs' reforms of development generated a new kind of governance in which private actors played important roles in determining the scope and content of policy, the legal mechanisms used to enforce those policies, and the implementation of those policies on the

[19] Mallaby, "NGOs," 57.

ground. NGOs flourished because of these transformations, and they established greater accountability of development institutions and inspired widespread awareness of the interconnection between environmental protection and development. However, taken together, NGOs' reforms of international development could not resolve the underlying issues that made environmental protection seem so pressing in the first place. The desire for continuous economic development and national economic self-determination remained powerful forces at the start of the twenty-first century. Many leaders in the developing world – much like their counterparts in developed countries – still prize rapid economic growth and often pursue environmentally destructive projects to achieve it, just as they had in the twentieth century.

All the while, fundamental questions persist over who should and will bear the costs of environmental protection for developing countries in a world defined by the legacies of past inequities. Those questions loom ever larger. The scale of contemporary ecological problems – climate change the foremost among them – requires national leaders, international institutions, and citizens around the world to rethink priorities and to address, as Barry Commoner once said, "the long-standing, unresolved conflicts that trouble the world."[20] Those conflicts are, at root, political and economic issues about poverty, inequality, and justice that demand cooperation and concessions between countries. Our ability to reconcile environmental protection with economic development in the future depends on our willingness to redress the nettlesome and persistent disparities of wealth and power in our own time. Many NGOs began to confront that fact decades ago. We neglect to do so today at our collective peril.

[20] Barry Commoner, "Motherhood in Stockholm," *Harper's*, Vol. 244, No. 1465 (June 1972), 54.

# Archives

UNITED STATES

**Environmental Science and Public Policy Archives, Harvard College Library, Cambridge, MA**
Maurice Strong Papers
Peter Thacher Papers

**George H. W. Bush Presidential Library, College Station, TX**
Jeffrey Holmstead Files
D. Allan Bromley Files
David Bradford Files
Nicholas Rostow Files
White House Office of Records Management (WHORM) Subject Files

**Gerald Ford Presidential Library, Ann Arbor, MI**
Gerald Ford Vice Presidential Papers
Stanley S. Scott Papers
H. Guyford Stever Papers
White House Central Files

**Jimmy Carter Presidential Library, Atlanta, GA**
Al McDonald Files
White House Central Files
RAC Project Files

**New Economics Institute, Great Barrington, MA**
E. F. Schumacher Archives

**Richard Nixon Presidential Library, Yorba Linda, CA**
Daniel Patrick Moynihan Papers
White House Central Files

Ronald Reagan Presidential Library, Simi Valley, CA
 Randall E. Davis Files
 White House Central Files
Special Collections and Archives, Frank Melville Jr. Memorial Library,
 Stony Brook University, Stony Brook, NY
 Environmental Defense Fund Papers
Special Collections Research Center, Georgetown University,
 Washington, DC
 Barbara Ward Papers
The Bancroft Library, University of California, Berkeley, CA
 David Brower Papers
 Sierra Club Records
 Sierra Club International Program Records
 Sierra Club Oral History Series
The Library of Congress, Washington, DC
 Russell E. Train Papers
 Daniel Patrick Moynihan Papers
United States National Archives, College Park, MD
 RG 59, Records of the Department of State
 RG 286, Records of the Agency for International Development
 RG 469, Records of the U.S. Foreign Assistance Agencies
Woodson Research Center, Fondren Library, Rice University
 Julian Huxley Papers
World Bank Group, Washington, DC
 Records of President Robert S. McNamara
 Records of President A. W. Clausen
 Development Committee Records
 World Bank Oral History Program
World Wildlife Fund-United States, Washington, DC

UNITED KINGDOM

Department of Manuscripts and University Archives, Cambridge
 University Library, Cambridge, UK
 Sir Peter Markham Scott Papers
Flora and Fauna International, Cambridge, UK
Royal Geographical Society, London, UK
 E. Max Nicholson Papers
 The National Archives, Kew Gardens, UK

The Nature Conservancy Council and English Nature (FT)
Department of Technical Co-operation, and of successive Overseas
  Development bodies (OD)
Prime Minister's Office (PREM)
Foreign and Commonwealth Office (FCO)


SWITZERLAND

**IUCN Library, Gland, Switzerland**
**United Nations Office in Geneva, Geneva, Switzerland**
  UN Registry Collection


KENYA

**Kenya National Archives, Nairobi, Kenya**
  Department of Wildlife Conservation and Management and Tourism
  Ministry of Environment and Natural Resources, Headquarters
**UNEP Library, Nairobi, Kenya**

# Index